Paracritical Hinge

CONTEMPORARY NORTH AMERICAN POETRY SERIES

Series Editors Alan Golding, Lynn Keller, and Adalaide Morris

Paracritical Hinge

Essays, Talks, Notes, Interviews

NATHANIEL MACKEY

UNIVERSITY OF IOWA PRESS, IOWA CITY

University of Iowa Press, Iowa City 52242

www.uipress.uiowa.edu
Printed in the United States of America

The University of Iowa Press is a member of Green Press Initiative and is committed to preserving natural resources.

Printed on acid-free paper

ISBN 978-1-60938-583-5 (pbk)
ISBN 978-1-60938-584-2 (ebk)

Cataloging-in-Publication data is on file with the Library of Congress.

Contents

Acknowledgments

The following pieces have previously been published, in some cases in a different version; their first appearances in print were as follows: "Phrenological Whitman" in *Conjunctions* 29 (1997); "Wringing the Word" in *World Literature Today* 68, no. 4 (1994); "Palimpsestic Stagger" in *H.D. and Poets After*, edited by Donna Krolik Hollenberg (Iowa City: University of Iowa Press, 2000); "Gassire's Lute: Robert Duncan's Vietnam War Poems" in *Talisman: A Journal of Contemporary Poetry and Poetics* 5 (1990), 6 (1991), 7 (1991), and 8 (1992); "Cante Moro" in *Disembodied Poetics: Annals of the Jack Kerouac School*, edited by Anne Waldman and Andrew Schelling (Albuquerque: University of New Mexico Press, 1994); "Blue in Green: Black Interiority" in *River City: A Journal of Contemporary Culture* 16, no. 2 (1996); "Sight-Specific, Sound-Specific. . ." in *Additional Apparitions: Poetry, Performance, and Site Specificity*, edited by David Kennedy and Keith Tuma (Sheffield, England: The Cherry on the Top Press, 2002); "Destination Out" in *Callaloo: A Journal of African-American and African Arts and Letters* 23, no. 2 (2000); "Expanding the Repertoire" in *Tripwire: A Journal of Poetics* 5 (2001); "Editing *Hambone*" in *Callaloo: A Journal of African-American and African Arts and Letters* 23, no. 2 (2000); "Interview by Christopher Funkhouser" in *Poetry Flash: A Poetry Review and Literary Calendar for the West* 224 (1991); "Interview by Edward Foster" in *Talisman: A Journal of Contemporary Poetry and Poetics* 9 (1992); "Interview by Peter O'Leary" in *Chicago Review* 43, no. 1 (1997); "Interview by Charles Rowell" in *Callaloo: A Journal of African-American and African Arts and Letters* 23, no. 2 (2000); "Interview by Brent Cunningham" in *Kenning: A Newsletter of Contemporary Poetry, Poetics, Nonfiction Writing* 3 (1998); "Interview by Paul Naylor" in *Callaloo: A Journal of African-American and African Arts and Letters* 23, no. 2 (2000).

Several of these pieces were first presented as papers or talks: "Cante

Moro" at the Naropa Institute in Boulder, Colorado, July 1991; "Blue in Green: Black Interiority" at the conference Miles Davis and American Culture at Washington University in St. Louis, Missouri, April 1995; "Paracritical Hinge" at the Guelph Jazz Festival Colloquium "Collaborative Dissonances: Jazz, Discrepancy, and Cultural Theory" in Guelph, Ontario, September 1999; "Expanding the Repertoire" at the conference Expanding the Repertoire: Continuity and Change in African-American Writing at the Small Press Traffic Literary Arts Center at New College in San Francisco, California, April 2000; "Editing *Hambone*" at the conference O Veículo da Poesia at Biblioteca Mário de Andrade in São Paulo, Brazil, May 1998.

Paracritical Hinge

Introduction

Door Peep (Shall Not Enter)

The present volume of essays, talks, notes, and interviews picks up where *Discrepant Engagement: Dissonance, Cross-Culturality, and Experimental Writing*, my previous book of essays, left off. I've continued to address the matrix of issues that the subtitle of that volume announced, doing so in relation to the work of the writers dealt with there as well as others while extending its recourse to music, chief among the nonliterary expressive practices it invokes and reflects upon. Many of the pieces contained herein continue, in quite obvious ways, concerns found in that earlier volume. "Wringing the Word," having to do with the foregrounding of language in Kamau Brathwaite's *Islands* and *Mother Poem*, extends the attention accorded his first trilogy, *The Arrivants* (of which *Islands* is the third book), and that accorded the language assault he calls "calibanization" in *Discrepant Engagement*'s "New Series 1 (Folk Series): Edward Kamau Brathwaite's New World Trilogy" and "Other: From Noun to Verb," respectively. Robert Duncan's poetry of the Vietnam War, touched on in passing in the two essays on Duncan's work found in *Discrepant Engagement*, is given extended treatment here in the lengthy essay "Gassire's Lute: Robert Duncan's Vietnam War Poems." (This piece, to vary the point made above, can be said to pick up prior to where *Discrepant Engagement* left off, having been first drafted in 1980 and published in serial form in the early 1990s. It could well, but for its length, have been included in *Discrepant Engagement*.) A footnote dealing with Federico García Lorca, Gypsy spirituality, African American spirituality, *duende*, Bob Kaufman, and Amiri Baraka in an essay on the latter's work included in *Discrepant Engagement* turns out to have anticipated the fuller treatment of those and other matters in the present volume's "Cante Moro." And so on.

There are also considerably less obvious continuities. The first piece herein, "Phrenological Whitman," though dealing with an author and a time period outside *Discrepant Engagement*'s purview, recalls, in its cross-cultural reading of the flag imagery in Walt Whitman's *Leaves of Grass*, Wilson Harris's importance to that earlier volume, his insistence on a "submerged and buoyant" vigilance, the work and relevance of a latent realm that contends with and unsettles ruling epistemes and assumptions, a reading of images as always partial and, as he puts it, "ceaselessly unfinished in their openness to other partial images from apparently strange cultures within an unfathomable, and a dynamic, spirit of wholeness."[1] Phrenology and Whitman's embrace of it are a case in point of a totalizing project quite at odds with unfathomability, wholeness's dissolve into latency. An externalist proposition committed to "conspicuosity," the conviction that "*all* the existing emotions of mankind *are legible* . . . [and] *come to the surface*," phrenology favored readable bump against occult recess, collapsing the distinction between surface and depth. In cross-cultural conversation or counterpoint with phrenology's belief in protuberant disclosure, the flag altars maintained by the Saamaka of Suriname, descendants of eighteenth-century maroons, sound a note from under in their valorization of undulant declivity, flutter, fold. An acknowledging regard for what gets away or for the fact that something, no matter what, gets away, the flags disburse maroon intangibles. Following their lead of intimating or eliciting low notes in otherwise or ostensibly high places, I read them into and against Whitman's surface calm, his assumed certainties and imperious assertions. To put it in terms proposed by *Discrepant Engagement*, such a reading, the supposition that—surface assertion and manifest inclination notwithstanding—a work, even such work as Whitman's, may sound notes from under, sings bass.

The low note or bass note is a discrepant note, a complicating play of endowment and disavowal, annunciative noise in deep league with silence. Both as reader and as writer, I look or listen for that note. Pablo Neruda, for example, has expressed great admiration for Whitman and is a poet whose work recalls Whitman's in significant ways. Like Whitman, he's characteristically a poet of large assertions and omnivorous claims. I find that his grand identifications and affirmations, celebrated though they are, aren't what resonate most for me. I likewise find, at the other end of the spectrum, that his encomia to the small mercies of everyday life (his artichoke, his lemon, his pair of socks and such, like William Carlos Williams's much lauded plums and red wheelbarrow) aren't—though they are widely endorsed—what speak most to me. I prefer the Neruda of "cera secreta," the secret wax he says filled his head and scattered ashes in his tracks. I think most, when I think of his work, of section 9 of *The Heights of Macchu Picchu,* an uncharacteristic section that begins (in Nathaniel Tarn's translation),

> Interstellar eagle, vine-in-a-mist.
> Forsaken bastion, blind scimitar.
> Orion belt, ceremonial bread.
> Torrential stairway, immeasurable eyelid.
> Triangular tunic, pollen of stone.
> Granite lamp, bread of stone.
> Mineral snake, rose of stone.[2]

It goes on for thirty-six more such lines, a succession of images (some concrete, some abstract, some plausible, some farfetched) regarding which no predication is offered, no argument advanced. Part litany, part stutter, it amounts to what Georg Lukács calls "the detour by way of speech to silence."[3]

Throwing something present throughout Neruda's work into bolder relief, the often dark dialectic between argument and image, the section's phanopoetic restlessness or waver recalls the Saamaka flag altar's flutter, a bass note Neruda sounds at the high point of a poem about heights. Wanting to say something about the unsayable, something about predicability's limits, it evokes Macchu Picchu as obdurate and impenetrable, an obstacle to speech or taunting speech, disavowing speech as in William Bronk's "The Beautiful Wall, Macchu Picchu," only not as serenely so:

> Looking at stones the Incas laid, abstract
> austerities, unimitative stones,
> so self-absorbed in their unmortared, close
> accommodation, stone to different stone,
> exactly interlocked, deep joined,
> we see them say of the world there is nothing to say.[4]

Section 9's repetition of "stone" (seven times within the first eleven lines, returning for an eighth four lines from section's end as "menacing stone") is fraught with a sense of impeded speech, as though the word were indeed stone, a wall the poem hurts if not breaks its tongue on.

The clipped, atactic nonsentences that comprise section 9 pointedly diverge from Neruda's hypotactic prolixity in the other sections of the poem, as though such prolixity were given pause by the critique of a monumentality built on human exploitation he advances, the questions he raises in section 10:

> Macchu Picchu, did you lift
> stone above stone on a groundwork of rags?
> coal upon coal and, at the bottom, tears?
> fire-crested gold, and in that gold, the bloat
> dispenser of this blood?
>
> Let me have back the slave you buried here!
> (*HMP* 57–59)

I quoted from this section in "New Series 1 (Folk Series): Edward Kamau Brathwaite's New World Trilogy" in *Discrepant Engagement*, suggesting that Brathwaite's "archaeology," his excavation of the lower strata of social experience and historic record, has a particular affinity with *Macchu Picchu.* "Wringing the Word," in the present volume, addresses what can be seen as the counterpart in Brathwaite's work, only more pointed, more extreme and more vigorously sustained, of the linguistic perturbation—the semantic, phanopoetic and phonological folds and flutter—found in section 9. Neruda writes in section 10, "allow me, architecture, / to fret stone stamens with a little stick" (*HMP* 57), lines that seem to anticipate Brathwaite's neologism "stammaments in stone" in *Sun Poem,* a "calibanism" that combines the words *monument, stammer, stamen,* and *testament* to suggest that colonial monumentality impedes the emergence of decolonized speech but that the stammer induced by such impediment is nonetheless germinal and generative. Brathwaite, in the very word *stammament,* frets as Neruda suggests, worrying the lines between words, bending words the way a blues musician bends notes, breaking words up and reassembling them.

Linguistic prioritization and play of the sort exemplified by the neologism "stammament" partake of what Brathwaite calls a "return to the pebble," a figure whose rendition of stone differs markedly from stone's deployment in monumental architecture, statuary, and such, the projects of totalization, immortalization, and aggrandizement monumentality traditionally serves. The pebble, a trope to which "Wringing the Word" devotes more than passing attention, restores a sense of mortal scale, a granular disposition quite the contrary of imperious consolidation, imperious (and imperial) presumptions of solidity, permanence, impermeability. Like the reading practice "Phrenological Whitman" brings to bear on Whitman's totalizing premises, the writing practice highlighted in "Wringing the Word" furthers a maroon impulse to leave such premises behind. Just as section 9 of *Macchu Picchu* limits itself to sentence fragments, nonsentences, Brathwaite's linguistic *marronnage* emphasizes language at reaches lower than sentence level, going in fact farther than Neruda to accentuate sublexical levels—the minims or the smallest particles of language, syllables and letters—that we're invited to regard as the pebbles of language.

Brathwaite's activity at these levels involves not only neologisms and "sound-word" coinages but anagrammatic rearrangement, idiosyncratic spelling, puns, malapropisms, and strained meaning. It also involves line breaks that occur in the middle of a word (sometimes marked by a hyphen, sometimes not) and the breaking of words by punctuation marks (slashes, periods, colons) inserted between syllables and even between letters within the same syllable. These practices insist upon and bring to light the provisionality of given arrangements, the noninevitability of presumably normative forms and procedures. They undermine monumental premises, the monumentality of language itself, by foregrounding the permeability of words, their susceptibility to alternate arrangement (at times a kind of derangement), their divisibility and alterability endorsing a possibility of change inside the province of language—and outside it as well. The prominence these practices accord variation, the blessing they bestow on divergence from standard, supposedly stable procedure, accents agency and variability, the viability of intervention in the interest of change. In this respect, they relate Brathwaite to H.D., my relationship to whose work is the subject of "Palimpsestic Stagger," the essay that follows "Wringing the Word" and concludes part 1 of the book.

We find something of a "return to the pebble," that is, in H.D.'s *Trilogy*, a work, like many of Brathwaite's, written in response to social distress—in this case the bombing of London during World War II. At pains to intimate change and transformation, a way out of the disruption and duress it's written under, it turns for hope to the variability of words, the fruitful instability of words, the presence of alternate, hidden words within a given word, thematizing anagrammatic and cryptogrammic resonance. While not as radically and unremittingly as the work of Brathwaite does, it too directs our attention to letters and syllables, the pebbles of language, the particles words are made of. As H.D. writes,

. . . I know, I feel
the meaning that words hide;

they are anagrams, cryptograms,
little boxes, conditioned

to hatch butterflies . . .[5]

She then gives an example, not only finding hidden words within the name Osiris but relating Osiris and Sirius (already related in ancient Egyptian thought due to Sirius's rising coinciding with the flooding of the Nile, whose waters brought crops, Osiris, back to life) orthographically, the two being near anagrams of each other:

For example:
Osiris equates O-sir-is or O-Sire-is;

Osiris,
the star Sirius,

relates resurrection myth
and resurrection reality
(*T* 54)

Hence the question, repeated in two variations, "O, Sire, is this the path?" (*T* 57)—a breaking up of the word to reveal and release the words within it.

I was thinking of passages such as these when I titled the essay "Palimpsestic Stagger," naming it with a phrase taken from a poem of mine, "Alphabet of Ahtt," in which anagrams figure, anagrammatic play ventured not only with Cecil Taylor, to whom the poem is dedicated, in mind but with H.D. in mind as well. I was thinking of passages such as these when I wrote the poem, the coinage in whose title, "Ahtt," rearranges the title of a composition by Taylor, "Taht," itself a rearrangement—the word *that* spelled backwards. The unlikely (some would say) intersection of H.D.'s work with African American improvisational music was something I meant to allude to with the use of the term *palimpsestic* in the lines "Palimpsestic / stagger, / anagrammatic / scat,"[6] *Palimpsest* being the title of one of H.D.'s books and the figure of the palimpsest being one she made use of many times. Taylor's anagrammatic title partakes of what amounts to a tradition of such titles in the music known as jazz. Examples include Dizzy Gillespie's "Emanon" ("no name" spelled backwards), Sonny Rollins's "Airegin" ("Nigeria" spelled backwards), Thelonious Monk's "Eronel" ("Lenore" spelled backwards—an allusion to Edgar Allan Poe?), and Miles Davis's "Selim" ("Miles" spelled backwards). Such titles appear to reiterate or reinforce a point made by the music, improvisation's insistence that the given is only the beginning, that arrangements as we find them are subject to change, rearrangement—variable in ways analogous to bebop's reinvention of popular tunes by way of a return to the pebbles that chord changes can be said to be. An explicit interest in the permutability of words and the spells cast by spelling can be found in Sun Ra:

> So Mercury is the first heaven, Venus is the second heaven, Earth is the third heaven. Have we got any basis for this? Of course we have, because if you take the word "earth" and write it the way the English wrote it some time ago it'd be something like e-o-r-t-h-e. You go back to Shakespeare. Today you've got the "a" in there because alpha is equal to omega. If alpha is equal to omega, anywhere you see an "a" you can put an "o." So somebody did that. They spelled it e-a-r-t-h, although you do not need the "a." Phonetically it could be spelled e-r-t-h. If we permutate that we get t-h-r-e. And what is that? It's three, of course. So this planet is named after three, because it *is* three. Of course, the way it's spelled now is e-a-r-t-h. If you permutate that it's t-h-e-r-a. That's "The Ra." That's my name. You've got a case where it says that God would send down a New Jerusalem from heaven, a new Earth. And here you've got me and I say I'm from outer space. That's The Ra, you see. You permutate it. It's all right to permutate things, if alpha is equal to omega. You can switch things around. Change the name of the planet to The Ra. That's all right. You'd be in a better *position*, because the Earth is going. The point is that if you change the name of the planet then it won't be here when God gets ready to destroy it.[7]

The point isn't that Taylor, Gillespie, Rollins, Monk, Davis, Ra, and other such musicians have read H.D. but that I have—and that I relate the interest of these musicians in alternative arrangements of letters and sounds to her suggestion that words "are anagrams, cryptograms."

"Palimpsestic Stagger" ventures the notion of a coastal poetics, a coastal knowledge or way of knowing in H.D.'s work, evoking Brathwaite's littoral precincts by invoking his neologism "tidalectical," a term whose revision of "dialectical" replaces the latter's totalizing, recuperative teleology with a more stoic recognition of erosion, oscillation, drift. "Dialectics with my difference," Brathwaite calls it: "In other words, instead of the notion of one-two-three, Hegelian, I am now more interested in the movement of the water backwards and forwards as a kind of cyclic, I suppose, motion, rather than linear."[8] The interface where terra firma meets dissolution, the seashore, H.D.'s "desolate coast," occasions and figures a "return to the pebble," sand's granularity a recognition of contingency and fleeting time, the ephemerality of solidity and structure, "the mortality," as Harris puts it, "of all assumptions." Coastal knowledge, the granular disposition I spoke of earlier, views truth as in colloquial parlance, available a grain at a time and, at that, never not near salt, the proverbial grain of salt.

Both grains are present in H.D.'s work and in Brathwaite's work, as well as in the work of Duncan, whose poem "The Continent" (to which an essay in *Discrepant Engagement* is devoted) comes up in "Palimpsestic Stagger" and whose writing from the Vietnam War period is the subject of "Gassire's Lute: Robert Duncan's Vietnam War Poems," part 2 of this book. Both grains are present in my reading of those poems and of relevant attendant writing, earlier and adjacent poems and such prose as *The H.D. Book* and "Man's Fulfillment in Order and Strife." The tale of Gassire's lute, told by the Soninke of Mali and brought most famously into Western literature by Ezra Pound—via Leo Frobenius—in the *Pisan Cantos*, is taken as a cautionary tale, gone to for both the truth and the salt it provides. In *The H.D. Book*, Duncan warns that "in every event of his art man dwells in mixed possibilities of inflation or inspiration," a precept or perception that the story of Gassire's vanity, a story of musical inspiration inflated or fed by blood and political ambition, bears out and helps bring to bear on Duncan's own work.

Jerome Rothenberg, in his commentary on the tale of Gassire's lute in *Technicians of the Sacred*, writes that its "statement about the artist remains chilling."[9] It's an odd myth to turn to, as Duncan does in "Orders," to inaugurate a poetry for "the good of the people." Gassire's wish to be king has nothing to do with wanting to serve the people, as his willingness to sacrifice his sons and his "Wagadu can go to blazes!" attest. Duncan's idealizing appropriation of the tale is complicated by an intuitive or subliminal acknowledgement of its unflattering portrait of the artist, an acknowledgement which perhaps accounts for the lines "I put aside / whatever I once served of the poet." His resolve in this regard, this "putting aside," however, is itself complicated or contradicted by a cosmologizing impulse or investment typified by the claim "my thoughts are servants of the stars, and my words . . . / come from a mouth that is the Universe."

Cosmology and morality, astral inflation and human scale vie with one another in "Orders" and in Duncan's poems of the Vietnam War. His outrage at the U.S. assault on Indochina and his protest against it are mixed with an acceptance of the war, an embrace of it as a revelatory, epiphanic event, a disclosure of "What Is." Whether as the coming into existence of a cosmogonic Spirit or the business as usual of a status quo conceived as cosmic, "What Is" bespeaks a higher order, a higher understanding or identification the poet embodies or aspires to, an understanding or identification which can take a misanthropic or masochistic turn, something quite distinct from the humanism his invoking "the good of the people" leads one to expect.

Duncan's ambivalences and mixed inclinations include but are not exhausted by such an understanding or identification, its grain of truth coexisting with other grains of truth as well as the requisite grain or grains of salt. He has described himself as a nineteenth-century mind, a Romantic, and something of the totalizing providentiality we see in Whitman and others we take to be typical of the nineteenth century and earlier periods adheres to his work and thought (as it also does to H.D.'s): the assertion "There is only the one time" in "The Continent," the attraction to Jacob Boehme's near-dialectical or protodialectical doctrine of "the Father's Wrath working to create Itself in the Son as Love" and such. His ambivalences and mixed inclinations, however, complicate such adherence, a complication whose moments and minutia "Gassire's Lute" takes great pains to track, advancing a sense of tidalectical drift or oscillation between moral outrage and cosmic acquittal, human pathos and cosmic acquittal, a discrepant waver nowhere more succinctly present than in the final two lines of his variation on Robert Southwell's "The Burning Babe." Looking at photographs of children mutilated by napalm in Vietnam and imagining himself in their position, Duncan writes, "I think I could bear it. / I cannot think I could bear it," an aporia on whose bass or low note "Gassire's Lute" concludes.

Duncan's two propositions tail off into silence, even amounting to a sort of silence in their cross-cancellation. A version of the silence whose league with discrepant noise I alluded to earlier, they explicitly worry thought's compass, what can or cannot be thought. They implicitly worry the limits of the speakable as well, albeit their cross-cancellation or self-silencing does indeed speak. The last word, that is, is given to morality, to a delimitation of the properly human and to human pathos, but to a certain vexation as well. The lines' courting of silence recalls H.D.'s "I do not want / to talk about it," touched on in "Palimpsestic Stagger," and the complex invocation of silence in the work of Brathwaite and Marlene Nourbese Philip attended to in "Wringing the Word." Silence is limit case but resource as well, symptom of language's limit and symbolic access to what's outside those limits, symbolic as well of social damage or devastation and a strategic relativizing term, the grain of salt with which permissible articulations are to be taken, and so on. Duncan's discrepant waver, complicating the transcendence or would-be transcendence of "I think I could bear it," is of a piece with the faltering of his voice that he writes of experiencing when reading "Moving the Moving Image," a poem calling for the assumption of a priestly voice or a godly voice in delivering lines from "The Perfect Sermon" of Hermes. The nonattainment of that godly or priestly voice, the vocal rending the failed attempt results in, is an erosive assertion or reassertion of human scale, a return to granularity—analogous, I point out in "Gassire's Lute," to the tearing of the voice, the singing "without voice," that Lorca writes about in his essay on duende. The blood feeding Gassire's lute, like duende's love of "the rim of the wound," bespeaks the rootedness of the singer's or the poet's voice in human appetency and passion, an appetency whose upward aspiration thins the voice, stretches or strains it to the breaking point, brings it to grief—passionate, pathetic, unfulfilled.

I've had recourse to Lorca's "Theory and Function of the *Duende*" on several occasions, including my essay "Limbo, Dislocation, Phantom Limb: Wilson Harris and the Caribbean Occasion" in *Discrepant Engagement.* It is the launching point for "Cante Moro," the piece that opens part 3 of this book, a section comprised of pieces whose focus is music, usually in relationship to writing, and in which my own work in poetry and fiction comes to the fore to a greater degree—"Palimpsestic Stagger" excepted—than in the first two sections. First presented as a workshop talk at the Naropa Institute's Jack Kerouac School of Disembodied Poetics in 1991, "Cante Moro" took the occasion of the school's weeklong focus on the "New American Poetry" to revisit Lorca's essay, noting its presence in Donald M. Allen and Warren Tallman's *The Poetics of the New American Poetry*—its anomalous presence, Lorca being the only non-Anglophone poet and one of only two non-Americans included. The piece thus has to do with cross-cultural inspiration and provocation, a concern that in this case involves intermedia inspiration as well, the models for writing or even mandates for writing found in music. Its rehearsal of Lorca's theory of duende leads to a treatment of Jack Spicer, Robert Duncan, Amiri

Baraka and Bob Kaufman, four poets who allude to Lorca and whose work has been touched by his.

Picking up on analogies—Lorca's among them—that have been drawn between flamenco's *cante jondo* and African American music, "Cante Moro" reflects on musical examples by La Niña de los Peines (about whom Lorca writes in the duende essay), Miles Davis, John Coltrane, Mississippi Fred McDowell, Rahsaan Roland Kirk, and Sonny Rollins, with a side excursion to a love song from the Luristan province in Iran. The piece takes its title from one of the places where that analogy is drawn, a Manitas de Plata recording in whose liner notes Nat Hentoff likens flamenco to the blues. The title, more specifically, is borrowed from and alludes to a piece on the recording called "Moritas Moras," after whose initial run of singing one of the members of the group exclaims, "Eso es cante moro," which means "That's Moorish singing." It is this recording, *Manitas de Plata—Flamenco Guitar, Volume 2*, that Stephen Jonas refers to in his poem "Cante Jondo for Soul Brother Jack Spicer, His Beloved California & Andalusia of Lorca":

Hey, Manitas, Jack Spicer says make with Meritas Moras
            & the Cantaer intones the blues
                        like it was early one Monday mornin'
    'n I was on my way to school
                  & it was the mornin' i broke my muther's rule
        "eso es cante moro"
                          this cat is *bad*
    'cause the blues is bad
                          from 'down home' southern Spain

Later in the poem we read: "that's black singing. 'eso es cante moro.'"[10]

"Cante Moro" takes the singing "without voice" of which Lorca writes as an admission of lack, insufficiency, limit, an expression of the need for an alternate voice and, further, the pursuit of a metavoice. As though voice, articulation itself, no matter how eloquent, were always insufficient, duende admits it to be "without voice" regarding what matters, desire's frustrated, frustrating wish to go beyond. Duende, if it could, would push voice into a realm of adequacy beyond voice, a realm in its own way "without voice," unavailable, just as the extremity cante jondo laments is often said to be *sin remedio*—without remedy. This need for an alternate voice, whether as a second, supplementary voice or as an attenuation intimating a wished-for beyond, is addressed with regard to musical practices that achieve rending and dialogic effects and to poetry's cultivation of the bivocality or polyvocality of multiple meaning, "the speaking more than one knew what," as Duncan puts it. Intermedia supplementation, the alternate voice one medium affords another or proffers the model of to another, also pertains to this need or pursuit, raising questions of translation or translatability and collaboration between media that, touched on in "Cante Moro," come up again in the other pieces in part 3.

The alternate voice that Miles Davis came up with on trumpet, the alternative to the trumpet sound that preceded his, is the subject of "Blue in Green: Black Interiority," originally presented at the Miles Davis and American Culture conference at Washington University in 1995. That one would rather hear Davis flub a note than a more virtuosic player perfectly hit nine or ten has something to do with duende's feeling or sense that what needs to be said can't be said. A regard for limits (Davis's own technical limitations among them) and something of an inverse extrapolation beyond limits come into his unprecedented feel for space, "the concept of space breathing through the music," as he put it, his parsimonious meting out of sound. As drummer Billy Cobham has commented, "He always played the ultimate musical phrase, even if it wasn't technically correct. It was unbelievable! When you listen to Freddie Hubbard you hear trumpet proficiency par excellence, and then you hear Miles and he had a way of taking what Freddie did and compacting it in five notes. Those five notes said it all. The air around them became musical, and the silence became more profound and important. . . . Not playing became more important than playing. But it had to be the right spaces at the right time! It was uncanny how he'd play one note, and that one note would carry through five or six bars of changes. That note would be *the* note."[11] "Blue in Green: Black Interiority" takes that space to be reflective space, an emanation of as well as a claim to an interiority not readily, if at all, granted to African Americans by the axioms of American racism. It notes Davis's cultivation of a new sound and of the altered spaces—social and psychic, as well as sonic—that went with it, positing Davis's music of the 1950s and '60s as an inward turn, a repudiation of the identification of African Americans, especially African American musicians and entertainers, with extrovert immediatism. The essay's valorization of interiority, its recognition of mediacy and complication, is of a piece with the critique of externalist presuppositions made by "Phrenological Whitman" as well as with the case made for a cool, undramatic reading style in "Sight-Specific, Sound-Specific . . ." later in part 3.

"Blue in Green" concludes by way of recourse to an alternate voice I've been pursuing in a multivolume work in prose, that of "my friend" N., the fictional musician whose letters and lecture-libretti comprise *From a Broken Bottle Traces of Perfume Still Emanate.* A work that wavers with regard to genre, by turns an alternate, fictional voice pursued by criticism and an alternate, critical voice pursued by fiction (keeping aside, for simplicity's sake, its emergence from the serial poem "Song of the Andoumboulou" and its relationship to poetry), *From a Broken Bottle* is quoted from where it touches on Davis before the essay confesses having been able to say less about his sound than it set out to. The subject of the alternate, intermedia voice writing provides or seeks to provide music, its pursuit of what John Clellon Holmes calls "the unnameable truth of music," implicitly arises as this confession, like what we hear in duende, gives the last word to limits, untranslatability or elusive translatability, admitting writing to be "without voice," only partially endowed. "Blue and Green" thus returns, in muted fashion, to the topic of alliances between writing and music taken up by "Sound and Sentiment, Sound and Symbol" in *Discrepant Engagement,* the first essay, significantly, in which *From a Broken Bottle* is quoted from. Citing William Carlos Williams's insistence that "the arts take part for each other," "Sound and Sentiment, Sound and Symbol" suggests that endowments are always only partial, that the endowments of particular genres and artistic media call out, in their partiality, for supplementation, collaboration.

Collaboration and dissonance was the subject of the 1999 colloquium at which "Paracritical Hinge," the third piece in part 3 and the piece from which this book takes its title, was first presented. Taking place in conjunction with the Guelph Jazz Festival in Guelph, Ontario, the Jazz Festival Colloquium was devoted that year to "Collaborative Dissonances: Jazz, Discrepancy, and Cultural Theory" and, in addition to inviting me to take part as a keynote speaker, cited *Discrepant Engagement* in its call for papers, inviting, among other possible topics, treatments of "the emancipatory potential of 'discrepant engagement,' of 'practices that, in the interest of opening presumably closed orders of identity and signification, accent fissure, fracture, incongruity.'" Risking incongruity, I chose to present a fiction reading as my keynote address, reading from *Atet A.D.,* volume 3 of *From a Broken Bottle,* following prefatory comments regarding my desire to have fiction "sit in" or collaborate, in keeping with the colloquium's theme, with the sorts of critical and analytic discourse typical of colloquia. *From a Broken Bottle*'s genesis, its hybridity with regard to genre, and its relationship to discrepant engagement are touched on in those prefatory comments, which also elaborate upon the concept, phrase, and figure "paracritical hinge," *From a Broken Bottle*'s desire to be or to support a door permitting flow between disparate modes of articulation. The letters from *Atet A.D.* which follow the prefatory, talk part of this talk/reading address "cognitive dissonance," "participatory discrepancies," "emancipatory potential," and other issues. Among these is the vexed question of translatability between music and writing, the emergence of comic-strip balloons from a band member's horn doing what it implies is the one thing one can with such vexation: laugh not to cry.

"Sight-Specific, Sound-Specific. . . ," the final piece in part 3, also has to do with collaboration. Written at the request of the editors of *Additional Apparitions: Poetry, Performance and Site Specificity*, it deals with *Strick: Song of the Andoumboulou 16–25*, the compact disc I recorded with musicians Royal Hartigan and Hafez Modirzadeh in 1994. Commenting on the relationship of writerly poets to the notions of performance associated with performance art, poetry slams, and such, it goes on to propose alternative senses of the term *performance*, less theatrical or spectacular senses, stressing the variety of performances a poem entails and the variety of sites on which they take place (the ear, the page, the mind's eye, etc.). Following these comments, which characterize the attitudes toward performance I brought to the collaboration that resulted in *Strick*, the essay recounts aspects of the collaborative process, highlighting the impact of technical and material, as well as philosophical, factors. The preference it expresses for a cool, undeclamatory reading style even when accompanied by musicians recognizes the assets of music and musical instruments as impressive—imposing, even—but not ultimate or to be envied as having it all, not to be imitated or felt inferior to by the reading voice, which instead adheres to its own virtues or advantages, "a counter stress," as Williams wrote in another context, "to keep its own mind."[12] This, again, is a recognition of partial endowments, the partiality or nonultimacy of endowments, positing horizontal rather than hierarchical relationships among them. As the comic-strip balloons emerging from instruments in *From a Broken Bottle* suggest, if writing can be said to aspire to the condition of music, music can be said to aspire to the condition of writing.

My emphasis on the writerly in the context of performance in "Sight-Specific, Sound-Specific. . ." complicates a racial division of labor that identifies African Americans with orality, the "speakerly," and with performance in its most extrovert manifestations. The bearing other facets of this division of labor have on the status of African American experimental writing, a concern of "On Edge" and "Other: From Noun to Verb" in *Discrepant Engagement*, is the context for the first two pieces in part 4. "Destination Out," written in 1994 for a symposium on African American experimental writing in a journal—*Muleteeth*—whose publication never came about, is a short statement on the marginalization of such writing and the need for it nonetheless. "Expanding the Repertoire," presented in 2000 at the conference Expanding the Repertoire: Continuity and Change in African American Writing, also deals with the canonization of certain assumptions and expectations regarding African American writing and the relative inattention to its experimental sides. These concerns are also among those addressed by the third piece in part 4, "Editing *Hambone*," a brief account of the history and the aims of the literary journal I edit. This account was presented at The Vehicle of Poetry, a conference on literary magazines, in 1998. It relates my intentions and my activities as an editor to *Discrepant Engagement*'s desire to widen the scope of discussions of experimental writing, to gain greater recognition of the cross-cultural, multiracial range of such writing and of innovative artistic practices more generally. It notes that relationship and makes that connection on its way to making the point that my work as a writer, as a critic, and as an editor have lent themselves to one another, gone hand in hand.

This latter point is also made by the six interviews that comprise part 5. Conducted between 1991 and 2000, they focus primarily on my poetry and fiction, but address my critical and editorial work as well. The point is also, one would hope, made by the book as a whole, which takes *Discrepant Engagement*'s interstitial play and nontotalizing drift a bit farther, making explicit what was merely implicit in the earlier volume. More varied in the kinds of pieces it includes and in the occasions from which those pieces are drawn, the present volume goes further toward insisting that critical and creative practice work together. The citation of *From a Broken Bottle* in "Sound and Sentiment, Sound and Symbol" moves *Discrepant Engagement* somewhat in that direction, as does the recourse to the Dogon "Creaking of the Word" (a staple, along with other Dogon lore, in my poetry and fiction) in "Poseidon (Dub Version)" and the very expression *discrepant engagement*. The present volume cites my work in poetry and fiction considerably more often, that work being expressly the subject of several of its pieces. That the book takes its title from a piece comprised primarily of an excerpt from *Atet A.D.* highlights this fact. It accents as well the attempt I mention in the interview conducted by Paul Naylor to learn from the high status accorded figural knowledge, the knowledge carried and generated by figures, in Wilson Harris's critical as well as creative work.

"I speak in figures," Williams writes in "Asphodel, That Greeny Flower," addressing his wife:

well enough, the dresses
you wear are figures also,
we could not meet
otherwise.
(*PB* 159)

This to me is a Dogon moment, recalling Ogotemmêli's discourse on fabric as carrier of the word, instilled with the word, dress and adornment as instigators of desire, invitations to knowledge, his comment that "to be naked is to be speechless."[13] Figures excite and sustain heuristic desire. The title of the present volume avails itself of a figure related to another Dogon moment, the "Creaking of the Word" already mentioned, a figure found at several points in *From a Broken Bottle*, where the letter and the ostensibly literal are said to "creak like the floorboards and doors in a haunted house,"[14] where the dreamer in a dream peeps through a door "hung on rusted hinges" that occasionally creak,[15] where "anagrammatic odor" pries open and rearranges "anagrammatic door" in a hotel whose doors never open or close without creaking,[16] where a lecture/libretto bears the title I've given this introduction, itself the echo of that of an early piece by reggae singer Burning Spear. The book wants to say, by way of recourse to that figure, something about the rickety fit of its parts, this introduction to say, by way of recourse to that title, something about the need to be participant-observer, anthropologist and informant both (ain'thropologist), something like Zora Neale Hurston's "you got tuh *go* there tuh *know* there,"[17] or Duncan's quotation of St. John of Ephesus, "If you have not entered the Dance, you mistake the event."[18] Doors are for going through.

PART I

Phrenological Whitman

Regarded as a pseudoscience nowadays and subject to parody and caricature, phrenology was "the science of mind" in the United States during the nineteenth century. It was taken seriously by a great number of people and Walt Whitman was one of those people; Fowler and Wells was a phrenological business whose Phrenological Cabinet Whitman visited frequently in New York. In the 1855 preface to *Leaves of Grass*, Whitman includes the phrenologist among those he describes as "the lawgivers of poets": "The sailor and traveler . . . the anatomist chemist astronomer geologist phrenologist spiritualist mathematician historian and lexicographer are not poets, but they are the lawgivers of poets and their construction underlies the structure of every perfect poem."[1] He reiterates this in "Song of the Answerer": "The builder, geometer, chemist, anatomist, phrenologist, artist, all these underlie the maker of poems." In "By Blue Ontario's Shore," he asks,

> Who are you indeed who would talk or sing to America?
> Have you studied out the land, its idioms and men?
> Have you learn'd the physiology, phrenology, politics, geography, pride, freedom, friendship of the land? its substratums and objects?

Earlier in the poem, he praises mechanics and farmers, particularly "the freshness and candor of their physiognomy, the copiousness and decision of their phrenology." Phrenological terms, terms such as *Amativeness*, *Adhesiveness*, and *Combativeness*, which were used to describe the phrenological faculties, are scattered throughout this and other poems.

Phrenology portrayed the brain as divided into different faculties that controlled the various aspects of personality. *Adhesiveness* was its name for the propensity for friendship and camaraderie, *Amativeness* its name for romantic, sexual love, *Philoprogenitiveness* its name for the love of offspring, and so on. There was disagreement among the different versions of phrenology as to how many faculties there were, the number ranging from thirty-five to ninety-six, but phrenological nomenclature pertaining to the faculties contributed significantly to the vocabulary of Whitman's poems. In "Mediums," regarding future Americans, truly fulfilled Americans, he proclaims: "They shall be alimentive, amative, perceptive, / They shall be complete women and men." *Adhesiveness* became Whitman's favorite phrenological term. In "Song of the Open Road," he writes, "Here is adhesiveness." And in "So Long!": "I announce adhesiveness, I say it shall be limitless unloosen'd." "A Song of Joys" doesn't explicitly name the phrenological faculties, but the joys that it catalogs are each related to a specific phrenological "organ" and, taken together, constitute a model of phrenological well-being. The poem was inspired by one of Orson and Lorenzo Fowler's phrenological manuals, *The New Illustrated Self-Instructor in Phrenology and Physiology*.

The documentation of Whitman's interest in phrenology dates back to 1846. An article on phrenology that he clipped from an issue of *American Review* that year has been found among his papers. In November of that year, while he was editor of the Brooklyn *Daily Eagle*, he wrote a review of several phrenological manuals, a review in which he announced, "Breasting the waves of detraction, as a ship dashes sea-waves, Phrenology, it must now be confessed by all men who have open eyes, has at last gained a position, and a firm one, among the sciences."[2] Four months later, in March 1847, he wrote an article called "Something about Physiology and Phrenology" in which he praised the leading proselytizers of phrenology in the United States, Orson and Lorenzo Fowler and Samuel Wells: "Among the most persevering workers in phrenology in this country, must certainly be reckoned the two Fowlers and Mr. Wells" (cited in *HH* 100). Whitman was not alone in his interest in phrenology. It was an interest he shared with most if not all of the writers and thinkers of his day, including Edgar Allan Poe, Horace Mann, and Ralph Waldo Emerson, as phrenology played an important role in various movements for self-improvement and social reform. Its basic precept was appealingly simple: the faculties within the brain display their degree of development by protrusions on the cranium, bumps on the head; hence the other name it was known by, "Bumpology." Phrenologists would read, as they put it, the bumps on a client's head, particular bumps corresponding to particular faculties. The head was thought to offer a map of the client's mind and personality. Whitman had his bumps read by Lorenzo Fowler in July 1849.

Orson and Lorenzo Fowler, who were to become publishers of the second edition of *Leaves of Grass* in August 1856, transformed phrenology into a business enterprise during the 1830s. Orson Fowler became interested in phrenology early in the decade while he was a student at Amherst College. In Vermont in 1834 he gave his first lecture on phrenology, and during the next few years, with his brother Lorenzo, he made a number of lecture tours around the country. In 1838 he set up an office in Philadelphia called the Phrenological Museum (also called the Phrenological Cabinet and the Phrenological Depot) and began to publish the *American Phrenological Journal and Miscellany*, which would eventually publish some of Whitman's anonymous reviews of his own *Leaves of Grass*. This was a year after his brother had set up the New York Phrenological Rooms on Broadway in Manhattan. In 1842 the two of them joined forces when Orson moved from Philadelphia to New York; there they established, with their brother-in-law Samuel Wells, who was married to their sister Charlotte, the Phrenological Cabinet that Whitman grew fond of visiting. Speaking of his return from New Orleans in 1848, Whitman wrote in one of his reminiscences, "One of the choice places of New York to me then was the 'Phrenological Cabinet' of Fowler & Wells, Nassau Street near Beekman."[3] It was there that he had his bumps read by Lorenzo Fowler, and he kept the chart all his life. It was published five times: in the Brooklyn *Daily Times* in September 1855, in the first, second, and third editions of *Leaves of Grass*, and posthumously by his literary executors, to whom Whitman had given it during the last year of his life, in a book called *Regarding Walt Whitman*.

Whitman published and republished his chart to credential himself; it was, according to phrenological opinion on the subject, a poet's chart. Wells and the Fowlers were interested, as were others, in the poetic personality and the making of the poet, and in the *American Phrenological Journal* they featured articles on the phrenological characteristics of poets. These articles stressed the balanced, well-rounded character of the poet, the equitable development of the poet's faculties and the manifestation of this equitability on the poet's head. The expression "well-rounded" had to do with the phrenological belief that the best head is a round head, a head whose bumps are equally developed and distributed. Whitman's chart describes his head as "large and rounded in every direction" and he offered it as evidence of his poetic qualifications. He makes his own case for the poet's well-roundedness in the 1855 preface when he writes, "The poet is the equable man." This, by then, was a phrenological commonplace. An article published in *The Phrenological Journal and Magazine of*

Moral Science in 1846, for example, argued, "Good Taste consists in the appropriate manifestation of each and all of the faculties in their proper season and degree; and this can only take place from persons in whom they are so balanced that there is no tendency for any one of them unduly to assume the mastery. When such a mind is prompted by some high theme to its fullest action, each organ contributes to the emotion of the moment and words are uttered in such condensed meaning, that a single sentence will touch every fibre of the heart, or, what is the same thing, arouse every faculty of the hearer. The power is known as Inspiration, and the medium in which it is conveyed is called Poetry" (cited in WWCB, 366). The power of poetry resides in an equitable development of the faculties; the mind should be a democratic ensemble in which no single faculty dominates. This idea is central to Whitman's sense of himself as poet and to his sense of the American poet's democratic vocation.

Phrenology's attention to cranial manifestation of mind, its postulation of a tangible, tactile availability of mental attributes, epitomized a physiological accent that had obvious impact on Whitman's work. In one of the Fowler and Wells publications we find the following: "Poets require the highest order of both temperament and development. Poetry depends more on the physiology than the phrenology. It consists in a spiritual ecstasy which can be better felt than described. Not one in many thousands of those who write verses has the first inspiration of true poetry" (cited in *HH* 73). Whitman's long song of bodily exuberance and appetitive touch tends at times, in ways that this formulation would have ratified, toward a hypersensitivity of a convulsive sort, bordering on ecstatic susceptibility: "You villain touch! what are you doing? . . . . my breath is tight in its throat; / Unclench your floodgates! you are too much for me." Likewise, his emphasis on bodily health and development was in keeping with the practical phrenology of Wells and the Fowlers, who were in the forefront of influential movements for social and individual reform. They not only advocated change in such areas as education and criminology but were proponents of vegetarianism, water cures, and the like. They conducted a campaign against tight clothing and rigid posture, whose influence can be seen in the famous photograph of Whitman published in the early editions of *Leaves of Grass*. This too was a self-credentialing move; his relaxed pose and his unbottoned shirt show him to be phrenologically correct.

A significantly commercial undertaking, practical phrenology marketed the idea that a person could change his character; bumps, like muscles, could be made bigger or smaller through more or less exercise. A belief in the changeability or, even, perfectability of personality was crucial to phrenology's program of self-improvement and social reform, a program whose commercial as well as ideological aspects we find Whitman very much in the thick of. Fowler and Wells sold and distributed the first edition of *Leaves of Grass*, which Whitman published himself, and then published the second edition the following year. Whitman had had an earlier connection with them; he worked as a bookseller in 1850 and 1851, and very prominent on his shelves were books published by Fowler and Wells. He reviewed *Leaves of Grass* anonymously, as previously mentioned, in their *American Phrenological Journal*, and for several months in 1855 and 1856 he wrote a series of articles called "New York Dissected" for another publication of theirs, *Life Illustrated*. His call, in *Leaves of Grass*, for a reformation of poetry and for poetry as a means of reformation partook of and took its place within a reformist atmosphere in which phrenology played a central part.

Before it could sponsor reform in the United States, phrenology itself had to undergo a reform of sorts, a revision in its migration from its place of origin, Europe. Under the name *cranioscopy*, phrenology was developed by the German physician Franz Joseph Gall, who began experimenting with it in the late 1700s and lecturing about it in the early 1800s; his book *On the Functions of the Brain and Each of Its Parts* was published in French in 1825 and in English in 1835. He advanced four basic principles: (1) the moral and intellectual dispositions are innate; (2) their manifestation depends on organization; (3) the brain is exclusively the organ of mind; (4) the brain is composed of as many particular and independent organs as there are fundamental powers of the mind. Gall asked, as a kind of corollary, "how far the inspection of the form of the head, or cranium, presents a means of ascertaining the existence or absence, and the degree of development, of certain cerebral parts; and consequently the presence or absence, the weakness or energy of certain functions."[4] This question occupied a peripheral position in Gall's original formulations but it was seized upon by later phrenologists and vigorously promoted in a series of revisions that popularized phrenology and brought it to the United States. No longer a question but a central tenet, an assertion, it became known as the doctrine of the skull.

It was Gall's assistant, Johann Caspar Spurzheim, who began to popularize cranioscopy, changing its name to phrenology and coining the phrase "phrenology, the science of mind." He formulated four basic tenets as well, though they're significantly different from Gall's, especially in their incorporation of the doctrine of the skull as a central principle: (1) the brain is the organ of the mind; (2) the mind is a plurality of faculties, each springing from a distinct brain organ; (3) in the same person, larger organs show more energy, smaller organs show less; (4) the size and form of the skull are determined by the brain. The doctrine of the skull, thanks to Spurzheim, became canonical wisdom for phrenologists and their followers. John Davies, in *Phrenology: Fad and Science*, characterizes the difference in outlook between Gall and Spurzheim, a difference that makes it clear why Spurzheim's revision of Gall lent itself to the democratic ethic phrenology became bound up with in the United States:

> Gall accepted the existence of evil in the world, and particularly of evil propensities in mankind, even labeling one region of the brain "Murder." The great majority of men, he thought, were composed of mediocrities, and he emphasized the creative role of genius and its destined function to command; his science would be the instrument by which the elite could govern effectively and rationally the mass of mankind. In keeping with the aristocratic clientele with which he had been associated, his was neither a democratic nor a liberal creed.
>
> Spurzheim, on the other hand, deliberately omitted from his categories all faculties which were inherently evil; on the contrary, all were intrinsically good and only from the abuse of them could evil result. Mankind was created potentially good, and in contrast to Gall's cynical pessimism, Spurzheim looked forward to the perfection of the race by the aid of phrenology.[5]

Spurzheim brought a sense of mission to phrenology. He learned English in six months in order to make a lecture tour of Great Britain in 1814. He published a book on his and Gall's findings, *The Physiognomical System of Drs. Gall and Spurzheim, Founded on an Anatomical and Physiological Examination of the Nervous System in General, and of the Brain in Particular*, that was harshly critiqued by the *Edinburgh Review*, thus occasioning a trip to Edinburgh to answer his critics. It was in Edinburgh, where he stayed for seven months, that one of the later proselytizers of phrenology heard him speak. Spurzheim eventually visited the United States, embarking on a lengthy lecture tour in August 1832, in the course of which, three months later, he died. He was given an elaborate funeral at Harvard University and was buried in Boston, his death contributing considerably to the popularization of phrenology in the U.S.

George Combe was a Scotsman who heard Spurzheim speak in Edinburgh and became a vigorous crusader for phrenology. (In his novel *The War of the End of the World*, Mario Vargas Llosa merges Combe with Gall; one of the characters, a Scottish phrenologist named Gall, goes to South America and inspires peasant revolts.) Combe was looking for a way out of Calvinism and later said that "phrenology conferred on me the first internal peace of mind that I experienced." He and his brother formed a phrenological society and began publishing the *Phrenological Journal* in 1823. In 1828 he published a book that became very influential, *The Constitution of Man Considered in Relation to External Objects*, a book that Emerson called "the best sermon I've read for some time." Combe toured and lectured in the United States from 1838 to 1840, further increasing phrenology's popularity. Thomas Hardy Leahey and Grace Evans Leahey comment, in *Psychology's Occult Doubles*, "To Gall's physiology Spurzheim wedded philosophy and Combe wedded reform. It only remained for Americans to wed this *ménage à trois* to business" (*POD* 64). Practical phrenologists like Wells and the Fowlers took up and marketed Spurzheim and Combe's idea that phrenology was the key to reform and self-improvement. It was a somewhat self-reflexive idea; phrenology itself had been the object of reform, "improved" by Spurzheim's revision of Gall.

Phrenology in the United States, in Whitman's text as well as outside it, became entwined with nationalist feelings and millenarian hopes. The Fowlers wrote of their *American Phrenological Journal* in 1849, "Its present desire is this—to PHRENOLOGIZE OUR NATION, for thereby it will REFORM THE WORLD. No evil exists in society but it sternly yet calmly rebukes, and points out a more excellent way. No reform, no proposed good, but it strenuously enforces. It is the very 'Head and Front' of that new and happy order of things now so rapidly superseding the old misery-inflicting institutions of society" (cited in *PFS* 46). Their optimism rested on an analogy between mental development and muscular development that they resorted to again and again. Like muscles, bumps put the degree of development of particular faculties on display; they also, again like muscles, make it possible to increase development through exercise. Phrenology thereby offered a way both to know oneself and to change oneself. "The exercise of particular mental faculties," Orson Fowler wrote, "causes the exercise, and consequent enlargement, of corresponding portions of the brain" (cited in *HH* 32). Madeleine B. Stern comments, "The Fowlers' statement that 'The organs can be enlarged or diminished . . . even in adults' was simply a technical way of saying that

'Man is not compelled to carry all his faults, excesses, and defects to the grave'" (*HH* 34).

Phrenology's mind/muscle analogy contributes, in Whitman's work, to an athleticization of mind, brain as brawn, and the trope of a gymnastic text. Thus, in "So Long!": "To young men my problems offering—no dallier I—I the muscle of their brains trying." In prose as well as verse he advances the figure of mind as muscle, calling for writing which would make reading a kind of calisthenic. In "Democratic Vistas" we read, "In fact, a new theory of literary composition for imaginative works of the very first class, and especially for highest poems, is the sole course open to these States. Books are to be call'd for, and supplied, on the assumption that the process of reading is not a half-sleep, but, in highest sense, an exercise, a gymnast's struggle; that the reader is to do something for himself, must be on the alert, must himself or herself construct indeed the poem, argument, history, metaphysical essay—the text furnishing the hints, the clue, the start or frame-work. Not the book needs so much to be the complete thing, but the reader of the book does. That were to make a nation of supple and athletic minds, well train'd, intuitive, used to depend on themselves, and not on a few coteries of writers."

He returns to this idea in the essay "Poetry To-day in America—Shakspere—The Future." The participatory-democratic ethic or ideal is obvious, but one of the more interesting things about Whitman proposing this role for the reader is that it's not a role that seems to apply to his own work. Whitman would appear to be a writer who does it all for the reader ("what I assume you shall assume"), offering an explicit, self-evident text of a prodigiously declarative, transparent sort. Is this a symptom of the ideological nature of Whitman's stance, the false consciousness doctrinal exuberance tends to be compromised by? The idea of the reader actively contributing to the construction of the text has become something of a commonplace by now, advocated by a range of twentieth-century experimental movements that includes the French "New Novel," the Fiction Collective, and the L=A=N=G=U=A=G=E poets, to name a few. The writing advanced by this idea is characteristically opaque, oblique, convoluted, often refractory—hardly "reader-friendly," however much it invites the reader's participation (or, more to the point, *because* it invites the reader's participation). The sort of work Whitman's advocacy of a gymnastic text might lead us to expect—recondite, elliptical work that catches us up in extended puzzlement and indeterminate exegesis, work we hermeneutically wrestle with, the sort of work offered in his own century, for example, by Emily Dickinson—is not what we get. Whitman teases the brain with paradox and contradiction on occasion, but his most characteristic manner is aggressively straightforward and accessible, requiring little of the reader beyond turning the page.

The demand is actually elsewhere—or directs the reader elsewhere. Whitman doesn't invite the reader to dwell on the text at great length. Rather, he cautions against exactly that, turning the reader away from the text. At the end of "Whoever You Are Holding Me Now in Hand" he admonishes,

> For it is not for what I have put into it that I have written this book,
> Nor is it by reading it you will acquire it, . . .
> For all is useless without that which you may guess at many times and not hit,
> that which I hinted at;
> Therefore release me and depart on your way.

Such admonition borders on abolishing the text. Whitman imagined world reform of such magnitude as to do away with the need for poetry. In "Thou Mother with Thy Equal Brood":

> Brain of the New World, what a task is thine,
> To formulate the Modern—out of the peerless grandeur of the modern,
> Out of thyself, comprising science, to recast poems, churches, art,
> (Recast, may-be discard them, end them—may-be their work is done, who
> knows?)

The work to be done goes beyond the page but takes up its image, for the gymnastic text is not the text as such but a turning toward the world as text. The athleticism resides in that turn, a conversion to the work of reform which is willing to envision poetry's abolition, poetry as literary text replaced by poetry as concrete action.

Whitman and phrenology shared a reliance on tropes of textuality, figurations of human character and action as forms of writing or printing. Phrenological prognosis was viewed and referred to in such terms; one had one's bumps *read.* A contemporary account of an afternoon at the Phrenological Cabinet contains the following: ". . . you hear some one reading rapidly. Looking up, you find that it is from a page of Nature's imprint, and that . . . the reader does it by the sense of touch. Standing beside a young girl, with his hands upon her head, forthwith that head under his deft manipulation turns tell-tale . . . betraying her idiosyncrasies" (cited in *HH* 200). This was consistent with the motto under which Fowler and Wells published the *Phrenological Almanac*: "Nature's Printing Press is Man, her types are Signs, her books are Actions" (*HH* 67–68). The presumed legibility of human beings was crucial to the promises of individual and social reform with which both Whitman and phrenology were involved. Democracy itself was believed to hinge on it. Democratic community, the argument went, depended on the ability of human beings to know one another; the democratic imperative was not only to know oneself but to know one's fellow citizens as well. The *American Phrenological Journal* insisted that nature aids this project of knowing by making people legible to one another, imprinting signs upon human surfaces. We read, "To this requisition—*imperious demand*—for knowing our fellow men, Nature has kindly adapted the *expression* of those mental qualities on the one hand, and our recognition of them on the other. Nature has ordained that we do not hide the light of our souls under the bushels of impenetrability but that we should set them on the hill of conspicuosity, so that all that are with insight may observe them. She even *compels* such expression. She has rendered the suppression of our mentality *absolutely impossible*. She has rendered such expression *spontaneous and irresistible*, by having instituted the NATURAL LANGUAGE of emotion and character . . . which compels us to tell each other all about ourselves. . . . It is desirable for us to know *all* . . . *all* the existing emotions of mankind *are legible. They come to the surface*" (cited in *POD* 106). Haunting such insistence is an anxiety over the limits of knowability, the specter of an opaque latency resistant to full disclosure. Phrenology's assurances of providential imprint sought to dispel that specter. According to Henry Ward Beecher, a friend at Amherst who introduced Orson Fowler to phrenology, "Men are like open books, if looked at properly" (cited in *HH* 2).

Whitman's famous "Camerado, this is no book, / Who touches this touches a man" is the converse of Beecher's formulation and bespeaks a two-way, phrenologically informed translation between body and book, person and poem. His assurance and exhortation in the 1855 preface that "your very flesh shall be a great poem" agrees with a statement made by Lydia Fowler, wife of Lorenzo Fowler and one of the first female medical students in the United States, that "every bone and muscle is an unwritten poem of beauty" (cited in *HH* 157). Castings of body as text and of text as body recur with notorious insistence throughout *Leaves of Grass*: "the expression of a well-made man" that "conveys as much as the best poem" in "I Sing the Body Electric"; the phallic "poem drooping shy and unseen that I always carry, and that all men carry" in "Spontaneous Me"; the assertion that "Human bodies are words, myriads of words" and that "In the best poems re-appears the body, man's or woman's" in "A Song of the Rolling Earth"; and so on. There is, though, more to this than there might seem, as phrenology's accent on textuality and self-improvement moves away, in Whitman's work, from simple surface cheer and celebration of health toward evocations of death and disappearance. The translatability of body and book subsists on writing as sublimation, compensation, the two-way traffic between text and flesh on a sense of the text as an alternate body, mind masquerading as body, flesh's death or sublimation as text.

There is a great deal in Whitman's work that suggests that writing is a kind of dying, a disappearance into (in order to live on in) the book, that the alternate body afforded by the book is an improved, augmented body, the page a place of alternate growth (grave plot and a compensative going forth: "leaves of grass"). In the same poem in which he writes, "I the muscle of their brains trying" and "Who touches this touches a man"—a poem tellingly titled "So Long!"—he writes, "I spring from the pages into your arms—decease calls me forth." And at the end, "I depart from materials, / I am as one disembodied, triumphant, dead." A poem whose final version was completed in 1881 and included in a section of the 1891–92 *Leaves of Grass* called "Songs of Parting," it can, of course, be read as Whitman, having entered his sixties, referring to an approaching and quite literal death. But the first version was completed twenty-one years earlier, in 1860, a fact suggesting that "decease" is also a figurative death afforded by writing, that writing was valedictory all along, a long rehearsal for death, and also that death equates with words as nondeeds, not doing. One of the notable things about Whitman's phrenological chart is that he was rated very high in "Cautiousness"; Lorenzo Fowler, evaluating the faculties on a scale that ran from 1 to 7, gave him a 6. Several critics and commentators on Whitman's relationship to phrenology find this surprising given the audacity of *Leaves of Grass*, but they miss the fact that in his written assessment Lorenzo Fowler says to Whitman, "You are more careful about what you *do* than you are about what you say" (cited in *HH* 103). Fowler may have, phrenology notwithstanding, happened upon an accurate characterization, for all the questions and doubts that have been raised as to what Whitman actually did rather than said he did or wrote about as though he'd done—questions and doubts about an affair in New Orleans, about the children he claimed to have fathered, about whether he was sexually active at all, and so on—suggest a relationship of compensation between words and deeds in his life and work. Words compensate for the not-done, improving on deeds hemmed in by caution and convention. In "Ventures, on an Old Theme," Whitman argues that poetic audacity, a disregard for social propriety of the sort found in *Leaves of Grass,* serves a necessary function. We read, "One reason [for not respecting the rule of society in my poems], and to me a profound one, is that the soul of a man or woman demands, enjoys compensation in the highest directions for this very restraint of himself or herself, level'd to the average, or rather mean, low, however eternally practical, requirements of society's intercourse. To balance this indispensable abnegation, the free minds of poets relieve themselves, and strengthen and enrich mankind with free flights in all the directions not tolerated by ordinary society."

Jorge Luis Borges is right: "There are two Whitmans: the 'friendly and eloquent savage' of *Leaves of Grass* and the poor writer who invented him. . . . The mere happy vagabond proposed by the verses of *Leaves of Grass* would have been incapable of writing them."[6] The idea of poetry as compensation explains, in part, Whitman's turning the reader away from the text and his willingness to envision poetry's extinction. If poetry subsists on lack and not doing, the reader, if there is to be substantive fulfillment and realization, mustn't be encouraged to linger with it.

Writing, self-improvement, and death form a matrix in Whitman's work that echoes phrenology's advocacy of writing—specifically, epitaph writing—as an aid to self-improvement. Lorenzo Fowler counseled his audiences, "Write your own epitaphs in legible characters on a slip of paper; make them as flattering and eulogistic as possible. Then spend the remainder of your lives, endeavoring not only to reach the standard . . . you have raised, but to go far beyond it" (cited in *HH* 188). Self-eulogy abounds in *Leaves of Grass.* A sense of the book as an epitaph is evident throughout, nowhere more explicitly than in the 1881 poem "As at Thy Portals Also Death": "I grave a monumental line, before I go, amid these songs, / And set a tombstone here." Whitman's investment in a compensatory sense of writing closes off the possibility of living up to and even beyond, as Fowler would have it, the standard such writing sets, but the specter it raises of textualization as a shortcut to self-improvement, a means to fraudulent self-improvement, applies to phrenology as well. Practitioners such as the Fowlers—who were, after all, running a business—appear to have sweetened their readings to make them appeal to their clients. A person who had undergone a reading wrote in 1835, "The faculties the phrenologist made mention that I possessed were in almost all cases very true so far as I can judge of my own mind. I am rather inclined to think he neglects to tell the evil passion as in my case and many others none were noticed which I am confident we possessed. Perhaps self-interest prompts him" (cited in *PFS* 35). The reading itself was an act of improvement. The Fowlers, responding in the *American Phrenological Journal* to questions regarding the accuracy and integrity of their readings, admitted that "if we must err, we prefer to err upon the side of charity."

Phrenology's sweetened readings remind us that both the advantage and the danger of textualization is the ability to erase and to revise. This sheds some light on Whitman's decades-long revision of *Leaves of Grass*, a process that included a revision of the phrenological chart he published with the first three editions, a revision in which he took a cue from the Fowlers. Finding his scores in some faculties not high enough, he changed them (not an altogether surprising move for someone "6 to 7" in "Self-Esteem"). After the first edition he edited Lorenzo Fowler's comments; among the phrases he excised was one describing him as "too unmindful probably of the conviction of others," a trait inconsistent with the democratic outlook he advertised. Reduced to textual manipulation, the project of self-improvement borders on self-parody, as does the frequently hollow ring of Whitman's exclamations in *Leaves of Grass*, but not without saying something real about nineteenth-century U.S. aspirations. "Self-made or never made," one of the Fowlers' most famous mottos, says more than they intended perhaps in its implication of an urgency (a desperation even) willing to risk vanity, self-aggrandizement, mere self-service.

Phrenological revision, both that of Gall's founding precepts and practical phrenology's willingness "to err on the side of charity," served an American optimism beginning to make a move on world ascendancy. It offered a hopeful hermeneutic, banishing the threat of dark recesses with an assurance that everything could be brought to light, everything seen, everything brought to the surface. The *American Phrenological Journal* in 1846 claimed that phrenology offered "*tangible, certain, absolute,* KNOWLEDGE," going on to exclaim, "Behold, then, the true SCIENCE OF MIND! Behold the study of this godlike department of our nature reduced to DEMONSTRABLE CERTAINTY!" (cited in *POD* 100). Uncertainty—doubt—was the serpent in the Garden that the New World was taken to be. (Whitman refers to "doubt nauseous undulating like a snake" in "Rise O Days from Your Fathomless Deeps.") Phrenology said no to that serpent. One of the critics of phrenology, Dr. Thomas Sewall, warned that "nature does not reveal her secrets by external forms" (cited in *HH* 23). Likewise, several major writers assumed a much more skeptical stance toward phrenology than did Whitman. Poe, though he favorably reviewed phrenological journals early on and used phrenological categories in some of the characterizations in his fiction, went on to write parodies of it. Mark Twain dealt skeptically with it as well. Herman Melville, in *Moby-Dick*, has Ishmael attempt to phrenologize the whale, only to conclude that it can't be done; a work having so largely to do with inscrutability would of course find phrenology's hopeful hermeneutic suspect.

If, as Allen F. Roberts observes in an essay on the epistemology of the Tabwa people of Zaire, black is "a looking inward at what is not apparent but is nonetheless the essence of being," an "artfully indirect suggestion or insinuation—the gnawing suspicion that an act or event has meaning beyond what one sees,"[7] phrenology was a white way of knowing. It valorized obtrusion, surface, apparency, warding off the obscurities and indeterminacies of recess, crevice, fold. It was also white in another sense, serving other senses of whiteness. While its advocates preached self-improvement and social reform, the emphasis was by and large individualistic, seeking to better society through individual cultivation of the virtues of self-help—thrift, hard work, purity, perseverance. Its advocacy of social reform, while populist in many respects, failed to offer its beneficence and promise of improvement to those who were not white; its will to reform didn't extend to reforming notions of racial determinism or the social relations upheld by such notions. Phrenology in fact shared with these notions an assumption that human surfaces offer incontestable evidence of the qualities, capacities, and traits not only of individuals but of groups. Its attention to cranial bumps is consistent with and occupies a place within a mode of reading human prowess that also attends to skin color, hair texture, and other phenotypic and physiognomic features. As the frontispiece to his *Phrenology: Fad and Science*, John Davies reproduces a phrenological diagram that compares, along an evolutionistic scale of development, the cranial shape and the forehead slope of eleven creatures. It shows four animals and seven humans; the animals, in order of development, are a snake, a dog, an elephant, and an ape; the human figures, in order of development, are designated "Human Idiot," "Bushman," "Uncultivated," "Improved," "Civilized," "Enlightened," and "Caucasian—Highest Type."

Racist evolutionism textualized earth surfaces as well, ascribing a providential imprint to bodies of land. Representative John A. Harper in 1812 employed a trope which was to be repeatedly taken up in the rhetoric of manifest destiny, arguing that the Author of Nature had "marked our limits in the south, by the Gulf of Mexico; and on the north by the regions of eternal frost."[8] The decimation of indigenous populations and the wresting away of their lands was an act of erasure and revision, a providentially mandated improvement in which a superior race vanquished and evicted an inferior one. Whitman, as he was with phrenology, was on intimate, speaking terms with such notions. He was an admirer of John L. O'Sullivan, whose *Democratic Review* he frequently wrote for and who, in support of annexing Texas in 1845, invoked the nation's "manifest destiny to overspread the continent allotted by Providence for the free development of our yearly multiplying millions."[9] In March 1846, Whitman

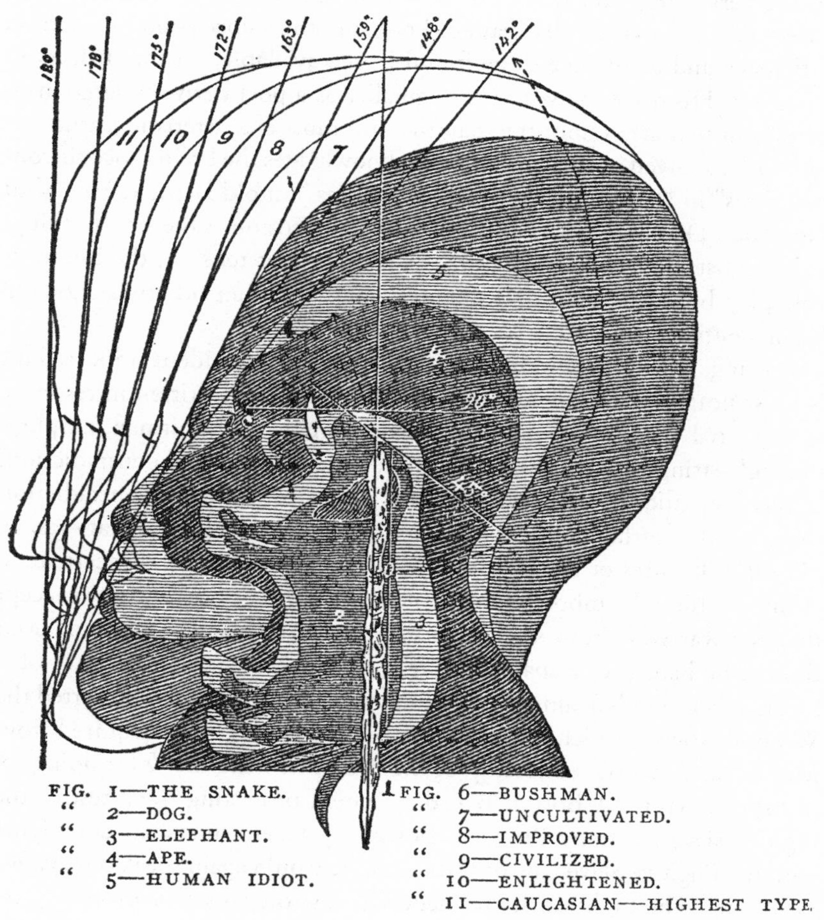

FIG. 1—THE SNAKE.
" 2—DOG.
" 3—ELEPHANT.
" 4—APE.
" 5—HUMAN IDIOT.
FIG. 6—BUSHMAN.
" 7—UNCULTIVATED.
" 8—IMPROVED.
" 9—CIVILIZED.
" 10—ENLIGHTENED.
" 11—CAUCASIAN—HIGHEST TYPE.

wrote in favor of acquiring Oregon, saying that "the name of 'American' must, in a few years, pale the old brightness and majesty of 'Roman'"; in the same year, when Yucatan seceded from Mexico, he wrote an editorial, "More Stars for the Spangled Banner," arguing that "she won't need a long coaxing to join the United States" (cited in *MD* 111); he supported the war against Mexico from its beginning in May of that year.

Like phrenology and along with phrenology, manifest destiny provided a hopeful hermeneutic, offering assurances of legibility, providentially mandated certainty, self-evident truth. Phrenology presented a version of manifest destiny at the individual level, mapping the head and making it readable, imprinted with a legible future, the individual's destiny manifest in the very bumps on her head. Whitman was greatly attracted to such externalist, self-evidentiary ways of knowing, the valorization of a certain articulacy and eloquence to be found in the available, on the surface, in the overt. His drive, power, and originality as a poet derive in large measure from that attraction; the majority and most characteristic features of his work are given over to it. Still, he acknowledges the brain's "occult convolutions" in "Song of Myself" and promises "untold latencies" in "Shut Not Your Doors." This makes for a certain tension. One of the things I find most interesting in Whitman's work is that tension, the unarrestable play between latent and manifest that brings an otherwise hopeful hermeneutic to grief.

It brings it to grief and into an order of non-self-evident import. This is most notably the case in "Drum-Taps," the poems written in response to the Civil War, whose outbreak was traumatic for Whitman, amplifying and setting in motion many an inner ambivalence and contradiction. It was a conflict in which the nation's most fundamental contradiction came to the surface and exacted its toll, a contradiction that—as he did other features of the nationality he said the poet should incarnate—Whitman himself embodied in various ways. For one, he refused to accept that the war was about slavery and the status of black Americans, even though he had, over a span of more than a decade before the war's outbreak, taken stands against slavery and its spread. In 1846 he supported the Wilmot Proviso, which prohibited slavery in any territory acquired from Mexico, and lost the editorship of the Brooklyn *Daily Eagle* for doing so; in 1854 he wrote "A Boston Ballad," a poem protesting the arrest of the fugitive slave Anthony Burns in Boston by federal marshals complying with the Fugitive Slave Law of 1850, a law he would again speak out against in 1856 in "The Eighteenth Presidency!"; he wrote an article exposing and condemning the illegal slave trade in New York for *Life Illustrated* in 1856. However, he was not, by his own admission, a "red-hot" abolitionist,[10] and his record was uneven, especially when the issue was not the status of the institution of slavery but the status of African Americans. While editor of the *Daily Eagle*, he let the voting down of black suffrage in Brooklyn in 1846 go without comment or condemnation; after the war, he was against universal suffrage, falling out with his longtime friend and admirer William Douglas O'Connor over this issue in 1872. In the 1850s he argued that blacks could never be assimilated into American life, invoking the familiar trope of providential imprint: "Nature has set an impassable seal against it" (cited in *WW* 132). For Whitman, the war that George Lamming calls the Slave War was fought not against the degradation of black Americans but against "devilish disunion." Whitman refers to it always as the Secession War and writes to O'Connor during the conflict, "In comparison with this slaughter, I don't care for the niggers" (cited in *WW* 291).

Repressed acknowledgment of the manifest cause of the war, the enslavement of African Americans, creates curious perturbations. In "Song of Myself," first published before the war, Whitman portrays himself aiding a runaway slave in section 10, professes love for a black coachman whose "polish'd and perfect limbs" he praises in section 13, then identifies with "the hounded slave" in section 33. In "I Sing the Body Electric," also first published before the war, he insists in section 7 on the pricelessness and humanity of a slave on the auction block: "In this head the all-baffling brain, / In it and below it the makings of heroes." However, in a postwar poem, "Ethiopia Saluting the Colors," included in "Drum-Taps" and first published in 1871, the inchoate and contrary sway of emotions and ambivalences tapped by the war has him wondering why a black woman salutes the flag, referring to her as "so ancient hardly human" and repeating it, "so blear, hardly human," but regarding her nonetheless as a "fateful woman," wondering, "Are the things so strange and marvelous you see or have seen?" More curious yet is the moment in "Song of the Banner at Daybreak" when, expressing love for the flag, he sees in it the undulant, serpentine quality attributed in "Rise O Days from Your Fathomless Deeps" to doubt:

> O you up there! O pennant! where you undulate like a snake hissing so curious,
> Out of reach, an idea only, yet furiously fought for, risking bloody death, loved by me,
> So loved—O you banner leading the day with stars brought from the night!

Albeit not altogether unvisited by sweetening, something moves here more than surface conviction. Whitman's optimism, under duress, wants to rebound, darkened by what the nation has been through. Unhinged hope and the recovery it seeks move into an embrace of captious flutter, a liminal epiphany coded in wavelike hiss (earlier in the poem: "hissing wave") and snakelike undulacy.

Cloth is cover, capricious cover, as fitful turning out as in. The flag's flutter and flap attest to agitant intangibles. Robert Farris Thompson, in *Face of the Gods*, discusses the Kongo derivation of the flag altars maintained by the Saamaka of Suriname, descendants of eighteenth-century maroons; he writes, "The Kongo contribution to the flag altar, the *nsungwa*, held by a processioneer at a funeral, is a towering staff onto which a narrow strip or strips of cloth are tied at the very top. To honor the dead, processioneers shake and elevate *nsungwa* in the air. The cloth strips atop these staffs encode *mambu* (words, matters, problems) that the living seek to communicate to the dead; one activates the attention of the other world by 'waving the words' (*minika mambu*), a basic Kongo metaphor for spiritually activated admonitions. This ritual act 'vibrates' (*dikítisa*) cloth-coded prayer, so that the ancestors cannot fail to comprehend. . . . Finally, for Kongo, motion imparted by wind to flags directly demonstrated ancestral presence. *Banganga* (ritual experts) phrased this belief in the following way: 'The wind on the flag is a vibration shared by the two communities, the living and the dead.'"[11] Earlier the poem, in its dialogue between Child and Father (speaking parts are also given to Poet, Pennant, and Banner), recalls section 6 of "Song of Myself," where the child's question, "What is the grass?" is answered: "I guess it must be the flag of my disposition, out of hopeful green stuff woven." The flags in "Song of the Banner at Daybreak" are woven of different stuff, threatening to woo the child away from acquisitive progress and material pursuit, "valuable houses, standing fast, full of comfort, built with money," what would eventually be called the American way of life. The child says of the flag,

O father it is alive—it is full of people—it has children,
O now it seems to me it is talking to its children,
I hear it—it talks to me—O it is wonderful!
O it stretches—it spreads and runs so fast—O my father,
It is so broad it covers the whole sky.

The father tells him, "Cease, cease, my foolish babe," tells him to look at "the well-prepared pavements" and "the solid-wall'd houses" instead. Then banner and pennant instruct the poet,

> Speak to the child O bard out of Manhattan,
> To our children all, or north or south of Manhattan,
> Point this day, leaving all the rest, to us over all—and yet we know not why,
> For what are we, mere strips of cloth profiting nothing,
> Only flapping in the wind?

Spiritually activated admonitions, the flags' flap and flutter disburse reminders of manifold latency, maroon intangibles ever bettering manifest capture. How striking that an African way of knowing should assert itself where the knowingness of Africans was anything but held to be self-evident.

Wringing the Word

Islands, the third book of Kamau Brathwaite's first trilogy *The Arrivants*, marks both an arrival and an embarkation. Following the diasporic panorama of *Rights of Passage* and the African focus of *Masks*, *Islands* initiates a return to the Caribbean, the undertaking of a groundedness long denied the "land- / less, harbour- / less spade."[1] The ground in question is literal (and, as the title of one of the book's poems reminds us, littoral), the Caribbean landscape and its characteristic features—shoreline, sand, coral, and so forth. The grounding undertaken is figural, a poetic investment in the specifics of place, a linguistic embrace and embarkation that asks the West Indies, "[W]here is your kingdom of the Word?" (*A* 222). Culture, the collective poesis that endows the habitation of a ground with meaning, is interrogated, meditated upon, and contributed to by a thematization of the word that *Islands* inaugurates. Accompanying this thematization is a tendency toward linguistic play and experimentation, a foregrounding of language that becomes even more prominent in the trilogy that begins with *Mother Poem*. *Chatter* rendered *shatter*, *umpire* rendered *empire*, and the lines "children / summer- / saulting in the park" (*A* 190, 202, 181) are among the few instances in *Islands* of a practice that escalates quantum-wise in the second trilogy. In this essay, looking at *Islands* and *Mother Poem* in particular, I will be discussing that escalation, the movement from landscape to wordscape, language thematized and acted upon.

The *chatter/shatter* and *umpire/empire* renderings are in fact a good place to begin. The former is one of many instances of an accent that falls on fragmentation from *Islands* on. Brathwaite writes in *Mother Poem* that "the child / is born to splinters // broken islands / broken homes,"[2] echoing an insistence we find in *Islands*: not only "cracked note," "cracked mother," "cracked ground," and "broken tongue," but also "history . . . / . . . stripped and torn" (*A* 162, 180, 187, 210, 216). Brathwaite grounds this insistence in the fragmentariness of insular topography, the islands' lack of the relative coherence possessed by larger land masses. As though the very ground, geography itself, underwrote and underscored such accent, he repeatedly, in the second trilogy, broods upon "this tilted cracked fragmentary landscape" (*MP* 41) in writing that amounts to a fractured wordscape, poems typified by idiosyncratic line breaks and syllabications:

> but can you ever guess how i
> who have wracked
>
> you wrong
> long too to be black
>
> be
> come part of that hool that shrinks us all to stars
>
> how i
> with all these loco
>
> motives in me
> would like to straighten
>
> strangle eye/self out
> grow a beard wear dark glasses
> driving the pack straight far
>
> ward into indigo and vi
> olet and on into ice like a miss
>
> ile[3]

The *chatter/shatter* rendering anticipates this later manner of speaking, both a broken mode and a breaking mode, as if to chatter were indeed to shatter. Broken speech, breaking speech, partakes of the ground, as announced in the invocation which concludes the next-to-last poem in *Islands*: "So on this ground, / write . . . // on this ground / on this broken ground" (*A* 265–66). It fulfills the announcement of "some- / thing torn // and new" with which the book concludes (*A* 270).

The phrase "broken ground," as the lines "history . . . / . . . stripped and torn" indicate, has historical as well as topographic meaning, referring to social divisions and social conflicts that have plagued the Caribbean since the advent of European expansion in the late fifteenth century. The *umpire/empire* rendering, as does much of Brathwaite's linguistic play, underscores the centrality of slavery, the plantation system, and colonialism to the history and the predicaments of the region. The verbal disruptions to which he resorts, together with his thematization of the word, address the cultural domination which accompanied and helped implement and sustain British imperialism. They not only address but also move to redress that domination. "I / must be given words to refashion futures / like a healer's hand," he writes in "Negus." And further on in the same poem,

> fling me the stone
> that will confound the void
> find me the rage
> and I will raze the colony
> fill me with words
> and I will blind your God.
> (*A* 224)

This aspiration gives a sense of prospect and promise to work which is otherwise a tally of deprivations. Broken speech, seeking to break new ground, brings a further sense of "broken ground" into play—the prospect and promise of a new beginning. (The fifth and final section of *Islands* is called "Beginning.") A sense of the emergence of an alternative cultural order, of being present at the inception of a new dispensation, pervades *Islands* and the second trilogy. Language, the cornerstone of cultural order, is accordingly prioritized. "My tongue is heavy with new language," the poet announces in the "Rebellion" section of *Islands* (*A* 221).

Brathwaite's work both announces the emergence of a new language and acknowledges the impediments to its emergence, going so far as to advance impediment as a constituent of the language's newness. This is one of the most distinctive features of the writing that *Islands* announces and inaugurates. The sense of an initiation into new orders of speech is in part what Brathwaite's repeated references to pebbles imply, calling to mind the practice of speaking with pebbles in the mouth to improve pronunciation. One of the poems in *Islands* is called "Pebbles"; and in "Eating the Dead" he writes, "I will return to the pebble" (*A* 196, 219). It is in this latter poem that he says his tongue is "heavy with new language," going on immediately, however, to add: "but I cannot give birth speech. // Pebbles surround me." The pebble is a multivalent figure whose meaning cuts more than one way. A figure for the resistances active in the encounter between conflicting orders of speech, the pebble simultaneously signifies promise and impediment. Even in the practice referred to above it functions antithetically, improving speech by impeding speech. Brathwaite's recourse to it carries even greater antithetic resonance, as he calls into question the very notion of proper speech, the elocutionary norm such improvement aspires to. In the Caribbean, of course, the notion of linguistic propriety is marked by colonialism and cultural domination, rooted in imposed, metropolitan models and canons that obstruct and delegitimate alternate modes of speech, the very modes Brathwaite is committed to advancing. The pebble signifies the diminishment and denigration of those alternate modes by a colonizing norm, by the biases intrinsic to imperial notions of propriety and improvement. It also signifies a resistance to so-called proper speech, a resistance that in Brathwaite's case is not, as in the conventional model of improvement, to be overcome, but rather encouraged, cultivated, carried farther. Hence the positive valence the figure carries as a symbol of linguistic and cultural self-determination. It comes to signify the vocalities and linguistic practices of Afro-Caribbean folk culture, tonalities and retentions Brathwaite tends especially to associate with women in a mothering role. "All that I have of her is voices," he writes of his grandmother in *Islands*,

> . . . And in the night, I listened to her singing
> in a Vicks and Vapour Rub-like voice what you would call the blues
> (*A* 240)

Depth and resonance accrue to the figure by the time we get to *Sun Poem*:

> mothers were *loa* were stone crabs were fish traps of no
> they were pebbles of sound down the floor of a well
> (*SP* 77)

The pebble is characterized in part by what it's up against, larger figures in stone that impede its emergence. In *Sun Poem*, Brathwaite coins a term to refer to one of the forms of material inscription whereby imperial authority sanctifies itself, statues monumentalizing the agents of colonial rule. As have other West Indian writers (Ismith Khan, for example, on Port of Spain's statue of Sir Ralph Woodford in *The Jumbie Bird*), he reflects critically upon the role of such statuary, its alienating impact upon the colonial subject. These monuments he calls "stammaments," a neologism that names a predicament while exemplifying the innovation that seeks to overcome it, the taking of linguistic liberties aimed at decolonizing the word:

and yet there are those stammaments in stone
that smile

are fat or romanesque, athletic like good traffic
cops

piercing or blind to the world but never look
ing like us
(*SP* 62)

Combining *monument* and *stammer, stammament* says that such material inscriptions obstruct autochthonous culture, impede the emergence of postcolonial speech. It also says that postcolonial speech begins in a stammer, as in one of the poems in *Islands*, "Negus":

It
it
it
it is not

it
it
it
it is not

it is not
it is not
it is not enough
it is not enough to be free
of the red white and blue
of the drag, of the dragon

it is not
it is not
it is not enough
it is not enough to be free

of the whips, principalities and powers
where is your kingdom of the Word?
(*A* 222)

A further component of the coinage *stammament,* the word *stamen* we see suggestions of, implies that obstruction and the stutter it occasions are germinal, generative. Brathwaite, at the end of *Sun Poem,* speaks of "beating . . . genesis // out of the stammering world" (*SP* 97).

The difference between the pebble and the statue is not simply one of size. The statue is representational. It appropriates the solidity and the durability of stone to give a look of permanence, unalterability, to what is merely a regime. Size matters, however, in that the scale of monumental statuary not only magnifies and bestows grandeur but also suggests a coherence, a totalization, of which the smallness and the dispersion of pebbles imply the opposite. The statue is integrative, the pebble particulate. The statue is symbolic, the pebble semiotic. In accenting the pebble, Brathwaite counters the apparent solidity, impermeability, and permanence of the social relations monumental statuary is meant to reinforce. His insistence upon the pebble is an insistence upon particles and provisionality, upon the gaps, fissures, and volatility masked by monumental appearance. His "return to the pebble" primarily alerts us to the monumentality of language itself, the role played by notions of a stable, standard English in the maintenance of metropolitan norms. Returning to the smallest particles of language, syllables and letters, he assaults the apparent solidity and integrity of words, destabilizing them (showing them to be intrinsically unstable) by emphasizing the points at which they break, disassembling them and reassembling them in alternate spellings and neologistic coinages.

The second poem in *Islands,* "Ananse," invokes its namesake trickster-creator as a "dry stony world-maker, word-breaker" (*A* 167). In *Mother Poem,* Brathwaite identifies the mother figure with Ananse, saying that "spiders make patterns in her mind" and having her say, "i is spiders weavin / away" (*MP* 25, 99). Both are word-breakers: "me mudda // brek / de word" (*MP* 59). Both are figures for an activity that increasingly takes place in Brathwaite's poems. Line breaks that occur in the midst of a word are the most persistent instance of such activity, occurring regularly throughout *The Arrivants* and continuing in more idiosyncratic fashion in the second trilogy. In *The Arrivants* and in *Mother Poem,* such breaks are hyphenated:

spark eye
crackle o' bone-

juice an de whole sing-
in forest on fire: whisp-

erin whips on de shiv-
erin stone o de kitch-

en where she turns
alone to the o-

ven burn-
in burn-

in world
without

world with-
out world

without
end
(*MP* 92–93)

Beginning in *Sun Poem*, however, the hyphens are frequently dropped, making the breaks more emphatic, as in this passage from *X/Self*:

chad sinks

sa
hara wakes out slowly

the dry snake of the harm
attan the harmattan reaches into our wells into our smiles in

to our cook
ing pot oil in

to the water re
flecting our walls in

to the bone
of the mutton in

to our dry
gully eyes[4]

Words are broken not only by line breaks but by punctuation marks inserted between syllables and even between letters within the same syllable. *Mother Poem* introduces a use of the slash that we see in *Sun Poem* and *X/Self* as well:

hear the pen/nies drop/in
lissen while they fall
ev/ry one for jee/sus
he shall have them all

drop/in drop/in drop/in drop/in
hear those pen/nies fall
ev/ry one for jee/sus
he shall have them all
(*MP* 11)

Colons are also employed in this way. We find "i:ron" and "us:ed" in *Mother Poem* (*MP* 45, 97), "us:ed" in *Sun Poem* as well (*S* 93), "immobil:e" in *X/Self* (*XS* 31). *Sun Poem* introduces the use of spacing to break words:

we're going to a wonderful place
we're going to a won der ful place
over the hills and far away
we're going to a wonder full place
(*SP* 40)

X/Self takes this farther, employing spacing and punctuation, a period, at the same time:

for if the laws be crook. ed
if pathways to the palace where/in
justice/es are not made strait

there will be
buildings rushing upwards on a scream of sand
(*XS* 20)

These practices remind us, at the graphic level, of the divisibility and the alterability of words, their permeability to alternate arrangement, variability, change. The visibility these practices accord variation, their graphic departure from standard, presumably stable procedure, undermines monumental premises. Again, landscape and wordscape correspond, the permeability of words recalling that of the poet's native ground. "This poem," Brathwaite writes of *Mother Poem*, "is about porous limestone: my mother, Barbados" (*MP* ix). The permeability of words, their susceptibility to alternate arrangement, is also made evident in the second trilogy by a recourse to anagrammatic rearrangement, a permutability that also leads to idiosyncratic spellings, puns, and "sound-word" coinages. In *Mother Poem*, *mane* anagrammatically alters *name* and *mean*, *nan* plays upon *ann*, *nam* upon *man* and so forth (*MP* 55, 74–75). Likewise, *glided* is rendered *gilded* in *Sun Poem*, where we also find *lion* and *loin* played upon one another and the neologism *godderal* derived from *doggerel* (*SP* 13, 49), while in *X/Self* we see *for/nicalia* derived from *california* and so on (*XS* 88).

Rearrangements of the particles—the pebbles—of language advance phonic and semantic as well as orthographic alterations. In "Ananse," Brathwaite says that the spider, the "word-breaker," "squats on the tips // of our language," going on to speak of it spinning "webs of sound" and "revealing . . . shadows of meaning" (*A* 165–66). His recourse to punning, the suggestion of *stairs* in the lines "he stumps up the stares / of our windows" (*A* 165), exemplifies the Anansean tactic the poem announces. Already in "Jah," the first poem in *Islands*, Brathwaite has referred to "bridges of sound" (*A* 162). He increasingly exploits these bridges, the "webs of sound" that connect a word to other words (*shatter* to *chatter*, *empire* to *umpire*), the echoes of other words and other meanings within a word. Words are reopened, broken open, their semantic integrity unsealed by "shadows of meaning" that are played upon and thereby shown to permeate "the Word."

Throughout the second trilogy, the meanings activated through wordplay do tend to be "shadowy," accentuating the negative, "dark," dysfunctional character of the status quo. Early in *Mother Poem*, in "Bell," a warehouse is called a "wear- // house," underscoring the damage done to the speaker's husband, who worked in it:

> i never did know when he start comin home
> wid a wheeze: wid a cough: wid a stone in e chess
> so he cud hardly breed, c'dear

when de duss dat e ketch in dat sun-
dayless wear-

house
brek e up like a stick
(*MP* 13)

In "Pig mornin," thirty-five cents become "dirty-five cents" (*MP* 30). Likewise, a shamrock is called a "shame- / rock," weekly pay is called "weakly pay," and the ill effects of being unable to read and write are orthographically highlighted in "Miss Own":

for the shoe is a safe cottage to the illiterate peasant
needing light, running water, the indestructible plastic of the soft ill
lit/erate present
(*MP* 35–36)

Further on in the book, the merchant/owner doesn't simply sit in the great house; we're told that he "shits in the great house" (*MP* 54). Farther still, grass rather than growing is said to be "growling along the hillside," panes of glass are called "pains of glass," steps that go no farther are said to "go no father," daily bread is "dearly bread," a kingdom is a "king/doom" and so on (*MP* 77–79, 83, 85). This tendency continues in *Sun Poem* and *X/Self.*

The phonic and semantic slippages Brathwaite cultivates resonate with reminders of injury and deprivation, wounds that run deep in the social fabric. These resonances are dissonances, reminders of discord, disharmony, disaster. In *Mother Poem* he coins a term, *skeletone,* that names and is an instance of this (*MP* 17, 40). The term recalls his announcement in *Islands,* "I will sing songs of the skeleton" (*A* 219). His work, that is, will disinter the dead and recall the injustices they were done, resound with the ringing of bones, the "skeletonality" evoked in "Cherries":

she will bend forward with the hoe: *huh*
and the gravel will answer her: *so*

she will swing upward with the hoe: *huh*
and the bones of the plantation will come ringing to meet her: *so*
(*MP* 77–78)

The ringing of bones redefines resonance, takes it in a direction contrary to expectation. It is a ringing which can only be imagined, a ringing that is difficult to imagine. Hearing the dull thud of bone as resonance epitomizes and offers an apt figure for Brathwaite's antithetic, oppositional poetics. Rooted in social disaffection and critique, "skeletonality" submits the ground to a qualitative audit, accenting the toll taken by the plantation past and its continuing repercussions.

In *Mother Poem*, bones ring in contrast and opposition to bells whose conventional resonance represents dominance and regimentation, the ruling order:

> quick step/chip step
> as punctual as cat'olic bells
> (*MP* 15)

The bells are those of school as well as church, the teacher Chalkstick's bicycle bells (*MP* 19, 22) and

> . . . the sound of schoolbells
> squares: triangles: hookey hockey matches
>
> desks: gas chambers: forward march
> (*MP* 24)

Brathwaite makes the intent of "skeletonality" clear very early: "bell that i will break and pour its sound in the vèvè" (*MP* 8). His writing, emulating the symbolic chalk designs that are drawn on the ground as part of *vodoun* ritual, will alter sound to mark the African presence in the West Indies. Through the figures of bell and bone he offers a thematization of sound that is concomitant with his work's phonic dislocations. Bone is an alternate bell, an antithetic bell suggesting not only victimization but also revolt, a movement toward liberation ("let freedom ring"). The deployment of these figures in *Mother Poem* recalls a conflation of corpse and bell at one point in *Islands*, where the hanged body of Paul Bogle, leader of a nineteenth-century revolt, is called a "dead bell":

> chapel bells bringing freedom's
> dark clash, bayonet's clangour of iron
> on chain, Bogle's legs swinging steep from their steeple of pain,

dead clapper, dead leader, dead bell,
leaden tongue, the snapped neck
slacker and slacker
(*A* 233)

This "dead clapper, . . . / leaden tongue" is an earlier version of "skeletone."

"Skeletonality" indicts and rebels against English, takes revenge on the language of empire, implicating English and its presumed norms in the subjugation of colonized people. Brathwaite, as have many colonial/postcolonial writers, critiques the role of the schools, disseminators of "the Word," in the maintenance of metropolitan dominance. In *Islands,* he writes:

they go to school to the head-
master's cries,

read a black-
board of words, angles,

lies;
they fall

over their examinations.
It is a fence that surrounds them.
(*A* 174–75)

He also speaks of the "cottonfields of Oxford" (*A* 168). In *Mother Poem,* the equation of colonial/neocolonial education with mystification and miseducation continues:

how can there be a carved trail
when schools teach their children blasphemies:
the blasphemy that the word is law when spoken by an english engineer
that our teaching must reflect these verities
(*MP* 31)

He speaks of "children locked up into their cell // blocks of school" (*MP* 25). His calling a student "another black hostage / of verbs" (*MP* 24) indicates the crucial, synecdochic relationship of language to the regimentation the schools impose. Liberties taken with language are thus acts of defiance.

They curse and condemn the language from whose norms they diverge. Brathwaite writes of the mother figure in *Mother Poem*, the word-breaker: "she crumples words into curses" (*MP* 47). He has already, on the same page, called her "black sycorax my mother," identifying the speaker in the poem with William Shakespeare's anagrammatic invention, Caliban. Her "curses" thus recall Caliban's lines in *The Tempest*, spoken to Prospero: "You taught me language, and my profit on't / Is, I know how to curse."

Brathwaite notes in *X/Self* that "Caliban has become an anti-colonial/ Third World symbol of cultural and linguistic revolt" (*XS* 116).[5] An identification of the second trilogy's linguistic license with Caliban's "profit" is explicitly made in the notes to *Sun Poem*, where he dubs the coinages to which he increasingly resorts "calibanisms." The term *cavicle*, for example, he defines as a "'calibanism' for clavicle; the cave between neck and collarbone" (*SP* 100). Brathwaite has argued that language was the area in which enslaved Africans most successfully rebelled against their masters, refusing to speak as they were taught but instead using—and abusing—English in ways that made it their own. He makes this argument in *The Development of Creole Society in Jamaica 1770–1820*, in a chapter titled "The 'Folk' Culture of the Slaves." As his use of the Ananse figure makes clear, in his linguistic experimentation he takes his cue from West Indian folk culture, the vernacular recasting of English he calls nation-language. His ability to sound and see *cave* in *clavicle* to fashion *cavicle* recalls a nation-language term such as *likkle*, which manages to sound a suggestion of *lick* and *trickle* one might otherwise not hear in the word *little*. The troubling accent he brings to bear upon English, the shadows of sound and meaning he brings out in a word, emulates the qualitative audit to which *down* seems to have been put to become *dung* in folk pronunciation.

It is not surprising, then, that nation-language itself assumes a much more prominent, pervasive role in the second trilogy than in the first. In *The Arrivants*, nation-language tends to be isolated, reserved for individual poems such as "The Dust," "Rites," and "Cane" (*A* 62–69, 197–203, 225–29), rather than dispersed and disseminated throughout the work as in *Mother Poem*, *Sun Poem*, and *X/Self*. In the second trilogy, Brathwaite addresses the challenge he spoke of in an interview conducted by Stewart Brown in 1989: "I think the real challenge for the artist who knows his English and mediates between the two languages is to develop an English which increasingly reflects the nature of nation-language."[6] His "calibanisms" do this, inventing a third lexicon that is neither English nor nation-language in work that, while continuing to use English, makes greater use of nation-language, of its particular syntax and grammar as well as individual words. English is shown to be subject to alternate arrangement at the phrasal and sentence levels as well as at the lexical level. Nation-language grammar and syntax do with words and parts of speech what anagrammatic rearrangements do with letters:

an to know that he hads was to walk down de noon
down dat long windin day
to we home
(*MP* 15)

Inspired by nation-language, Brathwaite increasingly takes grammatic and syntactic liberties with English, as when in *Sun Poem* he writes of the fishermen "walking out of the night down the street ahead of the sun and under the leaves of the seagrape and cordia trees whose flowers were fast fading stars in the touching them softly night" (*SP* 25). The adjectival placement of *touching them softly* reorders accepted usage, "the light which was touching them softly."

In addition to nation-language, Brathwaite has taken Afro-Caribbean religious and musical practices as models of cultural self-definition, examples of Calibanic resistance and a creative response to social dislocation. In *Islands*, the poem "Caliban" evokes two such practices, steel band music and limbo, thematizing "silence" as a limbo stick which must be gone under, a "long dark night" to be undergone. This thematization continues the emphasis put on non-speech in "Shepherd," the poem which precedes it, a poem in which the African pantheon is "dumb," awaiting and eventually, through music, achieving "speech" (*A* 185–90). The second section of "Caliban" ends:

Ban
Ban
Cal-
iban
like to play
pan
at the Car-
nival;
dip-
ping down

and the black
gods call-
ing, back
he falls
through the water's
cries
down
down
down
where the music hides
him
down
down
down
where the si-
lence lies.
(*A* 193)

The third section ends:

out of the dark
and the dumb gods are raising me

up
up
up

and the music is saving me

hot
slow
step

on the burning ground.
(*A* 195)

The play on dumbness, playing dumb and the double meaning of "the si- / lence lies" are tokens of a bifurcation between two types of telling: what is said and what is said through not being said. The dumb gods are not really dumb and to go down is to come back up. The silence lies in more ways than one.

Silence, as John Cage, Pierre Macherey, and others have pointed out, is unacknowledged sound. The Calibanic gesture is one of sounding silence, plumbing sounds that would otherwise not be heard. Brathwaite's thematization of silence is part and parcel of his thematization of the word, for silence is meaning and sound suppressed by a linguistico-cultural regime calling itself "the Word." We find his recourse to the figure of silence accompanied by images of hyperaudition, another aspect of qualitative audit. These images report a heightened auditory perception of the natural environment, implicitly critiquing the constricted hearing regulated by "the Word," an order of relative silence in which "men make noises / louder than the sea's / voices" (*A* 205). These images project sounds and acts of hearing we would otherwise not imagine. In *Islands*, "clinks / of dew in the grass," "the polyp's thunder," "the boom / of the mango bursting its sweetness," and "the creak of forests" in a carved block of wood are all said to have been heard (*A* 178, 232–33, 243). In *Mother Poem*, grass is heard "growling" (*MP* 77). In *Sun Poem*, we read of "a sun that he [Adam] heard in his ears" and are later told that "the sand always tinkled when he dived near the shore" (*SP* 6, 25). When, in *Islands*, we read of waves "lap- // ping these shores with their silence" (*A* 238), having already been told of human sounds outshouting "the sea's / voices," we know that *silence* is a relative term, referring to repressed articulacies whose mouthpiece the poet aims to become:

> and I see you, my wound-
> ed gift giver of sea
> spoken syllables: words salt on your lips
> on my lips
> (*A* 238)

Repressed articulacy is also emergent energy and anger, an apocalyptic return of the repressed whose harbinger silence becomes in the poem "Anvil," "dark, defeated silence" become "a destroying silence" (*A* 249–50).

The sea whose "lap- // ping . . . silence" Brathwaite invokes he calls "my mother / of water" (*A* 238). In the final poem in *Mother Poem*, "Driftword," he returns to this conjunction of mother, sea, and silence, writing of "her silent gutters of word-fall" and "the breaking of her flesh with foam" in the concluding lines of the book (*MP* 117)—giving silence, as it were, the last word. Tobago-born Marlene Nourbese Philip writes of silence in ways that are relevant here. In the introduction to her book of poetry *She Tries Her Tongue, Her Silence Softly Breaks*, she writes of "the anguish that is english in colonial societies." She argues that the acquisition of English by Africans brought to the West Indies was as much deprivation as acquisition. To speak English was to acquiesce to the subordinate position—"the non-being of the African"—it meted out, to silence one's Africanity, self-image, and experience. She writes, "The paradox at the heart of the acquisition of this language is that the African learned both to speak and to be dumb at the same time, to give voice to the experience and i-mage, yet remain silent. That silence has had profound effect upon the English-speaking African Caribbean artist working in the medium of words."[7] In a more recent work, *Looking for Livingstone: An Odyssey of Silence*, Philip gives silence a more positive, regenerative value, having the protagonist, identified only as The Traveller, reflect at one point, "in finding my own Silence I was finding my own power—of transformation." This reflection occurs following a conversation in which The Traveller is advised to weave "something new," composed of "word *and* silence":

> ". . . neither word alone, nor silence alone, but word and silence—weave, patch, sew together and remember it is *your* silence—all yours, untouched and uncorrupted. The word does not belong to you—it was owned and whored by others long, long before you set out on your travels—whore words." Then she laughed. "But to use your silence, you have to use the word."
>
> "Whore words?" I asked.
>
> "Yes, and there's the rub, my dear," she said, and gently drew me close and held me—"there's the rub—you need the word—whore words—to weave your silence."[8]

She is given this advice during her stay in the "land of needlewomen and weavers," the NEECLIS, a people whose name, like those of all the others with whom she stays during her travels, is an anagram of *silence*.

As Philip's Traveller moves from the land of the ECNELIS to the land of the LENSECI and from there to that of the SCENILE and so forth, the anagrammatic play induces a sense less of movement than of stasis, a sense of being stuck within orthographic permutations whose parameters are all too clearly defined. The book's liberatory assertions notwithstanding, we sense the limits imposed by verbal discourse, a sense of limits which makes its thematization of silence all the more understandable and compelling. This brings to mind a comment on Samuel Beckett's work made by Ihab Hassan in *The Literature of Silence.* He writes, "In a certain sense, all his works may be thought of as a parody of Ludwig Wittgenstein's notion that language is a set of games, akin to the arithmetic of primitive tribes. Beckett's parodies, which are full of self-spite, reveal a general tendency in anti-literature, one that Hugh Kenner describes brilliantly: 'the dominant intellectual analogy of the present age is drawn not from biology, not from psychology (though these are sciences we are knowing about), but from general number theory.' Art in a closed field thus becomes an absurd game of permutations, like Molloy sucking stones at the beach; and 'the retreat from the word'—the phrase is George Steiner's—reduces language to pure ratio."[9] Molloy sucking stones at the beach is not unrelated to Brathwaite's Caliban surrounded by pebbles—an absurdist kinship confirmed by a reference to the myth of Sisyphus, the founding myth of Albert Camus's absurdism, on the back cover of Brathwaite's recent book of poetry, *Middle Passages*: "It marks a Sisyphean stage of Third World history in which things fall apart and everyone's achievements come tumbling back down upon their heads and into their hearts, like the great stone which King Sisyphus was condemned to keep heaving back up the same hill in hell."[10] The Sisyphean strain, however, is nothing new. It has been a feature of Brathwaite's work at least since *Rights of Passage*, whose opening poem, "Prelude," exhorts, "Build now / the new / villages," and again, two pages later, "So build build / again the new / villages," only to announce at the end, "Flame burns the village down" (*A* 4–8). We find it again in the epigraph to *Islands* taken from James Baldwin's *Tell Me How Long the Train's Been Gone*, a passage in which a sense of long-awaited achievement is dispelled by the announcement "that it was all to be done again" (*A* 160).

It would be a mistake to read Brathwaite's work as a simple, triumphalist vindication of nation-language, a simple act of Calibanic restitution. The accent put upon silence at the end of *Mother Poem*—"so she lies / mutter of echoes, folded to silence" (*MP* 114)—issues a caveat regarding linguistic projects, a warning that applies to both conformity and revolt. This recourse to metaphoric silence, to a thematization of silence, is the Sisyphean strain brought to bear upon language. It problematizes not only English but language in general, revealing that Brathwaite's Calibanic play is not a positivist pursuit of an ultimate adequation afforded by a new, presumably unproblematic language. The all but fiendish delight Brathwaite takes in the slippage to which words are prone raises doubts as to whether such erosion could ever be curtailed. Hence the parodic tendency in the work, a tendency that appears to have turned on the work itself when we get to a parody of Calibanic revolt such as the following:

> and we marched upon the palace
> declaring that the governor was black
> and that his concubines would go abroad in naturelles or afro
>
> wigs
>
> we entered the holy carbolic echoing church
> cool clean heel heil
> and the madonna was made over in the image of my sister
>
> *hale mary full of grease*
> *the lard is with thee*
> (*MP* 106–7)

Likewise, the lisp with which Esse speaks in *Sun Poem* (*SP* 73–83) further dislocates an English already dislocated by nation-language, as if to suggest that language, all language, is irremediable drift—a suggestion already made by the title of the final poem in *Mother Poem*, "Driftword."

Woven into Brathwaite's linguistic liberties is a wish for what lies beyond language and sound. This is one of the further implications of "skeletonality." The "bell that i will break and pour its sound in the vèvè" signals not only a breaking of sound but a breaking away from sound, breaking away into synesthetic translation. In a note regarding this line, Brathwaite points out that in the Barbadian church "the bell is used as censer" (*MP* 120). The bell, chiming "with a sound like breaking glass," is swung from side to side as though wafting scent—a synesthetic swing into a silence of sorts, sound as incense. It is a swing that recalls the silent-synesthetic trajectories in *Islands*, where "the eye screams" but is admitted to be "dumb," an anesthetic-synesthetic order of "the closed eye / broken eardrum" (*A* 186, 256, 211). Images of silence and sensory deprivation conspire with images of hyperaudition, suggesting an appetite for meaning and sensation large enough to squeeze the last drop of sound and sense from the world and from words. "Skeletonality," the bell whose chime we can't quite hear, like Wilson Harris's "Well of Silence,"[11] wrings the word.

Palimpsestic Stagger

"I tend to pursue resonance rather than resolution, so I glimpsed a stubborn, albeit improbable world whose arrested glimmer elicited slippages of hieratic drift."[1] This was in 1979, in a letter inscribed above a signatory initial, one of the letters attributed to composer/multi-instrumentalist N. that comprise *Bedouin Hornbook*. I didn't consciously have H.D. in mind, but the fact that her initials are there in the last two words, "hieratic drift," seems appropriate. Helen says, in *Helen in Egypt*, "yes—I drifted here."[2] I'd had H.D. consciously enough in mind in an earlier letter, writing of *Ba* cutting itself off from *Legba* to hide out in Egypt like Stesichorus's Helen, but here her presence was more faint, more at a remove, written over as in a palimpsest—which also seems appropriate. No one, after all, has done more to bring that term to our attention than H.D.

The work this particular letter was prompted by, a pastel from Irving Petlin's *Lake as a Furnace* series, is itself palimpsestic, posing geologic features as inscriptions upon earlier features, revisions and partial erasures of earlier features. Furnace precedes lake in a series of pastels presenting surfaces water will efface, parched, arid landscapes that water will eventually cover or, if not entirely cover, differently articulate. It's as if the lake has been rubbed away to reveal a previous level of imprint, erased or partially erased as though geologic strata were a series of drafts. The revealed stratum itself partakes of a draftlike provisionality; differing kinds and degrees of definition and finish merge, coexist. The revealed stratum, in its unequal development, implies and partly reveals other coexistent strata. This is also true of the human or quasi-human figures populating these landscapes, just as in H.D.'s work human development is crippled and complicated by the palimpsestic presence of earlier steps along the way:

and anyhow,
we have not crawled so very far

up our individual grass-blade
toward our individual star.[3]

So it was that, years after seeing a Petlin pastel for the first time, I chose one of those in the *Lake as a Furnace* series for the cover of my compact disc *Strick: Song of the Andoumboulou 16–25*. The Andoumboulou, as I've explained elsewhere, are an earlier, failed form of human being in the cosmology of the Dogon of West Africa, a flawed, earlier form that I think of as a rough draft of human being, the rough draft we continue to be, compounded of starward reach and, as H.D. puts it, "the palimpsest / of past misadventure" (*T* 6).

It was Robert Duncan and his companion Jess who introduced me to Petlin's work. I first saw one of his pieces at their house in San Francisco in 1979. The pastel that prompted the *Bedouin Hornbook* letter I quoted from hung on the wall of a stairwell. It was also Duncan who ushered me into H.D.'s work, albeit indirectly. It wasn't that I hadn't read H.D. before meeting him nor that I hadn't read her prior to reading his readings of her in *The H.D. Book*. Though neither deeply nor especially well, I had read the Grove Press *Selected Poems* in my late teens. The image of her that has had so much currency—classical, chaste, austere—probably got in the way of that reading. It wasn't until some years later that I could recognize the discrepant strain running counter to that image, the mixed-metaphorical promiscuity of such lines as:

. . . inviting mountains
of snow-clad foam-tipped
green walls of sea-water

to rise like ramparts about her. . .
(*HE* 278)

Reading more and more of Duncan's work led me to read H.D. more deeply. Her importance to him had been made clear enough by three pieces in *Roots and Branches*, the first book of his I bought: "A Sequence of Poems for H.D.'s 73rd Birthday," "After Reading H.D.'s *Hermetic Definitions*," and "Doves." Still, it was my reading, during the early 1970s, of the sections of *The H.D. Book* that could be found in magazines and journals that led me to return to H.D.'s work. I went, this time, to the long poems *Trilogy* and *Hermetic Definition*, which had only recently, at last, been published, and *Helen in Egypt*, which had been in print for a while.

There is, however, a sense in which I'd read H.D. more deeply even before this, a sense in which I'd become a reader of her work upon becoming a reader of Duncan's work. When browsing in a bookstore in 1965 I happened upon a copy of *Roots and Branches* and pulled it off the shelf, I was drawn in by lines behind or beneath which lay, I found upon my return to H.D.'s work in the early 1970s, these lines from *Helen in Egypt*:

> there is no before and no after,
> there is one finite moment
> that no infinite joy can disperse
> (*HE* 303)

At the time I pulled *Roots and Branches* off the shelf I was in the habit of turning first to the backs of new, unfamiliar books, so the first lines of Duncan's I ever read were those at the end of the last poem in the book, "The Continent," the eleven lines of its concluding section, section 6:

> There is only the one time.
> There is only the one god.
> There's only the one promise
>
> and from its flame
> the margins of the page flare forth.
> There's only the one page,
>
> the rest remains
> in ashes. There is only
> the one continent, the one sea—
>
> moving in rifts, churning, enjambing,
> drifting feature from feature.[4]

These lines drew me in, reeled me in, immediately made me one of Duncan's readers, one of H.D.'s readers. They were lines in a sense I would later hear Duncan himself speak of: lines *cast*, as in fishing. I was caught.

Among the elements I was caught by, caught up in, was Duncan's much-remarked-on music. It was also the straight-out metaphysical wont of the first three lines that drew me in, an annunciative assurance whose willingness to advance vatic risk shows that it sees itself to be such once we get to "from its flame / the margins of the page flare forth." The order of statement loomed large among the elements that drew me in—that and the accumulative, incremental furtherance given to statement, the apparently confident assertions of singularity ("There is only the one time. / There is only the one god") whose apparency has to do with a subsequent mix of qualification and contagion. That there could be "only the one page" and an ashen remainder as well, "only the one time" but a reminder as well, reveals annunciative assurance to have been other than the declaration or proclamation it appeared to be, reveals it to have instead been a *proposition* (that word Duncan liked so much), having to do with lure, of course, but implicitly confessing lack. That the final assertion of singularity and totality ("There is only / the one continent, the one sea") is followed and refigured by lines that give the last word to rift, drift, fragment, fracture, ushers rhetorical swell into a rhythmic retreat into fractal subsidence, subtended ends of a tidalectical swing between annunciative ebb and annunciative flow.

Tidalectical is a term I borrow from another poet whose work has been important to me, Kamau Brathwaite. Another of his coinages comes to mind as well: "driftword." The bookstore I first read those lines of Duncan's in was in a shopping mall in southern California, in a town called Costa Mesa, not far from Newport Beach, but I felt I stood on an erosive, more remote coast. I've been drawn repeatedly to articulations of a coastal poetics, a coastal way of knowing, H.D.'s prominent among them. "An enclosure. Each wave is as to grasp / is an enclosure," I wrote in "Song of the Andoumboulou: 2." And later: "Wet sand and water / wet our feet, all / shore dissolves."[5] The "desolate coast" on which Helen and Achilles meet in *Helen in Egypt* poses coastal knowledge as dissolute knowledge, repetitive, compulsive knowledge, undulatory, repeatedly undone and reconstituted—dissolute enough to call Paris's knowledge into question:

But what could Paris know of the sea,
its beat and long reverberation,
its booming and delicate echo,

its ripple that spells a charm
on the sand, the rock-lichen,
the sea-moss, the sand,

and again and again, the sand. . .
(*HE* 304)

Coastal knowledge wants to be inoculative knowledge. It seeks to seal itself against antinomies of totality and dissolution, eternity and time, through recourse to a prolonged, rapaciously finite moment ("there is no before and no after") staged at an insular, eidetic remove. *Helen in Egypt* begins in retraction or retreat (Pallinode), avails itself of insular drift (Leuké), valorizes image in the end (Eidolon):

I say there is one image,

and slaves and princesses
and the town itself are nothing
beside a picture, an image, an idol

or eidolon . . .
(*HE* 243–44)

This reiterates its earlier assertion "I say there is only one image," an assertion echoed in Duncan's palimpsestic "only the one time . . . only the one god . . . only the one promise . . . only the one page. . . ."

Antonio Benítez-Rojo writes, in *The Repeating Island*, that "the culture of the Peoples of the Sea is a flux interrupted by rhythms which attempt to silence the noises with which their own social formation interrupts the discourse of Nature. . . . [T]he cultural discourse of the Peoples of the Sea attempts . . . to neutralize violence and to refer society to the trans-historical codes of Nature. . . . [T]he culture of the Peoples of the Sea expresses the desire to sublimate social violence through referring itself to a space that can only be intuited through the poetic, since it always puts forth an area of chaos. In this paradoxical space, in which one has the illusion of experiencing a totality, there appear to be no repressions or contradictions; there is no desire other than that of maintaining oneself within the limits of this zone for the longest possible time, in free orbit, beyond imprisonment or liberty."[6] This is what I felt or found in those lines on the last page of *Roots and Branches* and felt or found again a few years later in H.D.'s work. But the sublimation of social violence is only that, and the poetic knows it. Thus the need for a crosscut or cross-accentual tug between rapture and erosion, the tidalectical to-and-fro the poem gives the last word to. Hence the Soninke tale of Gassire's lute, in which the violence the poetic would otherwise sublimate is not only acknowledged but exulted in, the tale of a lute being fed by the blood of war. It is a tale Duncan had recourse to, a tale H.D., following a suggestion by Homer, offered a Greek version of:

> was Troy lost for a subtle chord,
>
> a rhythm as yet un-heard,
> was it Apollo's snare?
> was Apollo passing there?
>
> was a funeral-pyre to be built,
> a holocaust of the Greeks,
> because of a fluttering veil,
>
> or because Apollo granted a lute-player,
> a rhythm as yet unheard,
> to challenge the trumpet-note?
> (*HE* 229)

In 1980, I appended two epigraphs to "Gassire's Lute," my study of Duncan's Vietnam War poetry: René Char's "Art knows nothing of History but helps itself to its terror,"[7] and Charles Olson's "We drink / or break open / our veins solely / to know."[8] I meant them to suggest historical terror's ability to vex ostensible knowledge, ostensible witness, something the title of my book of poems *Eroding Witness* was also meant to suggest. I saw and see such vexation, a necessary vexation, answering or inoculative by turns, in H.D.'s as well as Duncan's work.

But noting such precedence as that of H.D.'s "Eros? Eris?" (*HE* 115) to Duncan's "Eris in Eros" wasn't all my return to her work entailed.[9] A confusion or a conflation of coastal sand with desert sand, undulatory premises with ambulatory premises, emerged from my reading *Trilogy* in close proximity to *Helen in Egypt.* The latter's "new Mortal" Achilles, having "limped slowly across the sand" (*HE* 10), would eventuate in *Bedouin Hornbook*'s conjugation of Legba, the limping god of West Africa, or, more exactly, of *Ba*, an amputated, Egyptian rendering of *Legba*, with

Stesichorus's Helen. Such ambiguation, early on, seeded itself in reflections on serial poetics nourished by H.D.'s use of the poetic sequence. Her insistence upon a singularity beyond or beneath seriality, the "one image" the sequencing of poems cannot capture but is included by, suggested that the gaps between poems in a sequence owned up to, if not advertised, a possibility of unitary consciousness beyond the sequence's reach:

> . . . I do not want
>
> to talk about it,
> I want to minimize thought,
>
> concentrate on it
> till I shrink,
>
> dematerialize
> and am drawn into it.
> (*T* 77)

Looking over my copy of *Trilogy*, I see that during one of my readings of it years ago I wrote out on one of its pages a passage from a book called *Frontiers of Consciousness*, edited by John White. From an essay by Keith Floyd, "Of Time and Mind: From Paradox to Paradigm," which likens our normal perception of time and motion (lower-case consciousness) to the cinematographic illusion of motion created by a succession of still frames, I copied the following: "In Consciousness, the one frame is every frame, storing an infinitude of images in an infinitely creative pattern of pure and perfect ambiguity." This I followed with an etymological note on the word *ambiguity*: "L. *ambigere*, to wander about." The advantage of the serial poem (or, more modestly, its honesty) appeared to lie in its not effacing the borders around frames, the break between frames, its acceptance of an itineracy and a multiplicity it would get beyond but admits it can't.

H.D.'s recursive, desultory way of moving through the long poems furthered the sense of a desert ethic, a nomadic measure I'd begun to be taken by. Alain Robbe-Grillet's work, which I'd read during the late 1960s, particularly *Jealousy*, *The Voyeur*, and *In the Labyrinth*, had already pointed me in this direction. The haunting, unpredictable way in which, in *Jealousy*, the squashing of a centipede comes up again and again, each time by an alternate route, a different chain of events, had especially stayed with me, charged with an air of obsession, ambiguations of possession and dispossession I recognized and took to in H.D.'s work as well. *Trilogy*, *Helen in Egypt*, and *Hermetic Definition* appeared driven, all their affirmations notwithstanding, by apprehensions of desertion or destitution. A sense of unremitting disquiet, unremitting extremity, susceptible to endless revisitation and variation, meandering transit through mixed emotional states, seemed as much of moment as those affirmations. (It wasn't until the early 1980s that I read H.D.'s prose. I found this quality even more evident there.) Her suggestion, in *Helen in Egypt*, that "Crete would seduce Greece, / Crete inherited the Labyrinth from Egypt" (*HE* 169), recalled Robbe-Grillet's use of the labyrinth as a figure for the predicament recursive movement seeks to be done with or to undo. She goes on to write, self-reflexively:

> my meanderings back and forth,
> till I learned by rote
> the intimate labyrinth
>
> that I kept in my brain,
> going over and over again
> the swiftest way to take
>
> through this arched way or that,
> patient to re-trace my steps
> or swift to dart
>
> past a careless guard at the gate;
> O, I knew my way,
> O, I knew my ways . . .
> (*HE* 265)

That the labyrinth, in her case as in Robbe-Grillet's, is also a figure for recursive movement itself shows nomadic measure to be desperate measure.

Reading *Trilogy*, *Helen in Egypt*, and *Hermetic Definition*, I was also particularly drawn to the prominence of Egypt in H.D.'s work. The black studies revolts of the 1960s had indicted racism on a variety of fronts, canonical renderings of history and cultural inheritance among them, particularly, in significant instances, as these had instituted and perpetuated a dissociation of Egypt from Africa. Egypt was contested ground, reclaimed for Africa in a range of texts I was then reading: Cheikh Anta Diop's *The African Origin of Civilization*, John G. Jackson's *Introduction to African*

Civilizations, E. A. Wallis Budge's *Osiris and the Egyptian Resurrection*, Ishmael Reed's *Conjure* and *Mumbo Jumbo*, Amiri Baraka's *In Our Terribleness* and "From the Egyptian." In addition, valorizations of Egypt were to be found in the music I was listening to. Sun Ra had been invoking Egypt in various ways for years, but there were also others: Cecil Taylor's *Nefertiti, the Beautiful One Has Come*, Pharoah Sanders's "Upper Egypt and Lower Egypt," John Coltrane's *Sun Ship*, Alice Coltrane's *Ptah, the El Daoud*, "Lovely Sky Boat," "The Ankh of Amen-Ra," and "Isis and Osiris," Wayne Shorter's "Nefertiti." And in Duncan's *Tribunals* I read

> . . . Egypt, the image of
> Heaven, Africa
> Her land, Her plants, Her animals,
> Osiris, the ever flowing
> returning river out of Africa . . .[10]

Egypt's Africanity isn't as explicitly acknowledged in H.D.'s work, but she clearly, consistent with Herodotus and others, views Egypt as importantly antecedent to Greece. She insists on pushing her immersion in Greek tradition back to Egypt, implicitly debunking the false beginning made of Greece by what Martin Bernal, in *Black Athena*, calls the Aryan model of Western civilization.

H.D.'s Egypt is a measure of lack, the excised ancestor on whose excision Western civilization Westernized itself. It persists like a phantom limb, advancing a critique of the rationalist-materialist premises Western civilization arrogates to itself, a critique of the arrogation if not the premises themselves. In *Trilogy*, these premises exact a toll during World War II, returning a repressed Egyptian disposition in the form of a pun:

> yet give us, they still cry,
> give us books,
>
> folio, manuscript, old parchment
> will do for cartridge cases;
>
> irony is bitter truth
> wrapped in a little joke,
>
> and Hatshepsut's name is still circled
> with what they call the *cartouche*.
> (*T* 16)

In *Helen in Egypt*, Egypt relativizes the reality and reach of such premises. It is more real, "*an ecstatic or semi-trance state*" (*HE* 109), "*another dimension*" (*HE* 112), "*a transcendental plane*" (*HE* 255), a way of looking at the world aslant: "Did her eyes slant in the old way?" (*HE* 245). The desire to "*bring Egypt and Greece together*" (*HE* 80) or to go "*back to Egypt but in a Greek mode*" (*HE* 178) gives way, as if in reference to the historical excision, to "Crete-Egypt must be slain" (*HE* 182).

But it cannot be slain. It is, along with everything else it is, the nomadic, recursive measure itself. It is returned to in "Winter Love":

O unseen and unknown,
wrap me round and round

with Egypt's linen as the dead are wrapped,
mystically cut, cauterise
as with fire, the wound from which

the heart and entrails were drawn out . . .[11]

It returns or is returned to not only as a carrier of cultural critique but as something personal, felt, a remnant, a reminder, some first, unfulfilled promise:

there is something left over,
the first unsatisfied desire—
the first time, that first kiss . . .
(*HD* 91)

I shouldn't end without saying that the sting of unrelieved longing spoke to me as deeply as anything in H.D.'s work—so much so I wasn't thinking of these lines when I wrote in "Melin":

Never another time
like the first but
to be free of its
memory.
This they'd pick their
hearts out aiming
for.[12]

PART II

Gassire's Lute

Robert Duncan's Vietnam War Poems

We drink
or break open
our veins solely
to know.

—CHARLES OLSON

Art knows nothing of History but helps itself to its terror.

—RENÉ CHAR

I

The tale of Gassire's lute, taken from an ancient epic known as the *Dausi,* comes into Western literature via the first of Ezra Pound's *Pisan Cantos.* Pound got it from the writings of Leo Frobenius, who heard it among the Soninke of Mali toward the end of the first decade of the twentieth century. Douglas Fox, who along with Frobenius edited *African Genesis,* a book of myths, legends, and folktales out of Africa, suggests that the *Dausi* dates back to around 500 B.C. and that the story of Gassire's lute as Frobenius gives it comes from the period between the fourth and the twelfth centuries A.D., during which time it was sung by griots. The tale is one I am continually intrigued by and attracted to. Not only is it one of the "dreams of the race" that, as William Carlos Williams warns us, make poetry "a dangerous subject," it is also a poem that alerts us to the dangers of poetry. I use the story of Gassire's lute here as a point of entry into Robert Duncan's "great theme of War."[1] It is a tale that fits his theme well, one to which he himself refers in "Orders" and *The H.D. Book.* An unsettling, highly suggestive piece of myth, the tale works as something of a primer for the concerns at work in Duncan's Vietnam War poems as well as for the concerns those poems give rise to in my response to them.

The story itself runs like this: There was once a city known as Wagadu, which was destroyed four times, once through vanity, once through dishonesty, once through greed, and once through strife. Each time it was destroyed it was rebuilt and each of its earthly manifestations took a different name—first Dierra, then Agada, Ganna, and finally Silla. But Wagadu was essentially immaterial, "the strength which lives in the hearts of men."[2] The first destruction of Wagadu, brought about by the vanity of Gassire and his lute's playing of the *Dausi,* ushered in the songs of the griots. A fierce warrior and the son of Nganamba, king of Wagadu, Gassire awaits the death of his father so that he can become king. Nganamba is very old, as is Gassire, whose eight sons are all grown and have children of their own. Nganamba hangs on, however, and Gassire, impatient, goes to an old wise man to ask when his father will die and bequeath to him his sword and shield. The wise man answers, "Ah, Gassire, Nganamba will die, but he will not leave you his sword and shield. You will carry a lute. Shield and sword shall others inherit. But your lute shall cause the loss of Wagadu" (*AG* 100).

The old wise man goes on to tell Gassire that his way will lead him to the partridges in the field, whose language he will understand. The next evening, following a battle in which Gassire outdoes all his earlier heroics, he hears a partridge singing the *Dausi* to a group of younger partridges. The bird sings of its battle with a snake and brags of the immortality of the *Dausi,* its ability to outlive heroes and kings. Gassire goes back to the wise man, tells him what he has heard and asks if humans can know the *Dausi* too. The wise man warns him again that, since he cannot become king, he will become a griot—and that this is why Wagadu will perish. "Wagadu can go to blazes!" Gassire answers (*AG* 102) and goes to the smith, whom he orders to make him a lute. The smith says that he will do it, but it will take the blood of Gassire's sons to make the lute sing: "This is a piece of wood. It cannot sing if it has no heart. You must give it a heart. Carry this piece of wood on your back when you go into battle. The wood must ring with the stroke of your sword. The wood must absorb down-dripping blood, blood of your blood, breath of your breath" (*AG* 103). He too warns that this is why Wagadu will perish, but again Gassire says in anger, "Wagadu can go to blazes!" For the next seven days Gassire goes into battle, with the lute slung over his shoulder and one of his sons at his side. Each day a son is killed and his blood drips down onto the lute. On the eighth day, the men of the city gather and tell Gassire that the killing must cease. They banish him from Wagadu; he leaves with his family, some friends, his servants, and his cattle, and goes into the Sahara. One night he has trouble getting to sleep, and when he finally does doze off he is awakened by a voice. The voice turns out to be that of the lute singing the *Dausi.* On hearing it, Gassire falls to his knees weeping; at that moment, his father back in Dierra dies and Wagadu disappears for the first time.

Presumably, other parts of the *Dausi* deal with the second, third, and fourth disappearances of Wagadu, but no such accounts appear in either *African Genesis* or the sixth volume of Frobenius's *Atlantis,* where we find the tale of Gassire's lute. A story called "The Rediscovery of Wagadu" follows that of Gassire's lute in both books; it tells us that Wagadu disappeared for seven years, was found again, and was then lost for 740 years. Nothing is said about dishonesty, greed, or strife causing this disappearance; the tale has wholly to do with the getting back of a great war drum known as Tabele from the devils who have stolen it and tied it to the sky. Once Tabele is recovered and beaten, Wagadu reappears. So what is available to us is an enigmatic picture of a spectral city that is both of the earth and not of the earth, visible at times and at other times invisible. Both tales suggest that war has something to do with making Wagadu visible. Only after the great war drum is beaten does the city reappear in the second tale; in the first, we read that Wagadu "is sometimes visible because eyes see her and ears hear the clash of swords and ring of shields" (*AG* 109). The first tale attributes the disappearance of Wagadu to "the indomitability of men" (*AG* 97)—or, in another translation, "the lack of human restraint"[3]—and the second describes at least one disappearance as the work of devils, the Djinns who steal Tabele and tie it to the sky. These may well be different ways of saying the same thing. The Djinns might be the embodiment of a human susceptibility to the daimonic.

There is also reason to see warfare as having to do with daimonic inspiration. The day after Gassire's first consultation with the wise man, he goes into battle against the Burdama and outdoes himself. "Gassire was greater than Gassire" is how it is put in the tale (*AG* 101). The shocked Burdama call him a Damo, which a note in the translation found in *Leo Frobenius, 1873–1973: An Anthology* describes as "a terrifying creature unknown to the singer" (*LF* 143). The separation the tale makes between what makes Wagadu visible ("the clash of swords and ring of shields") and what causes it to disappear ("the indomitability of men") is, perhaps, too easy, almost naive. If Wagadu is "the strength which lives in the hearts of men," it cannot help but be their "indomitability" too. Both the availability and the invisibility of Wagadu have to do with a rendezvous with vertical powers—the war drum, remember, is tied to the sky—a rendezvous that makes for unruliness. The capacity for invasion alive "in the hearts of men" is the openness to an otherness that cuts both ways. Our inspiration is also our peril, a risk of inflation whose would-be rise can take us down into hell. The singer of the tale is caught between cosmology (the claim that for better or worse this is how it is) and morality (the claim that were it not for human vices things would turn out well). The loss of Wagadu is told of in terms of human failings, but these failings are shown to be crucial to the destined order of things. "Gassire," the old wise man says, "you are hastening to your end. No one can stop you" (*AG* 102).

The splendor of Wagadu and the loss of Wagadu are variations on a single theme of inspiration. Wagadu is lost because of human vanity and Wagadu is itself a conceit of the human mind. Pound, in "Canto LXXIV," invokes it as a mental construct, "now in the mind indestructible." When at the beginning of the canto we see the infamous Benito Mussolini, hung by his heels in Milan, mourned as the first in history to be "twice crucified," we recognize the truth of Duncan's warning that "in every event of his art man dwells in mixed possibilities of inflation or inspiration."[4] Just as Gassire's vanity overlaps with his inspiration, Wagadu in *The Cantos* is a projection of Pound's vanity, the risk of inflation his inspiration takes and the stubbornness with which he dwells in that risk:

I believe in the resurrection of Italy   quia impossibile est
    4 times to be the song of Gassir
        now in the mind indestructible[5]

The indictment of the artist made by the tale of Gassire is a haunting one, so much so that Pound, if for no other reason than to acquit himself, directly addresses the content of his Wagadu projection in "Canto LXXXI." Not one to buckle easily, Pound repeats the admonition "Pull down thy vanity" seven times, only to end by denying the charge:

Pull down thy vanity
                How mean thy hates
Fostered in falsity,
                Pull down thy vanity,
Rathe to destroy, niggard in charity;
Pull down thy vanity,
                I say pull down.

> But to have done instead of not doing
> this is not vanity
> To have, with decency, knocked
> That a Blunt should open
> To have gathered from the air a live tradition
> or from a fine old eye the unconquered flame
> This is not vanity.
> Here error is all in the not done,
> all in the diffidence that faltered . . .
> (*C* 521–22)

One of the conditions of vanity is that it does not recognize itself, just as one of the terms of poetic inspiration is that the poet in its grips does not brood over its possible defects. The risk of inspiration may well be inflation, but the risk of brooding is one of inertia, not doing. However, Pound's gravitation toward the Soninke tale acknowledges, albeit subliminally, the grain of truth in its unflattering portrait of the artist.

Like Pound, Duncan in his appropriation of the tale vacillates between acknowledgment and self-acquittal, confession and aggrandizement, with affirmation winning out in the end. He makes two references to the tale in "Orders," a poem prompted in part by the U.S. Marines' invasion of the Dominican Republic in 1965. The poem in a sense heralds his poetry of the Vietnam War, being followed in *Bending the Bow* by "Up Rising," probably the most well-known and certainly the most angry of his Vietnam poems. It is notably a poem in which he appears to question his calling as a poet, coming close to disowning the kind of poetry he is most given to. The exaltedly mythic, rhapsodic vein he so masterfully works all but comes under fire. The poem begins almost like an oath of office, as if he were being sworn in as a more public, more political poet:

> For the Good,
>
> il ben dello intelletto, the good of the people,
>
> the soul's good.
>
> I put aside
>
> whatever I once served of the poet, master
> of enchanting words and magics
> (*BB* 77)

Is it a repudiation of poetry or the activation of a thwarted desire to rule that enters the picture here? Gassire does not come in until farther on in the poem, but in this resolve to speak for "the good of the people" we already hear the song of the would-be king. What we may tend to overlook about Gassire is that he wants to rule, that becoming a griot is something of an act of sublimation, an attempt at compensation. Duncan himself, as far back as "The Venice Poem," has spoken of poetry as a vain substitute for kingship:

> I no longer know the virgin mirror.
> Sometimes the diadems of poetry
>   —mock gold glories cut out from paper
> of an afternoon—
>   turn until my head turns, inflate
> a bulbous image of a world, a vulgar empire.
> And I can sit upon a throne,
>   cross-eyed king of one thousand lines.
> In the mirror of poetry I conjure
>   luxuries I can ill afford.[6]

Is it the unfulfilled desire to rule that indicts the mirror? Could the same desire have inflated it? Here, as in the opening of "Orders," the desire to put aside the vanity of poetry mingles with the vanity of a desire to be king. Why else would we get such lordly music from a poem that claims to disown music? Farther along in "Orders," Duncan writes of putting music aside, though all the majesty of his music is still there:

> I thought to come into an open room
> where in the south light of afternoon
> one I was improvised
> passages of changing dark and light
> a music dream and passion would have playd
> to illustrate concords of order in order,
> a contrapuntal communion of all things •
>
>   but Schubert is gone,
>   the genius of his melody
> has passt, and all the lovely marrd sentiment
> disownd I thought to come to
> (*BB* 78)

In Pound we see a poet hankering to get into government, wanting to dictate policy, to wield decision-making power, to sit in smoke-filled rooms. In Duncan we see not so much an eye to the actual grind of political authority as a Shelleyan sense of the poet as actual, though unacknowledged, king. He is also close to Williams, who in "The Basis of Faith in Art" insists, "Poetry is a rival government always in opposition to its cruder replicas."[7] Senses of rivalry and opposition run freely in Duncan's poems of the Vietnam War; the figural meaning he gives Wagadu in *The H.D. Book* clearly carries both. He writes there of the writers from whom he draws his poetic lineage, taking heart in his objection to the war from a sense of them having likewise opposed the warfare state. At one point, he evokes Wagadu as the "city . . . that those who are devoted to Beauty remember"[8]; later, he refers to it as something of a rival government in the hearts of his poetic elders. We read, "Pound, Lawrence, Joyce, H.D., Eliot, have a black voice when speaking of the contemporary scene, an enduring memory from this First World War that had revealed the deep-going falsehood and evil of the modern state. These had from their earliest years as writers a burning sense of the 'they' that ran the war and that accepted its premises and of the 'we' whose allegiance belonged to a Wagadu hidden in their hearts. . . . Their threshold remains ours. The time of war and exploitation, the infamy and lies of the new capitalist war-state, continue. And the answering intensity of the imagination to hold its own values must continue" (RP 50, 53). Here Wagadu is what Duncan elsewhere calls "the commune of Poetry" (*BB* vi). In his next mention of it, however, we notice a tension that troubles his use of the tale in "Orders." He suggests that "the Wagadu of the *Cantos* is the lost city not of a tribe but of a kindred among all men, 'an aristocracy of emotion' Pound called it" (RP 55). The communalist assertion is belied by the elitist ring of Pound's phrase, inclusiveness ("a kindred among all men") undermined by exclusivity ("an aristocracy of emotion"). Only the assertiveness of Duncan's poetics holds the two together. He writes a bit farther on, aware, one would think, of the irony involved: "The very heightened sense of the relatedness of everything sets poets apart" (RP 58).

We see the same tension in "Orders," where Wagadu is identified with the lute that destroys it. Referring to the U.S. Marines in the Dominican Republic, Duncan writes,

From house to house the armd men go,

in Santo Domingo hired and conscripted killers
against the power of an idea, against

Gassire's lute, the song

of Wagadu, household of the folk,

commune of communes

hidden seed in the hearts of men

and in each woman's womb hidden.

(*BB* 77)

Thinking back to the tale itself, we might balk at the yoking together of Wagadu and Gassire's lute. We are at least suspicious of the poetic conceit that wants to attribute a communal impulse—"the good of the people," "household of the folk," "commune of communes"—to Gassire, since we have heard him tell Wagadu to go to hell, watched him sacrifice his sons for his personal glory (having drafted them just as a government does), and seen him kicked out of Wagadu. Is this a case of unconscious distortion, Duncan altering a truth he cannot face? Or is he consciously presenting a reformed Gassire, a symbolic projection of his "putting aside" of a certain poetic stance? In either case, the inappropriateness of Gassire's lute as a symbol of "the folk" is a symptom of something else going on in the poem, something that the "putting aside" he announces both addresses and aggravates.

Duncan is not what we tend to think of as a populist poet. When he names a number of his poetic masters further on in the poem, we do not find—nor do we expect to find—Carl Sandburg or Langston Hughes, for example, among them. We do find an admirer of Mussolini and a self-proclaimed monarchist on the list:

Down this dark corridor, "this *passage*," the poet reminds me,

and now that Eliot is dead, Williams and H.D. dead,
Ezra alone of my old masters alive, let me
acknowledge Eliot was one of them, I was
one of his, whose "History has many
cunning passages, contrived corridors"

comes into the chrestomathy.

(*BB* 78)

(Is the earlier line "From house to house the armd men go," with its faint echo of "In the room the women come and go," an added homage to T. S. Eliot, who had recently died when the poem was written?) By announcing what appears to be a populist intent at the beginning of "Orders," Duncan leaves himself open to the sort of rebuke Charles Olson aims at Pound for his opening lines in "Canto LXXIV" ("The enormous tragedy of the dream in the peasant's bent / shoulder"):

And with no back references, no
floating over Asia arrogating
how a raiding party moves in advance of a nation thereby
eventually
giving a language the international power
poets take advantage of. As they also,
with much less reason, from too much economics speak
of the dream
in a peasant's bent shoulders, as though it were true
they cared a damn
for his conversation[9]

The tension between what I will roughly call "populist" and "elitist" impulses gives a telling quiver to Duncan's poem. We hear it in the slight note of apology—edged with a tinge of defiance—in his acknowledgment of Eliot. We hear it more expressly toward the beginning of the poem, where Duncan goes on to qualify his "putting aside" of an oracular, possibly inflated sense of his role as poet:

not to disown the old mysteries, sweet
        muthos   our mouths telling   •

and I will still tell the beads, in the fearsome
    street I see glimpses of   I will pray again
    to those great columns of moon's light,
        "Mothering angels, hold my sight steady
and I will look this time as you bid me   to see
            the dirty papers, moneys, laws, orders
            and corpses of people and people-shit."

(*BB* 77)

We see that the "putting aside" he announces does not so much repudiate as enlarge his art, bringing with it added rather than diminished risks of inflation. Acknowledging himself to be something of an ivory-tower poet, Duncan strikes out into new terrain, stepping into the world of current events, assuming a public, more oratorical, voice. But he is at the same time digging more deeply into the oracular, rhapsodic vein. Olson noted this in 1968 at Beloit College, where he said of some then-recent Duncan poems (apparently some or all of the "Passages" that later appeared in *Tribunals*): "Unbelievable, these new *Passages*. . . . I mean where Duncan . . . I mean he's moved into a—almost a status or something, if I may use that word—a condition of status. . . . He's become a BIG poet, like Yeats . . . he put on the robe."[10]

In spite of the dichotomy that Duncan apparently acknowledges with his "putting aside," the overall push of the poem is to have it both ways. The charge the poem is given is not one of abdicating the exalted mode but of bringing it to bear on more resistant matters. "Orders" continues Duncan's insistence on the relevance of myth and a sense of historical recurrence, in whose light he now looks at events on the six o'clock news. The lines preceding his acknowledgment of Eliot put into practice the sense of historical resonance and interconnectedness that he uses the term *passages* to evoke. With its intervention in the Dominican Republic, the United States reminds him of Herod and of the Abbé of Citeaux:

> They do not know where It is • at Béziers
>
> the Abbé of Citeaux orders *Kill them all—*
>
> *the Lord will know His own!*
>
> Pillars I saw in my dream last year, stand
>
> in my heart and hold the blood,
>
> my pulse rises and beats against its walls.
>
> In the streets of Santo Domingo Herod's hosts again
>
> to exterminate the soul of the people go
>
> (*BB* 77–78)

In the course of the poem, the communal feeling entered into at its beginning increasingly shows itself to open onto something other than a simple populist proposition. A mingling of vertical and horizontal inclinations inflates the words *commune* and *household.* The oracular mode, Duncan's urge to become a mouthpiece for cosmic truth, is such that his "household of the folk" gives way to or turns out to be "the great household," the cosmos itself. The "commune of communes" likewise inclines toward the "It" of the passage just quoted. What Duncan means by "It," his introduction to *Bending the Bow* tells us, is the "striving to come into existence" of a cosmogonic Spirit, the sense of the world he roots his poetics in: "This configuration of It in travail: giving birth to Its Self, the Creator, in Its seeking to make real . . . this deepest myth of what is happening in Poetry moves us as it moves words" (*BB* vii).

No simple humanism holds sway over "Orders." The poem's cosmic insistences border on misanthropy, a kind of masochism at times, as at the poem's conclusion:

There is no

good a man has in his own things except

it be in the community of every thing;

no nature he has

but in his nature hidden in the hearts of the living,

in the great household.

The cosmos will not

dissolve its orders at man's evil.

"That which is corrupted is corrupted with reference to
itself but not destroyd with reference to the universe;

for it is either air or water"

Chemistry having its equations

beyond our range of inequation.

There must be a power of an ambiguous nature
and a dominion given to choice: "For the

electing soul alone is transferrd

to another and another order . . ."

(*BB* 79–80)

Here "community" has more an ecological—with whose etymology his use of the word *household* has to do—than a populist ring, and the passage's assurance of the imperviousness of the cosmos repeats Duncan's conviction that "the universe is faithful to itself" (*BB* v). Like the teller of the tale of Gassire's lute, Duncan is caught between morality and cosmology, between outrage at human evil and a "higher" understanding of evil's place in the scheme of things. As he states in a passage that also explains the title of the poem, "The moralist must always be outraged by what God finds good; for God works, as the creative artist works, not with a sense of rewards and punishments, but to fulfill the law that he creates. He seeks in His Creation intensifications of Its orders. In the plenitude of His powers, He works always upon the edge of arbitrary alternatives; He could, we know, change the work if He would. But first among His powers is His Oneness in creation: the universe is faithful to itself" (*BB* vii–viii). The "orders" to which the poem's title refers, then, are "Its," "a power of an ambiguous nature."

The capitulation of what seems at first a political or an ideological imperative to a status quo conceived as cosmic, a sense of serving "It" or "What Is" (*BB* vii)—"my thoughts are servants of the stars, and my words . . . / come from a mouth that is the Universe," Duncan writes in one of the later "Passages" (*BB* 120)—seems to confirm the split between ideology and poetry that Roland Barthes writes of in *Mythologies*, where we read, "It seems that this is a difficulty pertaining to our times: there is as yet only one possible choice, and this choice can bear only on two extreme methods: either to posit a reality which is entirely permeable to history, and ideologize; or, conversely, to posit a reality which is ultimately impenetrable, irreducible, and, in this case, poetize. In a word, I do not yet see a synthesis between ideology and poetry (by poetry I understand, in a very general way, the search for the inalienable meaning of things)."[11] This capitulation, however, is only one moment, though a recurrent one, in Duncan's work. It can also be said that his sense of "What Is" is dialectical, evolutional enough not to postulate an "inalienable meaning." Barthes's formulation offers a way of looking at two poles between which Duncan maneuvers, particularly in the war poems, where he both objects to the U.S. assault on Indochina and accepts—even all but embraces—the war as a revelatory, epiphanic event, a showing forth of "What Is": "In a blast, the poem announces the Satanic person of a president whose lies and connivings have manoeuvred the nation into the pit of an evil war.

What does it mean? It is a mere political event of the day, yet it comes reveald as an eternal sentence" (*BB* x).

The tension between morality and cosmology, ideology and poetry in Barthes's parlance, bears the brunt of the troublesome impact the notion of inspiration makes on humanistic assumptions. The age-old sense of inspiration as an inspiriting, an invasion of a human vessel by a nonhuman daimon or spirit, carries the danger of a loss of touch with human realities and feelings. Taken seriously, the notion complicates and unsettles what we mean by "human," since if we are subject to such invasions, our susceptibility has to be a factor of what being human means. Ideology and morality tend to posit fixed notions of what is properly to be regarded as human, notions to which the otherness of inspiration may pose a threat. We see Duncan caught in this complication. He will make a morally inflected use of the terms *human* and *dehumanization* in his denunciations of Lyndon Johnson: "I have been criticized for dehumanizing Johnson in the poem *Up Rising,* but such men have dehumanized themselves, removed themselves from the human consequences of their acts and from the disorders that underlie their ratiocinations. Did they not have the immunity to the reality of what they are doing that the dehumanization of official identity and idealism gives, they would come into the full obsessional sickness of soul of the human state."[12] Duncan will also, as if to deny this removal the possible rationalization of having been prompted by inspiration, write, in "The Soldiers," "Johnson now, no inspired poet but making it badly, / amassing his own history in murder and sacrifice / without talent" (*BB* 113). But what if Johnson *were* inspired? Would the destruction of Vietnam be justified?

In the tale of Gassire's lute, it appears to be the artist who is dehumanized. Gassire becomes a Damo in battle before turning to his lute and the lute's appetite for blood might imply the more sinister, vampirish aspect of inspiration. Gassire does weep once the lute finally sings the *Dausi,* however, so there has not been a total removal from the possibility of a human response. In "Orders," it is exactly the human response, a mix of rage, grief, and dismay, that the blood shed by Gassire's sons—and by the people of the Dominican Republic—serves to further. The blood may well have inspired Duncan's song, but the song despairs of its inspiration. Duncan walks a tightrope; his exulting in the "lure for feeling" (to use Alfred North Whitehead's phrase) provided by that blood has to keep clear of celebrating beauty, the song, as though the blood were justified by it:

. . . a poetry
having so much of beauty
that in whose progressions rage,
grief, dismay transported— but these
are themselves transports of beauty! The blood

streams from the bodies of his sons
to feed the voice of Gassire's lute.
(*BB* 78–79)

The risk of inflation is also, as Duncan points out in his indictment of Johnson, the risk of insulation. Duncan in the office of poet—"BIG poet," no less—runs a risk analogous to that of Johnson in the office of president, the risk Duncan speaks of as ossification in his play on the word *office* in "The Multiversity":

In this scene absolute authority

the great dragon himself so confronted

whose scales are men officized —ossified— conscience

no longer alive in them,

the inner law silenced
(*BB* 70)

The poetic office's investment in whatever feeds it can become a kind of callous, a smugness in which the poet's "faithfulness in the poetry he creates" (*BB* viii)—the delight he takes in "transports of beauty"—doesn't adequately respond to the human misery those transports report. It is in acknowledgment of this risk that Duncan speaks of "putting aside" the office.

The problem of inflation tells in the voice itself, in the rhetorical ring we hear in lines like "There is no / good a man has in his own things except / it be in the community of every thing." Weary of high-sounding cant, of idealizations and preachments from public officials, are we ready for such a sermon coming from a poet? The mode is problematic—so much so that Ian Reid, citing a letter from Duncan, writes, "Duncan himself is aware of it, remarking that in them [the war poems] he seems unable to move outside the almost hypnagogic high tone."[13] It is a problem

Duncan has acknowledged elsewhere, in relation to another poem in the "Passages" series, one that even more directly relates the problem of an oracular, oratorical mode to the question of inspiration (or daimonic impersonation). In "Moving the Moving Image," the sermonizing voice of Hermes, forecasting the day when "this Vision of the Cosmos in which the Greatest Good is / will be in danger of perishing" (*BB* 61), takes over half the poem. Duncan has written about the difficulty this takeover presents in performing the poem:

> In "Moving the Moving Image," as Hermes speaks, delivering here his "Perfect Sermon," as it is called in the Hermetic Tradition, the poet performing must move into the high priesthood in which the official speaks in the god's person. My voice must move now in musical pitches so severely represst in every training our American speech lays upon us that, properly, each time, I dread my attempt. The mode itself is heretical; banned by the Puritans of the modernist movement as long before it had been banned by their Puritanical ancestors opposing the music of Papist incantations.
>
> Could I improve my delivery by rehearsing, initiating myself into the alien order of god's voice? But the speech of this persona of the poem must come each time out of the total ground of the poem in the presence of its auditors. The voice of the man falters and must brave the heart in which he fails to give himself over, inept as he is, to the sublimity of the concept. For this is the drama the poem projects.[14]

This faltering of the voice, which in its coming down cracks the possible hardening into "high priesthood," restores a sense of human proportion. The faltering is true to the condition the Perfect Sermon describes, a condition in which we "no longer cherish or abide in the Mind of the Universe / Nor take manhood in the music of its many powers" (*BB* 66), a state in which talk of these things is problematic.

The artist (as opposed, perhaps, to the office), however much he might opt for insulation or exemption, cannot help but suffer the content of the art. This is partly the meaning of the blood feeding Gassire's lute, something like Federico García Lorca's *duende.* The faltering of Duncan's voice, which David Bromige calls "the broken chant of yearning to be that other, of the will to be one with what is nearly forgotten,"[15] speaks from the heart of the condition it laments, tellingly fails to rise above that condition. We hear the pathos of an upward aspiration that we both identify with and are put off by, hearing the echo of our own resistance in Duncan's inability to keep the godly voice aloft. The aspiration caves in on itself as if to confess to what it wants immunity from. If poetry is a rival government, if it has a more compelling claim to our allegiance than its cruder replicas, it would have to be because of just such a capacity for confession, the acknowledgment of a richer play of response than etiquettes of office allow. It is in the richer play that the outlawed or unacknowledged pathos reasserts itself, that the passion of it, its keeping close to the heart of the matter, troubles entrenchment.

II

Charles Olson's poem "As of Parsonses or Fishermans Field or Cressys Beach or Washington, the Capital, of my Front Yard?" is a syncretic mix, a sort of gumbo in which, along with Gassire, the Norse Odin—specifically the fact that he drinks of the waters of wisdom from the underground Well of Mimir and, in the guise of an eagle, of a poetry-inducing mead stolen from the giant Suttung—figures prominently. The poem plays on the relationship of poetry to politics, a relationship that Olson was fond of asserting. The Odin-eagle merges with "Altgeld the Eagle," John Peter Altgeld, the governor of Illinois who, sympathetic to radical causes, pardoned the three anarchist leaders convicted of inciting the Haymarket Riot. (He also gets mentioned in Williams's *Paterson* and is the subject of Vachel Lindsay's "The Eagle That Is Forgotten.") The play on the eagle figure goes on to refer to the old, golden eagle (*altgeld* means "old gold" in German) that takes Geoffrey Chaucer up through the air for the dream-vision in *House of Fame*:

> . . . political
>
> agent of
> all other persons for a superior
>
> purpose, that
> their lives, all lives—Altgeld the Eagle, the Eagle
>
> always, the
> bird who <u>flies</u>   not necessarily can or does sing
>
> does Fish perfectly in the deep-cloven river's walls & all the Jungle Folk startle as the Golden Bird falls from the sky—fills the sky, to fish (to

lead—not I not any Son not any Poet we
as Chaucer in the eagle's feet, going up to see the
House of Fame is taught
                    by the eagle, Geoffrey
your meter & your mode's all right but
my dear Chaucer you don't speak well of what is important, you
shall, when I return you to Earth, I hope, know more[16]

The poem is difficult to pin down, but that it presents the actions of politicians as a challenge to the relevance of poetry seems clear enough. The need for poets to take up the challenge, to "speak well of what's important," sits alongside the assertion that poems are essentially of another dispensation, disdainful of the presumptions of political leadership ("not I not any Son not any Poet").

The poem goes on to allude to the story of Gassire, bringing in the partridge in the bushes as a bird that, unlike the imperial eagle, sings rather than flies (just as Osiris, in one of Ishmael Reed's poems, would "rather dance than rule"[17]). The part the partridges play in Gassire's case is taken by nightingales in Olson's poem:

in the night's air I alone
not partridges who drum as they fly coo or don't speak here?

  in any case any way always I was drummed ahead by
nightingales alone, here in the United States (part of America
—& wells are where our speech comes from
                                        we speak with water
                                        on our tongues when
                                                        Earth
has made us parts of the World again, Poets, & the Airs which belong to Birds have
led our lives to be these things instead of Kings
(*MP* 510)

One could play devil's advocate and dwell on the fact that Olson makes the poet's abdication of kingship less reluctant and less grudging than it actually is in Gassire's case, on the fact that his identification of the Poet with the Son backfires in light of what Gassire, himself a father, does to his sons. Olson's alertness to the complications involved puts him on a tightrope between praise for the innocence of poets and acknowledgment of the poet's complicity, as another human being, in the ways of the world. The poet is not exempt, he admits, from the father/son dialectic:

> . . . he'll
> sing from the Well of
> his own Sons'
> until his own sons' blood does
> awaken in the wood—the
>
> instrument of song carved by the smith from
> the trees' trunk:
> he was provoked—each man is
> (*MP* 509)

To say that "wells are where our speech comes from" recalls the sons' blood and the Well of Mimir from which Odin drinks. Where wisdom is a caution issued by the drinking of earthy truths, blood is a wisdom-giving water. The pull of the poem is between Airs and Earth. Its Way, the tightrope it has the poet walk, is the Sufi *sirat*: to be in the world (wells) but not of it (airs). Yet the word *airs* has its worldly aspect too, referring as much to vanity, the putting on of airs, as to song. The pull between Airs and Earth is the pull between vanity and feet of clay.

But Olson, unlike Gassire, willingly abdicated a political career, resigning in protest from the Office of War Information in 1944 and refusing the positions offered him by Democratic Party officials in 1945. (The poem refers to his residence in Washington, D.C., during the 1940s and early 1950s.) He continued, however, to be attracted to and repulsed by politics. At the Berkeley Poetry Conference in 1965 he called his reading "a political occasion," spoke playfully of "addressing a convention floor," said that Duncan was "caucusing" for him in San Francisco, and promised to make Allen Ginsberg his secretary of state if he became president. "Poetics is politics, poets are political leaders today, and the only ones," he said at one point.[18] He spoke with a good deal of irony and humor, but his playfulness had a serious, slightly bitter side to it. We hear the bitterness more clearly in the poems where he harps on what Pound called pejorocracy, complaining that the world is in the hands of the worst. Of Harry Truman he writes,

> I mean merchandise men,
> who get to be President

after winning, age 12,
cereal ad
prizes
(*MP* 58)

In Gassire, Olson sees a victim of pejorocracy, the poet deprived of his rightful power. Notably, when he delves into Mesopotamian studies to bring back a glimpse of more responsible rulers, he makes a point of the respect accorded the artist. In "The Gate and the Center," on his way to asserting that "the poet is the only pedagogue left, to be trusted," he quotes a passage written by Edith Porada in which she notes that "artists appear to have been so highly valued that they were spared in warfare."[19]

Olson's "archaeology of morning" partly tries to recover the archaic stature of the poet. In this he is like H.D., who in *The Walls Do Not Fall* reminds the Sword that the scribe in ancient Egypt "stands second only to Pharaoh."[20] It's against a background of past glory that the diminished importance of the poet is objected to. One of Olson's repeated complaints is that the poet's authority has been usurped, that pejorocracy is the reign of false, inferior "poets":

(o Statue,
o Republic, o
Tell-A-Vision, the best
is soap. The true troubadours
are CBS. Melopoeia

is for Cokes by Cokes out of

Pause

(*MP* 75)

At Berkeley he made the mishandling of language, the poet's instrument, the outstanding mark of the politician's incompetence: "And the trouble with our presidents, if you'll excuse me, is they can't talk or write" (*RB* 24). Poets of my generation tend to look askance at the large claims for the poet that poets like Olson and Duncan make, especially where they warm over romantic senses of the poet's mission or smack of moralizing self-aggrandizement. It is as though the analogy they draw between the poet and the politician boomerangs, what they say sounding like campaign rhetoric at times, as hollow as a political candidate's claim to integrity. What strengthens Olson's position and protects it against the charge of naïveté, however, is his willingness to acknowledge himself to be an heir to the corrupt power he condemns. He can own up to certain spoils the poet gathers from the workings of that power, can admit, as we have seen, that imperialism gives "a language the international power / poets take advantage of." In this we see the workings of not a clean but a troubled conscience.

Olson sometimes speaks of political power as something from which he is excluded, promoting a sense of a priori exclusion as a way of confirming his poetic vocation. But there is another side of his thought that admits that for a white male poet like himself, born in a white-supremacist, male-supremacist society, political power, relatively speaking, is a birthright from which he isn't excluded but about which he has to make a choice. A man who was once on the threshold of a political career, as he was in the 1940s, more believably speaks of renunciation than of exclusion. That is exactly what we find him doing, exhorting others to choose "to be these things instead of Kings." For him poetry is analogous to a vow of poverty, a moral act of renunciation, as he writes very early in *The Maximus Poems:*

In the land of plenty, have
nothing to do with it
                                        take the way of
the lowest,
including
your legs, go
contrary, go

sing
(*MP* 19)

The sense of poetry as something like a form of penance makes it a matter of conscience, his way of sublimating or attempting to sabotage his birthright, the complex of privileges and guilts we can, with Amiri Baraka, call white karma.[21] At the Berkeley conference Olson makes an interesting remark: "I'm the white man. I'm that famous thing, the white man. The ultimate paleface. The noncorruptible, the good. The thing that runs this country, or that is this country. And thank God—And in fact the only advantage I have is that I didn't" (*RB* 32). His righteousness, what here he calls his "advantage," consists only of abstention, of writing poetry in place of running the country.

But he also admits, as though his allusions to politics hadn't already done so, "I *crave* power." We understand the air of authority characteristic of Olson—the issuing of manifestos, the handing down of dicta, the sense of a movement to organize and get going—as the deflection of a politician's disposition into poetry. His observation that "poetics is politics" is autobiographical. He says the same thing in various other ways and in various other places, as in *The Maximus Poems*, where he proposes the construction, through writing, of "another kind of nation":

> having descried the nation to
> write a Republic
> in gloom on Watch-House Point
> (*MP* 377)

Olson's Republic, like the Wagadu of *The H.D. Book*, is an imaginal city, city-state, or nation over which poetry presides. A sense of the oppositional character of poetry, the sense of it as "a rival government" or "another kind of nation," is one that Olson and Duncan share. Duncan, even in poems prior to those of the Vietnam War, rails just as Olson does against pejorocracy. "The malignant stupidity of statesmen rules," he writes in "Ingmar Bergman's *Seventh Seal*."[22] Toward the end of section 2 of "A Poem Beginning with a Line by Pindar," he charges that no president since Lincoln has been worthy of a poet's affection:

> . . . What
> if lilacs last in *this* dooryard bloomd?
>
> Hoover, Roosevelt, Truman, Eisenhower—
> where among these did the power reside
> that moves the heart? What flower of the nation
> bride-sweet broke to the whole rapture?
> Hoover, Coolidge, Harding, Wilson
> hear the factories of human misery turning out commodities.
> For whom are the holy matins of the heart ringing?
> Noble men in the quiet of morning hear
> Indians singing the continent's violent requiem.
> Harding, Wilson, Taft, Roosevelt,
> idiots fumbling at the bride's door,
> hear the cries of men in meaningless debt and war.

Where among these did the spirit reside
that restores the land to productive order?
McKinley, Cleveland, Harrison, Arthur,
Garfield, Hayes, Grant, Johnson,
dwell in the roots of the heart's rancor.
How sad "amid lanes and through old woods"
echoes Whitman's love for Lincoln!
(*OF* 63–64)

He goes on in section 3, which is dedicated to Olson, to quote from the *Pisan Cantos,* whose line "the wind is part of the process," he says, "defines a nation of the wind" (*OF* 65), a Wagadu constructed of airs.

In the opening chapter of *The H.D. Book,* Duncan makes it clear that his study of H.D. will also be the story of his conversion to poetry. His sense of coming of age, coming to a sense of what his life's work would be, as he presents it there, is also his coming—his being brought by poetry—to a sense of the age in which his life and work unfold. The specific poems he mentions, H.D.'s "Heat" and James Joyce's "I hear an army charging upon the land," speak to him as omens of the age's coming of age, of a maturation toward crisis, a ripening at work in the times. What comes to a head in his perceptions is the apprehension of an assault on the creative spirit, on any cast of mind not given over to the pursuit of socially approved returns. He says of the life around him during the mid-1930s in Bakersfield, California, "All about one, one saw the process of the town's shaping unruly youth into its citizens, pressing desire into the roundness of its satisfactions, thickening the fire of the spirit into energetic figures that would be of public use. . . . Men hurried to satisfy ends in things, pushed their minds to make advances, right answers, accomplishments, early maturations. They contrived careers that they fully filled. They grew round and fat. . . ."[23] But feeling, which would be the poem's domain, contends with "public use." Duncan sees this rift in his recollection of a Miss Keough, the high school teacher he says "attended the possibility of a poet in me." It was she who, stepping outside the impersonality of her office, her role as teacher, would offer a genuine, heartfelt part of herself by reading "Heat," a poem not on the students' required reading list, aloud to the class. Or she would lend books to the young Duncan, nurturing him with D. H. Lawrence and Virginia Woolf, asking him what he made of what she lent. The transformative power of poetry, the distance between her obligations as a teacher, a representative of the state, and the more compelling authority she obeyed in her reading of "Heat," made an impression on him. He writes, "She could be a task mistress where the uninspired and uninspiring preparation for college entrance exams was concerned. She had, after all, to project an authority over us. She had her pay for that. She must have endured, we must have endured, a tedium then, but the dreary tests of accomplishment and graduation could vanish in moments when work itself took on another meaning" (*HD*I.1 11). Both the rigidity of "officization" and the answering release that poetry testifies to were there to be seen, even if, as it did for Duncan, this meant being done with "achievement." "But simple ends, direct uses of things, closing in one the opportunity, threatened the realization of some wholeness," he writes. "I felt I must be, the world must be, something more various and full, having more of flux and experience than the immediate terms of achievement around me disclosed. . . . The poem had something to do with keeping open and unfulfilled the urgencies of life" (*HD*I.1 15).

Already we see the seeds of an objection planted. The conviction that poetry opposes office, that the poet is at odds with the ossification of "public use," gives eventual rise to the attacks in "The Multiversity" on University of California President Clark Kerr, Chancellor Edward Strong, an unnamed "aging Professor," and Adlai Stevenson. A bit earlier, too, there is "The Fire":

Satan looks forth from
men's faces:
Eisenhower's idiot grin, Nixon's
black jaw, the sly glare in Goldwater's eye, or
the look of Stevenson lying in the U.N. that our
Nation save face •
(*BB* 43)

And there are the objections to Lyndon Johnson in "Up Rising" and again in "The Soldiers." Since the idea of office is intimately bound up with the state and the regimentation imposed by the state is nowhere more obvious than in the military, in this first chapter of *The H.D. Book* we see Duncan, while a student at Berkeley, make a choice between poetry and a compulsory class in military drill. The year is 1937; he sits on the grass with two young women, Athalie and Lilli, reading to them from Joyce's *Collected Poems.* The bells chime, announcing that it's eleven o'clock, the time for military drill. Duncan breaks off his reading, says that he has to go, but is told by his two listeners not to: "'You don't have to go,' Lilli commanded, raising her hand in a dramatic gesture that had been delegated its powers by our imagination of our company. 'Stay with Joyce.' What we had been enacting, the reader and the listeners—the muses, perhaps, for some serious amusement or enchantment was worked through our cooperation—celebrating this most high reading of the poem, was to become real. 'Rejoice with Joyce,' Athalie commanded. A poem was to take over" (*HD*I.1 27). The choice Duncan makes is to remain there on the grass reading to his two muses. The poem has taken over, "an eternal thing." We think of the poem "Orders" as he goes on to make the issue explicitly one of a clash between conflicting orders, those of the state versus those of the poem, the profane against the sacred. "The authority of the poem," he goes on to say, "was a voice of the spirit."

So a stream of students rushes toward the gym to comply with "public use" while he and his two companions obey the authority of the poem: "Away towards duty, the one command of the state over us, the students went." He goes on to refer to himself as "a deserter" and to say that much more than military drill alone had been opted out of. An entire way of life, utilitarian by society's sense of the word *useful*, had been deserted. The call to poetry had meant dropping out. We read, "Attended by two radiantly beaming women who had won me so into their company, their conspiracy, against the army, against the university finally. For I never went to Military classes again. I ceased going to other classes that I had found a sham. I had come into a poetic order more commanding than my fear of military authorities, but I had lost too the reality of graduating from school, of going on to take my place as a cultural authority. Towards something else, a reality where the poem, the little book of Joyce, the reading and the women, had survived time" (*HD*I.1 29). It is the power of poetry to disrupt, uproot, or unsettle any inert sense of achievement Duncan testifies to here, having put aside the pursuit of socially sanctioned goals and become more and more indifferent to socially sponsored motivations. The point carries back to what he writes earlier about feeling: "It was the sense of the necessity that what was felt be kept that filled the poet in writing. To find out feeling meant to evoke a new power in life. To feel at all challenged the course of everything about one. . . . It was . . . a trust in living, not only to use things but to be used by them, a drive that broke through the restrictions and depressions of spirit whereby men were shaped to a public purpose" (*HD*I.1 10–11). The willingness to get caught up in feeling, to celebrate intensity at the risk of appearing without purpose—"intensity, in itself, was uncouth," he says—is one mark of the poet's uselessness. To embrace the worthlessness of poetry, to rejoice in being useless, is to take a stand against what commonly passes for value. As with Olson, poetry for Duncan has to do with a renunciation, with warding off the uses to which we'd be put by the powers that be. Feelings of alienation from and defiance of those powers are central to the Vietnam War poems.

But the Vietnam War poems are not antiwar in a strict pacifist sense, perhaps not antiwar at all. They are clearly not against war in general, however much they object to this particular war. Duncan makes a point of distinguishing himself from those students who for pacifist reasons oppose military drill. He writes, "War! We were supposed to hate the thought of it, but to embrace the fact of it. Some students were opposed to whatever fact of war. There were pacifists, students who challenged the order to take Military and went on strike. . . . They had conscience. . . . I, too, believed that back of the army was a cult of War or a business or profession of War, an evil—for it stood against all hope of peace; but I had not righteous conviction to take a stand. I despaired myself of peace" (*HD*I.1 18). He goes on to conclude this first chapter of *The H.D. Book* by remarking, "The war, too, defines eternal measures." But however ambiguous their status as antiwar poems, the poems are decidedly antiauthoritarian, antiestablishment and antigovernment. Their oppositional stance has profoundly to do with an assertion of the poet's marginality to the reigning order's concerns. The war summons a more vigorous objection to the set of priorities that judges poetry useless; it calls forth a repudiation of those reigning senses of "use" conducive to profitable carnage. There is a thoroughgoing apologetics at work throughout the objection, for the reverse side of Duncan's grand, sometimes grandiose sense of the poet is a defensiveness, a fear of being diminished by the contrary thrust of conventional values.

We see this clearly in "A Letter," where Duncan writes of a dream in which he is in a crowd of people chased by a giant carpenter. The carpenter wants to convert them all to carpentry, to bring them over to worthwhile, socially useful work. The dream projects Duncan's doubts concerning his choice of poetry as his life's work. The letter is addressed to the carpenter, and very early in it he writes, "You made everything in my world small."[24] What the carpenter is demanding would amount to slavery, he says. He recalls a class called "woodwork" that he took while in high school; like the later military drill at the university, woodwork was compulsory. It was also a class in which Duncan, partly because of his crossed eyes, performed poorly. He laments that to try his hand at carpentry again would only take him "deep into failure." "Isn't my own work in poetry meaningful to you?" he asks, only to realize that in the dream he himself had forgotten about being a poet. The carpenter was intimidating enough and Duncan's resoluteness vulnerable enough to make for doubts:

> When I woke from the dream I thought at first about how well meant what you wanted was. I wonderd why I ran in such abject panic trying to get away from you. Carpentering was real work, it was for the good of all and without vanity. It seemd to me poetry was only an avocation and words were not needed things. The wood was real. No wonder in the dream I had nothing to turn to.
>
> Yes, I was running away from work, from the only real work to do. And nothing would hide me. (*RB* 18)

But more emphatically than it does Duncan's doubts, the dream projects the sense of persecution that is the source of those doubts. The carpenter embodies all the utilitarian biases of the social order the poet is an outcast from. He embodies as well the authoritarianism that makes those biases binding, what Duncan in the concluding words of the letter calls "the marches of relentless power."

Throughout *The H.D. Book*, much of whose writing runs concurrent with that of the Vietnam War poems, Duncan offers comments on H.D.'s responses to World War II. His remarks throw light on his responses to the Vietnam War, since here, as elsewhere in his work, Duncan is what he himself calls "a derivative poet," elaborately grounding himself in an inheritance left by previous poets. We have seen how one of his earliest experiences of H.D.'s work, the reading of "Heat" by his high school teacher, aligned her with a spirit contrary to the commercial, utilitarian, commodity-worshipping fixations of the dominant social order. "The new poetry," he writes in that first chapter, "was not to be a commodity, a thing of literature or culture, but an instrument in a process of spirit" (*HD*I.1 16). In later chapters he deals with H.D.'s own sense of herself as of a contrary order, returning again and again to her experience of the war as a deepening of her sense of exclusion. But the war is also, he points out, an event to be gloated over, if not celebrated, an event that bodies forth on a blatant scale what was suspected of the dominant order all along. The war provides H.D. with an opportunity, in *Trilogy,* to respond to that order's dismissal of poetry, to take the offensive with an "I told you so." The manifestly destructive, homicidal imperative of the reigning order elevates the outcast to a privileged position. The relegation of the poet to the absolute fringes of the dominant order allows her to dissociate herself from the war and from the suicidal values it brings to light. "This," she can say, "is not our field, / we have not sown this" (*T* 115).

Again and again we find H.D. responding to an adversary who indicts poets as useless, fielding the accusation only to turn it to her own advantage. In the section of *The Walls Do Not Fall* that ends with her saying that the scribe "stands second only to Pharaoh," she writes:

> . . . the double-plume or lotus
> are, you now tell us, trivial
>
> intellectual adornment;
> poets are useless,
>
> more than that,
> we, authentic relic,
>
> bearers of the secret wisdom,
> living remnant
>
> of the inner band
> of the sanctuaries' initiate,
>
> are not only 'non-utilitarian',
> we are 'pathetic':
>
> this is the new heresy . . .
> (*T* 14)

If the Vietnam War poems are at once public or political poetry and holdings forth on poetics, it is because Duncan, following H.D.'s lead, sees the war as both an attack on the claims of poetry and an occasion for reasserting those claims. By bringing out the nihilism of a worldview that denigrates the poet, the war fortifies the poet's position. The war provides the poet with a righteous anger that can be expressed in the name of poetry and, given the manifest misanthropy afoot, in humanity's name as well. The two can be presented as one, "Gassire's lute" aligned with the "household of the folk." The alignment, however, is troubled as well as secured by the will to revenge. Duncan has written about the way in which, in H.D.'s work, the scenes of destruction brought about by the war body forth psychic material that is both an attack and a counterattack, both the suffering inflicted on the heretic poet and the suffering the poet would inflict in return ("Wagadu can go to blazes"). We read, "Outer and inner conflicts enter into and surcharge the poetic. At odds with powerful influences, whether they be his own impulses or the opposing will of other men, the poet holds the new reality only by a heightened intensity. . . . The flaming cities are not only representations of persecutions suffered or punishments anticipated in heresy, they are also representations of a revenging wrath projected by the heretic, the stored-up sense of injustice and evil will over us raging outward. . . . Everywhere, we find at every level the content felt as psychic is manifest. . . . H.D.'s apocalyptic vision in the War Trilogy . . . provides an historical perspective in which the experience of London under attack in the Second World War becomes meaningful in relation to depths and heights of personal reality. . . ."[25] He comes to write the same thing in the poem "Before the Judgment," speaking not of H.D. with regard to World War II but of himself with regard to the Vietnam War:

> The poet turns in his sleep,   the cries of the tortured and of those whose pain
> survives after the burning   survive with him,   for continually
> he returns to early dreams of just retribution and reprisals inflicted for his
> injuries.[26]

We see that the way he reads H.D. is how he, too, would be read.

War is a profit-making tool and contingency for the military-industrial complex and other conglomerations of power, but there is a way in which the profit motive enters the poet's work as well—especially in H.D.'s and Duncan's cases, where war is capitalized on to yield a poetic return. H.D. admits this—not so much confessing as boasting—in *The Walls Do Not Fall,* where, reveling with a vengeance in the sense of herself as a pariah, she identifies with the worm, both in its lowliness or uselessness ("parasite" she calls herself) and in the inevitability of its transformation to butterfly ("industrious" she calls herself too):

> . . . I profit
> by every calamity;
>
> I eat my way out of it;
> gorged on vine-leaf and mulberry,

parasite, I find nourishment:
when you cry in disgust,

a worm on the leaf,
a worm in the dust,

a worm on the ear-of-wheat,
I am yet unrepentant,

for I know how the Lord God
is about to manifest, when I,

the industrious worm,
spin my own shroud.
(*T* 12)

The poem finds a way to feed itself, even thriving on war like Gassire's lute. Thinking of passages like the one just quoted, Duncan writes of *Trilogy* in *The H.D. Book*, "It is the 'unalterable purpose' of the poem to convert the War to its own uses; the bombings of London are read as signs in the Poem Effort which claims priority over the War Effort . . . the War is not to be taken for granted as simply an economic or political opportunity or as a disorder, but it is also a Mystery play or dream projection to be witnessed and interpreted, to be endured in order to be understood. The War rises from the dramatic necessity. . . ."[27] The same has to be said of his own war poems. Going at least as far back as "An Essay at War," written during the Korean conflict, we see the poem effort vying with the war effort, a transformative struggle or an alchemical operation that converts or seeks to convert the "lead" of destruction into the "gold" of poetic thought.

The "unalterable purpose" of "An Essay at War" is to follow Williams's injunction in the title of the book of stories he dedicated to U.S. troops in Korea, *Make Light of It.* The poem, which is much more clearly not an antiwar poem or a protest poem than the later work during the Vietnam War, tries to do just that—to provide "a lantern to read war by." The punning playfulness of Williams's title, exemplifying the very playfulness, lightness, or making light that its command encourages, carries over into Duncan's poem. An open, buoyant sense of meaning, to which wordplay is crucial, contends with the gravity of war. Duncan continues with Williams's play on the two senses of "making light," introducing one or two variations of his own. The connection, by way of fire, between light and heat catches him up in the closeness to one another, both in spelling and in sound, of the words *heat, heart,* and *hearth.* The fact that the last two words have to do with fire—one figuratively and the other literally—gives them, like *heat,* something in common with light, a further rapport the poem's variations play upon. The poem even, in a vein of self-reflexivity that carries throughout, comments on its own behavior, describing its act of illumination or of making light as a dance in which the words themselves heat up, flicker and catch fire:

> It is Love. It is a hearth.
> It is a lantern to read war by.
> I mean it has burnd all that we value,
> and we return to the burning itself,
> made savage by it, warmd by it,
> ears alert for the cave-lion or bear,
> as a company will gather about a burning house
> seeing the sparks fly up from their losses
> burning, brought together . . .
> only Love left.
>
> So, in Hell, imagine. All that we valued
> gone up in flames. Destroyd.
> There is a great light there.
>
> I mean the light of this war
> sweeps cities, a madness, laying waste.
> What remains is a hearth.
> What remains is the heart. Even
> out of Hell we demand it.
>
> Make Light. Gather about the flames
> and against the night recite
> as the words dance, dance
> as the flame flickers, burn
> as the language takes fire, revive
> the heat of the heart from its cold.[28]

In Claude Lévi-Strauss's discussion of the sorcerer-healer in *Structural Anthropology,* we are told that the healing art allows the sorcerer's overload or surplus of meaning to supplement the deficit of meaning suffered by normal thought. Duncan's word dance proposes a similar therapeutic. The poet, confronted by the dis-ease of war, likewise profits or proves useful by serving as a healer. He puts to work an otherwise renegade sense of the world as overwhelmingly charged with overtone and insinuation, rescuing the soul from the immobilization of semantic deficit and one-directional reference.

Healing here, as at its very root, has to do with making whole. "The writing triumphs," Duncan remarks, "for it most approximates the total configuration" (*HD*II.5 337). We recall him saying elsewhere that "the very heightened sense of the relatedness of everything sets poets apart." Throughout his writings he takes issue with any stance that would outlaw this feeling for connectedness. The once influential notion of "pathetic fallacy" comes under repeated attack in *The H.D. Book* as an example of an assault on poetic vigor by a rationalist, convention-ridden cast of mind epitomized by the New Criticism. The investment such a disposition has in the deficit of meaning it suffers from leads it to be protective of its predicament. It wants to confine thought to an acceptable containment of emotion and of the feeling for rapport Duncan so espouses. Eliot laments a "dissociation of sensibility," only to perpetuate it with the notion of an "objective correlative," his guarantee or would-be guarantee that emotions will not get out of hand; they are to be kept in check by agreed-upon ("objective") conventions and criteria as to the appropriateness of certain objects or situations to certain emotions. Yet even Eliot, in his very anxiety over emotions getting out of hand, acknowledges the risk of inflation that, inescapably, is a factor in "the total configuration." The threat of deflation, however, is Duncan's concern.

Returning to the first chapter of *The H.D. Book*, to what Duncan writes about H.D.'s "Heat," we see that what strikes him about the poem is her openness to and her giving in to feelings that might be criticized as uncalled for, inappropriate, excessive. That she gets worked up over pears, grapes, and the heat itself he sees as a matter of courage as well as necessity. But it goes against the grain of an overriding attempt to contain feeling and restrict meaning, to tame an intensity viewed as threatening or silly. "Being intense about trivial things like pears," he writes, "threatened the composure of household, gang, school and city or state, and was shamed, put down, as one must put away childish things" (*HD*I.1 10). One of Duncan's convictions is that nothing is trivial, that meaning and the potential for feeling permeate or saturate everything, no matter how apparently insignificant. Though we set up scales of priority that violate this fact, God's integrity, the universe's fidelity to itself, could have it no other way, as he asserts in "Moira's Cathedral":

. . . For in the Eye of the Creator

the trembling of a leaf
in the roar of gun-fire,

the fall of a tree, strikes dismay.
(*BB* 95)

The word dance of "An Essay at War," the multiplicity of meanings that its making light keeps aloft, is a dazzling enactment of what Baraka has called "meaning's possibility and ubiquitousness."[29] The poet's disaffection with or distance from a utilitarian, product-oriented social order shows in a difference of attitude toward words. Octavio Paz, in *The Bow and the Lyre,* observes that while the normal approach to language takes it as a tool, restricting the meanings of words in line with specific functions, goals, or jobs to be done, the poet liberates language by returning words to their natural, polysemous condition. The poet becomes a tool of the word's multiple meanings, serving the overload or surplus of meaning that resides in language as it does in the world.

Taking this further, we can say that the deficit of meaning suffered by nonpoetic thought is a frustration having to do not with a lack of meaning but with the variousness of meaning. What might be experienced as "meaninglessness" is the world's refusal to submit to a conclusive interpretation, to yield an ultimate meaning or to come to and abide by a final judgment. The common complaint against poetry's "obscurity," its "difficulty" or its "meaninglessness," is the reflex action of a desire for *the* meaning, for a single, unequivocally available, definitive message. "An Essay at War" flies in the face of such desire. Duncan explicitly writes, at one point, about the plurality of meanings that a single word is made to carry. The word, in this case, is *love*:

What do we mean when we say we're in love?
We use the one word
for tenderness, for passion, for enduring
devotion, or for the ocean-wide deep drawing
of the moon. We use the word
for a sexual madness, running

under the brimstone rain of fire
—so Alighieri described us—
backs bared, emotionally flayd,
        or, afraid,
crave love from statue-proud
        stone, or flesh
resistant as stone. . . .
(*D* 14)

To see that the word is not a containment but a contention of meanings is to see also that war isn't something existing only outside the poem, a fact to be simply referred to or dealt with as topic. War is also an internal characteristic of the poem, a fact of life at work within each word of which the poem is made. Not even the poem's title is allowed to rest in peace, for if we take the word *essay* in its multiple senses the poem is being said to be as much an effort at waging war as a composition having war as its subject—more so in fact, since it's called an essay *at* war rather than an essay *on* war. The poem effort and the war effort are one, or at least analogous.

The essay, whether as poetic or as martial effort, is also a trial. This becomes more evident if we go to the title of one of Duncan's books of the Vietnam period, *Tribunals,* the work in which "Before the Judgment" appears. And if we also go to the picture of trial and judgment we get in the Egyptian *Book of Coming Forth by Day,* where Thoth weighs the heart of the deceased against Maat's feather, we see that the poem's play on the words *heart, heat,* and *hearth* is also serious play, a weighing as well as making light. As a projection, a manifestation or a showing forth of psychic content, war puts us all on trial. The Korean War exists not as something to be disowned or objected to—"An Essay at War" hardly objects to it at all in any explicit way—but as a witness to what resides in the heart, a writing on the wall to be read by the light of the poem. What the reading brings to light is a deep-seated refusal to settle, to dwell peacefully in any one sense of what anything is. It reminds us that fire has both its malevolent and its beneficent sides. What makes the hearth can also destroy it. The comforting domestic fire carries the potential for holocaust:

. . . This blaze
is the same kind roar of flames
that destroys in terror Korea
and we

do not know how to make a light
pouring kerosene on the already burning paper.
(*D* 12)

The hearth, it says earlier, "is the first named incarnation of Love." But love, like any other fire, has a way of moving on. Its refusal, whether as word or as feeling, to be domesticated by or to come to rest in any single meaning, any one incarnation, eats away at the tranquility of the hearth. Aphrodite gets into an affair with Ares, as both love and war attest to an "indomitability" in the human heart. Their having to do with one another suggests an unrest or an estrangement at the heart of things, a quiver, an instability from which neither the poem nor any word inside it is exempt:

So, knowing or unknowing, the key
comes forward,   It lies in the speech
about us.   At ready response.   And within us.
It is in the air.
Everywhere.   The war is in the air.
(*D* 21)

"An Essay at War" tries the patience of any reader expecting a topical treatment of the Korean War, for while the poem does, at points, touch on one or two historical particulars of the conflict, its overall thrust is to regard the war as an occasion for a discourse on poetics. At no point is the "poemness" of what's underway, either in the words before us or in the conflict overseas, allowed to drop out of sight:

So this ordinary G.I. stript to the waist
        carrying the wounded
        American soldier in his arms
        repeats in his hot Korean summer
        a pièta.

He is like a nakedness of speech
        shedding its words; or
        an imaginary conclusion
        of acts or   of words;   without plan,
(*D* 21)

The pervasiveness of a poetic spirit, the rootedness of the poetic and the real in one another, makes the poem not a secondary fact of life reporting on an outside reality seen as primary, but an omnipresent participant in the thing it's "about." The poem is a war and the war is a poem. The G.I. fights in a war and is a figure in a poem in more senses than one. A free-floating, vagrant referentiality implicates any one thing in any number of other things. Proceeding by way of something that Olson, in reference to another work of Duncan's, calls "sets of positive and negative upsets" (*HU* 69), the poem agitates every settled sense of what's what and what refers to what. In one of the prose passages interspersed throughout the poem, Duncan writes, "It is the first named incarnation of Love. We burn with it. The fire of Hell. Pain. But it is also warmth. Demonic. But it is also light. The night is all about us. A darkness within which all known things exist. So, a moment before the appearance of one most feard or one most desired, or one most loved. Or . . . the centuries are all about us. A light to read by. Within us. A time within which all known things exist" (*D* 11). This gives the sense of a dance of transformations going on, a dance that could go on forever. But the poem tries the poet's patience, too:

> When does the poem end?   Why
> does it go on?   to exhaust
> what possibilities ?   Why does the war
> go on?
> (*D* 23)

The sense of the primal or primordial significance of the poetic, then, this inspiration in which the poem is the crux of things, is susceptible to doubts. Duncan's desire to approximate "the total configuration" demands that these doubts, the possibility of deflation, be given their due. Much as Williams does in "The Desert Music"—or as Duncan himself does in the later "A Part-Sequence for Change"—Duncan takes this crisis of inspiration, even the loss of inspiration, as a reality to be dealt with in the poem:

>   Anew?
>
>   Were we courageous to begin?
>
> Singing like troubadours in Albi or Toulouse
> as if in spite of . . .

listening to the nightingale
in the midst of the slaughter.

What good will this do?
(*D* 16)

He comes later in the poem to what he calls a "a breakdown, a failure of heart or of vision," where he looks with suspicion on his earlier figure of the language catching fire and dancing. The heat of inspiration, like the heat of love, moves on and leaves only cold in the hearth:

> You see, what I feel is needed at this point is a nadir, a breakdown, a failure of heart or of vision; and then, all longing left will be hopeless. Without a plan I was destined to come to this pass, to this foreclosing of all promise. The poem defeated. Yielding, without a war, we were bound to fail. Infatuates! Dancers! Once the music stopt, the effort to dance is painful to all concerned. What is left is despair. There is only the death of invention.

There is only the cold hearth.   The ashes
waste   .   it has all been said before.

The fire was the war.
We said burn with it.   We said
surrender all that we value to it,
to the burning   .   to the war
of words,   of the senses.

We did not make sense.
We made words dance.   Dance,
we said.   What is left is the hearth.
Dance by the light of the war.
(*D* 22)

It is here and at other such points in the poem that we come to what might distinguish the poem effort from the war effort, to the tentative sense in which this poem might be called antiwar. Its willingness to question or to corrupt its own inspiration is something like the faltering of Duncan's voice in his reading of "Moving the Moving Image." The chink it opens up in its armor allows for doubt and even desertion in a way that no army does. We're back to a sense of the poem as a foil to the rigidities of office.

There are momentary suggestions throughout "An Essay at War" of a possible reading in which such breakdowns as the one just quoted would seem to comply with such a sense. Section 2 of the poem initiates a highly charged opposition between inorganic, deathly perfection and the passional, untidy imperfections of actual living. The poem's way of posing the conflict—which, given Duncan's repeatedly acknowledged Freudian persuasion, can be stated as Thanatos battling Eros—is to represent the former, which it later calls "mineral perfection," as a rocklike or stone-like hardness. We see this in the already quoted lines in which we're said to "crave love from statue-proud / stone, or flesh / resistant as stone." The stanza following the one in which these lines appear introduces the figure of a rock crystal pitcher, a figure that is returned to a number of times throughout the rest of the poem. The complexity and the untidiness of what Duncan is doing, his recognition that in actuality so-called opposites don't always stand apart but often mix—he refers in his essay on Walt Whitman, for example, to "the deep co-inherence of Eros and Thanatos"[30]—can be seen in the fact that the pitcher is cracked. The crack makes it a figure of imperfection as well as perfection, of the perfection of imperfection and vice versa:

The Beauty of it!   we say.   The eye
catching fire, the hair luminous,
the torso like the Hapsburg's rock crystal
pitchers, flawd with its own wonder,
          shatterd visibly
with immutable perfection.
(*D* 14)

He goes on to say that we love imperfection as well as perfection, referring back to the pitcher:

But love—not of perfection
alone. The imperfections proposed, studied
in the cloudy stone, claims adoration.
(*D* 15)

Imperfection is perfect in that we love or desire it, just as perfection is flawed by the imposition of our desire. The poem proposes imperfection as a virtue, a form of honesty or truth, the flaw as a saving grace, a life-conducting shock. (The impossibility of going into this without resorting to what sounds like double-talk reminds us that flaws crack any word as they do the pitcher, giving it multiple meanings.)

In the final sections 5 and 6, the pitcher comes forward again. In these two sections Duncan makes the connection between it and the poetics the poem proposes more explicit, using the pitcher as a metaphor for the poem. At various points from section 2 on he plays with the idea of surrender, of "giving ourselves up . . . / falling away, / falling / face forward." "Let us resolve / the right surrender," he says at one point. This is what he aims for and claims to be doing throughout the poem—surrendering, for example, to the multiple meanings of words rather than wielding them as though he could diminish and thus master their meanings. In the first chapter of *The H.D. Book* as well, he articulates a poetics of surrender, speaking of a willingness "not only to use things but to be used by them" on his way to asserting that "instead of having ideas or feelings, the poet lets ideas or feelings 'have' him" (*HD*I.1 14). He writes there of the poem "taking over" and also writes of a desire for imperfection, hearing in H.D.'s "Heat" the "longing for a force that would break the ripening perfection" (*HD*I.1 14). In section 5 of "An Essay at War," he combines ideas of surrender and imperfection with the figure of the rock crystal pitcher, alluding to the poem's submission to the flaw of contradiction as an act of love, of "self-containd war":

Let there be no substitute for surrender to this
    ever about-to-be-realized, this
    imperfection in the cloudy stone, owl-wise
    perfect balancing of incongruities.

    only to fall!

(*D* 21)

To commit oneself to surrender is to be at odds with the central motive of war, so the poem can be said in that sense to be antiwar. Its poetics and its way of proceeding propose a warlike alternative to war, a "self-containd war" in which inconclusiveness removes the lure of victory. Doing battle, as Olson's Enyalion does (*MP* 405–7), with an image or a picture (a pitcher?) takes the place of blowing another human being to bits:

The figure was love as a transformation
of war, or
war without an enemy, or
war without a victory . . .
(*D* 22)

Section 6 offers another angle on the poem as pitcher, first proposing the cracks running through it as symptoms of a larger vision, of what Duncan earlier calls "a cosmic more-than-we-are. . . . A total vision. Exceeding the sensible." The larger the vision the more we need gaps to get it all in, as he says in a later poem, "Apprehensions":

"*Whenever the subject is not the earth*
but the universe viewd as a whole"
"*divergences appear*"
(*RB* 32)

The endlessness or ongoingness of creation makes any and every act inconclusive and thus imperfect, conclusiveness being beyond the sensible, no more than a lure for the imagination perhaps. Confusing the cracks in the pitcher with the lines of the poem, he secondly proposes them as lines of division, battle-lines drawn by the mind pulling away from itself in "self-containd war":

He conceives the poem
as a shatterd pitcher of rock crystal,
its more-than-language not in the form
but in the intrigue of lines, the shattering,
the inability .
tracing the veins of an imaginary conclusion,
the faults along which the tremor runs.

Or he conceives the poem as a mind dying
—that is, a mind dividing itself
from itself. The line divides.

Falling, face forward. .

(*D* 23)

Farther along in this section, having suggested that the idea of the poem as "a mind dying" is elegiac, "of things lost or about to be lost," he identifies the clear, unflawed portion of the crystal with the war. He poses the identification as a question, however, not at ease with the patness of a sense of the war as "unambiguous evil":

> The war is a mineral perfection, clear,
> unambiguous evil   within which
> our delite, our life, is the flaw,
> the contradiction?
> (*D* 23)

Throughout these last lines of the poem, Duncan plays with a less common, somewhat obsolete meaning of the word *flaw*, the sense of it as (quoting from the *Oxford English Dictionary*) "a burst of feeling or passion" or (from the *Merriam-Webster Eleventh Collegiate Dictionary*) "an outburst, especially of passion." So the word *rage* enters the poem, but in the unsettled and unsettling context of "positive and negative upsets," a sort of uncertainty principle that replaces the figure of war-as-mineral-perfection with one of elegiac-moment-as-flawed-perfection. The passage plays an image of rage not as flaw but as crystal purity against an image of the military strategist's lack of rage, a lack that is also posed as crystal purity. But the passage goes on to present rage as that which flaws the elegiac moment's purity (as it fails to do that of the military strategist's art?):

> . . . Or the elegiac moment
> —itself a mood as pure as crystal rage
> or the responsible traind military technician's art
> without rage   planning campaigns,
> organizing, ordering, giving   orders until
> the blood flows red from each page—
> the elegiac moment,
> the too-perfect-in-tone-to-be-sanctimonious
> moment of our pleasure in living grief,
> or living regret, the clear immutable pitcher
> flawd by our rage. . . .
> (*D* 23–24)

"An Essay at War" ends by referring overtly to the process of unsettling that it has been putting into practice. The variations and syncopations to which it refers contrast sharply with the characterization, in section 2, of the Alexandrine, the epitome of standardized, closed form in French poetry. Images of jewelry (stones that are overrefined, "precious" in the pejorative sense) suggest the obduracy of a will to perfection in the line's regularity:

> the repeated perfected
> Tanagra figure or pearl-rope
> twelve syllable measured Alexandrine line
> or rhyme like a fine jewel
> set in a regular reoccurring pattern . . .
> (*D* 15)

The "structure of rime" proposed at the end of the poem, on the other hand, invites a disturbance of repeatability and pattern, an agitation pulling the line away from any strict predictability. The poem ends with a return to its image of surrender, a "falling / face forward," the image which has been its way of speaking of an openness to irregularity and imperfection:

> . . . No calm
> unbroken by variations of the line
> or by the rime just off beat, repeated
> tokens for the listening ear of the endeavor
> to shape war.
>
> The skull forward.
> The flesh having melted into a dew.
> (*D* 24)

The poem turns out to have more to say about poetics than about the politics, economics, or any of what we would normally see as the primary dimensions of the war. The poem effort takes priority over the war effort, reducing it to a trope, a figure of speech with which it can play to get its poetics across. War is approached as an archetypal, ongoing fact of life and regarded cosmologically, in the manner of Heraclitus, rather than on the newspaper level—a level too attentive to only one dimension of current events, their timely, topical particulars, to suit Duncan's orientation.

The tenacity, the stubbornness even, of Duncan's sense of poetry as a fundamental fact of life makes him regard experience as at all points a pretext for and a revelation of poetic process. His tendency to poetize, to revel shamelessly in what some (even other poets) would call a poet's bias, is a challenge and an irritation to anyone expecting poems to bow to a reality not seen as indigenously poetic. His refusal to write about the war except in terms of a poetics, to accept or reject the war on what would seem to be its own terms rather than juggling and converting those terms, might even be seen as irresponsible, a refusal to submit to "public use" by being unequivocally for or against the war. Virtually any statement or apparent attitude one might extract from "An Essay at War" is either qualified or contradicted at some point. James F. Mersmann, in *Out of the Vietnam Vortex: A Study of Poets and Poetry against the War,* anxious to see it as an antiwar poem, makes its poetics the basis for his sense of "Duncan's objection to modern war." He writes, "We can hardly emphasize too much or too often the connection Duncan makes between the laws of the poem and all other activities. The proper poem is the paradigm, the universal signature of all action and being. Duncan's objection to modern war is that it is an atrocious poem written by bad poets *who have a plan*. . . . War necessarily operates under an entirely opposite poetic, and thus is anti-poetic not only by virtue of its unlovely *content,* but also by virtue of its blatantly anti-poetic *form*. . . . The bad poem is written *over* its matter and attempts to control and subjugate its parts."[31] The problem is that the poetics Mersmann bases this analysis on tends to militate against such one-sided statements. There is a grain of truth to these remarks, but it's only a partial truth. "An Essay at War" does speak, from its very beginning, of the poem as "a conception betrayd, / without a plan," and it does appear to make the war antithetical to its poetics with such lines as "The plan is the war" and "The war, or the plan, mocks us." But we also read, at one point,

> We are fighting over there.
> Without a plan   nor dream of conquest
> nor from love of humanity fighting.
> (*D* 17)

Are we to take it that Duncan approves of the Korean War, since here he sees it being fought "without a plan" and thus in agreement with his poetics? Couldn't the fact that wars rarely if ever go according to plan, even where there is a plan, make him a prowar poet if what Mersmann says is true across the board? I doubt that Duncan puts forth his poetics in order to argue against modern war. "An Essay at War" is less concerned with declaring itself either for or against the war than with declaring itself in favor of its own procedures—which is what any poetics-espousing poem tends to do.

III

So Duncan goes Barthes one better, calling on a third variously designated term that identifies history with poetry, ideology with poetics, and asserts that the inalienable meaning of things is that there is no inalienable meaning. Duncan's vision is as dialectical as that of any Marxist. Still, I recall him once remarking in conversation that what he could not subscribe to in Marxism was the idea that there could be an end to a dialectic. Nonteleological, his sense of time is that it's double-jointed. The war is both a sign of the times and "an eternal sentence." He adopts the Heraclitean sense of war as a cosmogonic, ever-active fact of life, the "Father of all" throughout all of time, but the historicity of our twentieth-century conflicts does not entirely fade from view. He repeatedly invokes a sense of war as a defining symptom, maybe *the* defining symptom, of the peculiarities of the times we live in. In the first chapter of *The H.D. Book* he describes the outbreak of World War I as an initiation into the age we now find ourselves in, the outbreak not of World War I alone but "of the war that we know now is not an incident but the continuum, the meaning of our nations, our politics, our labor unions, our masses" (*HD*I.1 31). He has referred to this as a time of another Hundred Years War, and in "Stage Directions" he writes,

Slowly the toiling images will rise,
Shake off, as if it were débris,
    the unnecessary pleasures of our lives
And all times and intents of peaceful men
Reduce to an interim, a passing play,
    between surpassing
Crises of war.
(*BB* 128)

Poetry, since it is also history, is likewise double-jointed, to be read for signs of the times but also defining eternal measures. Duncan, again in the first chapter of *The H.D. Book*, writes of poetry as a "fate," saying that its "quickening of vowels and consonants, the sequence and hidden design of voice that followed the sequence of emotion and intellection belonged now to an eternal order that challenged all the other timely conventions" (*HD*I.1 29–30). But the challenge itself is timely and tells of the times. So it is that he can suggest, a few pages earlier, that the contentiousness of Pound's *Cantos*, both the contentions among incongruous, heterogeneous elements within the work and Pound's tendency to rail, as in the usury canto, against things outside it, reveals that we are in an age of profound dislocations. He writes, "In *Kulchur*, relating his own Cantos to the music of Bartok and even, then, of Beethoven, Pound observed in these works 'the defects inherent in a record of struggle.' No other work so contains or shows forth the troubled spirit of our times: it is his genius that even where he presents flashes of eternal mind—veritas, claritas, hilaritas—he does not sublimate but remains involved, by defect, in the agony of the contemporary. A profound creative urge, like So-shu, churns in the sea of Pound's spirit everywhere, as it churns in the seas of our own history . . ." (*HD*I.1 19). Crucial to what one means by double-jointed is that things bend contrary to their customary courses, even to the point of appearing out of joint. The mystery of the seeming defect that paradoxically fits, of a destiny time works to fulfill through being out of joint, is something whose praises Duncan repeatedly sings. The points where things appear disturbed or disjointed, where "divergences appear," body forth and bear the brunt of a claim the eternal makes upon time. "It is towards what I have called the eternal that time is disturbed," he writes (*HD*I.1 30).

The idea of eternity, of an order of spirit, can have a comforting and reassuring aspect, but here we see something sinister announce itself, the specter of a grudge eternity bears against time. It is as though the spirit had a way of promoting unrest. Related to this is the idea that the artist, privy to the distempers as well as the dictates of the spirit, acts as an agent of apocalypse, a trumpeter of calamitous, misanthropic things to come. In *Art and Artist*, for example, Otto Rank presents a psychopathology of the artistic personality, writing that artists feel themselves to be set apart by an allegiance to a "spiritual-immortality idea" and that this allegiance makes for certain difficulties and conflicts. At one point in his *Tuscan Diary*, Rainer Maria Rilke describes the artist as "eternity protruding into time." He prophesies that the artist won't always live alongside ordinary people, that when the artist becomes active enough and strong enough actually to live what now she only dreams, the human race will degenerate and die out.[32] That the feeling of being bound "to an inner order of the spirit"—as *The H.D. Book* puts it—must entail dire, disruptive consequences is much attested to in Duncan's work. A strong line of assertion having to do with the inevitability of unrest, the willful instigation of dissonance, and the poet's special ability to dwell in dark, disturbed, or doom-ridden possibilities runs long and deep throughout what he has to say. The jeremiads he ventures into in his Vietnam War writings, where he says, "We enter again and again the last days of our own history" (*BB* i), and where he invokes Darwin, DNA, and a notion that evolution will eventually decide against human life, grow out of a long-nurtured predisposition toward crisis. What he says of Athalie in *The H.D. Book*, that she knew truth by its disaster, would also have to be said of Duncan himself.

The Vietnam War, then, is in part a fulfillment (in the sense in which we speak of prophecy being fulfilled) of Duncan's poetics. The first chapter of *The H.D. Book* makes it clear that, very early, poetry impressed him as the activation and the keeping alive of a feeling "that something more must impend" (*HD*I.1 21). The sense of an impending, of an investment in and even a wooing of "something more," whatever its risks of interference, has him write in "Letters" during the 1950s, "I attempt the discontinuities of poetry. To interrupt all sure course of my inspiration" (*D* 91). And in a notebook from the same period we read, "The poet, the adventurer, dreads achievement, eschews rest."[33] It is no accident that the Vietnam War becomes the occasion to reaffirm these earlier assertions in his introduction to *Bending the Bow*, where he writes, "Were all in harmony to our ears, we would dwell in the dreadful smugness in which our mere human rationality relegates what it cannot cope with to the 'irrational,' as if the totality of creation were without ratios. Praise then the interruption of our composure, the image that comes to fit we cannot account for, the juncture in the music that appears discordant" (*BB* ix–x). Much involved with this is a desire to bear witness to realities and truths whose acknowledgment business-as-usual tends to suppress. To the extent that the Vietnam War disturbs or dislocates the lulling, mind-constricting comforts of the American way of life, it is to be welcomed—even embraced—as the occasion for a widening, deepening, and raising of consciousness. In this, Duncan is in line with radicals and activists of the 1960s who hailed the war as an inevitable, instructive symptom of things that had long been wrong with the "American Way." That the war gave the lie to pat, reassuring assumptions of American righteousness, to the smug belief that American actions and motives could never be anything but innocent, was to be celebrated and used to demystify an American ethic felt by most to be exempt from question.

The feeling that, both for better and for worse, "something more" is there to be dealt with in the American reality than its official version admits participates in a larger campaign the poet undertakes to extend the boundaries of what we acknowledge to be real. Duncan writes with something of a Freudian sense of mission, discontent with the given terms of reality and testifying to depths and heights that exceed the limits of those terms. "To open Night's eye that sleeps in what we know by Day" is how he puts it in "Apprehensions," a poem in which he writes that the function of crisis is "to darken our intelligence" (*RB* 30–43). It is the sleep of a Day-lit reality principle that he sees the United States caught up in when he writes, in "Before the Judgment,"

> The president turns in his sleep and into his stupidity seep the images of burning
>   peoples.
> The poet turns in his sleep,   the cries of the tortured and of those whose pain
>   survives after the burning,   survive with him,   for continually
>   he returns to early dreams of just retribution and reprisals inflicted for his
>   injuries.
> The soldier gloating over and blighted by the burning bodies of children, women
>   and old men,
>   turns in his sleep of Viet Nam   or,
> dreamless, inert, having done only his duty, hangs at the edge of such a
>   conscience to sleep.
> The protestant turns in his sleep, setting fire to the hated images,
>   entering a deeper war against the war.   A deeper stupidity gathers.
> (*GW* 33)

Duncan's response to the war is complicated by the fact that he doesn't hold out much hope that we can awaken from this sleep. The best we can do, it seems, would be to awaken *to* it, to acknowledge it, thus coming to a fuller knowledge of ourselves. His art of healing traffics not in possibilities of a cure but in a predilection for dark truths, a Freudian pessimism couched in celebratory tones. So he writes in his notebook during the 1950s,

> Medicine can cure the body. But soul, poetry, is capable of living in, longing for, choosing illness. Only the most fanatic researcher upon cancer could share with the poet the concept that cancer is a flower, an adventure, an intrigue with life.

> The magnificence of Freud is that he never seeks to cure an individual of being himself. He seeks only that the individual may come to know himself, to be aware. It is an underlying faith in Freud that every "patient" is Man Himself, and that every "disease" is his revelation. (PN 403)

An apparent faith that all is well so long as it contributes to consciousness, to what—after Dante—he calls "the good of the intellect" ("il ben dello intelletto" in "Orders"), reveals the centrality of an intellectualist bias to Duncan's disposition.

But it is also a bias, via Sigmund Freud, in favor of repressed or unacknowledged psychic content. Duncan, in his approach to the war, continues H.D.'s intimation, also from Freud, that war represents the eruption of "something more," a surplus of meaning that has been repressed. Just as Freud feels the figures of ancient myth and legend to be not outmoded, abandoned realities but, like Oedipus or Electra, tenacious forces still to be found in the unconscious, H.D. in *Trilogy* experiences the bombings of London as a violent, explosive surfacing of these forces or figures. Gods and goddesses break in with a vengeance on a world which believes them nonexistent or, at best, irrelevant:

> saw with their very eyes,
> the battle of the Titans,
>
> saw Zeus' thunderbolts in action
> and how from giant hands,
>
> the lightning shattered earth
> and splintered sky, nor fled
>
> to hide in caves,
> but with unbroken will,
>
> with unbowed head, watched
> and though unaware, worshipped
>
> and knew not that they worshipped
> and that they were
>
> that which they worshipped. . .
> (*T* 68)

She likewise delights in the fact that the word *cartouche* refers both to the oval figure used in Egyptian hieroglyphs to encircle a divine name and to the explosive cartridge of a bomb or a bullet. The irrelevance of the first meaning to an increasingly secular world, she suggests, requires that the word impress itself on that world by manifesting the latter meaning, the rain of bombs speaking more intelligibly to our times than do the names of deities:

folio, manuscript, old parchment
will do for cartridge cases;

irony is bitter truth
wrapped up in a little joke,

and Hatshepsut's name is still circled
with what they call the *cartouche*.
(*T* 16)

Where the dominant order—in the name of reason, commodity worship, and the material comforts of the few—depresses, diminishes, and trivializes life on all fronts, the poet's invocation of a numinous realm is suspect and associated with fantasies better left unexplored. In H.D. we see a sometimes gloating sense of being vindicated by the powers the war lets loose. It is as though the poet's feeling for a passional seriousness or direness at work throughout life needed exactly such a cataclysmic intrusion, exactly such a disruption of business-as-usual, to attest to "something more." "If you do not even understand what words say, / how can you expect to pass judgment / on what words conceal?" she snaps back (*T* 14).

In Duncan's response to the Vietnam War there is likewise the sense that repressed, concealed, or simply unacknowledged powers are afoot. Such mythic figures as Okeanos, Kronos, Chrysaor, and the Hydra make their way into the poems, but on a more straightforward level the war is said to be involved with this country's refusal to come to terms with its own evil. In "Bring It Up from the Dark," which appeared as a broadside in 1970, we see something akin to the Jungian idea that by failing to acknowledge or to confront the Shadow, the illicit aspects of ourselves we seek to disown, we simply add to its destructive powers. The poem calls for a stripping away of every rationalizing cover, a looking into what our impulses actually are. Seeking the roots of the war in what's normally kept in the dark, Duncan demands an accounting and an excavation, a taking stock of the psychic contents motivating the assault on Indochina:

Bring up from the dark water.
It will be news from behind the horizon.
Refugees, nameless people.   Who are they?
What is happening?   I do not know.
Out there.   Where we can see nothing.
Where we can do nothing.   Men of our own country
send deadly messengers we would not send.
The cold wind of their desolation chills the first hint of morning,
rumors of burnd houses, smoking fields, and now wraiths
of the dead men daily they kill rise
against us.   It will go against us,
        pass, sweep on and beyond us.

The poem ends:

Dream disclosed to me, I too am Ishmael.
(*GW* 53)

But the news from Vietnam isn't only the news from below a threshold of the mind. It is also the suppressed, underlying truth of American individualism and capitalist "free enterprise," the deep truth that self-interest and the profit motive make for a pit in which each of us, like the biblical Ishmael, has his hand against everyone and everyone's hand against him. It is for this reason that Duncan so often invokes a sense of common and communal things, "the great house of our humanity," throughout these poems.

"Up Rising" speaks of America's "terror and hatred of all communal things, of communion, / of communism" (*BB* 81). The poem is normally thought of as an attack on Lyndon Johnson and, whatever else it might also be, it is unmistakably that.

Now Johnson would go up to join the great simulacra of men,
        Hitler and Stalin, to work his fame
        with planes roaring out from Guam over Asia,
all America become a sea of toiling men
        stirrd at his will, which would be a bloated thing,
        drawing from the underbelly of the nation
        such blood and dreams as swell the idiot psyche
        out of its courses into an elemental thing
        until his name stinks with burning meat and heapt honors
(*BB* 81)

Johnson never appeared to be more than a corny, wishy-washy rube whose mediocrity was his most decisive vice, so the profound evil of Adolf Hitler and Joseph Stalin that Duncan credits him with may not seem to fit. That the antiwar movement was able to harass him into not running for reelection would seem to suggest that his own "might and enduring fame," as it's later put, were not the maniacal obsession the poem makes them out to be. But this is the risk of inflated charges Duncan's excavation takes and deems it necessary to take, laying claim to a truth not entirely to be seen on the surface. Intent on bringing to light the deep "elemental thing" lurking beneath Johnson's harmless country-bumpkin façade, he can't help clashing with the image and the aura conjured by that facade. But this problem fades as the poem moves away from assertions about Johnson's ego or his personal ambitions and speaks of him as a pawn of the Pentagon and of men being "used like things." The poem speaks of a collective sleepwalk whose business-as-usual consists of "good people in the suburbs . . . / heaping their barbecue / plates with more than they can eat" and of warfare-developing "chemists we have met at cocktail parties, passt daily and with a / happy 'Good Day' on the way to classes or work" (*BB* 82). That the sources of the war are innocuously folded into the fabric of everyday life, into aspects of American reality we take for granted, is one of the more deep-reaching, disturbing possibilities the poem explores. Duncan digs beneath the narcotizing rhetoric that justifies the war, and he also raises the issue of the nation's refusal to confront its true history, its avoidance of such a confrontation through the adoption of cosmetic, jingoistic versions of the past, versions in which it credits itself with the creation of a "land of the free." He sees that American arrogance reaches all the way back, that the Vietnam War is part of a continuum, an accumulation of what he goes on to call "America's unacknowledged, unrepented crimes" (*BB* 83).

Thinking back to "Orders," we see that the relevance of Eliot's "History has many cunning passages . . ." to the poem's political occasion consists of the sense, advanced in "Up Rising," that a refusal to see what we are doing in the present comes out of refusing to see what was done in the past. The idealistic, rationalizing language that exonerates American actions in Vietnam is the same language that falsifies history in order to excuse or attempt to erase the deep taint of genocide. The genocidal and ecocidal assault on a Mongolian people in Indochina repeats an earlier such assault on a similar people here on the American continent. It is to this true but suppressed history, this "secret entity," that Duncan goes on to refer:

> . . . this secret entity of America's hatred of Europe, of Africa, of
> Asia,
> the deep hatred for the old world that had driven generations of
> America out of itself,
> and for the alien world, the new world about him, that might have
> been Paradise
> but was before his eyes already cleard back in a holocaust of burning
> Indians, trees and grasslands,
> reduced to his real estate, his projects of exploitation and profitable
> wastes
> (*BB* 82)

Throughout the war poems there is a move to restore a sense of history, and this restoration, as Duncan notes in "Before the Judgment," takes on the character of a confession:

> This Confession that struggles with you   and grows,
> this *History of My True Country*   that you have come to acknowledge,
> will not let you alone. . . .
> (*GW* 34)

If America's inhumanity partly consists of a denial of its share of human evil, an overly righteous sense of itself underlying its attempts to police the world, then confession might begin to restore more than a sense of history. The old truism that ignorance of history dooms us to repeat it combines with a surprisingly Christian sense on Duncan's part that failure to confess a crime is perhaps the greatest crime and that without repentance there can be no redemption. The final stanza of "Up Rising" hits hard on the score of "old evils arisen anew" and America's refusal to acknowledge the crimes it has already committed:

> this specter that in the beginning Adams and Jefferson feard and knew
> would corrupt the very body of the nation
>   and all our sense of our common humanity,
> this black bile of old evils arisen anew,
> takes over the vanity of Johnson;
> and the very glint of Satan's eyes from the pit of the hell of
> America's unacknowledged, unrepented crimes that I saw in
> Goldwater's eyes

now shines from the eyes of the President
in the swollen head of the nation.
(*BB* 82–83)

In "Man's Fulfillment in Order and Strife," an essay written in 1968, Duncan says that his writing of "Up Rising" was motivated by "the strong sense of belonging to this 'we,' of being American as a condition of being human, so that the crimes of the Nation are properly my own, of having, in other words, a burden of original sin in the history of the Nation." (So it is that he confesses in "Bring It Up from the Dark" that "I too am Ishmael," recalling Edward Dahlberg's characterization of America as a nation of Ishmaels, and of American artists—writers in particular—as "Ishmaels of letters" who are "cut away from the human vineyard."[34]) He goes on to write of the importance of acknowledgment, giving a sense that "Up Rising" might more aptly be thought of as an act of confession than as the protest poem it's normally taken to be:

> Think of the poem *Up Rising* then, not as it has often been taken as a reaction to the particular violation of our common humanity by the Johnson administration, think of this as an acknowledgement and potential repentance then of what America means. . . . My sense is that the vital thing is that we come into the present reality. The leaders deny that they are doing what they are doing. They act in the exterior social world as we recognize forces of repression act in the interior person to refuse to see what they disapprove of in themselves. . . . But acknowledging what we are doing is important. This is the importance we find in tragedy, where Man comes to know the depths of what he is doing, his righteousness is stripped bare. The bomber overlooks the reality he inflicts—he flies high as the politician who directs his action likes to fly high above the reality of his orders. . . . The lies of Johnson and his regime are terms of the language of a grand psychopathology of daily political life that belongs to their refusal to face the facts of what they are doing. (MF 247)

Elsewhere in the essay we see that not only questions of morality and the rehabilitative powers of repentance make for the weight Duncan attaches to acknowledgment. An unobstructed, unedited vision of the totality of what we are is essential to what he calls "il ben dello intelleto" in "Orders." The idea that "the good of the intellect," above all else, has to be preserved enters his discussion of Dante's *De Monarchia*, whose postulation of a world order he adapts for his own "emerging ideas of cosmos and life orders." He stresses Dante's sense of the world order as a work of art, a macrocosmic poem "in which the ultimate fittingness of every thing, being, or event, is its contribution to the intent of the whole," or, as he also puts it, "a poetry in which the actualization of each member's potentiality is remembered in the whole."

Just as in "An Essay at War" the sense of fulfillment, the filling full or the feeling full, has to do with the coexistence of multiple meanings, the filling up of words to the point of bursting with variabilities of meaning, the sense of world order Duncan reads out of Dante emphasizes multiplicity, potentiality, and variation. Central to the realization or apprehension of world order is human consciousness. "The good of the intellect" not only contributes to but also depends on keeping such an order in mind. The closest Duncan comes to teleology in his otherwise open-ended sense of this order—his Darwinian sense of it as endlessly evolving, endlessly in process—is his endorsement of Dante's emphasis on the cultivation of intellect as man's "proper function," the specifically human role in the scheme of things. He relates, at some length, the Darwinian and the Dantean aspects of his vision of creation, central to which is what Dante calls "apprehension by means of the potential intellect":

> I see Creation as a process of evolution of forms, and these forms in turn as arising and surviving in a ground of individual variations and mutations where the multiplicity is not superfluous but the necessary condition of potential functions. "No created being is a final goal in the intention of the Creator; but rather is the proper function of that being the goal." In Darwinian evolution the intention of the Creator is itself evolving, itself having identity in the process of the survival and perishing of potential functions. And the intention of the Creator, for Dante too, is larger than the creation of Man; it is posited in the universe, the sum of forms or form of forms in time and space: "The totality of men is a whole relatively to certain parts, and it is likewise a part relatively to a certain whole. That is, it is a whole relatively to special kingdoms and nations . . . and it is a part relatively to the whole universe." Not only is there no superfluous part in the process of the whole, but in turn the very multiplicity of parts, the variety of individualizations, races and species, is essential to the design, creative of the design: no one a goal but each a function in the creation at work. "There is, then," Dante continues, "some function proper to humanity as a whole for which that same totality of men is ordained in so great a multitude, to which neither one man, nor one family, nor one district, nor one city state, nor any individual kingdom may attain." Man's

> special mode of being, for Dante, is "*apprehension by means of the potential intellect*," the coming into being of an intellect; and in turn the potentiality requires the multitude of individualities: "And since that same potentiality cannot all be reduced to actuality at the same time by one man, or by any of the limited associations distinguished above, there must needs be multiplicity in the human race, in order for the whole of the potentiality to be actualized thereby." (MF 233)

The relevance of this to the Vietnam War poems is that American imperialism, the would-be hegemony of American biases and vested interests, is an assault on "multiplicity in the human race." The attempt to reduce the wide, various reach of human potentiality to the confines of what will serve the U.S. government and U.S. business leads Duncan to object in the name of "something more." In "Passages 32," among the quotations from John Adams's marginalia to a book called *Monde Primitif*, there is an early warning against America's potential for imperialist designs. Adams, as though he too were advancing these Dantean ideas, underscores Duncan's feeling that any such move wages war against, among other things, the freedom and flexibility of the mind, the "potential intellect":

> "   Americans!   Have a care   form no schemes of
> "   universal empire.   The Lord will always
> "   come down and defeat all such
>
>   projects."
>
> "Let the human Mind loose!   It must be loose!
>
>   It will be loose!"
>
> (*GW*, 14)

"Today the World Order that we know," Duncan goes on to say, "must be imagined in terms not of one civilization but of the multiplicity of civilizations; as the imagination of Man's potentialities must search out all we know and dream of Man's experience everywhen, everywhere" (MF 234). These ideas of a world order, especially the sense of it as a poetic order, a poem in process, are very close to and indeed overlap with the notion of a "world-poem" that Duncan advances in "Rites of Participation," chapter 6 of part 1 of *The H.D. Book*. The chapter begins with the announcement that "the drama of our time is the coming of all men into one fate, 'the dream of everyone, everywhere.'" It goes on to speak of *The Waste Land*, *Trilogy*, the *Cantos*, *Paterson*, and *Finnegans Wake* as instances of an analogous "drama" starting to take place in writing during the early decades of the twentieth century. All are examples of what Duncan calls the "world-poem," works in which a sense of the world as an available whole takes priority over political, geographic, and temporal divisions. The world-poem is a global, multiphasic work in which various times and places interpenetrate. It is no accident, as Duncan sees it, that this sort of work began to appear during the period of the two world wars, a time when national divisions and hostilities were at the forefront. He offers a sense of the world-poem as a dialectical, oppositional response to the disunity of a world at war, suggesting that the *Cantos*, for example, went against the grain in its refusal to honor national divisions: "It was the mixture of times and places, and especially the breakdown of all nationalistic distinctions that most angered the hostile critics and readers. Renaissance English or medieval Italian or modern French could enter into an American poem: not only Dante but Kung and even Gassire were to be our heroes in the new legend" (RP 55). A bit further on he writes, "These poems where many persons from many times and many places begin to appear—as in *The Cantos*, *The Waste Land*, *Finnegans Wake*, the War Trilogy, and *Paterson*—are poems of a world-mind in process. The seemingly triumphant reality of the War and State disorient the poet who is partisan to a free and world-wide possibility, so that his creative task becomes the more imperative. The challenge increases the insistence of the imagination to renew the reality of its own" (RP 66).

In "Man's Fulfillment in Order and Strife," Duncan admits to being "thoroughly a convert of such an idea of poetry." "Passages" fully takes part in this idea. That most of the Vietnam War poems should appear in that series reflects the fact that the war violates its internationalist assumptions, making objection a logical act of self-defense. But the objection also carries out the oppositional impulse Duncan sees as implicit in the world-poem idea. I recall hearing him describe "Passages" as a work "in which the mind can take place." Since his leanings toward a "world-mind" make any nationalism inherently "antimind"—"once we are people of a nation we are forced to surrender the authority of intellect" (MF 241)—it follows that "Passages" would be antinationalistic. We see this in "The Soldiers," where Duncan poses Whitman's version of the world-poem idea, his sense of "America" as a poem, a quality of the human spirit transcending both historical and political boundaries, against the blatantly nationalistic and imperialist reality of America in its aggression toward Vietnam. The ironic resonances history has inflicted on Whitman's idealistic, naive sense of the United States as "essentially the greatest poem," on his sense of "the Americans of all nations at any time upon the earth," are not lost on Duncan. In his essay "Changing Perspectives in Reading Whitman" he acknowledges the actual, historical America to be an embarrassment to Whitman's poetic, possibly inflated inspiration. He writes,

> He was a man of contradictions and he calls up inner contradictions in the reader. His ideals, as you will appreciate, the very ideals of the potentialities of Democracy, of "America," . . . have revealed potentialities of their own in the century since *Leaves of Grass* and *Democratic Vistas*. . . . In the late nineteen-thirties, as I came into some kind of social consciousness, ideas of Whitman's had come also to be the ideas of established and increasingly coercive governments. . . . Is it the deadly boast of the Chauvinist, the patriotic zeal of a spiritual imperialism, that fires Whitman's: "The Americans of all nations at any time upon the earth have probably the fullest poetical nature. The United States themselves are essentially the greatest poem"? Presidents, congresses, armed forces, industrialists, governors, police forces, have rendered the meaning of "America" and "the United States" so fearful—causing fear and filled with fear—in our time that no nationalistic inspiration comes innocent of the greed and ruthless extension of power to exploit the peoples and natural resources of the world that has spread terror, misery, and devastation wherever it has gone. (CP 79)

But when it came to the writing of "The Soldiers," he goes on to say, he was to lay such doubts and misgivings to rest, coming into what he calls "a new inspiration," an affirmative sense of Whitman's lines as "oracular," his "greatest poem" an anticipation of the world-poem.

But the ironies don't entirely disappear. In "The Soldiers," Duncan quotes the line asserting Whitman's notion of the United States as "the greatest poem" but adds a question mark. He goes on to affirm Whitman's vision as a way of undermining and proposing an alternative to the historical reality the United States has become. The discrete political and geographical entity we normally take it to be vies with a poetic, imaginal conception of "America." A "secret union," like the Wagadu of *The H.D. Book*, this "America" is a communal state so unconfined by national boundaries that it's more truly embodied by the Viet Cong than by the United States:

"The United States themselves are essentially the greatest poem"?

Then America, the secret union of all states of Man,

waits, hidden and challenging, in the hearts of the Viet Cong.

"The Americans of all nations at any time upon the earth,"

Whitman says—the libertarians of the spirit, the

devotées of Man's commonality.

(*BB* 113)

Given Duncan's belief that the cosmos, the totality of What Is, is the prototypical poem, the challenge of his poetics (and the challenge to it as well) is the necessity of acknowledging both the ideals of a poetic conception and the equally poetic perversions of those ideals. The objectionable, anti-"American" actions of the United States take part in the "greatest poem" the universe ultimately is, so however much Duncan might move to protest those actions the underlying assurance of his poetics is that they too belong to the scheme of things. But there is also a further sense in which the United States's betrayal of its own ideals, its failure to live up to the promise Whitman saw, conforms to Duncan's poetics. "The Soldiers" in a number of ways recalls "An Essay at War," in whose opening lines Duncan espouses a poetics of betrayal:

The design of a poem
constantly
under reconstruction,
changing, pusht forward;
alternations of sound, sensations;
the mind dance
wherein thot shows its pattern :
a proposition
in movement.

The design
not in the sense of a treachery or
deception
but of a conception betrayd, . . .
(*D* 9)

The special place provided for disturbance in Duncan's worldview, a sense of design in which things fail to go as planned, carries a feeling not only that "something more must impend" but that "something more" will carry seeds of a betrayal.

Very early in "The Soldiers" we're given a sense of the world as a poem that defies or betrays even a poet's expectations. Duncan struggles to hold to a vision of the fittingness of whatever occurs, to a conviction that everything, no matter how contrary to what we might wish, has its part in the overall poem. There is a certain humility in his attempt to understand the war as the opportunity for an epiphanic, poetic ensouling for the soldiers who are in it, an attempt consistent with his sense that everything human beings do enriches—however much it may complicate or even threaten to annihilate—consciousness. Rather than rigidify his own poetic disposition, which tends in many ways to be antimilitaristic, he chooses to see the war as a kind of poem, the soldiers as somewhat akin to poets:

> They've to take their souls in the war
>
> as the followers of Orpheus take soul in the poem
>
> the wood to take fire from that dirty flame!
>
> in the slaughter of man's hope
>
> distil the divine potion, forbidden hallucínogen
>
> that stirs sight of the hidden
>
> order of orders!
>
> They've to go into the war and have no other
>
> scene to make time to live •
>
> (*BB* 112)

The lines that follow these reveal the humility to be religious in certain respects, a bowing down before the mystery of a numinous intent. Duncan quotes Victor Hugo, speaking of "God, whose work extends farther than our dreaming," and again sees the soldiers taking part in a poem, the lines they make in marching forming "parts of a sentence":

Dieu, *dont l'oeuvre va plus loin que notre rêve*

Creator mysterious Abyss

from which there goes out a smoke
of men, of beings, and of suns!

so deep that he is blue with depth

containing without deception what so deceives us.

The extent of the shadow the weight of the fullness

measure

parts of a sentence they must make their long march to make

life writes we take as necessity.

(*BB* 112)

The phrase "their long march" brings Mao Zedong into the poem. As he also does in "An Essay at War," Duncan makes use of the fact that Mao is both a poet and a political leader. In "Man's Fulfillment in Order and Strife," he suggests, "The secret power of the demotic leader to arouse a people is that he impersonates the poetic content of his nation, he is driven by the unfulfilled consequences of a nation's history" (MF 240–41). The assertion of a connection between poetry and nationalism, poetry and politics, is underscored by Mao's involvement with both.

Yet in "The Soldiers" Mao serves as a double agent, allowing Duncan to reinforce but at the same time qualify the suggestion that political events make for a poetry of sorts. The same thing happens in "An Essay at War," where he brings Mao in partly to introduce the figure of the political-leader-as-poet and partly to differentiate the type of poetry the political leader writes—the war in this case—from the type of poetry he himself writes. Somewhat along the lines suggested by Mersmann in *Out of the Vietnam Vortex*, Duncan characterizes the politician as a "single-minded" poet, a poet unwilling to let the poem proceed "without a plan." The politician-poet's coerciveness and refusal to be swayed are inimical to the open poem Duncan aspires to, a poem in which many voices and many minds may freely enter, constantly disturbing and redesigning whatever plan there might be. The "medley of voices" and the "free harmony" of such a poem contrast with the regimentation of the war effort, the surrender of individual freedom the leader requires of his poem's constituents:

Stalin, over time, has shown determination.
Mao is an idea transforming an idea,
a poet with a war, a plan, an inspiration.
Cruelties, not to be corrupted;
terrors not to be turnd. Music
may tame the tiger, but these tigers
proceed to their own tune,
measure their own true scale expertly.
        What medley of voices, what free harmony,
can stand over against or answer
        single-minded tyranny?
Only a plan, a unanimous war, can win.
                An inspiration
not to be corrupted, not to be turnd.
(*D* 18)

That such a passage occurs in so early a poem shows that Duncan was long impressed by the analogy between poetry and politics. His sense of it goes back at least as far as the late 1930s. In his introduction to *The Years as Catches*, he remarks that along with his wary apprehension of the coercive energies of the modern state there also came a sense that the poetic impulse might have something in common with such powers. He writes that "in these years as I began to write, from 1937 on, the Roosevelt panacea for the ills of the profit system, the Permanent War Economy, began to emerge as a reality that would take over. My deepest social feelings then were irregular too—for I saw the State and the War as diseases, eternal enemies of man's universal humanity and of the individual volition. . . . However I went about it, I had to deal with elements in which I was not to be the master. The War itself and the power of the State I dimly perceived were not only a power over me but also a power related to my own creative power but turnd to purposes of domination, exploitation and destruction."[35] The relationship of poetry to the very powers it presumably opposes, the sense of its possible complicity with those powers, was not especially reassuring. It is exactly this sense that makes the story of Gassire's lute so unsettling.

Duncan takes the relationship seriously; he wrestles with its implications at a number of points. Throughout these wrestlings two contrary impulses intersect, one of them a desire to issue poetry a clean bill of health—to say, as H.D. does, that "we have not sown this"—and the other an assertion that even poetry bears something like "a burden of original sin." The latter impulse is the price of Duncan's insistence that poetry is not merely decorative, innocently after the fact, but initiatic and, accordingly, crucial, at the crux of things. To give poetry an absolute stake in the full span of What Is is to give it its shares of both good and evil, its shares of innocence and guilt. We find him very much immersed in these questions in "Man's Fulfillment in Order and Strife," where his exploration of the likeness of the demotic leader to the poet puts the poet on trial, quivers back and forth between indictment and exoneration. Perhaps the most immediately striking thing he has to say, especially to anyone who has come away from "An Essay at War" feeling that writing "without a plan" was being advanced as a virtue—moral as well as aesthetic—is that the poet's susceptibility to seizures, to inspirations that defy purposes and plans, makes for a sinister power. "I had started to go back to the beginnings of a sense of an aura in language," Duncan writes, "to a rhythmic and tonal seizure in words where I found suddenly I was not using language but used by language, not saying something I meant to say but being carried away to things I had not thought to say—amazed or ashamed of what I was saying. Here the beginnings of song and prophecy, of trance and imagination, are very close, and how much, and rightly, we are afraid of them. Unspoken and unacknowledged purposes of our own rush in. 'Poetry,' Ezra Pound wrote, 'is language charged with meaning to the utmost degree' . . . . In that charge there are meanings we are not prepared for. Language so charged is not simple, it is multiphasic. And there is a sinister, a duplicit, possibility in the charge" (MF 239). Here Duncan writes with misgivings concerning the excited, polysemous possibility he so often extols, finding in language a dangerous ability to fascinate, seduce, and enthrall, a power through which it uses its users. He goes on to speak of this power's ability to "release the demonic in politics."

Duncan's description of Hitler as "a poet of the public soul" and his discussion of nationalism as an effect of language, an "overcharge of language with popular apprehensions," are also striking. Throughout the essay he describes political phenomena in terms generally reserved for poetry, even suggesting that the threat of nationalism to "the good of the intellect"—its requirement that we "surrender the authority of the intellect"—results from a sinister poetry in which "language suddenly runs loose, out of bounds, and so does knowledge." The argument that Duncan objects to war or any other fact of political life because it embodies a poetics contrary to his own begins to sound naive in the face of these remarks. We see him describing nationalism, even Nazism, in terms that employ his own notions of poetic inspiration, his pet ideas on the poet's relationship to language. The sense of being taken out of oneself, of losing oneself in the upsurge of poetry, the sense of becoming a creature of language, used by words to further some obscure intent of their own, is central to the poetics he advances. What he calls "the demotic inspiration," "the poetic content" that erupts to galvanize a people, he describes in the same way: "The demotic inspiration converts us, beyond ourselves, into the people of a language, into a flow, a current of destiny" (MF 241).

These descriptions of the demonic in politics, the analogies with a clearly Duncanesque poetics, ricochet and generate currents of self-incrimination. Duncan takes pains, then, to differentiate the poet from the demotic leader. The distinction he makes has mainly to do with the difference between the media in which the two work, between the materials they make use of. "What is the difference between Hitler as the demotic leader and the poet?" he asks. "In following the political leader our will is to become converted to the purposes of a political force in history; our 'selves' here are our very lives, our individuating personal purposes. The poem of the political genius, what he is making, is the very state in which we live. I mean here the political dominion we call the State, and in that the state of being that we feel in all the relationship of the pronouns 'we' and 'they' to the nation. . . . The leader of the people must convert actual men to his purposes, to be killed upon the battlefield of his cause or to be conscripted or coerced from their individual willfulness into the service of a new order, as the poet uses words, converting them from their history as the language of other men into their particularity as his own language" (MF 241). The innocence or the virtue of poetry, its "only advantage," has to do not with the embodiment of realities so different from those at work in politics, but with the fact that it confines itself to the medium of language, not making use of people. It is as though the usually pejorative idea of the poet as someone who sublimates a will to action, does with words and images what others do in "real life," were being invoked to the poet's advantage. (This is like Olson celebrating Enyalion, saying that he "goes to war with a picture," suggesting that at the level of instincts he isn't any less warlike than others, but that he deals with those instincts differently, directing them at images rather than people.) Duncan goes so far as to admit, contrary to his usual tendency, that poets do use language, however much they may also be used by it, that their relationship to words can be as coercive as that of a general to the army he commands, as that of a Hitler to the people he arouses. The difference is that words are not people and don't react like people, but what it would mean if they were and did still bothers him—sufficiently so, at least, that he leaves off as he begins to explore that possibility, refuses to complete or continue with the sentence: "If words slashed from the composition of a paragraph could bleed, as men do, or, removed from their original intent into the blinding intent of a new poetry, could cry out in protest . . ." (MF 241; ellipsis in the original).

Likewise, in "The Soldiers" it is the fact that the politician-poet's "verse" consists of the coercion, maiming, and murder of actual people that makes it objectionable, not that it fails to comply with Duncan's poetics. (I once heard him suggest, in fact, during a reading, that one of the techniques used by the United States in Vietnam did so comply. He likened saturation bombing to open field poetics.) With one possible exception, no passages like those which, ambiguous though they are, contribute to Mersmann's misreading of "An Essay at War" show up in this later poem. It is probably a measure of the differences a decade and a half can make that none do. Duncan's response to the Vietnam War is more overtly one of outrage and appears, at points at least, to issue from a more conventionally humanistic ground. It is not that the politician-poet's "verse" is coercive rather than open or free, but that it coerces *people.* It is the human carnage that stands out in the passage having to do with Mao, even though Mao's enemies are not being sided with:

> And in order to liberate the New China
> from Chiang Kai-shek, Presbyterian warlord, his bankers
>   raiding the national treasury, his armies
>   paid with bribes (aid) from Roosevelt and Stalin,
>   against Mao, exterminating cities,
>
> Mao's own mountain of murderd men,
>
> the alliteration of ems like Viet Nam's
>
>   burnd villages . . .
>
> (*BB* 113)

The passage following this one contains the possible exception I referred to above. Duncan describes Johnson as a poet lacking talent as well as inspiration, making for a reading which might focus on this lack as his most objectionable fault:

(Johnson now, no inspired poet but making it badly,
    amassing his own history in murder and sacrifice
  without talent)
    . . . irreplaceable   irrevócable   in whose name?
      a hatred the maimd and bereft must hold
against the bloody verse America writes over Asia
  we must recall   to hold   by property rights that
    are not private (individual) or public rights but
      given properties of our common humanity.
(*BB* 113)

The picture of Johnson given here doesn't entirely agree with the one we get from "Up Rising," where he is portrayed as demonically inspired, inhabited by a Satanic spirit. (The question of whether or not he has talent doesn't enter there.) There would appear to be no systematic, consistent set of equations (inspired = good, uninspired = evil, etc.) at work throughout Duncan's condemnations of the politician-poet. (In "An Essay at War," he calls Mao "a poet with . . . an inspiration," but that doesn't seem to make him a positive figure.) All the use of these terms amounts to is name-calling. What makes Lyndon Johnson's "verse" bad is that it's bloody, not that it's uninspired.

But Gassire's verse is bloody too. Is he a poet or a politician? One suggestion that the Soninke myth and Duncan's politician-poet figure coincide to make is that Rilke's active, power-hungry artists may already be among us. Or is it that the poet and the politician are two halves of a whole, opposite sides of a single coin? At one point in *The H.D. Book* Duncan writes of Pound's refusal to look at the possibility that the ideal might be a party to what betrays it, "that the sublime is complicit, involved in a total structure, with the obscene—what goes on backstage."[36] The juxtaposition of America's "bloody verse" against Whitman's "greatest poem," Johnson's obscene against Whitman's sublime (or, for that matter, saturation bombing against open field poetics), may intimate exactly such a total structure. Whitman's megalomaniacal sense of "America" has to have more than a casual, coincidental relationship to U.S. arrogance in world affairs. And doesn't Duncan's own world-poem idea reflect a distinctly American sense of privilege, the American feeling of being entitled to everything the world has to offer? It may well be the aesthetic arm of an American sensibility of which CIA-arranged coups, multinational corporations, and overseas military bases are more obvious extensions. The apprehension of an intimacy between the ideal and that which perverts it, a sense that the inescapable fate of the ideal is to undergo perversion, is strong throughout Duncan's work. Allusions to gnostic beliefs in debasement as a condition of life, a feeling for life as an ordeal in which the soul plumbs abysmal depths before it can have its ascent, recur throughout *The H.D. Book*. We read at one point of an "ambivalence of the sacred in which travesty and honor contend."[37] At another, we find Duncan eliciting from Apuleius's "Cupid and Psyche" the insight, crucial to his worldview, that "the story turns, as life itself turns. The light spills. Eros is burnd or betrayed."[38]

At yet another point, we see that the title of the poem "Up Rising" might be announcing such a turn: "The underground uprises into the place of what is above-board. Justice demands it. The verse appears, so vivid that we see the surface of things had faded in the sunlight, and what we most feared we might be we become. . . . The Above and the Below, the Left and the Right—Hermetic doctrine and Cabalistic lore suggested a reality that was duplicit."[39] Does the word *verse* tell us why on occasion it would tend to be bloody? What about *strophe*? Is the root charge of poetry a power to partake of a gnostic "version" of things, catastrophic events wherein we know truth by its downward turn? At one point in "The Soldiers" Duncan raises a rather idealized conception of soldiership, only to go on to overturn it in order to show its not-so-sublime side. Following the passage in which he quotes Whitman, he imagines an army composed of the "devotées of Man's commonality," looking at the etymology of the word *soldier* and relating it to *solder*, a near homograph, as well as to *sodality*, another like-sounding word. The words *sol* and *solidarity* echo as well, the latter furthering the communalist assertion at work in the poem. But it is a communism he sees as having been betrayed, numbering himself among those who have betrayed it:

"To unite ourselves with you we have renounced
All creatures of prey: False gods and men"

l'oeuvre qui va plus loin que notre rêve

Solidarius   :   so*l*derd   this army having its sodality
in the common life,   bearing the coin or paid in the coin

solidum, gold emblem of the Sun
tho we fight underground
from the heart's volition, the body's inward sun,
the blood's natural
uprising against tyranny •
And from the first it has been communism, the true
Poverty of the Spirituals the heart desired;
I too removed therefrom by habit.
(*BB* 113–14)

The second section of the poem opens with a look at modern soldiership, the soldiers on both sides of the Vietnam War falling short of the ideal. The emphasis falls on the U.S. troops, who do not even, Duncan almost playfully points out, conform to the root meaning of the word *soldier*, which has to do with being paid ("bearing the coin or paid in the coin / *solidum*"). His snide, punning assertion that they're not really "sold" on the war recalls the earlier word *soldered* both by negation and by likeness of sound:

They fight the invader
or cower, fear so striking them, unmanned by hunger or having
no dream of manhood, the Sun
does not last in them;
or conscripted, the pay being no goal, they are not true soldiers,
not even sold on the war
but from fear of punishment go, compelld, having no
wish to fulfill in fighting
but killing, killing, to be done with it.
(*BB* 114)

The two lines beginning "To unite ourselves . . ." are taken from *The Hymns of Zarathustra* and make for one of the doors through which

Persian cosmologies enter the poem. The placement of these lines just before the exploration of the Latin roots of the word *soldier*, together with the sacrificial bull Hadhayans in the poem's opening lines, might be hinting at the impact of Persian ideas on the legions of the Roman Empire. We recall that Mithraism was the religion of the imperial army, that it originated in Persia and that it involved the sacrificial slaughter of bulls. The identification of Mithras with the sun agrees with the poem's advancement of the *solidus* as both a form of payment and a form of sun-worship. The fact that he was the god of contracts and thus of social bonding goes along with its concern with community. Although Zarathustra himself rejected the worship of Mithras and the bull sacrifice, blendings of his teachings with Mithraism eventually came about. Zoroastrianism absorbed aspects of the cult of Mithras and vice versa. In Manicheism, yet another Persian cult, we find elements of both, Mithras playing the role Ohrmazd plays in Zoroastrianism, doing battle with the powers of darkness. The network of motifs introduced by these bits of information connects with a number of the poem's concerns. The theme of empire is touched on by the latent allusions to Rome. The figure of a "frontier" of which the poem goes on to make use, recalling remote Roman legion outposts as well as American ideas of manifest destiny, conjures an image of military operations extending the borders of empire. The contrast between the ideal and the actual continues, however, since this is not the "frontier / of Truth" it would be were the soldiers fighting for "the body's inward sun," the volitional, revolutionary Mithras of Duncan's humanist army:

> O you, who know nothing of the great theme of War,
> fighting because you have to, blindly, at no frontier
>   of the Truth but in-
> structed by liars and masters of the Lie, your own
>   liberty of action
>   their first victim . . .
> (*BB* 114)

The Zoroastrian dualism at work in the poem begins to be stated more explicitly here, evoking the conflict between Truth (*Asha*) and Lie (*Druj*) found in Zarathustra's hymns.

Zoroastrian rhetoric, which, in another phrasing of the conflict between truth and lie, asserts that the good mind opposes the worst mind, lends itself to Duncan's concern with "the good of the intellect." The war brings to light the pejorocratic powers that oppose free thought, the "masters of the Lie" who manipulate, constrict, and obstruct the free growth of the mind. The words *good* and *mind* both recur throughout the Vietnam poems, usually in proximity to one another and often with uppercase initials, advancing Duncan's view of the war as a crime against consciousness, his awareness of the investment the powers behind it have in closing off thought. In the early part of "The Soldiers" he entertains the idea that the war might provide the soldiers with a visionary experience, a mind-expanding rite of passage through ordeal ("forbidden hallucínogen / that stirs sight of the hidden / order of orders"), but the larger portion of the poem asserts that since they fight out of compulsion rather than choice such an ensouling is not very likely. He describes them as zombies, fighting with no goal in mind, no dream or wish to fulfill, no knowledge of "the great theme of War"—simply doing what they are told, following orders. But this is a tendency he sees pervading all of American society, not just the military. Soldiers fighting mindlessly and blindly, like so many robots, belie the "freedom" the war-supporting rhetoric says they're fighting for:

> youth, driven from your beds of first love and
>   your tables of study to die
> in order that "free men everywhere" "have the right
>   to shape their own destiny
> in free elections"—in Las Vegas, in Wall Street,
>   America turns in the throws of "free enterprise",
>   fevers and panics of greed and fear.
> (*BB* 114–15)

The drafted, volitionless troops are symptomatic of the bondage that enslaves everyone, whether civilian or soldier, the deep, all-pervading submission to the profit motive in American life.

In Zoroastrianism the principle of evil that opposes Ohrmazd is known as Ahriman, the name Duncan applies to the manipulative, war-invested push of the American economy. His indictment of the war spares neither organized labor nor the American worker-consumer, the "good people in the suburbs" whose high standard of living has roots in unseen misery elsewhere in the world:

The monstrous factories thrive upon the markets of the war,
and, as never before, the workers in armaments, poisond
    gasses and engines of destruction, ride
high on the wave of wages and benefits. Over all,
the monopolists of labor and the masters of the swollen
    ladders of interest and profit survive.

The first Evil is that which has power over you.

    Coercion, this is Ahriman.
(*BB* 115)

As in "Bring It Up from the Dark," a psychologizing note enters the poem when Duncan asserts that the coercion comes from within as well as without, that the manipulation of consciousness by advertising and the media is the outward projection of an "inner need" not to know, a need to beat back "something more," the shadowy side of truth which might prove disturbing. He makes reference to the American fetish for deodorants, identifying the much-advertised wish to repress "offensive" odors with an antilife impulse. We get a sense of people not only reduced to mannequins or robots but made complicit in that reduction by a need to evade the fullest meaning of being human (which, as Duncan has it here, includes the divine):

In the endless Dark   the T. V. screen,
    the lying speech and pictures   selling its time and produce,
corpses of its victims burnd black by napalm

    —Ahriman, the inner need for the salesman's pitch—

the image of the mannequin, smoking, driving its car at high speed,
    elegantly dresst, perfumed, seducing, without

    odor of Man or odor of sanctity,

in the place of the Imago Xristi;

    robot service in place of divine service;

the Good Word and Work   subverted by the Advertiser,

    He-Who-Would-Avert-Our-Eyes-From-The-Truth.
(*BB* 115)

At the end of the first section of the poem Duncan speaks of communism, lamenting that he too has been "removed therefrom by habit." Habit enters the poem again to be equated with Ahriman, as it is the hypnotic sameness of the American routine, the robotizing business-as-usual, which domesticates and diminishes consciousness. But, again, the specter of complicity figures prominently, Duncan taking us to task for our cooperation with Ahriman:

> Habit, this is Ahriman.
>
> The first Evil is that which conscripts you,
>
> spreading his "goods" over Asia. He moves in, you let him
>
> move in, in your own interest, and it serves you right,
>
> he serves you as you let him. Glimmers of right mind
>
> obscured in the fires he scatters.
>
> (*BB* 115–16)

The connection between the above and the below—the dark, unacknowledged ties between high-sounding, reassuring rhetoric and the lowly actions the rhetoric justifies—gives a pointed inflection to Duncan's use of the word *high* throughout the poem's second section. The word resounds, as the word *habit* also does, with suggestions of drug use, going along with the sense we get throughout of a narcotized, mindless stupor dictating American actions. (Also, we know that the war gave rise to an increase in the drug traffic out of Indochina and that large numbers of U.S. soldiers became addicts as a means of coping.) Beyond that, there is a play on the phrase "high standard of living," which hints at the numbing, narcotizing effects the sense of one's own well-being can have, as with the workers who "ride / high on the wave of wages and benefits." The blindness conducive to sleepwalk, the high that presumptions of height induce, ignoring what's below, is epitomized by the U.S. bomber squadron, flying so high above the destruction they inflict that they can't even see it: "The bomber overlooks the reality he inflicts—he flies high as the politician who directs his action likes to fly high above the reality of his orders." Ahriman is this high of not looking, the blindness induced by habits of not seeing what's below, letting it remain in the dark:

Master of Promises, Grand Profiteer and Supplier!

the smoking fields, the B-52s flying so high no sound no sight
of them gives warning, the fliers dropping their bombs
having nor sight nor sound of what they are bombing.

This is Ahriman, the blind

destroyer of the farmer and his ox at their labor.

The Industrial wiping out the Neolithic! Improver of Life

flying his high standards!

Who makes the pure into wicked men,
Who lays waste the pastures and takes up arms against the righteous.
(*BB* 116)

IV

The tale of Gassire's lute promises that through strife the lost Wagadu will be found again, that a fifth, everlasting Wagadu will arise: "Dissension will enable the fifth Wagadu to be as enduring as the rain of the south and as the rocks of the Sahara, for every man will then have Wagadu in his heart and every woman a Wagadu in her womb" (*AG* 109–10). Duncan suggests in *The H.D. Book* that out of the turmoil and the dissension of the two world wars a new poetic revelation, a world-poem that he identifies with Wagadu, appeared in the work of H.D., Williams, and Pound. Taking his cue from Pound, who in Canto LXXIV speaks of Wagadu as "now in the mind indestructible," he sees in *Trilogy, Paterson,* and the *Cantos* the creation of an imaginal, paradisaic Wagadu that serves as a refuge from the hellishness of war:

> It seemed to me then that . . . in London, in Pisa, in Paterson, there had been phases of a single revelation. . . . Was it that the war—the bombardment for H.D., the imprisonment and exposure to the elements for Ezra Pound, the divorce in the speech for Williams—touched a spring of passionate feeling in the poet that was not the war but was his age, his ripeness in life? They were almost "old"; under fire to come "to a new distinction."

> Where the fullness of their age was also the fullness of an historical age, as if the Second World War were a trouble of the times, unprepared or prepared for its old age?
>
> They give, these three works out of the war, a text for the historian of our contemporary spirit; as Shakespeare gives text for the Tudor Renaissance; as Dante gives text for the thirteenth century catholic world.
>
> In the light of these works I write today. Taking them as my immediate ancestors, as they in turn took Swinburne, the Pre-Raphaelites Rossetti and William Morris, and Robert Browning, as theirs.[40]

It is as though the war were a sort of muse—a taunting muse, to be sure, but a muse nonetheless. A challenge and a dialectical goad, it elicits acts of the imagination that envision its abolition. Looked at from this angle, the connection between the above and the below takes an upward turn. The ordeals of hell give birth to a vision of heaven.

Not surprisingly, we find this view advanced quite explicitly by one of these three poets. In 1941 Williams wrote a piece entitled "Midas: A Proposal for a Magazine," a piece in which he speaks of the war then raging in Europe as "the Death" and calls for a flurry of artistic activity to combat it. "The Midas touch, the alchemy of the mind which cannot be seduced by political urgencies" is how he describes the imagination, and in the war he sees a release of usable energy, a leaden power to be transmuted into gold:

> One of the purposes of the Death among us is to terrify the world, to use a destructive ideology to push our culture so far back that it will take a full generation. another crop of flesh and mind, before it can begin to regenerate. . . .
>
> But we on our part will stay on the heels of the Death, baying and snapping, never giving it a moment's rest, driving it among the rocks, to keep it there at bay. . . .
>
> War elevates the artist, the builder, the thinker to the peaks of the stars, trebles his significance. In times of peace he is, at best, a humdrum worker not because he must be so, but because he is perpetually laboring under weights to inflame and to magnify. But in times of war—helplessly split off in the cyclotron of the times—he becomes inevitably king of men. (*SE* 241–42)

Here we get something of the "black voice" Duncan refers to, the acidic, oppositional rant that comes out in *Paterson* with even greater virulence:

You come today to see killed
                                   killed, killed
as if it were a conclusion
                                   —a conclusion!
a convincing strewing of corpses
—to move the mind

                              as tho' the mind
can be moved, the mind, I said
by an array of hacked corpses:

                                        War!
a poverty of resource . .[41]

Williams's is one of the precursors of Duncan's own "black voice," the bitter, militant outrage we hear in poems like "The Fire," "The Multiversity," "Up Rising," and "The Soldiers." Williams relates this bitter voice to alchemy, a correspondence ratified by the alchemical acrostic formula: *V*isita *i*nteriora *t*errae; *r*ectificando *i*nvenies *o*cculturn *l*apidum: VITRIOL. ("Visit the interior of the earth; through purification thou wilt find the hidden stone.")

H.D. also invested in this connection. As early as section 28 of *The Walls Do Not Fall* she speaks of "bitter thought," and in section 3 of *Tribute to the Angels* she sees bitterness as a condition of renewal:

but *I make all things new,*
said He of the seven stars,

he of the seventy-times-seven
passionate, bitter wrongs,

He of the seventy-times-seven
bitter, unending wars.
(*T* 65)

Tribute to the Angels opens with a reference to "Hermes Trismegisthus / . . . patron of alchemists," the psychopomp who leads the way into the underworld. By section 8 the connection between alchemy and the bitter, vitriolic voice that winds in and out of *Trilogy*—between alchemy and the bitter, vitriolic reign of wrath she feels the bombings to be—is even more explicit:

Now polish the crucible
and in the bowl distill

a word most bitter, *marah,*
a word bitterer still, *mar,*

sea, brine, breaker, seducer,
giver of life, giver of tears;

Now polish the crucible
and set the jet of flame

under, till *marah-mar*
are melted, fuse and join

and change and alter
(*T* 71)

In section 16 of *The Flowering of the Rod* she again speaks of bitterness in relation to processes of transformation:

she was a stricken woman,
having borne a son in unhallowed fashion;

she wept bitterly till some heathen god
changed her to a myrrh-tree;

I am Mary, I will weep bitterly,
bitterly . . . bitterly.
(*T* 135)

The alchemist's belief in the transformation of lead into gold, together with the age-old conviction that misfortune might be a transformative ordeal, that affliction might carry the seeds of its own cure, serves here to preach a gospel of poetry, to assert its ability to turn adversity to its own advantage ("I profit / by every calamity"). The bitterness is not simply the suffering endured, but the answering bitterness of a vitriolic voice that eats away at what ails it, an acidic power dissolving the walls of an otherwise hegemonic hell. The hellish voice enters the poem to cry down hellish behavior, object to hellish conditions. The descent into the interior of the earth is a prelude, not a terminus, an initiatory visit that, as in Dante's *Comedy,* leads to heavenly things.

In Duncan's work we hear this gospel preached even more overtly. The poems that follow "The Soldiers" and its bitter vision of Ahriman in *Bending the Bow* turn to a celebration of poetry's ability to resist history. "An Interlude" speaks of a release from having "to contend with the / lies and dreams of Generalissimo Franco" and of "measures of an old intoxication that leads into poetry" (*BB* 117). In the "Rites of Participation" chapter of *The H.D. Book*, where he posits Wagadu as a creative rejection of an adverse world, he speaks of "an insistent creation, the tenacity of a day-dream to outlast the reality principle" (*HD*I.6 45). We see the same idea at work in "Transgressing the Real," where he makes a case for the imagination as both a survival aid and a subversive power. The sense of not being totally confined to the earth, of acting as a medium for extraterrestrial powers, prompts him to write, "In the War now I make / a celestial cave," and, a bit later,

> . . . it seems no man   but a world speaks
>
> for my thoughts are servants of the stars, and my words
>
> (all parentheses opening into
>
> come from a mouth that is the Universe   *la bouche d'ombre*
>
> (*BB* 120)

An insistent feeling of having access to an other world, a remote or even an "irreal" world, is especially strong where he confronts the political realities of the day, for those realities give rise to the need for an alternate reality. In "The Fire," making use of the biblical opposition between Christ and Caesar, he poses Christ as the visionary dreamer of an alternative world, diverging from and closing His eyes on *this* world:

> The Christ closes His eyes,   bearing the Cross
>
> as if dreaming.   Is His Kingdom
>
> not of this world, but a dream of the Anima Mundi,
>
> the World-Ensouling?
>
> (*BB* 43)

Likewise, in "Passages 32," he writes, "Your name, Jesus, has begun in my heart / again an allegiance to that Kingdom / 'not of this World'" (*GW* 15).

The biblical rhetoric, the distinction between this world and some other, is at work in "Transgressing the Real" as well. Here, however, the reference is not so explicitly Christian, but cast in terms of magic, an allusion to "the poet-magician Dr Dee." It is perhaps for this reason that the "pastoral stillness" we see on Christ's face in "The Fire" gives way to something more active, an act of withdrawal which would hasten the collapse of Caesar's world:

For now in my mind all the young men of my time
    have withdrawn allegiance from *this world,* from public things •

    and as their studies in irreality deepen,

        industries, businesses, universities, armies

                shudder and cease

(*BB* 120)

Duncan makes the same claim for these "studies in irreality" in "Before the Judgment," where he invokes "il ben dello intelletto" again, but in a saboteur's role this time:

    And that there are islands in Time,

        and even in War,   and in the Time of Retribution

                            (his Hell   our commonwealth)

                they return to us,
ἔσθλοι   abounding,   Mind returning, a Child,   to the Goods of the Intellect

    as if to his Paradise, a secret state of Mind we obey,
            shaking the powers of this state from within.

(*GW* 30)

The word *transgressing* has to do with going beyond limits, exceeding bounds or breaking a law. Here it serves to assert that "the real" is a human concoction, bounded by limits imposed by commonly held assumptions and reinforced by artificial conventions. As such, "the real" is at odds with the universe, which is boundless and of which Duncan writes, in an earlier poem, "unhindered, the vast universe / showing only its boundaries we imagine" (*BB* 74). The point is that we live in a world whose limits we make up, and that those limits are therefore subject to unmaking. The "irreality" the poem refers to is not so much a stepping outside as an extending of reality. This is the meaning of the cosmic impulse or aspiration, the cosmic medium to which the poem lays claim. An unbounded "something more" dictates that we erase whatever limits we impose.

Magic posits a world conditioned only by will and desire, imagination and feeling. Its claim to the ascendancy of mind over matter, the irresistibility and the efficaciousness of ardor, is very close to Duncan's conception of the imagination. Where the mind becomes an agent of the Anima Mundi, chaos and cosmos join forces to overcome distance:

> Chaos / and the divine measures and orders
>
>   so wedded are
>
> we have but to imagine
>
>   ourselves the Lover
>
>   and the Beloved appears
>
> (*BB* 121)

Caught in the embrace of a world-ensouling Eros, the erasure of whatever distance would come between, lines of division blur to the point of extinction. By the end of the poem, the last word, *unreal*, is descriptive not of the act of overstepping bounds or of the realm into which that overstepping leads, but of the bounds themselves. The shores that border the river of feeling, the limits that would contain and condition that feeling, are made to recede into nonexistence by an erotic magic, the creational insistence of a feeling so large as to become coextensive with the universe itself:

>   In this rite the Great Magician stirs in His dream,
>
>   and the magician dreaming   murmurs to his beloved:
>
>   *thou art so near to me*
>   *thou art a phantom that the heart*
>   *would see—*
>
> and now the great river of their feeling grows so wide
>
>   its shores grow distant and unreal.
>
> (*BB* 121)

Going back to "Man's Fulfillment in Order and Strife," we see that this cosmic, erotic dreamer might embody Duncan's sense of a world order, for there he writes of just such an unbinding of feeling, such a loosening of the bonds that would hold back Eros: "Only in the love-feast of the agape and in the love-wedding in which desire was liberated in sensual delight would the work be done. . . . It is not in political right-thinking or in political power that we come into the apprehension of a World Order but in falling in love. It is in the very act of love, in the marital union, and then in the love-banquet of brotherhood—at once ideal and sexual—that the meaning of freedom and fulfillment is at work" (MF 244).

The three poems that follow "Transgressing the Real," both in the "Passages" series and in the order of their appearance in *Bending the Bow,* contribute to the plausibility of such a reading. "The Light," "Eye of God," and "Stage Directions" all tend toward assertions regarding the mission of poetry, the first two in particular proposing liberation as quintessential, at the crux of what the poet envisions. The possibility of envisioning bondage as a two-way affair, one side imprisoning crypt and the other a womb from which freedom is born, of seeing through to what dwells inside but otherwise outlives bondage, is hinted at by way of figural and mythological equivalents of the antinomy of wrath and love, Old Testament Jahweh and New Testament Christ. In "Man's Fulfillment in Order and Strife," Duncan refers to "a doctrine of the meaning of wrath, read out of Jacob Boehme, a theosophist of the seventeenth century, who saw the Father's Wrath working to create Itself in the Son as Love" (MF 244). Likewise, in the introduction to *Bending the Bow*, he writes, "the Father, first known as He named Himself to be Wrath, Fiery Vengeance and Jealousy, to be made or revealed anew as Love, the lasting reason and intent of What Is—this deepest myth of what is happening in Poetry moves us as it moves words" (*BB* vii). H.D. again provides precedent, for she works the same opposition, the same sense of advance or transformation through this opposition, in *The Walls Do Not Fall.* In section 21, she casts the distinction between Father and Son in terms of Ram and Lamb, exploiting the fact that the advent of the Christian era, the age of the Lamb, the Fish, or the Son, was announced astrologically by Pisces, due to the precession of the equinoxes, taking over the initial slot in the zodiac from Aries. The age of the Ram gave way or gave rise to the age of the Lamb. She wants the war to portend a similar giving way to the law of love:

time, time for you to begin a new spiral,
see—I toss you into the star-whirlpool;

till pitying, pitying,
snuffing the ground,

here am I, Amen-Ra whispers,
Amen, Aries, the Ram,

be cocoon, smothered in wool,
be Lamb, mothered again.
(*T* 30)

H.D. and Duncan both advance a Freudian understanding of this opposition, eliciting echoes of the conflict between Thanatos and Eros. The sense of wrath as Thanatos, unfulfilled desire, the thwarting or the denial of Eros, appears in "The Light" and "Eye of God" as the figure AntEros, the god of unhappy love, avenger of unrequited affection, and brother of Eros, portrayed in some mythological traditions as opposed to and struggling against Eros. In "The Light," Duncan resorts to the myth of Pegasos and Chrysaor's birth from the beheaded body of Medusa (as he does in "Stages Directions" as well). His assertion is that poetry projects the unbinding of Eros, that it not only preaches "the new law" but is that law, a new testament of love:

From the trunk of whose gorgon-wild head flying up
Pegasos / that great horse Poetry,   Rider

we ride, who make up

the truth of What Is;

and, as if Eros unbound, AntEros / bound
free to love, Chrysaor / of the golden sword—

twins of that vision in which from the
old law's   terrible sentence

wingd   the new law springs
(*BB* 122–23)

But "as if" suggests that only in the imagination is such an unbinding to be brought off. Is Duncan arguing for poetry as a form of compensation, that the work of AntEros in the manifest world makes for an imagined release, a binding of AntEros that obtains only in the mind, remaining "not of this world"? Or is he prophesying actual, manifest "wonders to come" (as he puts it in "Transgressing the Real"), an eventual heaven-on-earth in which wrath will be a thing of the past and only love will rule?

The former is more likely the case. In an unpublished piece with which he considered prefacing *Ground Work,* Duncan writes of Norman O. Brown's *Love's Body* at one point, putting forth a sense of the book that tells us a great deal about the meaning of his own work. Disposing of the idea that the book calls for a sexual revolution, the liberation of the libido and the physical body in unrestrained coitus, he argues that *Love's Body* employs the sexual as a metaphor, the narcissistic, even onanistic lure of a deeply self-serving, self-referential poetics:

> The writing of *Love's Body* is not the proposition of a radical change in love or in the body; it is not the proposition of a revolution in sexuality, but the proposition and demonstration—idea in action—of a radical change in the body of writing. . . . It is his writing that is compeld toward nakedness; his sentences that disclose and clothe, touching upon and luring toward—an encounter in poetry that his supposed encounter in the sexual is a screen-image for. . . . He does not seek to free us from bondage, from the depths of a sexual trouble or brooding—he no more comes to harrow Hell than did Dante in his Comedy—but to free *from us,* in that very Hell, that poem. It is to convert us to the purposes of a poetry, to make us his readers not his lovers, that he brings us deeper and deeper, admits us more and more, darkens our counsel, into the tension, the attention—that the arrow of song spring from the bent bow of our body—in agony! but this *body* is an image, and its agon we find belongs to the formations of the work he is creating, the sequences and resonances of each part in every other of a music in *Love's Body* as a prose poem.[42]

Likewise, what Duncan writes has only tangentially to do with *Love's Body,* for, given the terms of his own argument, the poetizing intent that would advance "poetry as the prime reality" (as he puts it at one point) works to upstage any subject matter other than itself. What these remarks do tell us is something Duncan announces repeatedly throughout his work. "The poetry that most moved us moved us to a need for poetry," he observes in his preface to *Caesar's Gate.*[43] The poem's promise of "Eros unbound" is only as good as that of a politician campaigning for office, except that Duncan is more straightforward, honest enough to add an "as if."

There is also the question of what is to be made of Chrysaor, the giant warrior wielding a golden sword. He would appear to be "the old law" to Pegasos's "new." The pairing of the two seems to echo the opposition in *Trilogy* between the sword and the word. But they are referred to as twins, and the manner of their birth suggests intimacy, kinship, and near-identity, something more complicit, more symbiotic, than a strict opposition. They may well be Greek mythology's way of asserting that close ties exist between poetry and war, its way of hinting at such a sense as we get from the myth of Gassire's lute that the two nourish each other. There is a tradition in Western literature that has to do with this, and of which Duncan is well aware. In the sixth book of the *Iliad* Homer all but declares that the Trojan War was fought so that he could write his poem, having Helen refer to herself and Hektor as "us two, on whom Zeus set a vile destiny, so that hereafter / we shall be made into things of song for the men of the future."[44] H.D. takes this up in *Helen in Egypt,* where Helen asks,

was Troy lost for a subtle chord,

a rhythm as yet un-heard,
was it Apollo's snare?
was Apollo passing there?

was a funeral-pyre to be built,
a holocaust of the Greeks,
because of a fluttering veil,

or because Apollo granted a lute-player,
a rhythm as yet unheard,
to challenge the trumpet-note?[45]

Jean Giraudoux's answer in *La guerre de Troie n'aura pas lieu* (translated into English by Christopher Fry as *Tiger at the Gates)* is a confident *yes.* Just when it appears that Helen will be given back and war with the Greeks averted, the Trojan poet Demokos bursts in to accuse the negotiators of cowardice. His fellow Trojan Hektor angrily strikes him down, inflicting a fatal wound, but Demokos has enough life left to blame Ajax for the blow, provoking an attack on the Greek that touches off the war. The final words of the play are spoken by Cassandra: "The Trojan poet is dead. And now the Grecian poet will have his word."[46]

The point is not that all or even most poets are as hawkish as Demokos. Obviously the dominant tendency in poetry having to do with war has been antiwar. The sense of "collusion" is much more dialectical, an inverse function in which war feeds the poet's imagination by giving rise to the need for an alternative vision. There is also the related sense of war's contribution to the poet's task that Williams gives, where the energies let loose by strife actualize an intensity that the poet, "perpetually labouring under weights to inflame and to magnify," is otherwise at pains to bring to bear on a humdrum world. The surplus of meaning to which the poet attests may seem less fanciful when such energies are afoot. Duncan, who acknowledges war to be a "great theme" of poetry, proposes love as an alternative mode of intensification, falling in love as a way of coming into an order of intensities, a richness of intent otherwise unavailable. With his next breath, however, he tells us that neither love nor wrath can rest as a final resolve, one as an unentangled choice against the other. He reminds us of "the deep co-inherence of Eros and Thanatos" and as we think back to "An Essay at War," to its confounding of love's fire with the flames of strife, he goes on in "The Light" to speak of "Love, light *and* dark" (*BB* 122; emphasis in the original). The saving grace of poetry is not a return to an edenic world, but an ambidextrous, even duplicit capacity for counterpoint, the weaving of a music that harmonizes contending terms. We think back to "Orders":

> passages of changing dark and light
> a music dream and passion would have playd
> to illustrate concords of order in order,
> a contrapuntal communion of all things •
> (*BB* 78)

We think back to the introduction of *Bending the Bow,* where Duncan speaks of "the trouble of an Eros," having already written, "I saw, long before this war, wrath move in the music that troubles me" (*BB* iii, vi).

In the course of his comments on *Love's Body* Duncan refers to Freud as a poet who proposed "a new poetry using the seductive lure of our trouble with sex, even as poets have used man's trouble with religion or with social orders and nature as lures to involve us with the poetic." He too makes this use of trouble. The case he makes for poetry borders on the notion of a fortunate fall, for in the mired world in which ostensible opposites mix poetry bridges a fault, a navigable breach between contrasting poles in which the poem's peculiar way of "making light" comes into play. "The Light" opens with an allusion to Victor Hugo's *La Fin de Satan,* specifically the poem "La Plume de Satan," in which as Lucifer falls one feather escapes his wing. Instead of falling with him, the feather is seen by God and by His glance transformed into the angel Liberty:

> now down-falling doom's darling,
> one feather of his wing / lost
>
> in God's gaze found *Libertas*
>
> the Master Victor Hugo saw in that dream
> Poetry is / or at his singing tables
>
> heard rumor of
>
> an angelic being true to Lucifer
> as Satan was false to his Self / and fell,
>
> brooded in the roots of power as if
>
> it be his own,
>
> divorced from that Love, light *and* dark,
> source of all we call
>
> Wing of our Mothering Universe
>
> (*BB* 122)

The angel Liberty embodies not only the unbinding of love, the freedom of an "Eros unbound," but also, self-reflexively, the ability of poetry to concoct—its being free, at liberty to concoct—exactly such a figure. Lucifer's fall both ignites and inaugurates an otherwise invisible arena of play wherein the contrapuntal maneuvers of a poetry—its light-bearing, shadow-casting way of going from "lost" to "found" and of harmonizing other such opposing terms—can and do take place. Again the pun is crucial and exemplary, for the word *down* in "down-falling" refers as much to the feather as to the direction in which Lucifer falls, as much to what doesn't fall as to what does. The poem at once refers to and puts into practice the unique liberty we have recourse to in language, the ability to violate the lines between opposite or incongruous meanings, to transgress the distance between otherwise disparate things. "The Light" sums itself up by concluding with two opposing words it reconciles (highlighting each with an introductory pause): "darkling" (slightly echoing "darling") and "lumen."

"Eye of God" likewise alludes to Victor Hugo's poem. Duncan even incorporates a translation of one of its stanzas at one point. The poem continues and elaborates on the concerns and motifs at work in "The Light," so that in its opening lines we get a repeat of the old-law-becoming-new-law theme, along with a figure of Eros unchained and another reference to God's gaze giving rise to liberty:

Cao-Daï

gold and crystal of the Sky's reaches!

First from the Father   glance that lit

New love in Liberty   whose law

dissolves in its coruscations
(rainbow) (lapis lazuli)

the chains of Eros and the Old Law!
(*BB* 124)

Among the new elements in the poem is the reference to the Cao-Dai religion of Vietnam, which relates to the other strains running through the poem in a number of ways. A syncretic religion that arose in Vietnam in the 1920s incorporating aspects of Buddhism, Taoism, Confucianism, Christianity, traditional Vietnamese spirit worship, and other spiritual traditions, Cao-Daism, with its attempt at such a global synthesis, fits in well with Duncan's world-poem idea. In addition, the fact that Cao-Daism was a major material as well as spiritual force in the anticolonialist struggle that ousted the French lends itself to a series of poems expressing solidarity with the Vietnamese resistance to the United States. (The church maintained an army of several thousand troops that fought against the French in the 1945 coup that brought Ho Chi Minh to power, only to find itself persecuted by Ho's government within a couple of years.)

On a more immediate level, Cao-Daism shares with the poem the image or symbol that gives it its title. The symbol the church uses to represent the Supreme Being (the meaning of "Cao-Dai") consists of a single eye surrounded by and emanating solar rays. This relates it to the divine gaze or glance brought in from Hugo's poem. The connection between Cao-Daism and the French poet is not arbitrarily Duncan's doing. Both were significantly involved in table-tapping séances. Cao-Daism arose from the messages received via table tapping by a Vietnamese clerk named Ngo Van Chieu as early as 1919. It was during such a séance in 1925 that the Cao-Dai directed Ngo Van Chieu to set up the formal church Cao-Daism went on to become. Hugo became involved in séances during the 1850s, and they had a crucial impact on the visionary side of his work from which Duncan borrows, such books as *La Légende des Siècles, La Fin de Satan,* and *Dieu.* Duncan alludes to this in "The Light" with the figure of Hugo "at his singing tables," and in "Transgressing the Real" he follows the mediumistic assertion that his own words "come from a mouth that is the Universe" with the phrase *"la bouche d'ombre"* ("the mouth of shadow"), a reference to Hugo's "Ce que dit la bouche d'ombre," a theological poem derived from table-tapping sessions. As educated French colonials, Cao-Dai leaders were acquainted with Hugo's work, and he seems to have been a strong influence on Ngo Van Chieu in particular. During a séance on Christmas Eve in 1925 Ngo Van Chieu made contact with Hugo, which is largely why the church eventually included the poet in its lowest-ranking order of saints (which also includes Sun Yat-sen, Winston Churchill, the Vietnamese prophet Trang Trinh Le, and Joan of Arc) and chose the anniversary of his death, May 22, as the date on which to dedicate a new temple at Long Thanh in 1937.[47]

During that same Christmas Eve séance Ngo Van Chieu also made contact with Jesus Christ. This is the descent to which Duncan refers near the poem's beginning:

Christmas Eve, 1925.   The Spirit descended
    to bring the Truth to Viet-Nam.

            Réjouissez-vous de cette fête,

                anniversary of my coming to the West
to give my Sign

                that certain hearts tremble
and pour out from their reserves

                enduring Love . . .

(*BB* 124)

"Eye of God" in a sense recapitulates the séance, for in it, too, the voices of both Hugo and Christ take part. In addition, Duncan quotes from a

Cao-Dai hymn, glossing its French with English translations and playing on a number of interconnected motifs. (The hymn's phrase "l'étoile d'un matin," for example, might also refer to Lucifer, the morning star.) The poem again goes into the matter introduced in "The Light," the feather transformed by God's glance in Hugo's poem:

> And the black opend up,   a god
>
> in trouble came, like an eye   opening
> lids of the sorrow and the cold   trembling,
>
>   into a glance,   striking . . .
>
> it was no more than a feather lost in the tumult
>
>   turnd,   high in the up-wind
>
> he fell so far from her
>
>   (as if a hand   sustaind me
>
>   Day opend in the Abyss
>
> his glance awakening   flames in the under ground
> (*BB* 124–25)

Duncan's earlier words tell us that, however else we may also read it, the trouble out of which the godly glance emerges is a lure for the poetic, the glance itself created by and significant of a poetic vision. Cao-Daism's inclusion of a poet among its saints, along with the copresence of Hugo and Christ in the poem as at the séance (which copresence all but merges the poet and the Son, as Olson does in "As of Parsonses. . ."), confirms the overlapping of religious and poetic orders essential to Duncan's work. As with George Oppen, for whom poetry is involved with keeping the faith ("I don't mean he despairs, I mean if he does not / He sees in the manner of poetry"[48]), with Duncan the godly, transformative glance may be the work of a true believer's creed, but it is also the "up-wind" or inspiration of a poet's way of looking, rising up though conditions counsel despair.

The feather, then, is the all-but-lost, virtually imperceptible, easily overlooked inversion of an overshadowing fall, the hidden stone of an alchemizing descent. Like the biblical grain of mustard seed H.D. recalls throughout *The Flowering of the Rod*—the "infinitely tiny grain," "least of all seeds" the Kingdom of Heaven is likened to—the feather is a mereness that, easily missed, puts faith and vision to a test. Its relationship to the surrounding tumult of Satan's fall both anticipates and parallels that of the Cao-Dai prayers to the louder noise of the bomber attack that drowns them out. The all-but-invisible feather both prefigures and is analogous to the "inaudible bell" at the poem's end:

At the Saint-Siège Caodaïste   at Tay-Ninh,

in the roaring din of American planes
performing their daily missions to destroy
the Viet-Cong's strongholds of the Holy Spirit

the prayers of the shaman-priests at the altar

rise / and in the crescendo of the War,

exact the line of a melody / as if

the faith of Schubert would enter the Heraklitean truth,

the polemic

father of all,   harsh necessity

in the roar and fire-fall,

bear

this sonance,   his son

and the Note to mount

they sound

sentences of an inaudible bell.
(*BB* 126–27)

Recalling Heraclitus's Fragment 54 ("The hidden harmony is better than the obvious"[49]), we see that the trouble is also the lure for a Heraclitean bias which might favor hell because there the stone is *hidden* (as distinct from "*there* the stone is hidden"). This would be the more hellish, masochistic twist of a poet's bias for the esoteric, the paradoxical, the obscure (itself the pretext for the poem as a hermeneutic), for again, as in "Orders" and in the tale of Gassire's lute, we meet the specter of a bloodthirsty music. The "sonance" borne by the prayers of the Cao-Dai priests is the martyred Son, just as earlier in the poem the massacred Albigensian martyrs at Montségur are said to "enter as notes of a sublime sweetness / the resounding chords of wrath and woe":

> The President of the Grand Symphony
>
> for the sake of a dread calm and harmony
>
> sets into motion a counter-point of contending elements,
>
> music's divine Strife. At Montségur,
>
> that the heart be tried . . .
> (*BB* 126)

Duncan goes on to name ten of the over two hundred martyrs and ends by exclaiming, "Grandeur!"

What this exclamation celebrates is the tautologous propriety of the Albigensians' fate, its gruesome confirmation of their view of the world. To posit an irreconcilable split between spirit and matter, to advance and adhere to the idea that one's true home is "not of this world," virtually invites extinction. Is it that the hell-on-earth the burnings at the stake manifest, the hellishness so blatantly there to be seen, confirms—by way of a process of inversion—an all-but-invisible, not-so-easy-to-see heaven? But the poem is exultant because it, too, holds to or holds out for "something more" not readily available to the senses. The heaven it celebrates, notwithstanding what it may have been for the Albigensians, is a hidden, esoteric harmony apprehended through the authority of an aesthetic faith ("the faith of Schubert"). The poem, using the Albigensians and the Cao-Dai priests to objectify itself, exults in its own ability to assert the existence of such a harmony, to hold to the sublimity of its own conception. It sides with the Albigensians or the Cao-Dai priests only in a limited sense, for its deification of counterpoint requires that it honor their adversaries as well, that it look both ways. The "divine Strife" it bows down before elevates contention above either of the terms it is constituted by. It promotes the dynamic, oscillatory character of experience. When we look back to the earlier point in the poem where Duncan translates a stanza from Hugo's "La Plume de Satan," we see that duality and instability prevail. The angel Liberty, born of the opposing powers of heaven and hell, embodies a freedom to volley back and forth between contending terms ("falters, returns, falters . . ."):

And the angels, shaking with love, regarded her.
The Xerubim, the great twins, who cleave one to the other,

the legions of anger and the hosts of wrath,

the constellations of morning and of evening,
the Powers, the Intelligences, longd to see
this sister born of paradise and of hell

l'Ange Liberté.

The visage of the Father undergoes changes in the thought of her,

his rage falters, returns, falters . . .

in the chains of the First Eros, AntEros / longs to be free.
(*BB* 125)

Despite the otherworldliness of much of the material Duncan brings into the poem, there is a sense in which the oscillatory rhythm he evokes remains true to experience, empirically apt. However much the idea of a grand symphony may sublimate history, it emulates it as well. Just as events vary between turbulence and calm, a piece of music as it unfolds varies tempo and intensity, building tensions it goes on to resolve, following crescendo with decrescendo, ever changing. In "Stage Directions" Duncan continues to look at events in terms of an art form, but in this case, as the poem's title announces, the art form is drama rather than music. We recall him saying in *The H.D. Book* that "the War rises from the dramatic necessity." In "Man's Fulfillment in Order and Strife," he observes at one point, "We must acknowledge how deeply the intent of the whole is dramatic" (MF 248). The holistic vision that asserts the universe's fidelity to itself, which seeks to see (as Heraclitus puts it in Fragment 51, from which *Bending the Bow* takes its title) "how that which is at variance with itself agrees with itself,"[50] now puts in terms of plot what before it spoke of as counterpoint. In his now dramatic sense of the distribution of dark and light, Duncan is like Ramakrishna, whose answer to the question "Why is there evil in the world?" was "To thicken the plot."[51] He sees the plot thickening toward increasingly war-torn times as the poem begins:

Slowly the toiling images will rise,
Shake off, as if it were débris,
the unnecessary pleasures of our lives
And all times and intents of peaceful men

Reduce to an interim, a passing play,
  between surpassing
Crises of war.
(*BB* 128)

But the poem is in many ways a meditation on the nature of creativity, a speculative, elliptical inquiry into the sources of artistic vision. Duncan returns to the birth of Pegasos and Chrysaor from the beheaded Medusa, seeming to suggest poetry and war as alternative, even hand-in-glove responses to a dire, deadly intent at work within time. He speaks of them as "children of adversity":

Upon the stage before:

He brings the camera in upon the gaping neck
  which now is an eye of bloody meat   glaring
  from the womb of whose pupil   sight

springs to see,   two   children of adversity.

The Mother's baleful glance in romance's
  head of writhing snakes haird

  freezes the ground.

  Okeanos   roars,

wild oceanic father,   visage   compounded of fury and of wind
(*BB* 128)

The entrance of Okeanos into the poem has to do with Poseidon having fathered the two. There may also be an allusion to Olson's "Maximus, at the Harbor," for in that poem as well we meet with Okeanos as a figure of fatherly wrath—a transformative wrath "working," as Duncan says, borrowing from Boehme, "to create Itself in the Son as Love":

  Okeanos rages, tears rocks back in his path.

Encircling Okeanos tears upon the earth to get Love loose . . .

  * * *

The great Ocean is angry. It wants the Perfect Child
(*MP* 240–41)

The fact that Pegasos's name refers to his birth "near the springs of Ocean" is also relevant and is referred to in the poem. Duncan plays on the word *springs*, using it to suggest the winged horse's bounding upward into the sky, as well as to recall the line "the new law springs" from "The Light." He also tends not to draw a line between the springs of Ocean and the springs of blood flowing from Medusa's neck, so the suggestion that the sources of poetry touch upon depths of affliction, a bloody descent into adversity, comes across very strongly.

In addition, the poem's reference to the pair of arteries that pass up though the neck to supply the head with blood, the carotids (whose name derives from the Greek *karos,* meaning "heavy sleep"), allows Duncan to identify these depths with the unconscious, to which we get access through dreams and sleep. Pegasos is a figural version of the admonition "Bring it up from the dark," for Duncan goes on to speak of his springing upward as an awakening:

> And Pegasos springs "born near the *springs* of Ocean"
>
> ὅτ Ωκεανου περι πηγας γενθ
>
> He-who-spurts-up from the broken arteries carotids out of
>
> deep sleep the blood carries upward
>
> (Ocean then, the drowsy deep)
>
> awakend
>
> flies
>
> to Zeus-Father above,
>
> Lord of the Deep Skies, whose House
> awaits him,
>
> the pressure of whose tides
>
> upon the shores of life is like a horse raging,
> thunderous hooves, striking
>
> flashes of light from unbright matter.
>
> (*BB* 129)

The sense of poetry as a power that, sourced in or born of the deep, bridges the gap between the above and the below is very active here, nowhere more succinctly than in the expression "Deep Skies." The sense, too, of an alchemizing investment the poetic makes in "unbright matter" carries the seeds of a possible conception of Pegasos as a fifth horse of the Apocalypse. Among the things, we now see, that Chrysaor represents are apocalyptic, calamitous times, "surpassing / Crises of war." The poem goes on to speak of genius, suggesting that an ability to dwell creatively in mixed possibilities, to revel, however fearfully, in the cocontamination of ecstasy and horror, sets genius apart. The twin birth of Pegasos and Chrysaor, reinforced by lines quoted from Edmund Spenser and an earlier reference to Chrysaor's sword as "two-edged," comes to represent the "double nature" genius is said to have:

> the twain rise to form for this moment
> the head of a new monster
>
> Genius
>
> so starts up, affrighted, of sudden stroke
>
> *"the which a double nature has"* (Spenser
>
> telling his syllables here)
>
> that from the Garden verse addresses each word
>
> *"It sited was in fruitfull soyle of old,*
> *"And girt in with two walles on either side;*
> *"The one of yron, the other of bright gold,*
> *"That none might thorough breake, nor ouer-stride:*
> *"And double gates it had, which opened wide"*
>
> the wound become so wide a door
>
> a deed
>
> (the skull fragments and brain splattered over the car's
> upholstery, the red of blood and roses mixing
> in a flash)
>
> (*BB* 129–30)

Compounded of base as well as exalted metal, iron and gold, the "flash," the "sudden stroke" of genius, mixes the splendid with the horrific, "the red of blood and roses." Like the crack in the pitcher in "An Essay at War," the wound is portrayed as opening opportunely, a door admitting access to untidy truths, a door, as Duncan goes on to say, "in which the nation's secreted / sum of evil is betrayd" (*BB* 131).

The second part of "Stage Directions" returns to the matter of "America's unacknowledged, unrepented crimes" brought up in "Up Rising." Laying claim to prophetic powers, Duncan charges American evil with having brought the world to the brink of apocalypse. But prophecy here is decidedly aligned with recollection and aesthetic doctrine, for what Duncan glimpses omens of is the resurfacing or "up rising" of an "old pageant," "portentous rimes" from the past invading the future if not already the present:

> The nation has gone so far in wrong / Truth grows fateful
> And true song gives forth portents of woe.   Sublime
>
> Forbidden intensities convert the personal,
>   and from what *I* am
> Masks of an old pageant, from my world and time
> Portentous rimes, foreshadowings history become a plot demands.
>   The dramatist
> Would not misunderstand the *melos* "romantic and sensational,
>   with both song and instrumental music interspersed"
> Taking over the place of the Real, dims humanity and moves us
>   toward its own End.   *Melodramatic*
>
> (*BB* 131)

The symphonic and dramatic analogues for history active in "Eye of God" and in this poem combine in the word *melodramatic*, a possible confession on Duncan's part that his grave predictions may be overstated, inflated as a thematic imperative by the claims of his poetics. There is a similar hedge in the phrase "dims humanity and moves us / toward its own End," for more immediate than its possible forecast of the end of the world or the end of the human race is its restatement of an abiding assertion of Duncan's aesthetic: art has a life of its own and thus ends—purposes—of its own, and in being admitted into its powers we surrender our intentions to *its* will, dim our humanity as we "convert the personal," for art is a transpersonal, transhuman power that takes us out of ourselves. It is as though the apocalypse were not so much a prophetic, historical claim as a trope for the art experience, being taken out of oneself by way of art.

We sense this again when we go to *Tribunals,* comprised of the five "Passages" (numbers 31 through 35) that follow "Stage Directions." There too we meet a strong apocalyptic strain, a sense of being, as the title right away tells us, on trial and even on the verge of a Last Judgment. But we find it so entwined with Duncan's aesthetic preoccupations, so entangled with recurrent claims regarding the workings of art, that it is impossible to separate what is being said about the times and our possibly imminent extinction from the aesthetics that are being proposed. "Passages 33" opens on the ostensible theme of "the death of Man" but finally has more to say about the "dying upward," self-transcendence, or taking leave of ourselves provided by art:

And in the whole community
the death of Man at work,   bee hive
cells a-buzz with it,

the thriving of Death among us

the work of Art to set words

jiving   breaking into crises

in which a deathless strain moves thru

means without ends
Brancusi's towering column

moving into its true power,
into an imagined "endlessness",   each stage of the form

dying upward,   giving way
(*GW* 19)

Mention is also made of Aleksandr Scriabin, Algernon Charles Swinburne, Robert Creeley, Le Corbusier, Fernand Léger, Piet Mondrian, the de Stijl school, Gustave Moreau, and Pound (whose "Let the line surpass your uses!" Duncan quotes to make the point that art has "its own End"). We get such passages as

We pretend to speak.   The language is not ours
and we move upward beyond our own powers into

words again   beyond us   unsure measures

the poetry of the cosmos
(*GW* 21)

We wonder at the end of the poem whether he is talking about the end of the world, art's "own End," or both:

over this gateway of a whole civilization

carved the words: *unless the grain die.*

A million reapers come to cut down
the leaves of grass we hoped to live by

except we give ourselves utterly over to the

end of things.
(*GW* 24)

With its figure of art as a "dying upward," "Passage 33" reaches back to "The Concert," the first of the poems comprising *Tribunals.* "The Concert" in turn reaches into Duncan's involvement with music, the sort of involvement that posits a grand symphony in "Eye of God" and speaks of "a contrapuntal communion of all things" in "Orders." Among the assumptions at work in the poem is the idea that life as we commonly know it represents a descent into separation, a fall from unboundedness into limitation, a thwarting of majesty. He speaks of "the isolated satyr each man is / severd distinct thing" at one point, the overall thrust of the poem going to suggest music as an ascending power that breaks the bonds of limitation, ecstatically lifting each "severd distinct thing" beyond itself:

. . . He bends his head
to hear the sound he makes
that leads his heart upward,

ascending to where the beat breaks
into an all-but-unbearable whirling crown
of feet dancing, and now he sings or it is
the light singing, the voice
shaking, in the throes of the coming melody,
resonances of meaning exceeding what we
understand, words freed from their origins,

obedient to tongues (sparks) (burning)
speech-flames outreaching the heart's measure.
(*GW* 12)

The analogy he means to draw between music and his own art is made clear by these last lines especially. The phrase "resonances of meaning exceeding what we / understand" speaks of what Duncan repeatedly asserts to be the magic of poetry. The poem's repeated references to the stars not only point to "the harmony of the spheres" but also recall the claim in "Transgressing the Real" that "no man but a world speaks / for my thoughts are servants of the stars." The images of death and apocalyptic extinction that pervade these poems, whether "the death of Man" or "the / end of things," are, whatever else they may also be, figural projections of such self-transcendence, for here, as in the *vodoun* possession rites of Haiti, the spirit arrives only when the human departs.

This age-old belief that a divine or demonic presence requires the absence of man, that extinction is the door to an other world, makes the apocalyptic thrust of these poems, given Duncan's view of inspiration as a form of possession, a foregone conclusion. It is in such a belief that the blood feeding Gassire's lute is rooted. Such a belief led the Aztecs to feel that "the harmony of the spheres" depended on human blood, to offer up the heart of a sacrificial victim on a periodic basis to keep the universe going. It is no accident that in the concluding lines of "The Concert" Duncan speaks of his release into celestial orders in bloody terms:

                                        I saw

willingly the strain of my heart break
    and pour its blood thundering at the life-locks

to release   full   my man's share of the stars'

        majesty   thwarted.
(*GW* 13)

These lines declare that to be human is to be cut off from true being, to have descended into a perversion of celestial roots. Blood is unavoidably the price of "dying upward." There is a strong sense of fallenness, a gnostic bias against the world, throughout all of this. We see it again in "Passages 32," where the reaffirmation of an "allegiance to that Kingdom / 'not of this world'" tells us that the annihilation or evacuation of the world as we know it, however much it may be predicted as an historical eventuality, is, whether it ever occurs or not, built into the definition of such a Kingdom. Whether as Wagadu, the New Jerusalem, or the other names it goes by, the Kingdom *is* the negation of this world, inimical to it by definition. The evocation of it cannot help but be attended by images of death.

There is an important sense, then, in which the apocalyptic in Duncan's work is not so much a prophetic or historical claim as an eternally present possibility, the "eternal sentence" given birth to and kept alive by imagining an other world. It is, that is, inescapably among "the dreams of the race," part of our poetic baggage. Duncan himself remarks, in "Man's Fulfillment in Order and Strife," "We are in apocalyptic times. But this crisis is not at some particular time or place; it is the condition of man and we find it wherever men have been awake to that condition. This feeling of coming to the end or the beginning of things never comes to an end and is always beginning"(MF 231). The imagination of another world is itself a judgment of this one, perhaps punishment as well as judgment, for it is impossible to imagine that other world without wanting to go there. The result is what Duncan calls "a life-spring of dissatisfaction in all orders from which the restless ordering of our poetry comes" (*BB* x), an inability to come to rest where we are. The imagination, the potential intellect, is intrinsically apocalyptic, inherently judgmental. The "old pageant" may very well be its "eternal sentence," the brink of extinction we feel to be an enticement even as it is also a threat. The twin births of Pegasos and Chrysaor, the intimacy between poetry and apocalypse, are a reflection of this, for their births are brought about by the primal crime of Perseus beheading Medusa, as a result of which the poem presents him "hounded" by guilt. (The poem earlier presents Macbeth, a similarly "hounded" figure, on its way to getting at "America's unacknowledged, unrepented crimes," "the nation's secreted / sum of evil.") The imagination's judgment has to do with this guilt, the sense of a fall that prompts its projection of an alternate world. Poetry is both haunted and sustained by, "hounded" and sustained by, recollections and confirmations of this primal taint. The misdeeds of men, the specter of "old evils arisen anew," again and again conspire with and confirm the imagination's judgment, adding fuel to its apocalyptic fires, alerting us to the brink on which we live. The misdeeds of the United States take us there in this instance, recapitulating the primal crime:

And from the dying body of America I see,
or from my dying body,
                                        emerge

children of a deed long before this deed,
seed of Poseidon, depth in which the blue above
is reflected
released

huge Chrysaor and Pegasos sword and flash

Father of Geryon, of him
who carries Dante and Virgil into Hell's depths,

and Steed of Bellerophon

beneath whose hooves once again
new springs are loosed on Helicon.

(*BB* 132)

New springs are loosed on Helicon. The poem effort gets the last word again. History is a tortured womb whose utmost issue is inspiration, a two-way release heading up and down at the same time. But up and down are finally reflections of each other; familial ties between plunge and flight give rise to "a life-spring of dissatisfaction." Winged Geryon, Chrysaor's three-headed, three-bodied son, takes Dante and Virgil down into hell, but the outcome of that we already know. "This very brink in which we despair of the unity in multiplicity of humanity is the brink in which we had the vision of that unity," notes Duncan (MF 235). All but a foregone conclusion, history flirts time and again with a visionary brink of extinction, only to be eclipsed by the vision it provokes. History takes a backseat here, for Duncan writes in *The H.D. Book*, quoting Jacob Burckhardt, "all that art will accept from religion or any other themes is a stimulus" (DB 27). All that poetry will accept from history, the only thing it asks of hell, is a charge. And the charge, as we see insistently throughout *Tribunals,* is both energy and accusation. Thus the Golden Ones, the muses Duncan calls "the ancestors of our Good," bear two-way witness in "Before the Judgment." They look on, allowing us to look beyond:

Children of Kronos, of the Dream beyond death,

secret of a Life beyond our lives,

having their perfection as we have,

their bodies a like grace, a music, their minds a joy, abundant, foliate, fanciful in its flowering,

come into these orders as they have ever come, stand,

as ever, where they are acknowledged,

against the works of unworthy men, unfeeling judgments and cruel deeds.
(*GW* 34–35)

Responding to these deeds, to "the presidents, governors, mayors / this profound Evil has placed over us" (*GW* 31), affirming "an allegiance to that Kingdom / 'not of this World,'" Duncan agrees with another of Burckhardt's assertions, though I know of no text where he either quotes or refers to it. (Burckhardt is cited in the poem "An Interlude" as well as in *The H.D. Book*.) "The only lesson to be derived from the successful misdeeds of the strong," Burckhardt writes in *Reflections on World History*, "is to hold life here and now in no higher esteem than it deserves" (cited in *DM* 88).

V

Among the excerpts from *The H.D. Book* published in *Origin* under the title "From the Day Book" there is a discussion touched off by H.D.'s lines in *The Walls Do Not Fall*:

The Christos-image
is most difficult to disentangle

from its art-craft junk-shop
paint-and-plaster medieval jumble

of pain-worship and death-symbol
(*T* 27)

The difficulty, Duncan argues, has to do with prying the image loose not only from "pain-worship and death-symbol," but from any use of it obtrusive to the truth of, as he elsewhere puts it, "the Christ who impends" (*HD*II.3 131), the "something more" of an ever-yet-to-be-created Christ. "The *persona* of the Christos is continually created in the imagination," he says. "This god Christ will not rest in an historical identity, but again and again seeks incarnation anew in our lives." He speaks of the Christ as "the fullness of a person that is hidden in the creative life, . . . a dangerous source," and suggests that "creation and persuasion contend" wherever we use it. At one point he warns, "We sense it right away when a poet or painter is using a doll of Christ to project a given attitude, for the figure postures to present suffering or brotherly love and has no other life of its own. Even a master like El Greco obsessed with attitude will lose the persona to the conceit that emerges as if to triumph. The doll of Christ—the expressionist or Beat Christ, becomes filled with a sanctioned grievance that can readily be allied with the sanctions in grievance the artist has already taken in his own role. The exchange or interaction within What Is is closed off, and an inflation of attitude is drawn from the hubris involved. . . . In the inflation, the man makes a place for his grievance or guilt, his being unloved or his being unloving, to be deified in the doll" (DB 34–35). What the "doll" approach—the inflation—overlooks is another Christ, the logos Christ of the Gnostic Christians; he goes on to explain, "For the Gnostic Christians, their teacher was two—one who suffered in the man Jesus, and one who did not suffer in the logos Christ. Here again there is truth, for to know suffering is something other than suffering, is a happy thing. In searching out what we suffer and undergo, taking our strength there, we discover a new person who does not suffer" (DB 42). Throughout this section of *The H.D. Book*, Duncan makes a number of references to what he quotes Burckhardt as calling the "high and independent selfhood" of art. It does not take long to see that the "other life of its own" the "doll" misses the point of, the logos Christ or the Word, is none other than this selfhood, the transformative and transcendent, forceful and fateful thrust of a poem:

> But for the poet, for the man already transformed in making some work of art, for the carpenter, the meaning of the crucifixion scene is not that of a lynching party, nor of a passion, but of a poem in the actual world, the fulfillment of a prophecy or story-form. There is in the man and in the god a perfume and a radiance, a flower that portends; and in the passions of the two in One upon the cross or tree, we see the ripeness of what the story demands, the mystery of the whole thing in which nails, blood, and cry, the *Eli, Eli lama sabachthani,* is the crisis of the poem enacted.
>
> In our work we lose our selves, our independence, the *Jesus* of each one, or it is fused, enters into the radiance of another power of the same being, another person we find in the community of language and our work there that we call the poet. It is in passion, in suffering, that, even as we cry out, we become

> workers, organs, instruments of our Art that is fateful or formal. The Christ is the music, the sense of needed form. . . . (DB 42–43)

It is exactly here that we are likely to reflect that bringing it all back to poetry is itself an attitude—a very familiar, insistent one in Duncan's case—and that the danger of inflation he warns against moves in this direction, too. I have already suggested that throughout the Vietnam War poems Duncan walks a tightrope between humanist outrage and a cosmologizing acceptance of the war, even a poetics-advancing embrace of it. The tightrope is not so much a choice against either as an attempt to remain true to both, the two poles which tighten this rope corresponding to the man Jesus and the logos Christ. The outrage has to do with the suffering of actual men and women and the cosmology, the poetics, with our being other than the suffering part of ourselves. The war is a more than ample occasion for the "inflation of attitude," the "doll" approach Duncan warns against, and in the opening lines of "Before the Judgment" it is his own excessive anger that he moves to keep within bounds:

> Discontent with that first draft.   Where one's own
>   hatred enters   Hell   gets out of hand.
>
> Again and again   Virgil   ever standing by Dante
>   must caution him. . . .
> (*GW* 28)

This reminds us that for all of his dwelling on the self-transcendence of art, all of his insistence that "the glory is to be universal, not personal" (DB 35) or that "Sublime / Forbidden intensities convert the personal," there is an acknowledged, recognizably personal strain running through these poems. The uprising referred to by the title of the poem "Up Rising" and "the blood's natural / uprising against tyranny" spoken of in "The Soldiers" refers as much to the high blood pressure that Duncan was suffering from at the time as to the other meanings we have seen. In "Stage Directions," we get the lines, "And from the dying body of America I see, / or from my dying body. . . ."

What is interesting is that what Duncan does in his articulation of this personal strain is just what he says takes place in the "doll" approach, where "the man makes a place for his grievance or guilt, his being unloved or his being unloving." The war poems open a vein of self-accusation through which guilt and unloving, though not so much grievance and being unloved, make their way—be it the "Dream disclosed to me, I too am Ishmael" of "Bring It Up from the Dark" or the "I too removed therefrom by habit" of "The Soldiers." One of the first poems in *Bending the Bow,* "Such Is the Sickness of Many a Good Thing," deals with an early refusal to love, initiating on an autobiographical level the "contrapuntal communion" of Eros and AntEros that the book returns to again and again. The "deep co-inherence of Eros and Thanatos" is gotten at here by way of the near-identity, on the level of sound and spelling, of Eros with Eris, the goddess of discord, sister of Ares. Again we hear H.D.'s influence, for in *Helen in Egypt* the question "Eros? Eris?" occurs a number of times and at one point she elaborates,

> Is there another stronger than Love's mother?
> is there one other, Discordia, Strife?
> Eris is sister of Ares,
>
> his unconquerable child is Eros;
> did Ares bequeath his arrows
> alike to Eros, to Eris?
> (*HE* 190)

So in "Such Is the Sickness of Many a Good Thing" we read,

> Was he then Adam of the Burning Way?
> hid away in the heat like wrath
>   conceald in Love's face,
> or the seed, Eris in Eros,
>   key and lock
> of what I was?   I could not speak
>   the releasing
> word.   For into a dark
>   matter he came
> and askt me to say what
>   I could not say.   "I. ."
>
> All the flame in me stopt
>   against my tongue.
> My heart was a stone, a dumb
>   unmanageable thing in me,

a darkness that stood athwart
his need
for the enlightening, the
"I love you" that has
only this one quick in time,
this one start
when its moment is true.
(*BB* 6)

Duncan returns to this matter of wrath, this difficulty with the word *love*, in the final poem in the book, "Epilogos," which begins,

I have grown from a wrathful bough of the tree.
When I say *Love* the word comes out of me
like a moan—life-sap. From broken wood.
Yet I would not have it come easily.
(*BB* 134)

In between, there is the sort of unmasking or demystification of himself that we see in "A Lammas Tiding" and "My Mother Would Be a Falconress," where what's brought up from the dark is Duncan's own warlike, bloodthirsty instincts. In what may have been the dream referred to in "Bring It Up from the Dark" he sees himself as a falcon treading his mother's wrist, anxious to draw blood, and awakens with the opening lines of "My Mother Would Be a Falconress." He explains, in "A Lammas Tiding," that "searching out the poetic lore of what America is, I had been reading Blake's *Vision of the Daughters of Albion* these last few nights just before going to sleep. '*With what sense is it that the chicken shuns the ravenous hawk?*' I had read, and I said to myself, yes, there are bloody men, and I am not one of them but of chicken-kind, for I would never draw blood. Which goes to show one should be careful of vain self-delusions entertained at bedtime. For now my dream would have me a hawk" (*BB* 51). In the poem he goes on to confess, "I tread my mother's wrist and would draw blood" and "I tore at her wrist with my savage beak" (*BB* 52–54). Here Duncan practices what he elsewhere preaches. The idea that the war puts us all on trial, not just as a nation but as individuals, that it brings us to the revelation of a personal "burden of original sin," works to erode presumptions of exemption and righteousness, eat away at the vanity of self-congratulation. The chicken sees himself to be a hawk underneath it all. Even the exalted aura Duncan usually bestows upon the poet comes down somewhat as he writes, "And, hearing my account, Jess comments: 'Especially since chickens do draw blood.' Whereupon, I recall those horrible cannibalistic hens I tended at Treesbank, that needed only the first sign of blood that might be left after egg-laying to tear at each other, bloody not from hunger but from malice, like so many poets furious in their pecking order" (*BB* 51). It was this insistence upon a personal, psychological accounting that led to the cooling of Duncan's friendship with Denise Levertov, the stirring up of bad air and hard feelings regarding their slightly different approaches to the war. Both his and her accounts of the matter agree that the trouble began with his questioning the image of "skinned penises" in her poem "Life at War," which he insisted on reading psychoanalytically, debunking what he saw as the poem's public pretensions by bringing it back to the issue of a personal, psychosexual disturbance. With a righteously, rigidly Freudian eye for latent content, Duncan saw the image not as a fact of the war—he challenged Levertov to prove that the skinning of penises was among the atrocities committed in Vietnam—but a projection of her troubled state of mind, behind which lay the troubled state of her marriage. This is an odd thing for someone who encourages conversions of the personal to be doing, but evidently Levertov's increasingly public stance, more overtly and actively political than his own, raised a specter of her succumbing to what he saw as the self-delusions of "public use," the "officization/ossification" (*BB* 70) syndrome in which private grievances, not recognized as such, inflate themselves and masquerade as public concerns.

The public and the private being so difficult to disentangle, the specter is easy enough to see. It is visible in Duncan's case as well; it is in order to confront it that he brings the personal, almost confessional strain so explicitly into his own poems of the war. We sense, however, that what alienated him most was that Levertov's displacement of the personal (if that is in fact what it was) was being done in the name of politics rather than poetry. In her Vietnam War poems we at times hear something close to a questioning of poetry's right to go on, a sense of it as trivial or vain, diminished by the urgencies brought about by the war. "And all I can bring forth out of my anger is a few flippant rhymes," she writes in "An Interim."[52] Or it is a questioning of her own ability to go on, a complaint that these are not particularly poetic times. "Advent 1966" contrasts Robert Southwell's "The Burning Babe" with the burning, napalmed children of Vietnam, Southwell's vision of redemption with a grim reality that calls it into question if not negates it outright. The war attacks the possibility of seeing in the manner of poetry, Levertov laments:

> my clear caressive sight, my poet's sight I was given
> that it might stir me into song,
> is blurred.
>   There is a cataract filming over
> my inner eyes. Or else a monstrous insect
> has entered my head, and looks out
> from my sockets with multiple vision,
>
> seeing not the unique Holy Infant
> burning sublimely, an imagination of redemption,
> furnace in which souls are wrought into new life,
> but, as off a beltline, more, more senseless figures aflame.
> (*RA* 4)

This must have sounded like backsliding to Duncan, something close to apostasy. In her account in *Scales of the Marvelous*, Levertov gives the impression that Duncan took her at her word in such poems as this, agreed with her that the war was taking over, that she was capitulating, surrendering the authority of her poet's eye. She appears to have objected to him agreeing with what she herself was saying, objected that he could only do so disapprovingly (*SM* 110–12). For Duncan the war was an occasion to be risen to with increasingly fervent, assertive, and confident affirmations of the validity of the poet's vision. Though he appears to waver somewhat with the "putting aside" he announces in "Orders," no such abdication ever really takes place—not even in that poem. By the time we get to the last of the war poems we hear a very eloquent, self-conscious pitch for poetry, something quite different from what we hear in Levertov's poems of the war.

Duncan's campaign for poetry, the zeal and the excitement he brings to bear on the very idea of poetry, makes for one of the most distinctive, compelling characteristics of his work. He describes himself as a man who took poetry to be his fate, and the sense of him we get not only from his writings, but from his activities as a teacher, a speaker, and a contributor to poetry concerns and events (often in an organizing role), bears his description out. But his energetic advertisement for poetry makes a large, difficult-to-miss target. No doubt the easiest and most often made criticism of Duncan is that he is intoxicated with the idea of poetry, pushing a romance of the poem at the expense of everything else a poem could be about. His tendency to write poems about poetry, even when they are ostensibly about something else, runs the risk of inflating a poetry "doll." His friendly relations with "What Is," alongside his sense of poetry's privileged access to "It," appear too complacent at times, especially in the context of political and social problems like the war. He sometimes appears to be saying that whatever is is right, especially if—or exactly because—it contributes to the writing of poems. The delight he takes in poetry, his own "riding high," runs its particular risks of narcosis. This is a point I have made before. I make it again because it pertains to the poem with reference to which I would like to conclude—as does everything in this section from the Christos image on.

The poem appears in *A Seventeenth Century Suite,* which was first published privately by Duncan in 1973. Written in homage to the English metaphysical poets, the *Suite* is described by Duncan as "Imitations, Derivations & Variations upon Certain Conceits and Findings Made among Strong Lines." He takes a number of seventeenth-century poems and writes poems of his own based upon them. Among the poems he does this with is Southwell's "The Burning Babe." Despite the literariness of its occasion, the variation on "The Burning Babe" is quite straightforward, one of the most moving of Duncan's poems, for the war intrudes on that literariness, setting off a questioning and a confrontation, an emotional friction at the very heart of its conceit. The poem cannot help but recall Levertov's "Advent 1966," turning, as does Levertov's poem, upon a contrast between Southwell's epiphanic Babe and children burned by napalm in Vietnam. But here the confrontation is less an either/or proposition than an interaction of "the two in One," the man Jesus and the logos Christ at once adding to and subtracting from each other. Duncan insists on acknowledging both. The way in which he does so requires a lengthy quotation. Here is the second half of the poem:

"*A pretty Babe*"—that burning Babe
        the poet Southwell saw—
a scorching, a crying, that made his cold heart glow,
        a fuel of passion in which
the thought of wounds delites the soul.
        He's Art's epiphany of Art new born,
a Christ of Poetry, the burning spirit's show;

He leaves no shadow, where he dances in the air,
        of misery below.

Another Christ, if he be, as we are,
Man, cries out in utter misery;
and every Holy Martyr must have cried
        forsaken in some moment
that from Christ's "Why hast Thou forsaken me?"
        has enterd our Eternity
or else is not true to itself.   But now

        I am looking upon burnd faces
that have known catastrophe incommensurate
        with meaning, beyond hate or loss or
Christian martyrdom, unredeemed.   My heart
        caves into a space it seems
to have long feard.

I cannot imagine, gazing upon photographs
        of these young girls,   the mind
transcending what's been done to them.

        From the broild flesh of these heretics,
by napalm monstrously baptised
        in a new name, every delicate and
sensitive curve of lip and eyelid
        blasted away, surviving. . .
        eyes?   Can this horror be calld their
fate?   *Our* fate grows a mirroring face
in the accusation beyond accusation
        of such eyes,
a kind of hurt that drives into the root
of understanding,   their very lives
        burnd into us   we live by.

Victor and victim know not what they do
        —the deed exceeding what we would *know;*
the knowledge in the sight of those eyes
        goes deep into the heart's fatalities.
And in our nation's store of crimes long
        unacknowledged, unrepented,

the sum of abject suffering, of dumb incalculable
        injury increases
the sore of conscience we long avoid.

What can I feel of it?   All hurt
rushes in to illustrate that glare
and fails.   What can I feel of what was done?
All hatred cringes from the sight of it
and would contract into self-loathing
to ease the knowledge of what no man
can compensate.   I think I could bear it.

I cannot think I could bear it.
(*GW* 75–76)

I don't know if poetry can do much more than bring us to this brink. The deep entanglement of word and humankind, the difficulty of disentangling "I think I could bear it" from "I cannot think I could bear it," bears witness to a truth to be faithful to which the poet runs a two-way risk. The hubris of an easy gesture of commiseration, the assertion of solidarity through presumptions of suffering only vicariously suffered, vies with the hubris of a callous transcendence of suffering, the narcotizing lure of holding life "in no higher esteem than it deserves." The difficulty, the meaning, is in the mix, the holding aloft of an unresolved dilemma. The meaning, more exactly, *is* the mix, the intertwinement and the intensification; the entanglement taunts our wish to conclude.

PART III

Cante Moro

I would like to touch on the topic of the "New American Poetry" where it opens onto matters we wouldn't necessarily expect it to entail—not necessarily "new," not necessarily "American," not even necessarily "poetry." What I would like to touch on is the New American Poetry's Spanish connection: Federico García Lorca's meditation on the "dark sounds" of *cante jondo*, deep song, the quality and condition known as *duende*. I will discuss that in relation to an array of "dark sounds" that bear on a cross-cultural poetics intimated by the inclusion of Lorca's "Theory and Function of the *Duende*" in Donald M. Allen and Warren Tallman's anthology *The Poetics of the New American Poetry*, an espousal of not only cross-cultural but intermedia fertilization and provocation, which I'll relate to the work of a number of writers.

The title "Cante Moro" goes back to a recording that came out in 1966, a recording by Manitas de Plata, probably the flamenco musician best known to listeners in the U.S. at that time. At one point during one of the pieces on the album, "Moritas Moras," after the opening run of singing by José Reyes, a member of the group says, "Eso es cante moro," which means "That's Moorish singing."[1] Calling deep song *cante moro* summons the past rule and continuing cultural presence of the Moors in Spain; it acknowledges the hybrid, heterogeneous roots not only of cante jondo but of Spanish culture generally, of, in fact, culture—collective poesis—generally. A Gypsy doing so, as in this instance, allies outcast orders, acknowledging hybridity and heterogeneity to entwine the heterodox as well—heterodox Gypsy, heterodox Moor. *Cante moro* bespeaks the presence and persistence of the otherwise excluded, the otherwise expelled.

Let me begin by saying a bit about Lorca. Of the twenty-five writers in *The Poetics of the New American Poetry*, Lorca is one of the anomalies, perhaps *the* anomaly—the only non-Anglophone poet and one of only two non-Americans included. It's fitting he should give the volume its heaviest cross-cultural, cross-pollinating touch. He himself was drawn to the marginalized, the anomalous, to those relegated to the outskirts of sanctioned identity and culture. A large part of his importance to Spanish poetry is the respect he accorded the vernacular culture of southern Spain. He sought instruction in the mixed cultural inheritance of Andalusia, in the music of outcast Gypsies, in reminders of the expelled Moors. The book that made him famous is *Gypsy Ballads*, published in 1928. There is a correspondence between what Lorca was doing in Spain and what was going on in this country among black writers during the Harlem Renaissance of the 1920s and '30s. The tapping of vernacular resources was a defining feature of the Harlem Renaissance, and it's no accident that one of its most prominent poets, Langston Hughes, was one of the first translators of *Gypsy Ballads* into English. Lorca in fact had direct contact with Harlem and the Harlem Renaissance writers while studying at Columbia in 1929 and 1930. The work that came out of that stay, *Poet in New York*, contains a section called "The Blacks" that celebrates Harlem. The translation of that work by Greg Simon and Steven F. White includes letters Lorca wrote his family from New York. In one of them he tells of meeting the Harlem Renaissance novelist Nella Larsen, author of *Quicksand* and *Passing*, and of the party she gave for him at her house at which "there were only blacks." Of the music they played and sang he writes, "Only the *cante jondo* is comparable."[2]

In his essay on duende Lorca is working with the black aesthetic of Spain. One of the things he does early in the essay is quote the Gypsy singer Manuel Torre as having said, "All that has dark sounds has *duende*." That, at least, is how it's translated by J. L. Gilli in the version that appears in *The Poetics of the New American Poetry*.[3] Christopher Maurer, in the more recent translation that appears in *Deep Song and Other Prose*, renders it, "All that has black sounds has duende."[4] Maurer also points out, in a footnote, that when Lorca met Torre in 1927, Torre, evoking the Gypsies' fabled origins in Egypt, said to him, "What you must search for, and find, is the black torso of the Pharaoh" (*DS* 140). He meant that one has to root one's voice in fabulous origins, find one's voice in the dark, among the dead. The word *duende* means "spirit," a kind of gremlin, a gremlin-like, troubling spirit. One of the things that marks the arrival of duende in flamenco singing is a sound of trouble in the voice. The voice becomes troubled. Its eloquence becomes eloquence of another order, a broken, problematic, self-problematizing eloquence. Lorca also quotes Torre as having told a singer, "You have a voice, you know the styles, but you will never triumph, because you have no duende" (*DS* 42). So duende is something beyond technical competence or even technical virtuosity. It is something troubling. It has to do with trouble, deep trouble. Deep song delves into troubled water, troubles the water. As a character in Leon Forrest's novel *Two Wings to Veil My Face* puts it, "Still waters don't run deep enough."[5]

Lorca tells a story of the Andalusian singer Pastora Pavón, also known as La Niña de los Peines. He tells of her singing in a little tavern in Cádiz one night before a group of flamenco aficionados. He says that when she finished singing she was met with silence. Her voice, though technically perfect, and her virtuosity, though impressive, didn't move anyone. "When Pastora Pavón finished singing," Lorca writes, "there was total silence, until a tiny man, one of those dancing manikins that rise suddenly out of brandy bottles, sarcastically murmured 'Viva Paris!' as if to say: 'Here we care nothing about ability, technique, skill. Here we are after something else'" (*DS* 45). Which is not to say that one gets there by not having skill. One gets there by not being satisfied with skill. It is the other side, the far side of skill, not the near side. Then Lorca goes on to say, "As though crazy, torn like a medieval weeper, La Niña de los Peines got to her feet, tossed off a big glass of firewater and began to sing with a scorched throat, without voice, without breath or color, but with duende. She was able to kill all the scaffolding of the song and leave way for a furious, enslaving duende, friend of sand winds, who made the listeners rip their clothes with the same rhythm as do the blacks of the Antilles when, in the 'lucumí' rite, they huddle in heaps before the statue of Santa Bárbara" (*DS* 45–46).

It is interesting that Lorca makes the Old World–New World connection, a black connection, a connection between duende, black song in Spain, cante moro, and black song in Cuba, the music of the Yoruba-Catholic mix known as *lucumí*. This is one of the reasons Lorca is relevant to new American possibilities, to an American newness that is about mix, the meeting of different cultural styles and predispositions. He was interested in Old World predecessor mixes like those in Andalusia, whose further inflections in the Americas he recognized and embraced.

Lorca doesn't so much define duende as grope after it, wrestle with it, evoke it through strain, insist on struggle. He writes, for example, that "one must awaken the duende in the remotest mansions of the blood" (*DS* 44), that "the duende loves the rim of the wound" and that it "draws near places where forms fuse together into a yearning superior to their visible expression" (*DS* 50). He notes that "[e]ach art has a duende different in form and style but their roots all meet in the place where the black sounds of Manuel Torre come from—the essence, the uncontrollable, quivering, common base of wood, sound, canvas, and word" (*DS* 52). One of the ongoing challenges of Lorca's essay is how to bring duende, which he discusses mainly in relation to music, into writing—how to relate it to writing. I would like to touch on four American poets whose work intersects with Lorca's and then remark on a few pieces of music that pertain to these matters. Three of the four poets were included in the anthology *The New American Poetry 1945–1960*: Jack Spicer, Robert Duncan, and Amiri Baraka. The fourth, Bob Kaufman, was not included, though he should have been.

First, Jack Spicer, who was based in the San Francisco Bay Area, a San Francisco poet. Though he began writing in the 1940s, he felt that his real work began with *After Lorca*, which was published in 1957. It is a book of poems and prose pieces, poems that are presented as translations of poems by Lorca—translations in a very loose sense. Some of them are translations in an even looser sense in that they are translations of Lorca poems that do not exist. Interspersed among these translations are the prose pieces, which are written as letters addressed to the dead Lorca. Lorca was killed during the Spanish Civil War, executed by Francisco Franco's troops, which is another reason he has attracted a lot of attention—as a symbol, a sign of those times and the times we continue to live in. He is a poet of cultural openness, cultural mix, cut down by the emergence of fascism. A lot of writers have identified with Lorca and the position, implicit and explicit, he took against fascism. Remember that the Gypsies he so celebrated were one of the targets of fascism; a million Gypsies were killed in concentration camps.

Lorca was killed in 1936 near Granada. Spicer, a very playful writer, albeit a bit grim, begins *After Lorca* with an introduction attributed to "Federico García Lorca / Outside Granada, October 1957."[6] The gremlin, the imp, is very active in what he is doing. As well, Spicer picks up a certain insistence in Lorca's discussion of duende, which is that it is a conversation with the dead, intimacy with death and with the dead. "The duende," Lorca says, "does not come at all unless he sees that death is possible. The duende must know beforehand that he can serenade death's house and rock those branches we all wear, branches that do not have, will never have, any consolation" (*DS* 49–50) The disconsolate character and tone of Spicer's work agrees not only with this but with the fact that one of the phrases that recur a great deal in cante jondo is the phrase *sin remedio*, "without remedy." The assertion *no hay remedio*, "there is no remedy," also occurs. Pepe de la Matrona, who has one of the darkest, gruffest voices one will ever hear (more an extended, variegated growl than a voice), sings a song called "Remedio No Tengas," which means "You Would Have No Remedy." Duende often has to do with a kind of longing that has no remedy, not simply loss, unrequited love and so forth, but what Lorca calls "a longing without object" (*DS* 112). He discusses this in relation to *Gypsy Ballads*, to a poem that has to do with a woman named Soledad Montoya, who "embodies incurable pain." "The Pain of Soledad Montoya is the root of the Andalusian people," writes Lorca. "It is not anguish, because in pain one can smile, nor does it blind, for it never produces weeping. It is a longing without object, a keen love for nothing, with the certainty that death (the eternal care of Andalusia) is breathing behind the door" (*DS* 112).

So Spicer opens *After Lorca* with an introduction written by Lorca, at that time some twenty years dead. In it Lorca says that several of the pieces in the book are translations of poems he has written since his death, though he does not say which. In the essay on duende he writes, "A dead man in Spain is more alive as a dead man than any place else in the world" (*DS* 47). Spicer seems to have taken him at his word. Impish play and disconsolate spirit—"The dead are notoriously hard to satisfy," we read (*CB* 12)—repeatedly embrace in an introduction whose antic humor gathers troubling undertones. The words *execution* and *executed*, used in reference to Spicer's technique, resonate with and are darkly inflected by the circumstances of Lorca's death. So too does the joke with which the introduction ends, where we read, "But I am strongly reminded as I survey this curious amalgam of a cartoon published in an American magazine while I was visiting your country in New York. The cartoon showed a gravestone on which were inscribed the words: 'HERE LIES AN OFFICER AND A GENTLEMAN.' The caption below it read: 'I wonder how they happened to be buried in the same grave?'" (*CB* 12).

Another poet who was engaged with Lorca's work, and another San Francisco poet, is Robert Duncan, an associate of Spicer's. In his book *Caesar's Gate: Poems 1949–50* there is a preface Duncan wrote in 1972, the year the book was published, and in that preface there is a section called "Lorca." The book includes a poem called "What Have You Come to Tell Me, García Lorca?" and in the preface Duncan recalls the 1940s and '50s when he was reading Lorca. He writes for several pages about Lorca's importance to his development, and he mentions Spicer as well. He discusses the historical predicament, the historical moment that was Lorca's fate, the Spanish Civil War and the rise of fascism. He discusses duende. He also discusses Lorca as a gay poet, a troubled, conflicted gay poet who was important to him and Spicer as gay poets. It is not that Lorca advanced a gay poetics, but that they saw in him and his work some of the trouble, for him, of being gay—a certain depression and self-censure, a censuring of his own homosexuality. Duncan writes this about duende:

> In his lecture "Theory and Function of the *Duende*," Lorca tells us: "The dark and quivering *duende* that I am talking about is a descendant of the merry demon of Socrates." The madness, then, however it may relate to the practice of deliberate alienation which Lorca's intimate friend from student days, Salvador Dalí, had brought into Surrealist circles of Paris from their Spanish conversations, and which led to the work of Breton and Eluard in *L'Immaculée Conception*, contemporary with Lorca's *Poeta en Nueva York*, with Breton's essay on the simulation of verbal deliriums from various categories of insanity—this madness is not ultimately a surrealist simulation drawn from a clinical model in a program of systematic alienation but, past that state, means to return to the divine madness of daemonic inspiration, the speaking more than one knew what, that Plato tells us his Master, Socrates, thought to be at once the power and the dementia of the poet in his art.[7]

He speaks of duende as a "mode of poetic dissociation" and of "disturbed meanings." The poet speaks in tongues, multiply, troublingly: "Freed from reality, the trouble of an unbound reference invades the reader's sense of what is at issue" (*CG* xxii).

So duende, for Duncan, is "the speaking more than one knew what," the taking on of another voice, and that is very much what duende is in cante jondo. It is a taking over of one's voice by another voice. This wooing of another voice, an alternate voice, that is so important to duende has as one of its aspects or analogues in poetry that state of entering the language in such a way that one is into an area of implication, resonance, and connotation that is manifold, many-meaninged, polysemous. One has worked beyond oneself. It is as if the language itself takes over. Something beyond the will, the conscious design or desire of the poet, is active, something that goes beyond univocal, unequivocal control. That is what Duncan means by "the trouble of an unbound reference"—an inordinacy, a lack of adequation that is to language what *sin remedio* is to a longing without object. Bound reference, univocal meaning, is no solution to the riddle of language.

Amiri Baraka cites Lorca as an influence in his statement on poetics in *The New American Poetry*. There is an early poem of his called "Lines to García Lorca," which he prefaces with an epigraph taken from an African American spiritual: "Climin up the mountain, chillun, / Didn't come here for to stay, / If I'm ever gonna see you agin / It'll be on the judgment day."[8] By doing so he not only acknowledges Lorca's interest in African American music and culture but furthers the analogy, the sense of rapport, between African American spirituality and Andalusian spirituality. Gypsies, though they do not appear explicitly in this poem, come in elsewhere in Baraka's early work to embody a mobile, mercurial noninvestment in the status quo. One of the things going on in "Lines to García Lorca" is the implicit connection between that mercuriality, that nomadism, and the line "Didn't come here for to stay," behind which lies a well-known, resonant history of African American fugitivity and its well-known, resonant relationship to enslavement and persecution. Thus the resonant apposition of the poem's opening lines, "Send soldiers again to kill you, García. / Send them to quell my escape." At the end of the poem Lorca's voice, "away off," invested with fugitive spirit, laughs:

> But, away off, quite close to the daylight,
> I hear his voice, and he is laughing, laughing
> Like a Spanish guitar.

The way in which fugitivity asserts itself on an aesthetic level, at the level of poetics, is important as well. The way in which Baraka's poems of this period move intimates fugitive spirit, as does much of the music that he was into. He writes, of a solo by saxophonist John Tchicai on an Archie Shepp album, "It slides away from the proposed."[9] That gets into, again, the cultivation of another voice, a voice that is other than that proposed by one's intentions, tangential to one's intentions, angular, oblique—the obliquity of an unbound reference. That sliding away wants out. Musicians like Tchicai and Shepp were called "outside" players. Robin Blaser called Spicer's work "the practice of outside" (*CB* 269). Let me, though, let another poem of Baraka's, "History As Process," say it, show it. Lorca does not explicitly come in, but the Gypsies do and so does the guitar:

1\.
The evaluation of the mysteries by the sons of all
experience. All suffering, if we call the light a thing
all men should know. Or find. Where ever, in the dark folds
of the next second, there is some diminishing beauty we might one day
understand, and scream to, in some wild fit of acknowledged Godliness.

Reality, is what it is. This suffering truth
advertised in all men's loveliest histories.

The thing, There As Speed, is God, as mingling
possibility. The force. As simple future, what

the freaky gipsies rolled through Europe
on.

(The soul.)

2\.

What can I do to myself? Bones
and dusty skin. Heavy eyes twisted
between the adequate thighs of all
humanity (a little h), strumming my head
for a living. Bankrupt utopia sez tell me
no utopias. I will not listen. (Except the raw wind
makes the hero's eyes close, and the tears that come out
are real.)[10]

One hears the pronouncements, the propositions. One also hears the slips, the slides, the shifting ratios—rhythmic, predicative, quick.

The last of the four poets is Bob Kaufman. His work was not included in *The New American Poetry*, even though it was very important to the Beat movement. He was very involved in the development of the Beat movement in San Francisco, in North Beach, and is said to have coined the term *beatnik*. Some people consider him the prototypical Beat poet. Steve Abbott has called him "the hidden master of the Beats."[11] A poet of African American and Jewish descent to whom Lorca's work was very important, he refers to Lorca in a number of poems, echoing lines from his work, sometimes quoting or paraphrasing them outright. In "Lorca," for example, we find the line "Give Harlem's king one spoon,"[12] harking back to *Poet in New York*, where "The King of Harlem" begins with the lines "With a wooden spoon / he dug out the crocodiles' eyes" (*PNY* 29). What spoke most to Kaufman was Lorca's valorization of African American presence. In his lecture on *Poet in New York*, Lorca argued that "the blacks exercise great influence in North America," that "they are the most delicate, most spiritual element in that world" (*PNY* 186). The "great sun of the center" (*PNY* 35) that he encourages black people to seek in "The King of Harlem," to continue seeking, is, among other things, the covert centrality of an otherwise marginalized people, a "sun" that cross-linguistically puns on "soul" ("el gran sol del centro").

Kaufman's apocalyptic, ironically patriotic prose-poem "The Ancient Rain" generously samples, as we would say nowadays, "The King of Harlem" and "Standards and Paradise of the Blacks." Its embrace of Lorca's endorsement of new American possibilities, new American mixes, resounds in telling counterpoint not only with Kaufman's noninclusion in *The New American Poetry* (only one nonwhite poet's work was included) but with the negligible attention accorded him and his work in the numerous writings on the Beat generation as well:

> At once I am there at the great sun, feeling the great sun of the center. Hearing the Lorca music in the endless solitude of crackling blueness. I could feel myself a little boy again in crackling blueness, wanting to do what Lorca says in crackling blueness to kiss out my frenzy on bicycle wheels and smash little squares in the flush of a soiled exultation. Federico García Lorca sky, immaculate scoured sky, equaling only itself contained all the distances that Lorca is, that he came from Spain of the Inquisition is no surprise. His poem of solitude walking around Columbia. My first day in crackling blueness, I walked off my ship and rode the subway to Manhattan to visit Grant's tomb and I thought because Lorca said he would let his grow long someday crackling blueness would cause my hair to grow long. I decided to move deeper into crackling blueness. When Franco's civil guard killed, from that moment on, I would move deeper in crackling blueness. I kept my secrets. I observed those who read him who were not Negroes and listened to all their misinterpretation of him. I thought of those who had been around him, those that were not Negro and were not in crackling blueness, those that couldn't see his wooden south wind, a tiltin' black slime that tacked down all the boat wrecks, while Saturn delayed all the trains. (*AR* 80–81)

"Crackling blueness," out of "Standards and Paradise of the Blacks," is the sky cracked by lightning, the imminence of thunder and rain, wrath and redemption, "the bitter freshness of . . . millenary spit," as Lorca puts it (*PNY* 25). It is also the raspy, cracked voice of duende, the ominous, black vocality of the blues and of cante jondo.

Those, then, are four instances of American poets making use of the work of Lorca. They relate to the question of how one's writing can draw upon that of predecessors, the sense of tradition, a lineage one creates for oneself, that one seeks out in the work of others. Call it influence without anxiety. As a writer, one has to find one's tradition, create one's tradition, and in doing that one creates lines of affinity and kinship that can cut across national boundaries, ethnic boundaries, and so forth. They also relate to the question of how one's writing can be informed and instructed by other artistic media, how one can create or pursue lines of kinship and conversation with nonliterary media. That's one of the useful senses the phrase I used earlier—"cultivation of another voice"—has. A different medium is a different voice, an alternate vocality. Lorca's sense of duende comes out of his engagement with music, the Andalusian music he was obviously moved and inspired by. Attentiveness to those other, alternate voices that speak to you—painting, sculpture, whatever—can make you susceptible, impinge upon you in ways which alter your own voice.

My work has a pronounced relationship to music. I was always struck by Louis Zukofsky's definition of poetry as a function whose lower limit is speech and whose upper limit is song. He uses the integral sign from calculus to suggest that we are integrating that lower limit, speech, and that upper limit, song. Poetry is an integral function. But even before I came across Zukofsky's formulation of it I heard poetry as a musical deployment of language, the music peculiar to language, language bordering on song, speech bordering on song. From doing a lot of listening I have gotten certain ideas about music, a thematics of music, but also an impulse toward a musicality in the writing. Years ago I wrote a poem for John Coltrane, "Ohnedaruth's Day Begun," in which there is this passage:

I grope thru smoke to glimpse New
York City, the Village Gate, late
'65. I sit at the bar drinking scotch between
sets, some kid comes up and says he'd
like to hear "Equinox."

We play "Out Of
This World" instead, the riff hits

me like rain and like a leak in my
throat it won't quit. No reins whoa
this ghost I'm ridden by and again
I'm asking
myself what "climb" will Nut ask of
me next? . . .[13]

This has to do, among other things, with a surge, a runaway dilation, a quantum rush one often hears in Trane's music, the sense that he's driven, possessed—*ridden*, as it is put here, which recalls the African possession religions in which worshippers are spoken of as horses and the gods, the spirits, are spoken of as horsemen, riders. To be possessed is to be mounted and ridden by a god. You find that imagery in *vodoun* in Haiti, in *candomblé* in Brazil, in *lucumí* or *santería* in Cuba. Possession means that something beyond your grasp of it grabs you, that something that gets away from you—another sense in which fugitivity comes in—gives you a voice. Like Lorca, who, remember, refers to lucumí, I think of this as related to duende.

That is one place in my work where ideas having to do with duende come in. Another place is *Bedouin Hornbook*, which even more extensively and graphically has to do with music. It is prose, written mainly in the form of letters addressed to an angel by a musician/composer, N. *Duende* is a term that comes up a number of times in these letters. One instance is this one, toward the end of a letter that accompanies the tape of a composition that N. has written, where we read, "The name of the piece is 'Opposable Thumb at the Water's Edge.' Its basic theme I'd put this way: Graspability is a self-incriminating thirst utterly native to every hand, an indigenous court from which only the drowned hope to win an acquittal. The piece makes use of two triadic phrases which I call utility riffs: 'whatever beginnings go back to' and 'an exegetic refusal to be done with desire.' These generate a subtheme which could be put as follows: Thirst is by its nature unquenchable, the blue lips of a muse whose refusals roughen our throats with *duende*."[14] Unquenchable thirst is a longing without object. Blue, the color of its ostensible object, plants a disconsolate kiss.

Let me now refer to several musical examples that relate to these matters. The first is a piece by the singer whom Lorca writes about in his essay on duende, Pastora Pavón, La Niña de los Peines. Found on the album *La Niña de los Peines*, it is called "Ay Pilato" and is a type of song known as a *saeta*. The saeta is a song heard in Andalusia during Holy Week, the week before Easter. A procession takes place through the streets, a procession that includes musicians—sometimes playing nothing but muffled drums, but often including horns, brass instruments. The procession carries an image either of the Virgin Mary or of Christ, sometimes both. At each point where the procession stops there is a singer on a balcony overlooking the street. The procession stops right beneath the balcony and the singer sings to the image they carry. *Saeta* means "arrow." The song is piercing, heartrending. We hear the singer singing from a position of being pierced. What we also hear is a Gypsy-Moorish-Arab substrate piercing—breaking through from underneath—the occasion's Christian surface.

Another saeta, the first one I ever heard, is by Miles Davis, one of the pieces on his album *Sketches of Spain.* Miles was very attracted to flamenco. On the *Kind of Blue* album there is a cut called "Flamenco Sketches," and on a later album, the famous *Bitches Brew* that came out in 1970, there is a cut called "Spanish Key," all of which lends itself to the Andalusian/African American rapport we have seen Lorca and others get at. In late 1959 Miles teamed up with pianist/composer/arranger Gil Evans and recorded *Sketches of Spain.* One of the five pieces on the album is a saeta, with Miles, on trumpet, playing the role of the *cantaor*, the singer on the balcony. They go so far as to simulate a procession, opening and closing the cut, simply called "Saeta," with march music. One hears that tremulous, piercing sound Miles gets out of the trumpet, which there have been various attempts to describe. One critic called it the sound of a man walking on eggshells, and there is the story of a little girl who said he sounded like a little boy crying in a closet.

The next piece does not relate as explicitly to Andalusia but it still has to do with the things I have been discussing. It is John Coltrane with Miles Davis's group, from the last concert tour that Trane made as part of Miles's band. It was recorded in Stockholm in 1960 and released on the album *Miles Davis and John Coltrane Live in Stockholm 1960.* The solo he plays on Miles's composition "All Blues" has the quality of reaching for another voice, stretching the voice, passionately reaching; it has the quality of duende that Lorca talks about as a tearing of the voice, a crippling of the voice that paradoxically is also enabling. I have discussed, in an essay called "Sound and Sentiment, Sound and Symbol," the connection between limping and enablement in relation to the African god Legba, one of the gods of vodoun, candomblé, and lucumí. Legba is the god of doorways, gateways, entrances, thresholds, crossroads, intersections. Legba is crippled, the limping god who nonetheless dances. That conjunction of limping disability with the gracefulness of dance is one of the things I hear coming through in Trane's solo. This also relates to a forking of the voice, so that we hear the intersection of two lines of articulation—doubling the voice, splitting the voice, breaking the voice, tearing it. There is a dialogical aspect to African American and African music that is very strong. It comes across in call and response, the antiphonal relationship between lead singer and chorus, preacher and congregation. It comes across in the playing of musicians like John Coltrane, who use the upper and lower registers of the instrument as though they were two different voices in dialogue with one another, in a sometimes quarrelsome conversation with one another, competition with one another. In this instance Trane gets into doing some things with overtones, multiphonics, that make it sound as if he's playing two different horns, trying to play in two different octaves at the same time. It makes for an unruly, agonistic sound in which it seems that the two lines of articulation are wrestling, that they are somehow each other's contagion or contamination. It is appropriate that that solo should come in a piece called "All Blues."

This business of the pursuit of another voice, an alternate voice—in *Bedouin Hornbook* N. calls it the pursuit of a metavoice—is very much a part of the African American musical tradition, very much a part of the African musical tradition. The dialogical quality in music of this disposition can be heard in a number of different idioms and forms. The blues is certainly one of them, as can be heard in the next two pieces, both by a blues musician from the Mississippi delta, Mississippi Fred McDowell. One of the striking things about the blues tradition is the way the instrument becomes that other, alternate voice. Everyone talks about the speech-like qualities of instruments as they are played in African American music. Built into that is some kind of dissatisfaction with—if not critique of—the limits of conventionally articulate speech, verbal speech. One of the reasons the music so often goes over into nonspeech—moaning, humming, shouts, nonsense lyrics, scat—is to say, among other things, that the realm of conventionally articulate speech is not sufficient for saying what needs to be said. We are often making that same assertion in poetry. This is one of the reasons that in poetry we seek out "the trouble of an unbound reference" about which Duncan writes, as well as one of the reasons this music has been so attractive, so instructive, such an inspiration to poets.

In the music of Mississippi Fred McDowell one hears an interaction between voice and guitar, a slide guitar, the way the line between speech and song is very fluid, frequently blurred. This is very much a part of the tradition. There is an album called *Singing Preachers* that features preachers whose sermons would taper off into singing, speech into song, and vice versa, back and forth. In "Everybody's Down on Me" on his album *I Do Not Play No Rock 'n' Roll*, McDowell starts off talking and works talk into song. We get a mini-lecture, a sermonette as to what this recourse to *sound*, a sound peculiar to the slide guitar, a raucous, unruly wail, is about, what it comes out of. He talks about being betrayed, saying that you need an unruly, outrageous sound when you feel there's no other way you can get satisfaction. What you can say, what can be stated within the limits of conventionally articulate speech, is not enough. What you need is this *sound*. Notable too is the fact that he starts stumbling, the way he stumbles as he tries to talk about that sound until the sound itself comes to his rescue. The sound itself rescues crippled speech, which, again, is the eloquence of Legba, the limping eloquence or enablement of Legba.

Another context in which to think about this recourse to an alternate voice, this movement into a voice beyond one's voice, into a metavoice, is shamanism, the shamanic roots of music evoked by the Cuban writer Alejo Carpentier in his novel *The Lost Steps*. It was published in the 1950s and has to do with the journey of a composer/musician into the jungles of South America in search of the origins of music, something of an ethnomusicological expedition. Carpentier was, among other things, a musicologist. He did research, for example, into the African roots of Cuban music and culture, into lucumí and so forth, and his first novel, *Ecue-Yamba-O!* has to do with that. The recourse to another voice, the need for an alternate voice, is something he goes into in several passages in *The Lost Steps*. In the depths of a South American forest the narrator witnesses a shamanic rite performed over the body of a hunter who was killed by a rattlesnake bite. He takes this to be the origin of music; he sees the shamanic confrontation with death as the birth of music:

> . . . the shaman began to shake a gourd full of pebbles—the only instrument these people know—trying to drive off the emissaries of Death. There was a ritual silence, setting the stage for the incantation, which raised the tension of the spectators to fever pitch.
>
> And in the vast jungle filling with night terrors, there arose the Word. A word that was more than word. A word that imitated the voice of the speaker, and of that attributed to the spirit in possession of the corpse. One came from the throat of the shaman; the other from his belly. One was deep and confused

> like the bubbling of underground lava; the other, medium in pitch, was harsh and wrathful. They alternated. They answered each other. The one upbraided when the other groaned; the belly voice turned sarcastic when the throat voice seemed to plead. Sounds like guttural portamenti were heard, ending in howls; syllables repeated over and over, coming to create a kind of rhythm; there were trills suddenly interrupted by four notes that were the embryo of a melody. But then came the vibration of the tongue between the lips, the indrawn snoring, the panting contrapuntal to the rattle of the maraca. This was something far beyond language, and yet still far from song. Something that had not yet discovered vocalization, but was more than word.[15]

He later speaks of this as his having seen "the word travel the road of song without reaching it," and later still of "its verbal exorcism turning into music when confronted with the need for more than one intonation" (*LS* 200, 217).

Think about that in relation to La Niña de los Peines, whose voice breaks and seems intent on some higher octave, some higher voice. Think about it in relation to the John Coltrane solo, where, working with multiphonics, he voices discontent with the given intonation, bent on going beyond it. Think about it in relation to antiphony, the call-and-response, dialogical impulse that can be heard even in music played by a lone performer, the interplay between voice and instrument especially within the blues tradition, in the music of someone like Fred McDowell. One of the reasons for the development of slide guitar was the need to get a more human (but not quite human) sound out of the guitar, out of the instrumental line—human-but-not-quite-human speech as well as human-but-not-quite-human cry.

In the second piece by Fred McDowell, "Jesus Is on the Mainline," also on the *I Do Not Play No Rock 'n' Roll* album, one of the striking things is the way he lets the guitar speak, actually lets it take parts of his lines. He will begin singing a line only to break off and let the guitar finish it, suggesting a continuum, a complementarity, between human voice and instrumental voice, an interchange between speech and song, verbal articulation and nonverbal articulation. If you have read Ishmael Reed's novel *Mumbo Jumbo*, you may remember the episode in which he writes about an ancient musician named Jethro, an ancient Egyptian musician whose sound he describes as a kind of muddy, delta sound, blurring—muddying—the distinction between the Nile delta and the Mississippi delta. Fred McDowell's guitar has the kind of sound Reed has in mind.

Another example of multivocality is from an album with the shamanic title *I Talk with the Spirits*, recorded in the 1960s by Rahsaan Roland Kirk, who plays flute on it throughout. On a piece called "The Business Ain't Nothin' but the Blues," Rahsaan hums while playing, which is something other flute players sometimes do as well. Yusef Lateef is one of the first I ever heard do it. The technique has become something of a standard in the repertoire of jazz flutists. On the current scene, James Newton is a flutist who uses it a lot. Interestingly, it was not something that Eric Dolphy, who was a great flutist, did that much with, but that's another story. Rahsaan, though, hums and even speaks as he plays. Again, the play of voices, a move into multiple voices, is analogous to speaking in tongues. One hears a braiding of vocal and instrumental lines that holds a great deal of attraction for jazz musicians. I have even heard saxophone players hum while playing. Pharoah Sanders does it from time to time, and I have heard Dewey Redman do it as well. There is a piece in Amiri Baraka's book *Tales* in which he writes, "The dialogue exists. Magic and ghosts are a dialogue, and the body bodies of material, invisible sound vibrations, humming in emptyness, and ideas less than humming, humming. . . ."[16]

One of the things I have been discussing is cross-culturality, sensing rapport across cultural lines, picking up on rhymes between cultures, dialogue between cultures. A piece that presents Rahsaan's multivocal technique of humming while playing the flute in another context is a love song from Luristan, in Iran, found on the album *Folk Music of Iran*. It is performed by a singer accompanied by a flutist playing a reed flute known as a *nay*. The nay has quite a special place in the mystical traditions of that part of the world. Rumi, for example, writes of the nay, "Hearken to the reed-flute, how it complains, / Lamenting its banishment from its home."[17] He goes on to say that the reed was cut from rushes and that what we hear in the sound of the nay is the remembrance of that cutting, that the very sound calls to mind the cutting which brought it into being and which it laments. The sound subsists on that cutting. The nay not only mourns but embodies separation. Fittingly, the song from Luristan, simply called "Love Song" on the album, contains the lines "I am burning, / I have the taste of separation." In this song the flutist hums while playing the nay. In Iran this technique is known as *zemzemeh*. In this piece the splitting of the voice, the cultivation of a multiple voice, seems to embody at the instrumental level the "taste of separation" that is complained of in the lyrics. So again one hears humming, the additional voice and vibration it brings in, the buzz it elicits.

Think about that buzz, that vibration, that multiply-aspected vocality, in relation to poetry, to the cultivation of multiple meaning in poems, the play of polysemous articulation. A poem's order of statement is what has been called a buzz of implication, something one can hear in even a very brief passage. Take, for example, these lines of Robert Kelly's in a book called *Songs I–XXX*:

I was not a tree,
I hung in my bones like a man in a tree,
the tree talked . I said nothing[18]

The play of assertion against a recanting of assertion amounts to a buzz. The changes it registers concerning the status of treeness, the status of the speaker, and the status of speaking make the passage what Rahsaan took to calling his band: a vibration society. The words buzz, whisper among themselves, vibrate with such implicit assertions as that the tree that talks is a skeleton, that the man is not his bones, that bones are gallows, and so forth. I think of this also in relation to the cultivation of resonance in African music. In Zimbabwe, for example, they not only place the *mbira*, the so-called thumb piano, inside a calabash gourd, which they call a resonator, but they also attach cowrie shells to the outside of the gourd. The shells rub against the gourd and make a raspy, buzzing sound when the mbira is played. The African predilection for a burred, "dirty" sound, which the Camerounian musician/musicologist Francis Bebey, among others, has commented on, is reluctant to let a tone sit in some uncomplicated, isolated, supposedly pure sense of itself. Poems likewise buzz with meanings, implications, and insinuations that complicate, contaminate, "dirty" one another.

A piece that brings us full circle, back to Andalusian/African American resonances, is Sonny Rollins's "East Broadway Rundown" on the album of the same name. The bass player Jimmy Garrison takes a solo, playing the bass like a big guitar (which it is), playing it, more specifically, like a Spanish guitar—playing the flamenco riffs that came to be one of his trademarks. When Sonny Rollins comes in, what takes place is an interesting interchange that has remained a suggestive, poetic image for me over the years. Rollins removes the mouthpiece from his saxophone and plays it, sans horn. So, again, we have separation, severance, amputation. *Bedouin Hornbook* opens with the idea of music as a phantom limb, a phantom reach with/after something you have but do not have. It is a kind of re-membering, a mended dismemberment. This is one of the pieces that put that idea, that figure, into my head—a bassist playing flamenco while a horn player makes a voice, a high, falsetto voice, out of breakage, an alternate voice out of separating the mouthpiece from the horn.

I will finish by mentioning some further extensions and elaborations of cante moro. One of the interesting things that have been happening lately with flamenco in Spain is the assertion of its ties to the Moors, to some of the Arab musics of North Africa. This includes collaborations between flamenco musicians and North African performers of a type of music whose roots are in Muslim Spain, a type of music still known as Andalusian throughout the Maghreb. Two recorded instances are José Heredia Maya and the Andalusian Orchestra of Tetuan's *Macama Jonda* and Juan Peña Lebrijano and the Andalusian Orchestra of Tangier's *Encuentros.* In the 1970s and '80s Lole Montoya, of the group Lole and Manuel, recorded a number of songs in Arabic, traveling to the Sono Cairo studios in Egypt in 1977 to record a song made famous by the legendary Om Kalsoum, "Anta Oumri." Also interesting are the connections some of the younger flamenco musicians have made with New World extensions of the African-Iberian mix. A group called Ketama blends flamenco with Cuban rumba, Brazilian samba, and so forth. They have also collaborated with a kora player from Mali, Toumani Diabate. One of their influences is a musician named Manzanita, whose 1978 album *Poco Ruido y Mucho Duende* presented him accompanied by, as its liner notes explain, "dos músicos de color en razón a su sentido improvisatorio y a su 'feeling,' muy próximo al gitano" ("two black musicians because of their improvisatory sense and their 'feeling,' very close to that of the Gypsy"). The two musicians are bassist David Thomas, from the United States, and percussionist Pepe Ebano, from Cuba. Another of Ketama's influences is singer Camarón, who in the late 1970s expanded his instrumental accompaniment to include trap drums, keyboards, and electric bass. Finally, a few years ago a group called Pata Negra released an album called *Blues de la Frontera.* As is clear from the title, they play a flamenco-blues mix. It builds on the rapport that has long been noted between the two. I remember hearing a radio documentary on Jimi Hendrix. One segment was a tape from a recording session, maybe a jam, and Hendrix was talking to the other musicians and said, "What I want is a Muddy Waters/flamenco sound." The other musicians said, "Yeah!" Everyone knew exactly what he meant. No problem.

Blue in Green

Black Interiority

> It's in the crackling blue,
> blue without a single worm or sleeping footprint . . .
>
> —FEDERICO GARCÍA LORCA

I'd like to talk a bit about what brought us all to this conference: Miles Davis's sound. By the early 1950s that sound was unmistakable, uniquely and recognizably his, a sound that would become *the* sound, the timbral concept influencing trumpeter after trumpeter, both those established and those coming up. "A round sound with no attitude in it" is what he said he was after, but it was a sound a great deal of attitude would attach to. Wayne Shorter recalls himself and his friends hearing Miles for the first time in Charlie Parker's band in the late 1940s; "the guy with the strange sound on the trumpet," they called him. The image of a man walking on eggshells and that of a little boy crying in a closet are two of the best-known attempts to describe that strangeness, that oddly familiar strangeness—what Walter Bishop Jr. called "this haunting kind of a sound."

Miles took the horn in a distinct direction that, while not entirely new, moved it farther along a path it was already on. It was the path from reveille to reverie—extrovert, heraldic axe turned introspective. "He changed the tone of the trumpet for the first time since Louis Armstrong," Gil Evans once remarked. "Everybody between Louis Armstrong and Miles Davis basically came from Louis Armstrong, but that sound, that timbre, hadn't been changed until Miles did that. . . . That's what's known as a sound innovator. And there aren't too many."[1] It was an inward turn, an expansion of ruminative space—vulnerable, confidential, prayerful at points. In the prologue to *Invisible Man*, Ralph Ellison has the narrator marvel over the way Armstrong "bends that military instrument into a beam of lyrical sound." Miles took that bend even further, wresting hard-won reflective space from a notoriously demanding instrument, hard-won interiority, black interiority, from a social sphere and performance venues invested heavily in assumptions of black outwardness. As is well known, he turned his back on showmanship, a turn concomitant with the sound he got from the horn. His comments on his predecessors in this regard bear repeating:

> As much as I love Dizzy and loved Louis "Satchmo" Armstrong, I always hated the way they used to laugh and grin for the audiences. I know *why* they did it—to make money and because they were entertainers as well as trumpet players. They had families to feed. Plus they both liked acting the clown; it's just the way Dizzy and Satch were. I don't have nothing against them doing it if they want to. But *I* didn't like it and didn't *have* to like it. . . . I was younger than them and didn't have to go through the shit they had to go through to get accepted in the music industry. They had already opened up a whole lot of doors for people like me to go through, and I felt that I could be about just playing my horn—the only thing I wanted to do. I didn't look at myself as an entertainer like they both did. I wanted to be accepted as a good musician and that didn't call for no grinning, but just being able to play the horn good.[2]

The point is that the two went together, the change in sound and the change in stage demeanor.

Contrasting Dizzy Gillespie's bravura introduction to his 1946 big band recording of "'Round Midnight" with Miles's introduction to his 1955 quintet recording of the same tune, as Jon Faddis did a few years back on "The Miles Davis Radio Project," typifies the difference. Faddis commented,

> Dizzy was definitely a big influence on Miles's life. He had him study the piano for harmony, and that, of course, is one of Miles's big contributions to jazz, his harmonic concept. Taking a line like the introduction that Dizzy wrote to "'Round Midnight"—it goes something like this, the original line:

> That's the way Dizzy wrote the line. But Miles, because of his, I guess, great creative sense, his sense of harmony and his sense of space, took . . . the most important notes and played around with them. . . . Instead of going

Dizzy's introduction does indeed introduce; it comes close to fanfare. We're at the start of something, something being heralded, an announcement that something's coming. Miles's introduction introduces in another way. It introduces *us* into what's already underway, already there. We're not so much addressed as allowed to listen in, given the sense that he's completing a thought whose beginning we've not been privy to. This approach puts more night into the piece. It broods. It brings reflection to the fore. It's a characteristic move, the meaning of all that blue in so many of his titles: "Bluing," "Blue in Green," "All Blues," "No Blues," "Trane's Blues," "Blues No. 2," "Blue Haze," "Vierd Blues," "Red China Blues," "Blues by Five," "Blue Xmas," "I'm Blue," "Out of the Blue," *Kind of Blue*. James Hillman suggests that blue "deepens the idea of reflection beyond the single notion of mirroring, to the further notions of pondering, considering, meditating."[3] William Gass writes that blue is "the color consciousness becomes when caressed."[4] That's what we hear when we hear Miles, who said he saw colors when he played, and who would seem to have seen blue a lot: the sound of consciousness being caressed. Just as a certain withholding we hear in Billie Holiday's voice heightens, by way of contrast, the emotional extremity her lyrics announce, Miles's less-is-more approach appears to make deliberative thought audible, palpable—deliberative thought itself, not simply the decisions at which it has arrived. This is partly what he meant when he spoke of "playing what isn't there."

Miles's approach—"the concept of space breathing through the music" he called it—highlights analysis, dissection, the act of selection, discernment, choice. "Back in bebop," he said, "everybody used to play real fast. But I didn't ever like playing a bunch of scales and shit. I always tried to play the most important notes in the chord, to break it up" (*M* 70). In so doing, he made the music more palpably a vehicle for thinking out loud, though the "out loud" was in fact an effect of his use of silence—reticent sound, it seemed, making cognition a manifest presence. That he took to painting later in life makes perfect sense; there was something painterly, sculptorly, in the rhythms of implication, the pace and placement with which he stroked out a solo, carved out a solo, worked sound as a thick medium, texturable, shaped. His music during the 1950s and '60s recalls Rainer Maria Rilke referring to music as "breathing of statues," and it's worth noting that another poet, Kamau Brathwaite, invokes Miles to make a point about the visual aspect of African oral tradition, writing that "it is there in the Griot, that is the man who does the singing and the history, orally. It is also there in the sculpture. It is a very intimate relationship between what he has to say and what he carves. There is always a visual underpinning. You think of Egypt and the Sphinx and the pyramids and all that. It is a strong oral tradition, which is underpinned by this remarkable visual monument. The monument itself is an abstraction, like a Miles Davis solo. It is a skeleton of the song."[5] Such abstraction flies in the face of condescending notions of immediatist, nonreflective blackness.

Ornette Coleman writes of having heard Eubie Blake tell of times when he was playing in black bands for white audiences and they would have to go on stage without any written music. They would look over the music backstage, then leave it there and go out on stage and play it. "He was saying," Coleman writes, "that they had a more saleable appeal if they pretended to not know what they were doing. The white audience felt safer."[6] A fearful, grudging acknowledgment of black intelligence (the "hive of subtleties" that Babo's head is said to be in Herman Melville's "Benito Cereno") haunted such audiences. Just as going on stage with written music would have done in that situation, to insist, as Miles did, on presence of mind in black music went contrary to prevailing divisions of cultural labor, broke with notions of black creativity as raw, unstudied instinct. Bebop had already moved in that direction and Miles took it further. "We were like scientists of sound," he remarked (*M* 63)—a trope that occurs in even more pronounced form among later musicians such as Lester Bowie, who appears on stage in a lab coat, or Anthony Braxton, with his diagrammatic titles, "Kelvin" compositions, and the like.

"From reveille to reverie," I said earlier, but I don't mean to suggest there was anything unawakened about it. The music has a distinct nocturnal atmosphere, a decidedly dark feel to it, an atmosphere and a feel explicitly advanced, for example, by the lullaby-like saxophone line that opens "All Blues," the rocked-cradle figure on bass underneath. But the sound, even so, is one of emergence—on speaking terms with dream, without a doubt, but awake nonetheless. On a piece like "Blue in Green," whose title I've taken for this talk, the squeezed-out, put-through-a-strainer sound Miles gets with the mute builds like something culled from lengthy immersion, deep sleep even, Ellington/Ellison's Jack-the-Bear coming out of hibernation. It has the sound of a yawn and a stretch, an emergent mix of inward and outward redefining the horn: horn yes, but beyond being horn, gnostic host. Cassandra Wilson heard it this way, harking back to Miles's Spanish ruminations in the lyrics she put to the tune, where she echoes Pedro Calderón de la Barca's title, *La vida es sueño*: "And life is but a dream of blue and green."[7] Then, later: "We'll always sail this way, until we find our home." The being "tossed between the sky and sea" that she sings about images the forlorn, refugee sound coming out of the horn, the play between tone and toneless texture, the timbral chill he cloaks the higher notes in.

But before I make too much of a mystic out of Miles, let's not forget the renegotiation of social and commercial arrangements that accompanied his "concept of space breathing through the music." He was responsible, for example, for reducing the number of sets expected of musicians by club owners, eliminating the "forty-twenty" sets (play forty minutes, rest twenty, every hour) that could add up to four or five a night. He simply refused to go on playing them. The reflective space that he made a place for in the music is not unrelated to the demands he made for more pay, fewer sets, and the like. These too were demands for more space, for greater latitude and leverage, a conscious renegotiation of the terms defining the black musician's place in American commerce and culture. Such demands, as was the music itself, were participant in senses of black emergence during the 1950s and into the '60s, in what would come to be called black consciousness. They were also participant in the growth of consumer culture and consumerist consciousness during the postwar period. The successful commoditization of jazz was the "action" of which Miles demanded—and got—a bigger piece, becoming one of the most financially successful jazz musicians ever. ("He plays all right for a millionaire," Cecil Taylor once quipped [*M* 251].) And with that commoditization, not only the music but Miles himself became a consumable artifact, a consumable image at least—consumable as model consumer, connoisseur. As inward as his music was or seemed to be, he also became famous for his attention to outward things. His taste in fine clothes, fine cars, and fine women, at a time when a new venture such as *Playboy* was lucratively extolling "gentlemanly" discernment in exactly such matters, was as much a part of the package as his impeccable choice of notes. That outward attentiveness and appetite led to a desire for an even bigger piece of the action, for access to spaces beyond those jazz could offer. Miles's desire, in the 1970s and '80s, to move away from jazz venues and jazz audiences, to gain access to larger, more lucrative spaces and larger, more lucrative audiences, led him to a music whose clutter was antithetical to the reflective space in which he carved out the authority that clutter cashed in. Blue got lost in green.

But that's another story. I'm here not to judge the later music so much as testify to what of Miles's music speaks most to me, that of the 1950s and '60s in particular, music I cut many a reflective tooth on. Amiri Baraka once wrote something about John Coltrane's music that applies to Miles's as well: "If you can hear, this music will make you think of a lot of weird and wonderful things. You might even become one of them."[8] Though I'm not a weird and wonderful thing myself, I've met a few. The Boneyard Brass Octet, for example, the band my friend N. sat in with one night:

> By now time was of course beside the point, my own bovine persistence with regard to the skirt the mirrored image of the Octet's "baby elephant walk." What I mean is that the trombones had been joined by the rest of the band, the vamp taken up with the ruminative patience of some lumbering beast. The staggered entrance of the trumpets made for a certain halo around the figure, something almost like a spray which if one were not "awake" would tend to overcome "sleep." But here "sleep" moved thru an atmosphere so absolutely one with its own hypnotic arousal as to activate an army of otherwise overt, albeit rhapsodized obstructions. Dewey, that is, came on with the sputtering eloquence (if not opulence) of a Bill Dixon, while Tyrone nicked one's ears with a knifelike pointedness worthy of muted Miles. The self-predicating ordeal of Dewey's Dixonian approach rubbed against the slickness of what Tyrone proposed, the result of which was a splintered voice which came off like an elapsed or elusive aspect of itself. Under their care the vamp grew to be poetically graced in such a way as to suggest that to adorn, whatever else it might also be, is to adore. It was some of the most heartfelt trumpet work I've ever heard.[9]

Or my friend N.'s friend Derek:

> He teaches music out at Cal Arts and he's planning a symposium, at which he's invited me to give a talk. He got interested in something he calls "propositional positionality" a few years back. He was in a workshop run by Joseph Jarman at

the Creative Music Studio in Woodstock. Jarman, it seems, turned to a horn player at one point and asked him to stand up and play something. The horn player stood up but before he could start playing Jarman stopped him, saying, "Wait a minute. Notice the stance. It's a statement. The instrumentalist as sculpture. *Notice* it. We usually take it for granted but we can *use* it." This clicked with an idea Derek had been carrying around for some time—namely that people weren't being precise enough in discussing Miles Davis turning his back on his audiences, that sufficient note had yet to be made of the fact that the angle at which his back addressed the audience tended to vary in relation to a host of contextual factors and coefficients. The upshot was that he set about quantifying and chronologizing—based on photographs, films, second-hand accounts and first-hand observation—the positional/propositional variables attendant upon Miles's posture, or, as he himself puts it, the "semiotemporal calculus of Miles's postural kinematics." He's published two or three monographs discussing his findings. Anyway, this developed into a more general interest in the "semantics of movement and posture," one of the results of which is the symposium he's planning for the spring having to do with "Locus and Locomotivity in Postcontemporary Music," the one at which he's invited me to speak. (*BH* 111–12)

Or my friend N. himself, his shattered cowrie shell attacks:

I have . . . had occasion to do some reflection and self-diagnosis these past few days. A remark my mother made the other day sparked it. We were talking on the phone, me telling her about the latest round of attacks, the quandary they've got me in, the dizziness, trances and so forth, when she said, "It's all that music, all those records you've been buying all these years." I laughed. "No, seriously," she went on, "all those records doing all that spinning have made you dizzy." I laughed again, my only defense. It was an old axe, one she's been grinding ever since I was a kid. My mother, as I may have told you already, has never really understood my becoming a musician. Virtually nothing, as far as she's concerned, could be more impractical. I recall times as a kid when I'd buy a record and have to sneak it into the house, so upset would she get at my "throwing away good money."

Still, it's an axe I've come to take more seriously than my laughter let on. It set me to thinking. Are the attacks a self-sentencing conviction the music fosters and feeds, even if only as the occasion for a reprieve? Are self-sentencing conviction and self-commuting sentence merely symbiotic halves of a self-cycling ordeal? Do I knock myself down in order to be picked up?

> Someone I once read remarked on the need to produce an inventory of traces. What better place to begin, I've been thinking, than with those discs I used to smuggle into the house? Records we call them. Rightly so.
>
> I've been listening a lot these past couple of days to one such disc, Miles's *Seven Steps to Heaven*, one of the first I ever bought. I can't help hearing it as a repository of imprints which long ago went to work on me, set up shop (tenuous hope, tenuous heaven) in my perhaps too-impressionable heart (foolish heart). The title of one of the cuts, my favorite in fact, practically jumped off the album jacket at me: "I Fall In Love Too Easily." There it was. A complete sentence. This indeed was one of the cuts which made me.
>
> And the other titles, even when only fragments or phrases, likewise had a sentencing effect. "So Near So Far" gave an apt enough description of the tenuous heaven it whetted one's appetite for. It was an old dialectical story: possibility paradoxically parented by prohibition. Not only did vertigo set in, a quixotic dizziness and discontent, but one's heavensent stagger turned into a blue compensatory strut. Blue earth itself was made even bluer by the tenuous ladder one took it for. Listen, if you don't believe me, to "Basin Street Blues."
>
> My mother's axe notwithstanding, I accept it all, even the scratches and the nicks, the points on the record where the needle skips. Noisy reminders of the wear of time they may very well be, but I hear them as rickety, quixotic rungs on a discontinuous ladder—quixotic leaps or ellipses (quantum lump in one's throat) meted out by contraband heaven having set up shop.[10]

N.'s shattered cowrie shell hits are the shards of heaven he hears breathing through the music, blown but still alive in the music. Not unlike N., I was assisted by Miles early on to imagine not only that such a heaven exists but that there are steps, rickety rungs notwithstanding, one might take to reach it. That at times his pursuit of such steps took a turn through hell I would find out later, but that's also another story.

"It's not about notes, it's about sound," Roscoe Mitchell once said. Miles Davis, his painstaking choice of notes notwithstanding, implicitly said the same. I've ended up saying less about his sound than I set out to, a fact that itself says something about that sound. Something about it, perhaps everything about it, defies definitive capture, akin to what, painterly smudge and bent note both, *kind of* in the title *Kind of Blue* allows blue to do. It's as if notes—and, in this case, words—were at best a wager. When that sound hits, all bets are off.

Paracritical Hinge

When I received the invitation to speak at this colloquium the theme "Collaborative Dissonances: Jazz, Discrepancy, and Cultural Theory" struck a responsive chord. It seemed to be or to propose to be a colloquium after my own heart, a colloquium attentive to the role of improvisation in advancing collaborative/discrepant encounters and to the bearing of such encounters on the theorization of cultural agency and value. When I read, among the topics for consideration in the call for papers, of "the 'cognitive dissonance' that results when creative practitioners enter collaboration from different disciplinary and/or cultural locations," I said yes. When I read of "the extent to which the dissonances that result from collaborative practices might be seen to reduce the effects of hierarchies in the production and valuation of knowledge," I said yes. When I read of "the cultural work of 'participatory discrepancies' (Charles Keil) . . . the implications of Keil's claim that 'Music, to be personally involving and socially valuable, must be 'out of time' and 'out of tune,'" I again said yes. When I read of "the emancipatory potential of 'discrepant engagement,' of 'practices that, in the interest of opening presumably closed orders of identity and signification, accent fissure, fracture, incongruity' (Nathaniel Mackey)," I again, of course, said yes, but the quotation from my book of essays *Discrepant Engagement* and the recourse to the coinage that gives the book its title made me fear my presence here might be redundant. I wasn't sure that simply reiterating my call for discrepant engagement was quite what was in order.

What I decided was to highlight the practice of mine out of which, more than any single other, the critical formulation I call discrepant engagement emerged. That practice is the writing of fiction, specifically that of a work called *From a Broken Bottle Traces of Perfume Still Emanate*, running through which are installments of a scribal-performative undertaking known as "The Creaking of the Word," a name borrowed from the Dogon of Mali that I see as related to—a parent or an ancestor to—discrepant engagement. In the introduction to *Discrepant Engagement* I put it this way: "Recalling the derivation of the word *discrepant* from a root meaning 'to rattle, creak,' I relate discrepant engagement to the name the Dogon of West Africa give their weaving block, the base on which the loom they weave upon sits. They call it the 'creaking of the word.' It is the noise upon which the word is based, the discrepant foundation of all coherence and articulation, of the purchase upon the world fabrication affords."[1] The writing of *From a Broken Bottle*, I want to emphasize, played a large part in what led me to this. I want also to suggest that the promise of collaborative dissonances that the colloquium seeks, I assume, to advance as well as examine might accrue to bearing that discrepant foundation in mind.

From a Broken Bottle grew out of my interest in the relationships between literature and the improvisatory music we call jazz, an interest reflected in *Discrepant Engagement*'s repeated recourse to jazz (and African American music more generally) as an instructive model of artistic and cultural experimentation, a music whose lessons have not been lost on a number of the writers dealt with in the book nor on me in my role as writer-critic. One such lesson is a discontent with categories and the boundaries they enforce, with the impediment to social and aesthetic mobility such enforcement effects. Saxophonist Oliver Lake writes, in the poem "Separation" on the jacket to his 1976 album *Ntu: Point from which Creation Begins*,

> first it's the salad
>   then the meat
>   then the vegetables. . . .
>   "WAIT"
> bring all my food at one time on the same plate!
> dixieland, be-bop, soul, rhythm & blues, cool school, swing, avante-garde, jazz, free jazz, rock, jazz-rock
>
> WHAT KINDA MUSIC U PLAY?
>
>   "GOOD KIND"
>
> Aretha franklin & Sun Ra is the same folks,
> Coltrane & the Dixie humming birds same folks
> Miles & muddy waters same. there is no. . . . . there is no . . . .

LABELS DIVIDE! SEPARATE
THE ORAL AND THE LITERARY

> One music—diff feelings & experience, but same. . . . the total sound—mass sound—hear all the players as one[2]

Lake's insistence accents a history of boundary crossing that resonates throughout the music, a history that begins with the contributions made to the development of early New Orleans jazz by the closer association between the black middle class of the time—Creoles, *gens de couleur*, mulattoes—and working-class black people from whom they had held themselves apart. That history includes Charlie Parker's famous quotations from such disparate material as Woody Woodpecker cartoons and Georges Bizet's *Carmen*, Yusef Lateef's recourse to non-Western instruments and traditions, Archie Shepp's inclusion of march music in his avant-garde classic "A Portrait of Robert Thompson (as a young man)," John Handy's collaborations with Ali Akbar Khan, Don Cherry's use of Balinese gamelan instruments on his *Eternal Rhythm* album, and so on.

Boundary crossing and its implied if not explicit critique of categorization deeply informed *Discrepant Engagement* and *From a Broken Bottle* both. I used a line from Bessie Smith's "Black Mountain Blues" as the title of the former's introduction, explaining, "I have . . . offered its fortuitous, figurative title, 'And All the Birds Sing Bass,' as a discrepant note meant to call attention to the problematics of rubric-making, a caveat meant to make the act of categorization creak. Such creaking is always present, even in the case of more customary groupings—groupings that appear unproblematic, proper, only because we agree not to hear it" (*DE* 21). Improvisation, in its divergence from the given, frequently will not allow us not to hear noise, the creaking of categorization, the noise categorization suppresses and the noise, not admitting doing so, it makes. The cacophonous element of the avant-garde jazz of the 1960s is an obvious example, a relativization of the very notion of noise that reflected critically upon the term's employment as an instrument of dismissal and derogation. Such relativization valorizes noise as the antidote to the derogation the term conventionally conveys, not unlike the manner in which Cuban poet Nicolás Gullén reclaims the Spanish term *algarabía*, "noisy chatter," as what Vera Kutzinski calls a "master trope for cross-cultural exchange." *Algarabía*, Kutzinski points out, literally means "Arabic" and its etymological origins go back to the Moorish occupation of Spain, to associations with the oriental bazaars that came to be commonplace in medieval Spain.[3] The equation of Arabic with "noisy chatter," of the bazaar's linguistic and cultural heterogeneity with "noisy chatter," reminds us that the notion of noise is often freighted with xenophobic predilections (some of Thelonious Monk's early detractors accused him of playing "Chinese music"), the very predilections cross-cultural dialogue and discrepant collaboration seek to overcome. An attribution of otherness available to xenophobic recoil and cross-cultural espousal as well, dismissive predilection as well as discrepant embrace, noise, whether derogatorily engaged or affirmatively engaged, frequently functions as the sign of alterity, the sound of alterity.

The creaking of the word's boundary crossing, its critique of categorization, entails a critique and a complication of genre. *From a Broken Bottle*'s conversation with improvisatory music necessarily involved me in a practice of writing that, in terms of genre, was multiform if not indeterminate. The work, as James Weldon Johnson said of the early ragtime songs, "jes' grew." What began as brief, prose-poetic, manifesto-like letters of an *ars poetica* sort grew into longer excursions that, while for the most part maintaining the epistolary form, availed themselves of aspects of conventional as well as experimental narrative, essayistic analysis and reflection, diaristic and anecdotal elements, literary-critical techniques and a variety of influences ranging from mythology to anthropology to album liner notes. The work's multiformity, its improvisatory sampling or juggling of different discourses, genres and forms, involved me in a practice of discrepant engagement spurred or inspired by characteristics of the music it sought, so to speak, to be in concert with. Art Lange and I, in the editors' note to our anthology *Moment's Notice: Jazz in Poetry and Prose*, wrote, among other things, of "writings which blur the line between genres, bending genre in ways which are analogous to a musician bending notes."[4] *From a Broken Bottle* increasingly declared itself, early on, to be of that order. The music's origins among people policed by racial categorization suggest that it bends notes in an effort, as Ralph Ellison puts it, to hear and see around corners, outmaneuver the rigidities of a taxonomic grid. Think, in this regard, of writing that similarly bends genre while indicting racial taxonomy, such multiform, mixed-genre writing as W. E. B. Du Bois's *The Souls of Black Folk*, Jean Toomer's *Cane*, or Ishmael Reed's *Mumbo Jumbo*, and of the insistency with which it invokes African American music.

The creaking of the word's critique of categorization also, of course, entails a critique and a complication of language, a critique and a complication of which those of genre are necessarily part and parcel, a critique and a complication of that which is nothing if not an instrument of categorization. The creaking of the word critiques and complicates the word, spurred in part by instrumental music's wordlessness, the apparent dispensability of words, and in part by the music's emulation of speech, its deployment of speechlike rhythms and inflections as if in possession of words or aspiring to be so. As Lange and I wrote,

> It is particularly unsurprising that a music which so frequently and characteristically aspires to the condition of speech, reflecting critically, it seems, upon the limits of the sayable, should have provoked and proved of enormous interest to practitioners of the art of the word—writers. . . . In addition to offering tributes to and portraits of individual musicians, depictions of and meditations upon the social and cultural milieu in which the music exists, evocations of the music's import for specific audiences and so forth, writers have been moved to inspect, as artists witnessing other artists wrestling with the limits of their particular medium, the possibilities and resistances peculiar to writing. Mack Thomas once wrote, in liner notes, of Eric Dolphy confronting "the barrier that begins with what the horn will not do." Writers, tracking what John Clellon Holmes calls "the unnameable truth of music," have had to deal with a similar confrontation. Charles Lloyd, asked to comment on a piece of his music by a radio interviewer, answered, "Words don't go there." Writers influenced by jazz have been variously rising to the challenge of proving him wrong. (*MN* i–ii)

That challenge is also, I would add, a contagion, an infectious testing of terms and limits that wants not to hold itself apart, wants to close, among other distances, conventional critical distance. It wants to be anthropologist and informant both, participant-observer.

So this will be more a reading than a paper or a talk. I'd like to try, in line with the colloquium's theme of collaboration, to get fiction to "sit in" with the kinds of critical and analytic discourse characteristic of colloquia, to pursue the possibility of fiction collaborating with those kinds of discourse. The fiction in question, *From a Broken Bottle*, perhaps enhances that possibility by being fiction that, as I've already stated, doesn't entirely reside within the genre of fiction. It's a type of fiction that wants to be a door or to support a door or to open a door permitting flow between disparate orders of articulation. It wants to be what I call a paracritical hinge, permitting flow between statement and metastatement, analysis and expressivity, criticism and performance, music and literature, and so forth. It traffics in a mix—a discrepant, collaborative mix—of idioms, genres, registers, dispositions. (*Paracritical* is meant, of course, to echo and to be analogous to such terms as *paramedical* and *paralegal*, its prefix indicating an auxiliary, accessory relationship to criticism, a near equation with or a close resemblance to criticism. *Merriam-Webster's Eleventh Collegiate Dictionary* defines a hinge as "a jointed or flexible device on which a door, lid, or other swinging part turns." I'd like to suggest a translative project or prospect in a quality so often attributed to the music, the quality—the verb, not the noun—known as swing. *Hinge*'s work as verb highlights contingency, haunted by tenuousness and risk, an intransitive creaking well worth bearing in mind. The coinage wants to suggest that improvisation, the pursuit of new expressivity, whether musical or literary, is an operation best characterized by the prefix *para-*, an activity supplemental to more firmly established disciplines and dispositions, an activity that hinges on a near but divergent identity with given disciplines and dispositions. The given is just the beginning.) It's a work in which, while not a musician, I write as a musician. Comprised of letters written to an "Angel of Dust" by a composer/multi-instrumentalist who signs his letters "N.," it began in the late 1970s and consists, so far, of three volumes, *Bedouin Hornbook*, *Djbot Baghostus's Run*, and *Atet A.D.* I'd like to read a selection of letters from the latter that bear on the colloquium's concerns (intermedia and interdisciplinary conversation, improvisation's utopic horizon, cultural theory's diagnostic desire—all shaded by a blue, dystopic truth), but let me, before I do that, say a bit about the work's genesis.

The work began, no doubt, in the dreams I had during my late teens and early twenties of playing with some of the greats of the music. These were literal dreams in which I played alongside John Coltrane, Ornette Coleman, Thelonious Monk, and others. I repeatedly had these dreams. But that was fantasy, not yet fiction, albeit the letter that begins *Bedouin Hornbook*, the first volume in the series, grew out of a related dream I had one night in my early thirties, a dream in which, although I played alone, the presence of Eric Dolphy seemed implied by the fact that I played a bass clarinet, that of John Coltrane by the fact that the tune I intended to play was "Naima," that of Archie Shepp by the fact that what I actually played was "Cousin Mary" done the way he plays it on *Four for Trane.* The catalyst for the work took place several months prior to this dream however. I was living in Los Angeles at the time and had already written a couple of "Angel of Dust" letters as part of a serial poem called "Song of the Andoumboulou"; they were really short statements on poetics. What planted the idea of N. writing as a musician and prompted, eventually, the

"Cousin Mary" letter I just mentioned—which is the letter that got the series going on a track of its own, apart from "Song of the Andoumboulou," the letter in which N. announces the formation of a band—was an odd concert I went to one night.

This was in 1977. There was a concert series at the Century City Playhouse that presented "outside" music on Sunday nights. I saw posters announcing a concert by a group called A Love Supreme, a name that piqued my interest, so I decided I'd go, which I did. What was odd about it was that I was the only person to show up. I got there to find that, besides the band, there were only three people there: the fellow I bought a ticket from at the ticket window, the fellow who took my ticket at the door, and me. Even so, I went in and sat down and before too long the lights lowered and the band came onstage and played—for me. It was a strange experience, as though I was there on a special assignment or by special appointment, an appointment I didn't know I had, an odd appointment of an almost mystic sort. The band played and I sat, an audience of one, listening, wondering why in a city of over two million people and a greater metropolitan area of several more million, I was the only person to show up to hear a band called A Love Supreme. (I later learned that the band was led by a fellow named Shamsu-'d-Din. I was told this by saxophonist Ghasem Batamuntu, who sat in with the band that night. I don't know what's become of Shamsu-'d-Din, but Ghasem later moved to the San Francisco Bay Area, where he started a band called the Nova Ghost Sect * Tet, and then on to Amsterdam, where he currently lives. The Nova Ghost Sect * Tet recently released a CD, *Life on Uranus*, on a Dutch label, A-Records.) I felt as though I'd been summoned. It felt almost as though I was part of the band, had been inducted into the band. It started me wondering, at least, what being in such a band might be like. That one of the members of the band read poetry from a notebook at one point during the concert not only seemed intent on saying the music invited poetic support, literary assistance or accompaniment, but seemed as well to be directed at me. That, along with wondering what being in a band like that might be like, led eventually to *From a Broken Bottle* and the fictional band in which N. plays, known first as the Deconstructive Woodwind Chorus, next as the East Bay Dread Ensemble, next as the Mystic Horn Society, most recently as the Molimo m'Atet.

So I'd like to read from this work that in a sense responded to what I felt was a call. I'll read four letters from the third volume, *Atet A.D.* Before doing so, I should note that the band began as a quintet, consisting of reedmen Lambert and Penguin, violinist/percussionist/bassist Aunt Nancy, and keyboardist/vocalist Djamilaa in addition to reedman/trumpeter N., and that the second volume, *Djbot Baghostus's Run*, is largely taken up with the decision to add a drummer to the group and the decision that the drummer would be a woman. A search ensues, during which the three men in the band are beset by the same dream, a collective dream that seems to announce that the drummer will be named Djeannine, and the two women in the band are likewise beset by a shared dream, one that appears to announce that the drummer will be named Penny. When they find the right drummer her name turns out to be Drennette. Penguin, in the course of Drennette's first few weeks in the band, takes a liking to her and eventually makes an aborted romantic overture, out of embarrassment over which he goes into hiding. *Djbot Baghostus's Run* ends with no one in the band knowing where Penguin is. In *Atet A.D.* he returns, comes out of seclusion. Penguin's primary horn is the oboe, whose "high wood" root (*haut bois*) is construed, given his quixotic bent, as "high would." He turns out to have been in retreat in a place called Wouldly Ridge. The first letter I'll read is written a few months after his return from Wouldly Ridge, during a gig in Seattle.

•

_________________ 5.VI.82

Dear Angel of Dust,

The other shoe finally dropped. We're in Seattle playing a three-night stint at a club called Soulstice. Last night, the first night of the gig, new repercussions on a number of fronts came to light. Foremost among them is that the wouldly subsidence in which Penguin and Drennette's embryonic romance had gotten hung up seems to've given way, exacting a ledge, an atomistic ledge, from the lapse it rescinded. You've no doubt noticed that since Penguin's return from Wouldly Ridge it's been as though his embryonic courtship of Drennette had never occurred. He's not only not pursued it further, he'll neither speak nor hear talk of it. Whenever I've brought it up he's acted like he had no idea what I was talking about, staring at me with a blank, uncomprehending look on his face, as though English were a foreign language, as if I spoke some unheard-of tongue. Aunt Nancy, Lambert and Djamilaa say it's been the same with them.

Drennette likewise has acted like nothing ever happened. She and Penguin have been nothing but normal in their dealings with one another.

It's hard to say what it was, why it was wouldly subsidence took this occasion to exact wouldly ledge. My guess is that the air of anticlimactic futurity pervading this town had something to do with it, the datedness of what was once thought of as "things to come." I'm referring, of course, to the Space Needle. That the future has no place in which to arrive but the present, that its arrival is thus oxymoronic, is the sort of reflection one can't help entertaining in the shadow of such a monument as that—a monument, when it was built, to the future, a future it prematurely memorialized, prematurely entombed. Today it's more properly a monument to the past, a reminder of the times in which it was built, tomb to the elapsed expectancy it all turns out to've been. I remember my aunt and uncle driving up for the World's Fair twenty years ago—hopelessly long ago it seems now.

But by no means to be ignored is the reinforcement given elapsed or outmoded future by us happening to hear "Telstar," the early sixties hit by the Tornadoes, on the jukebox in a diner we had lunch in yesterday. The tinny, strained, "futuristic" sound of it said it all, spoke to a sense of lost occasion elapsed future began infusing us with the moment we laid eyes on that Needle. I thought of every wish which had seemed to miss the mark in being fulfilled, though I corrected myself at once, admitting the case to be one of an "it" which could only be projected, never arrived at. Anticlimactic "it," I reminded myself, allotted virtual space, an ironic investiture missed opportunity couldn't help but inhabit. Disappointment, the needling sense of a missed appointment, couldn't help but be there. This we knew before "Telstar" came on. We knew it all the more once it did.

The weather played a part as well. It hasn't rained outright since we've been here but it's been overcast and drizzling, a thin mist coming down pretty much all the time. That mist, it seemed, went with us into the club last night. It adopted a low profile for the occasion, close to the floor like a carpet so intimate with our feet we'd have sworn we dragged it in. What had been of the air was now oddly underfoot. In a way it was like the world had turned upside down, the way the mist, instead of falling from the sky, came up from the floor, ever so lightly addressing the soles of our feet. The difference this would make in our music was evident at once. No sooner had we taken the stage than the low-lying mist was an atomistic ledge we stood on which made our feet feel as though they'd fallen asleep—not entirely numb but (you know the feeling I'm sure) put upon by pins, subject to a sort of pointillist embrace. Point had become a hydra, its pinpoint tactility multiply-pinned. We couldn't help knowing it was "missed" on which we stood (missed mark, missed opportunity, missed appointment), no less real, no less an actual mist even so. What it came down to was an odd, pointillist plank-walk, notwithstanding we walked in place if it can be said we walked at all. The ledge onto which we stepped calibrated a tenuous compound or compaction of low-lying spray with spreading phantasmality (phantom feet and/or the phantom ledge on which "missed" insisted we stood).

We stood on lost, oddly elevated ground, elegiac ledge. This was no mere materialization of loss even so, no glib legitimation of lack, elegy (lapsed eligibility) notwithstanding. We stood upon or perhaps had already stepped across an eccentric threshold, thrust, or so it seemed, into a post-expectant future, the anti-expectant gist of which warned us that "post-" might well turn out to've been premature. What expectant baggage did we weigh ourselves down with even now? What ingenuous out did we disingenuously harbor hopes of having secured? The needling mist which addressed our feet multiply apprised us of an inoculative boon we sought even as we disavowed all promise, all prepossessing "post-." Post-expectant futurity stood accused of harboring hope. Nonetheless we stood by it, one and all, atomistic ledge an exemplary rug allotting endless rapport, unimpeachable aplomb.

Post-expectant futurity stood its ground. It was this of which our feet grew multiply-possessed before we hit a single note. Though its multiply-pinned massage ostensibly comforted the soles of our feet, the needling mist became a goad of sorts. The quantum-qualitative lift it afforded gave an operatic lilt and leverage to the post-expectant ground on which we stood. Ground and goad rolled into one, it coaxed an abrupt, acquiescent grunt from each of our throats, an abrupt, expectorant exhalation whose fishbone urgency furthered itself once we began to play. Part seismic splint, part psychic implant exacting an auto-inscriptive lilt, it put the phrase "inasmuch as what we want is real" on the tips of our tongues, amending our attack and our intonation in ways we'd have not thought possible had it not been so palpably so. What this meant was that "want" walked arm in arm with "real" across bumptious ground. We knew it all at once, it seemed, an instantaneous jolt as though the needling mist were an electric mace.

We were several bars into our opening number before fishbone urgency let go of our throats. The ripped, expectorant permission it apprised us of abruptly left us on our own, ushered albeit we were that much farther along the pointillist plank on which we walked. Djamilaa, Penguin, Aunt Nancy, Lambert and I stood in staggered array, stumbling in place while Drennette sat as though caught in a suspended spill. She looked as if she'd fallen backwards, as if her fall had been broken by the stool on which she sat. She too, it appeared, stumbled in place.

Our collective stumble suspended us in time it seemed, notwithstanding the atomistic ledge had a decidedly glide aspect and sense of advance running thru it. This was its odd, contradictory confirmation of post-expectant premises, the odd, post-expectant way it had of rolling promise and prohibition into one. The piece we opened with was Lambert's "Prometheus." The expectorant, post-expectant permission the occasion laced it with put one in mind of Charles Davis's "Half and Half," the rash, rhythmelodic treadmill effect Elvin Jones and Jimmy Garrison's band exact on the *Illumination* album. Still, it went way beyond that in the anticlimactic refractivity, the visionary hiccup we fostered and factored in. It was this which tallied with while taking elsewhere the iterative carpet-ride on which we ran in place. Iterant weave and itinerant rug ran as one. Atomistic ledge came on as though steeped in deep-seated conveyance, *run* so deeply woven into wouldly arrest it was all we could do to keep our feet on the floor. The conveyor-belt bridge and the bedouin breach it addressed introduced a deep, irredentist quiver to the needling mist, an ever so agitant feather's touch tickling our feet.

What struck us most was how quickly we'd moved onto mixed-metaphorical ground. Where was it we stood if stand could be said to be what we did? Where was it we stumbled if stumble said it better? So many different sensations complicated one another: mixed-metaphorical conveyor-belt/carpet-ride, mixed-metaphorical mist/pointillist plank, mixed-metaphorical feather/pinpoint massage, mixed-metaphorical splint/ low-lying spray . . .

The other shoe I spoke of to begin with fully partook of this dispensation, a mixed-metaphoricality which brought off being a hammer, a broken pedal and a shoe at the same time. It seemed a Cinderella fit or effect wherein hammer, broken pedal and shoe were now showcase items, encased in or even constituted of glass. Hammer had been placed under glass by the Penny dream. Broken pedal had been placed under glass by Drennette's concussive spill, shoe (slipper, to be more exact) by the presumption of fairy-tale artifice, fairy-tale fit. These three were one, a see-thru insistence upon breakage, atomization, the meaning, however chimeric, of atomistic ledge. The other shoe, the newly shod alterity onto which or into which or invested with which we now stepped, came down with a resounding report it took us a while to realize was us—a new sound which, unbeknown to ourselves, we'd come up with (or which, "unbeknown" being the case, had come up with us).

Other shoe mixed-metaphorically segued into other shore, the floor sliding away like sand when a wave retreats. Suppositious wave, I turned around and saw, was intimated, ever so exactingly meted out, by the drumroll Drennette now sustained, a roll which required all but acrobatic skill, so at odds with the suspended spill it appeared she was in. Suppositious retreat, the spasmic thumps thrown in on bass drum, tended to be consistent with suspended spill, suppositious wave rolling back upon itself so as to pull what ground one thought there was back with it. Thus it was that Drennette played out the mixed-emotional endowment her final bicycle ride with Rick had left her with, the promise and the putting aside of promise her critique of "antique emotion" so insisted on. Promise and resistance to promise rolled pregnancy and post-expectancy into one, the bass drum pedal sounding the post-expectant "floor" the broken pedal had introduced her to.

Drennette's anti-foundational patter recalled the fact—recalled while commenting upon the fact—that it was Lambert's debut of "Prometheus" which had launched us on our quest for a drummer. Whatever hope he might have had of bedrock solidity had long since been given an antithetic spin, made to comply with and to confirm or anticipate (or so it seemed in retrospect) the sense of anticlimactic futurity we've been under since getting here. The rhythmic anchor Lambert announced he wanted had turned out to be exactly that, turned out to be a *rhythmic* anchor. Rhythmicity, Drennette insisted, contends with bedrock foundation, the sense of an unequivocal floor anchorage implies.

That the atomistic ledge on which we stood entailed wouldly subsidence having been rescinded became clear the more one listened to Penguin. The piece's "love slave" thematics, the subtextual strain having to do with Epimetheus's "hots" (as Penguin put it) for Pandora, was the thread he pulled out and pursued. It took us a while to realize it, but this was largely what was new about the way we sounded. Never before had we so equated Promethean fire with Epimethean "hots." While at first it was difficult to pick out Penguin's advancement of that equation from the avalanche of sound we put forth, his needling insinuation that "Pandora" was an apter title than "Prometheus" gradually came to the fore. Gradually he blew louder, needling insinuation becoming more blunt, less innuendo than hammerlike assertion. The more assertive he became the more Drennette encouraged the equation he advanced, quickening the pace with rabbitlike rolls as though they were wheels for him to ride. Penguin, in turn, grew bolder, swifter, quickening the pace to play Epimetheus to what he took to be Drennette's Pandora (or took, it turned out, to be Djeannine's Pandora, took to be Drennette's Djeannine).

It was a blistering pace which Penguin handled without the slightest loss of articulacy. With each note he did as he wished. He clearly had something to say, something which all but leapt out of him, so Lambert and I backed away from our mikes, letting him solo first. Drennette's rabbitlike rolls continued to feed the Epimethean heat with which he blew, heat which was all the more astonishing considering the finesse with which he played, the nuanced ability to speak which, notwithstanding the frenzy it appeared he was in, he maintained. His oboe spoke. It not only spoke but did so with outrageous articulacy, so exquisitely so a balloon emerged from its bell. Lambert and I looked at one another. We traded looks with Aunt Nancy, Djamilaa and Drennette as well. It was hard to believe one's eyes but there it was, a comic-strip balloon enclosed in which one read the words Penguin's oboe spoke: *Drennette dreamt I lived on Djeannine Street. I walked from one end to the other everyday, back and forth all day. Having heard flamenco singers early on, I wanted in on duende.* Penguin took a breath and with that the balloon disappeared.

Another balloon took the first balloon's place when Penguin blew again, a balloon in which one read: *A long-toed woman, no respecter of lines, Drennette obliged me by dreaming I walked up and down Djeannine Street, stepping, just as she or Djeannine would, into literality, notwithstanding the littered sidewalk and the unkempt yards.* He took another breath and when he blew again the third balloon read: *Sprung by her long toe, Drennette (part gazelle, part tumbleweed) leapt away as I reached out to embrace Djeannine. Among the weeds in a vacant lot a half-block away, she ran a few steps and turned a cartwheel. All I wanted was to bury my head between her legs, press my nose to the reinforced crotch of her white cotton panties.* He took another breath and when he blew again the fourth balloon read: *Something I saw, thought I saw, some intangible something led me on. Something I saw not so much as in some other way sensed, an audiotactile aroma, the synaesthetic perfume Djeannine wore which was known as Whiff of What Was, a scent like none I'd otherwise have known.*

While this fourth balloon hung in the air several people in the audience stood up and came forward to get a better look, not stopping until they stood in front of Penguin, squinting to make out the last few words. I had already noticed that *a* and *scent* were written somewhat close together, so I took it they were trying to determine whether what was written was *a scent* or *ascent.* They returned to their seats when Penguin took another breath and the fourth balloon disappeared. In its place, when he blew again, was a fifth which read: *The salty-sweet, sweating remembrance of Drennette's long-toed advance animated the street with an astringent allure, a ruttish funk I fell into which was more than mere mood. Drennette's advance made the ground below the sidewalk swell, cracking the concrete to release an atomistic attar, dilating my nostrils that much more.*

This went on for some time, a new balloon appearing each time Penguin blew after taking a breath. There was a sixth, a seventh, an eighth balloon and more. How many there were in all I can't say. I lost count. In any case, I understood them as a ploy by way of which Penguin sought to gain relief, comic relief, from the erotic-elegiac affliction of which the oboe so articulately spoke. By way of the balloons he made light of and sought to get leverage on the pregnant, post-expectant ground Drennette so adamantly espoused or appeared to espouse. The leverage he sought gave all the more torque to the dream-projection he projected onto her, the "street" he later admitted to be based on the housing projects he lived in as a child. There was a regal touch to it as well, each balloon both cartoon and cartouche, this latter aspect very much in keeping with the stately tone the oboe wove into its erotic-elegiac address. Wounded kingship came thru loud and clear, an amalgam of majesty and misery, salty-sweet. Love lost was as easily loss loved it intimated, a blasé spin the blue funk it announced increasingly came to be amended by. Such grim jest or indifferent gesture increasingly infiltrated courtly ordeal, cap and bells inaugurating an alternate crown, King Pen's cartoon/cartouche. Laughing to keep from crying some would call it, but in fact it went much deeper than that.

Penguin wrapped up his solo with a round of circular breathing which introduced an unexpected wrinkle to what had by then become a pattern: blow/balloon emerge, take a breath/balloon disappear, blow/balloon emerge, take a breath/balloon disappear, blow/balloon emerge, take a breath/balloon disappear . . . The breath he now took was continuous with the one he expelled and the balloon, instead of disappearing, hung in the air above the bell of his horn growing larger the longer he blew. The steady enlargement, however, was only partly what was new about the new wrinkle he introduced. Two-dimensional up to this point, the balloon acquired a third dimension as it grew, becoming a much more literal balloon. What was also new was that there were now no words written inside it. By making it more a literal than a comic-strip balloon Penguin put aside the comic lever he'd made use of up to this point. He was now nothing if not emotionally forthright, the empty balloon all but outright insisting, the way music so often does, that when it came to the crux of the matter, the erotic-elegiac fix one was in, words were beside the point.

The admission that words fail us would normally not have been so unexpected, normally come as no surprise. Music, as I've said, does it all the time. But in this case it seemed a new and unusual twist, so persuasively had the comic-strip balloons insisted it could all be put into words. It's a measure of Penguin's genius that he could endow something so close to cliché with new life. The balloon not only swelled like a pregnant belly but, thanks to the mixed-metaphorical ground onto which we'd moved, it appeared to be a sobriety-test balloon as well. Penguin blew into it intent on proving himself sober even as he extolled the intoxicant virtues of Djeannine's audiotactile perfume. Whiff of What Was notwithstanding, the vacant balloon seemed intended to acquit him of drunken charges, the admission of words' inadequacy a sobering descent from the auto-inscriptive high to which the earlier balloons had lent themselves. Even so, this descent could easily be said to have been further flight, so deciduously winged was the winded ferocity with which Penguin blew, what falling off there was reaching beyond itself with a whistling falsetto—stratospheric screech and a crow's caw rolled into one.

So it was that sobering descent mounted higher and higher. The balloon grew bigger and bigger, a weather balloon pitting post-expectant wind against pregnant air. Penguin put a punning spin on it, wondering out loud whether it might also be the other way around, pregnant wind encountering post-expectant air. With us crescendoing behind him all the while (Lambert and I had now joined back in), he eventually answered his own question when the balloon swelled and swelled and finally burst with a loud bang, pricked by a post-expectant needle, the needling mist which was now not only on the floor. It was with this that he brought his solo to an end, whereupon the audience went crazy, loudly applauding the release he'd had them hungering for, the release he now at last let them have.

Penguin timed it exactly right. The audience couldn't have stood another beat, much less another bar, couldn't have held its collective breath a moment longer. We too, the rest of us in the band, breathed easier now, inwardly applauded the release we too had begun to be impatient for. All of us, that is, except Drennette, who quickly apprised us, with the solo she now insisted upon taking, of the fact that the ground on which we stood was, if anyone's, hers, that impatience had no place where post-expectancy ruled.

Post-expectant futurity brought one abreast of the ground, Drennette announced, annulled, in doing so, any notion of ground as not annexed by an alternate ground. This was the pregnancy, the unimpatient expectancy, she explained, Penguin, albeit put upon and perplexed, had been granted rare speech, rare fluency by. Djeannine Street, alternate ground par excellence, inflected each run of heavy bass drum thumps with ventriloquial spectres, Drennette's recourse to the sock cymbal insistent that she and Djeannine, long spoken for, had spooked (her word was "inspirited") wouldly ledge, atomistic ledge.

It was a wild, outrageous boast, but she had the chops, it turned out, to back it up. The drumset had become a wind instrument by the time she finished her solo. A gust of wind arose from each roll and with each roll the storm she brewed grew more ferocious. We felt it at our backs when we joined in again, pressing as it pestered us toward some occult articulation only Drennette, not looking ahead, saw deep enough to have inklings of. Not so much needling as pounding us now, the needling mist partook of that wind—mystical hammer rolled into one with atomistic pulse. Wouldly ledge, needling mist and Penguin's auto-inscriptive high would all, post-expectancy notwithstanding, turn out to have only been a beginning.

Suffice it to say we made some of the most ontic, unheard-of music we've ever made. Say what one will about unimpatient expectancy, I can't wait to play again tonight.

As ever,
N.

•

________________ 10.VI.82

Dear Angel of Dust,

We're back in L.A. Got back from Seattle a few days ago. The Soulstice gig, all in all, went well, though the last two nights were a little bit disappointing. It's not that we didn't play well or that the music wasn't well received. We played with characteristic fluency and fire both nights and both nights the crowd, noticeably larger than the first night, got into it, urged us on. Even so, the post-expectant ground we stepped onto the first night was nowhere to be found on nights two and three. The pointillist tread, the wouldly "one step beyond" with which we'd been blessed, pointedly avoided us the next two nights. No atomistic plank-walk lay before us, no needling mist massaged our feet. It was ground we couldn't get back to no matter how hard we tried, ground we couldn't get back to perhaps because of how hard we tried.

The most conspicuous difference was that no balloons emerged from Penguin's horn. It was this which left the audience a bit disappointed, notwithstanding the applause and the hip exhortations they repeatedly gave the music. Word of the balloons had quickly gotten around town after night number one and it was this which in large part accounted for the larger turnout the next two nights. Clearly, people came hoping to see the balloons emerge again. Though we've never thought of ourselves as crowd-pleasers, never been overly concerned with approbation, we'd have been happy to oblige them had it been up to us. But that the balloons didn't emerge amounted to an anti-expectant lesson which, while not exactly the same, was consistent with the post-expectant premises onto which we had stepped and again hoped to step. The air of anticipation the audience brought with them was so thick that before our final number the second night, the balloons not having reappeared and, clearly, to us in the band, not likely to, Aunt Nancy stepped forward and spoke into the mike. "Remember what Eric said," she admonished them. "'When you hear music, after it's over, it's gone in the air. You can never capture it again.'"

It was a lesson we ourselves have had to ponder. Post-expectant ground was clearly evaporative ground, but it was hard not to be disappointed we couldn't find it again. It had been a lapse to expect otherwise we admitted, but that's been easier to say than to accept. Lambert, in any event, said it best as we were discussing this at rehearsal the other night. "It's about digesting what you can't swallow," he said at one point.

As ever,
N.

•

_________________ 17.VII.82

Dear Angel of Dust,

The balloons are words taken out of our mouths, an eruptive critique of predication's rickety spin rewound as endowment. They subsist, if not on excision, on exhaust, abstract-extrapolative strenuousness, tenuity, technical-ecstatic duress. They advance the exponential potency of dubbed excision—plexed, parallactic articulacy, vexed elevation, vatic vacuity, giddy stilt. They speak of overblown hope, loss's learned aspiration, the eventuality of seen-said formula, filled-in equation, vocative imprint, prophylactic bluff. They raise hopes while striking an otherwise cautionary note, warnings having to do with empty authority, habitable indent, housed as well as unhoused vacuity, fecund recess.

The balloons are love's exponential debris, "high would's" atmospheric dispatch. Hyperbolic aubade (love's post-expectant farewell), they arise from the depth we invest in ordeal, chivalric trauma—depth charge and buoy rolled into one. They advance an exchange adumbrating the advent of optic utterance, seen-said exogamous mix of which the coupling of tryst and trial would bear the inaugural brunt. Like Djeannine's logarithmic flute, they obey, in the most graphic imaginable fashion, ocular deficit's oracular ricochet, seen-said remit.

The balloons are thrown-away baggage, oddly sonic survival, sound and sight rolled into one. They map even as they mourn post-appropriative precincts, chthonic or subaquatic residua come to the surface caroling world collapse. They dredge vestiges of premature post-expectancy (overblown arrival, overblown goodbye), seen-said belief's wooed risk of inflation, synaesthetic excess, erotic-elegiac behest. The balloons augur—or, put more modestly, acknowledge—the ascendancy of videotic premises (autoerotic tube, autoerotic test pattern), automatic stigmata bruited as though of the air itself.

Such, at least, was the insistence I heard coming out of Dolphy's horn. "The Madrig Speaks, the Panther Walks" was the cut. I sat down to listen to it only minutes ago and found myself writing what you've just read. Never had Eric's alto sounded so precocious and multiply-tongued, never so filled with foreboding yet buoyant all the same, walk (panther) and talk (madrig) never so disarmingly entwined.

Listening, more deeply than ever, bone-deep, I knew the balloons were evanescent essence, fleet seen-said equivalence, flighty identity, sigil, sigh. This was the horn's bone-deep indenture, wedge and decipherment rolled into one. This could only, I knew, be the very thing whose name I'd long known albeit not yet found its fit, the very thing which, long before I knew it as I now know it, I knew by name—the name of a new piece I'd write if I could.

What I wouldn't give, that is, to compose a piece I could rightly call "Dolphic Oracle." It would indeed ally song (madrig) with speech, as well as with catlike muscularity and sinew—but also with catlike, post-expectant tread, oxymoronically catlike, post-expectant prowl, post-expectant pounce, an aroused, heretofore unheard of, hopefully seen-said panther-python mix . . .

Yours,
N.

•

________________ 26.VII.82

Dear Angel of Dust,

Could be. Yes, possibly so. The balloons, for all their outward display and apparent address of popular wish (literal access, legible truth) may well, as you say, signal an inward turn. As I've said before, the last thing we want is to be a lonely hearts band, but that may in fact be what, under Penguin and Drennette's influence, we're becoming or may even have already become. Are the balloons' apparent roots in problematic romance, their repeated erotic-elegiac lament, a default on collectivist possibility, a forfeiture of possible bondings greater than two, an obsessed, compensatory return (would-be return) to pre-post-romantic ground?

I don't know. I'm not so sure, for one thing, it can all be laid at Penguin and Drennette's feet. To whatever extent the balloons embody a retreat from more properly collectivist wishes, an introspective move masquerading as wished-for romance, costume-courtly complaint, the larger social, political moment we find ourselves in would have to have had a hand in it, no? I don't much subscribe to the increasing talk, in these dreary times, of "empowerment," "subversion," "resistance" and so forth. I once quoted

Bachelard's line, "Thirst proves the existence of water," to a friend, who answered, "No, *water* proves the existence of water." I find myself more and more thinking that way. I find myself—and this goes for everyone else in the band, I think—increasingly unable (albeit not totally unable) to invest in notions of dialectical inevitability, to read the absence of what's manifestly not there as the sign of its eventual presence. To whatever extent hyperbolic aubade appears to have eclipsed collective "could," the balloons' going on about love's inflated goodbye should alert us to the Reaganomic roots of that eclipse.

I drove down to Santa Ana yesterday. An old friend and I went to the store at one point and on our way we passed a neighborhood park which has more and more become a camp for the homeless. Park Avenue people now call it, irony their one defense. Anyway, as we drove past, my friend, looking out the window, sneered, "Look at them, a bunch of dialects." He meant "derelicts." So much for malaprop speech as oppositional speech, I couldn't help thinking, so much for oppositional *any*thing.

That's how I sometimes feel, how we all sometimes feel. Not all the time, but often enough to nourish what you call an inward turn. I don't altogether buy your inward/outward split, but if you're saying the balloons' erotic-elegiac lament mourns the loss of larger bonding as well, I agree.

Yours,
N.

PS: What the two occasions the balloons have emerged on have in common is the ur-foundational/anti-foundational sense and/or apprehension we had—atomistic ledge/needling mist/pointillist plank-walk in Seattle, subterranean strum/"collapsed" contour/tar pit premises at Keystone Korner. Each entailed an excavation of substrate particles or precincts, erstwhile plummet or plunge. Are the balloons mud we resurface with, mud we situate ourselves upon, heuristic precipitate, axiomatic muck, unprepossessing mire? I ask because of my acquaintance with earth-diver myths—myths in which an animal plunges into primeval waters and brings up a mouthful or a beakful of mud, mud from which the world is then made. In some the animal is a tortoise, in others a boar, in others a duck, in others a loon. Could the balloons, I'm asking, be a pseudo-Bahamian play on the latter, namesake play with B'-*Ba* overtones, the spirit or the embodied soul of namesake play going by the name B'Loon?

I say yes. B'Loon, not unrelated to Djbouche, is our murky, mired cry, a call for world reparation. It muddies our mouths with the way the world is even if only to insist it be otherwise. Such insistence notwithstanding, it implicates us (myth advancing mud, mouth proving mud) in the pit we'd have it extricate us from.[5]

Sight-Specific, Sound-Specific . . .

Performance is a bothersome word for writerly poets. Performance art, poetry slams, and the like have made the term synonymous with theatricality, a recourse to dramatic, declamatory, and other tactics aimed at propping up words or at helping them out—words regarded, either way, as needing help, support, embellishment, deficient or decrepit or even dead left on their own. Writerly poets, advocates or devotees of what Wilson Harris calls "the innate life of the word," shy away from the implied subscription to such a view of language, resistant to the presumed deadness of the word, an apparent deadness *to* the word by those who advance it. We're less comfortable speaking of the poetry reading as performance or the poet as performer than of the words themselves performing, the words being made to perform by the poet, allowed or trusted to perform. Kamau Brathwaite, in a 1989 interview conducted by Stewart Brown, responded to a question regarding "the importance of performance" in relation to his work by saying, "I *don't* perform at all, it's my poetry that does it. . . . The words on the page have a metaphorical life of their own. I do not depend upon walking up and down on the stage and doing things. People have the impression that I'm performing when in fact they are actually dealing with poetry as they ought to, that is, the poetry is singing in their ears."[1] I've heard Clayton Eshleman, Lyn Hejinian, and others make a similar distinction, likewise insist on the animacy of the word. I, too, view the matter that way.

I recall a Robert Duncan reading in 1979 that at one point conjured an image of a stairway beneath eyelids, a stairway a star ascended. It was an image I found startling, arrestingly so, all but grotesque or etymologically grotesque in the way it put a flight of stairs inside the eye or between the eyelid and the eye, on the eye, throwing in a star to boot. The piece was the prose-poem "Structure of Rime XIX." The passage in question, I found on looking it up later, goes as follows:

> At the turn of the path where it is steep we saw Jupiter climbing ahead of us and turnd his image in the hand mirror. As a lone brilliant in the thick of eyelashes. As a star in the stare under the closed lids.[2]

I'd read this poem a number of times in the years prior to attending the reading but I'd evidently forgotten that the word was *stare.* I heard it as *stair.* To hear it so was to "mishear" it—in quotes because to hear it so was to be true to the passage's play on the fact that a stare under closed lids is no stare, an eclipsed or suspended stare if not the inversely capable, inner sight or ascent suggested by *stair,* the mind's eye the passage both advocates and opens. The life of the word resides in such variable apprehension, a congeries of apprehension its power to perform concatenates. Writing that's alive to this power needn't be performed or declaimed. It needn't be read with a pointed effort to be dramatic, emotive, hortative, expressive, and such. There's enough going on already. There's no need to ham it up.

One of the benefits of readings is that things of the sort I just recounted can occur. I could give other such examples, but my aim isn't to extol, in isolation, the power of the spoken word, the heard word. Language's ability to perform is variable and site-specific, mind, ear, eye, air, page, and other sites conducing to particular powers and effects. Ezra Pound's "phanopoeia, melopoeia and logopoeia," echoed by Louis Zukofsky's "sight, sound and intellection," touches on this multisitedness to an extent, but by congeries of apprehension something more multiple and involved than a trinarism is gotten at. Taking not only eye, ear, and mind into consideration but acknowledging mind's eye, mind's ear, and, further, mind's nose, mind's tongue, and mind's touch as well, to say nothing of synesthetic amalgams and exchanges, considerably complicates the mix. Look, for example, at Lorenzo Thomas's poem "The Leopard":

> The eyeballs on her behind are like fire
> Leaping and annoying
> The space they just passed
> Just like fire would do
>
> The ground have no mouth to complain
> And the girl is not braver herself
>
> She is beautiful in her spotted
> Leopard ensemble. Heartless so

To keep her fashionable in New York
Leopards are dying

Crude comments flutter around her
At lunchtime. She sure look good
She remembers nine banishing speeches

More powerful than this is the seam
Of the leotard under her clothing

Her tail in the leotard is never still
The seam!
She feels it too familiar on her leg
As some crumb says something suggestive

The leopard embracing around her
Is too chic to leap and strike

Her thoughts fall back to last semester's *karate*
Underneath, the leotard crouches up on her thigh
It is waiting for its terrible moment![3]

The reader's literal, physiological eye alights on the near identity, orthographically, of *leopard* and *leotard,* which are roughly to the eye what *stare* and *stair* in Duncan's poem are to the ear (these last two having an orthographic nearness as well but an "unstated" one, "stair" not actually on the page). Appeals to suggestive tactility factor in as well, erogenous mind touching or touched by intimate cloth and animality as well as the nearness (phonologically and in the movement the poem reports) of *crouches* to *crotch.* There's other action, other performance going on as well, but these brief comments will suffice.

I try to write poems whose words perform on multiple fronts. I'm as attentive, to speak only of two such fronts, to the placement of words on the page (the use of variable margins, intralinear spacing, page breaks, and such to advance a now swept, now swung, sculpted look, a visual dance down the page and from page to page) as I am to the rhythms and inflections with which they're to be read when read aloud. It's not that the former serves as a score for the latter, as Charles Olson, Denise Levertov, and others have insisted. Such placement, to the silent reader, can suggest the unfolding of thought or composition (its hesitancies, tenuities, accelerations, leaps, and so forth) while speaking, by way of the eye, to a mind's ear that hears every line break as a caesura, every break between sections or pages as an amendment or an addendum or even a new beginning, additional space between words as a pause. This is the poem performing on the stage the page amounts to (and on the stage the reader's mind amounts to by way of the page). I don't, however, feel obligated to read the poem aloud in the manner such placement might suggest—obligated or even able. What, after all, do varied margins sound like? (What, for that matter, does an unvaried margin sound like?) To avail oneself of graphic amenities peculiar to the page is not to disallow the poem behaving differently when read aloud but to recognize that it does. The ultimate untransmissibility of vocal dynamics (timbre, accent, pace, volume, inflection, and so forth) by print—and vice versa—makes variance inevitable. The poem's articulation is as various as its locations.

All this goes as lead-in to saying that when it came to working with musicians, the collaboration with Royal Hartigan and Hafez Modirzadeh that resulted in the CD *Strick*, I didn't particularly think of the project as a move into performance—certainly not performance in the hyped, hortative sense I associate with stage adaptations of Walt Whitman, performance art, poetry slams, and such. On the contrary, I had misgivings about the equation of music and poetry collaborations with a more hopped-up or heated-up reading style, the declamatory mode that is often, perhaps typically, the staple and fare of such undertakings. This isn't to say performance in that sense is without its powers and attractions, but simply that it's not what I do. When Royal contacted me in the fall of 1993 and said he was interested in collaborating with poets and that David Bindman, a tenor saxophonist with whom he'd worked, had suggested he get in touch with me, I thought of Carleen Robinson's oratorical reading of Sonia Sanchez's poem "A Blk Woman Speaks" on the *Tomorrow Is Now!* album by Fred Ho and the Afro-Asian Music Ensemble (Soul Note, 1985). Royal, I knew, was a member of the ensemble and although it turned out when I later looked it up that he wasn't yet in the band at the time of that recording, I associated him with that reading. I thus took it that he was used to working with a type of poetry and a style of reading quite different from mine. He said he wasn't familiar with my work, that he'd phoned solely on the basis of Bindman's recommendation, so I wondered if he would find it work he could collaborate with. (Bindman had written me some time prior to this and I knew that he'd read my fiction, specifically *Bedouin Hornbook*, a copy of which he'd been given by his grandmother, Joyce Adler, a literary critic with whom I'd been in touch due to a shared interest in Wilson Harris's work. Whether he'd read my poetry I didn't know, but with his not having mentioned it, I assumed he hadn't.)

Wariness notwithstanding, when Paul Naylor got in touch to say that he and Lindsay Hill were launching a spoken-word recording venture, Spoken Engine Company, a project that would issue CDs of poets reading with musical accompaniment, and that they were interested in recording my work, I thought right away it was worth giving a try. Music, after all, had from the beginning figured prominently in my work as reference and inspiration. Hearing from Paul only a couple of weeks or a month or so after hearing from Royal, moreover, seemed especially auspicious. In any case, when I contacted Royal to tell him about the recording possibility and to ask if he'd be interested in taking part I asked him to wait until he'd gotten acquainted with my work to decide, saying I'd like him to hear some of my work and my reading style and to think about whether he could do something with it musically and, if so, what that something might be. I was determined that my reading style with musical accompaniment remain essentially the same as when reading alone, a determination I talked about, conveying thoughts along the line of those I opened this essay with. I sent him a tape of a reading I'd given at the Woodstock Guild in Woodstock, New York, a few months earlier, a reading that included installments 16 through 25 of the "Song of the Andoumboulou" series, the ten poems that were later to comprise the "Strick" section of *Whatsaid Serif* and which I was already thinking of devoting the recording to. Royal got back to me after listening to it, saying yes, he liked the work and was interested in collaborating, that he had some ideas about what could be done with the poems musically. We agreed to get together over the coming months to see what we could come up with, aiming for a recording date sometime early in the summer. The two of us would start the process and later bring in Hafez, whose work with the Afro-Asian Ensemble, like Royal's, I was already familiar with.

I was interested in getting beyond the generic jazz and poetry sound: musicians noodling nonchalantly behind fairly transparent verse. While I wanted there to be room for improvisation I didn't want it to sound as if the musicians just happened to be there. I wanted to plan what, within certain limits, would be going on when, to sketch out an approach to each poem with regard to instrumentation, atmosphere, color, pace, and so forth, to map out who would come in doing what where, who would pull back giving way to what when, to determine how each piece would begin and how it would end, to decide on the place of purely instrumental stretches, and so on. Among the advantages and attractions of working with Royal and Hafez was their proficiency on a wide range of instruments, including instruments other than those typically played in jazz. In addition to the traditional drum set, Royal brought an array of African and Oriental percussion instruments to the project; in addition to tenor saxophone and Western flute, Hafez contributed work on a variety of Oriental reeds and flutes. The cross-cultural musical possibility and palette they afforded not only helped get outside the jazz and poetry box but accorded well with the poems' cross-cultural references and reach, a cross-culturality not only in such areas as history, mythology, and lore but in that of music itself. References, that is, to John Coltrane, Lester Young, and Johnny Mbizo Dyani sit, over the course of the poems, alongside references to flamenco singer Juan Peña Lebrijano, the Ethiopian "harp of David," Algerian chaabi singer Hsissen, reggae singer Burning Spear and the reggae band Culture, Sudan's Abdel Gadir Salim, Mali's Rail Band, and Brazilian sambista Paulinho da Viola.

It wasn't, however, that Royal and Hafez's playing would "illustrate" such references. It wasn't that they would represent or sample the cultures or the music alluded to in the poems. The rendering of "Song of the Andoumboulou: 21," which begins "Next a Brazilian cut came / on" and is backed by a drums-and-flute bossa nova that turns into a samba in the section mentioning samba, was a pointed exception, an exception intended to highlight the rule it departed from. The role of the music was more atmospheric than referential, its cross-cultural work's accent falling on *cross*, an offhand or loose congruence if not incongruence. Cultural specificity or exhibition was not the aim, music and cultural amenities valued no more for what they avail than for what they ameliorate or mask. The point was to partake of the salvage operation the poems assert music and cultural amenities to be, to invoke while applying a balm to the primordial devastation the Andoumboulou represent:

> who, asked his name, gave only his
> middle, "Music,"   mask made of
>   wind, of wrack,   by which if
> by wind it meant soul it meant
>   salvage[4]

A transcultural caution, a certain wariness of culture masks and identity masks, would have its say. The music, for all its energy, assertion, and performative presence, would be laced with or subjected to a subjunctive ascesis or abeyance, a relay work of qualm and qualification that would verge on evacuating the acoustic masquerade (performance also, then, in that sense) that music is, the graphic and acoustic masquerade that poetry is.

On the phone after listening to the tape I sent him and again when we first got together, Royal remarked on the layering in the poems and their multiple strands of exposition, drawing analogies with Cecil Taylor's music and West African drumming. We talked about the poems a good deal before working on the music, and later, when Hafez came in, we returned to that discussion. I talked about my approach to writing and about the particular poems we were working with, elaborating on the place of the Andoumboulou in Dogon cosmology, commenting on some of the references and allusions, detailing some of the concerns driving the work. Royal and Hafez spoke of their senses of the poems, especially where their responses or readings prompted ideas as to how to accompany them musically. Royal, for example, noted early on the fraught sensuality of the people in the poems, their sexual strain and striving, and suggested resorting at times to putting the drumsticks aside and simply laying his hands on the snare drums' heads (their skins) and rubbing—a pun or a play on the head-and-heart, head-and-skin harmony sought by the people in the poems, the tension or tug between mind and body they're beset by. Hence the sound that opens the CD, a sound of abrasion as much as caress that some have heard, due to the words it introduces, as the sound of the sea. The hands-on-drumhead tack anticipates and would be echoed or returned to—rhymed with—by the use of the *bendir*, a Turkish frame drum played with the fingertips and heel of the hand, on the rendering of "Song of the Andoumboulou: 19" and "Song of the Andoumboulou: 22," two of the poems most fraught with senses of bodily lure and largesse. Likewise, Hafez heard and read a theme of possessed or problematic speech, spooked or impacted speech, that led him to suggest removing the mouthpiece from the tenor sax, playing it with no mouthpiece. (Conch sax he called it.) Hence the garbled or haunted or ghostly sounds he contributes on the CD's initial track.

Hafez and Royal's playing not only underscored such themes and motifs but also added further layers and further strands. Their accompaniment to the poems was worked out by way of a process involving trial and error, conversation and rehearsal, a process that took place over a number of months. They both wrote out the arrangements we arrived at on their copies of the poems, notes as to what instrument was to be played when, where to come in, where to cut off, tempo, attitude, and such. Royal's notes were very detailed, Hafez's a bit more sparse. Their copies of the poems, in both cases, became something of a score. We consciously worked, in these arrangements, to knit the set together musically in a way that reflected, somewhat, the recursive nature of the poems, returning to specific instrumentations and aural textures (usually with slight variations) for a kind of leitmotif effect at points.

As for my part, I simply tried to read the poems as I normally do, aiming to enunciate clearly though not dramatically and to render the rhythms, inflections, and accents the way I heard them when writing the poems. I found it a challenge to do so, especially at first. The presence of the music does exert an influence, an influence it took some getting used to. I came to see why poetry and music collaborations are so often in the declamatory mode. Simply the volume or insistency musical instruments are capable of can impart a driven, hortative quality, a sense of goad it's difficult not to be affected, impelled, or even overwhelmed by. Although the tenor of the poems and their diction and syntax tend not to lend themselves to declamation, I found I needed to resist that sense of goad nonetheless. It took an effort to maintain a cooler approach. Royal and Hafez made it easier by listening, letting me set the tone—attempting to, at least. Our biggest challenge, that is, was a practical one, that of my rather low-key, soft-spoken reading style being difficult to hear amid the instruments—especially the louder ones, tenor sax and drum set. It was difficult for me to be heard and to hear myself, difficult for all of us to hear the overall sound. This was especially the case during the period of working things out through rehearsals, which took place in a small room at Royal's house without benefit of microphones, monitors, and the like. We learned to accommodate each other, however, Hafez and Royal keeping their volume down and me striving to project a bit more than usual.

By the time we went into the recording studio, which brought such amenities as monitor headphones with levels mixed to our individual dictates ("I feel like I'm fully hearing the poems for the first time," Hafez remarked), we'd gotten a lot better at hearing one another under less than ideal circumstances, which included a presentation of the first five poems of the set at the University of California, Santa Cruz, a month prior to the recording. Such amenities notwithstanding, the demands I'd gotten used to under those other circumstances and, I think, a certain force field intrinsic to ensemble interplay, made for a charge or an edge or a hint of urgency in my voice even on the recording, subtle differences from the way I sound when simply reading alone. Since making the recording we've had occasion to present the poems at the Monterey Jazz Festival, Rutgers University, and Seton Hall University, venues where technical provisions less ideal than those in the studio continued to teach us how to listen better, how to hear one another better, but also not to be put off by not hearing, the occult clamor that sound, whether words or music, often is.

PART IV

Destination Out

Centrifugal work begins with good-bye, wants to bid all givens good-bye. It begins with what words will not do, paint will not do, whatever medium we find ourselves working in will not do. Amenities and consolation accrue to a horizon it wants to get beyond, abandoning amenities and consolation or seeking new ones. It will, of course, suffer marginalization, temporary in some cases, unremitting in most.

Black centrifugal writing has been and continues to be multiply marginalized. Why would it be otherwise? At a time when academic and critical discourse battens on identity obsession (even as it "problematizes" identity), black centrifugal writing reorients identity in ways that defy prevailing divisions of labor. In the face of a widespread fetishization of collectivity, it dislocates collectivity, flies from collectivity, wants to make flight a condition of collectivity. It says that "we" was never a swifter fiction—not so much a war between family and flight as the familial song of one's feeling for flight. It says that only such admitted fugitivity stands a ghost of a chance of apportioning prodigal truth. This is one of the lessons it has learned from black music. It remembers that Coleman Hawkins felt no identity crisis playing an instrument invented by a Belgian, that Lester Young referred to the keys of his horn as his people.

Black art, like any other, is innovative, demanding and/or outside to the extent that it addresses the wings and resistances indigenous to its medium qua medium, address ranging from amorous touch to agonistic embrace, angelic rub. To don such wings and engage such resistances as though they were the stuff of identity and community is to have taken a step toward making them so.

Expanding the Repertoire

I'd like to address the question of what characterizes innovation and the question of how the term impacts or fails to impact critical approaches to African American writing. I'd like to make the point, to begin with, that the term *innovation* is a relative one, that it's haunted by the question, Compared to what? There are a variety of ways in which it can apply, a variety of ways in which to innovate or be seen to innovate. Still, there's a general tendency to think of innovation, especially where it's taken to be related to or synonymous with experimentation, as having to do with method, as having, more specifically, to do with the pursuit of greater complexity and sophistication in technical and formal matters, greater self-consciousness and complication with regard to questions of mediation. The pursuit of a more complex accommodation between technique and epistemological concerns, between ways of telling and ways of knowing, especially where knowing is less the claim than a nervousness about it, is what tends to be thought of as innovation, experimentation, avant-garde.

Understood in this way, these terms have not had a very prominent place in the discourse attending African American writing. The innovation that's granted African American writing, where there's any granted at all, tends to be one of content, perspective, or attitude. The newness African American writing is most likely to be recognized and valorized for, credited with or taken to be characterized by, is the provision of an otherwise absent or underrepresented (thus new) perspective, conveniently known as the black perspective, its report on the one thing African Americans are regarded as experts on—racial victimization. Along with this tendency go canons of accessibility and disclosure that are viewed as diametrically opposed to the difficulty attributed to formally innovative or experimental work. One of Langston Hughes's most popular creations is a character named Jesse B. Semple—a lightly veiled way of saying, "Just be simple," the credo of quintessential blackness. Charles Olson, on the other hand, uses the phrase "the blessing / that difficulties are" in *The Maximus Poems*,[1] a phrase one of the L=A=N=G=U=A=G=E poetry magazines later took its name from. The distinction between a formally innovative willingness to incur difficulty, on the white hand, and a simple disclosure of innovative content, on the black, is a simple or simplistic one, but telling nonetheless. Oversimplifications along exactly such lines have had an enormous impact on the questions we're here to address and can even be said to be what brought us here. They contribute to the relative invisibility of African American writing that seeks to advance content outside the prescribed or expected limits and/or to be formally innovative or experimental. They contribute to the neglect that gave rise to the need for a conference like this, to the constriction of the repertoire we're talking about expanding.

Racialized dichotomies between content and form, accessibility and difficulty, conventionality and innovation, and the like rest on a division of cultural labor black experimental writing has to contest and overcome. The grid of expectations enforced by such dichotomies has had a great deal of influence on the critical legitimation of African American writing and experimental writing as well, categories that are generally treated as entirely separate, nonoverlapping. When I was looking for a publisher for my book *Discrepant Engagement*, which deals with experimental writing by African American authors, white American authors, and Caribbean authors, I was told by one university press that the book's "problem" is that it's not really one book but potentially three: a book on experimental writing, a book on African American writing, and a book on Caribbean writing. I eventually found a publisher for the book, but this made it clear that the investment in segregated categories dies hard, that it's still not quite done dying. My experience with and relationship to notions of innovation and experimentation and the question of categorization they give rise to for nonwhite writers go back to my earliest years as a reader of contemporary writing, my earliest years as an aspiring writer. Ed Roberson and I were part of a discussion of this question a few years ago at Rutgers University, and we both found ourselves having to insist that the category "black experimental writing" that was being picked at and problematized wasn't a problem, that for both of us, very early on, each at a different time and in a somewhat different way, the overlap between African American writing and experimental writing had been so clear that we simply took it for granted.

Amiri Baraka, no doubt the best-known black experimental writer in recent memory, figured prominently in both our accounts of what fostered that recognition. I first read Baraka's work when I was seventeen and he was LeRoi Jones. The first book of his I read was *The Dead Lecturer*, the back cover of which said, among other things, "Like Pound and Olson, LeRoi Jones is not an 'easy' poet, for he too is searching for new ways of expression and rejecting any preconceived notion of what a poem ought to be."[2] Statements like this, along with Baraka's inclusion in the discussion of projectivism in M. L. Rosenthal's *The New Poets* and other things I was then encountering, didn't suggest that African American writers could not or should not be experimental, could not or should not be difficult, could not or should not be included in discussions of innovative writing. Baraka proved to be a signal example not only of what was possible but also of certain constraints that racialized dichotomy and the grid of expectations help keep in place. His anxieties over the anomaly he took himself to be bespoke the power of that taxonomy and its attendant simplicities, their power even over someone whose existence and work prove them wrong. "Having been taught that art was 'what white men did,'" he wrote in the introduction to *Home* in 1965, "I almost became one, to have a go at it."[3] He called himself "sammy davis / for allen ginsbergs frank sinatra" around the same time.[4] He dismissed Ralph Ellison's work as an "extraliterary commercial . . . about European literature, the fact that he has done some reading in it" (*H* 123), which is an odd comment coming from the author of a novel called *The System of Dante's Hell* and poems with titles like "Valéry as Dictator," "HEGEL," "Don Juan in Hell," and "The Return of the Native." The comment's implicit self-indictment became explicit when Baraka rejected the predominantly white avant-garde context in which he and his work had come to prominence, a move that was celebrated and canonized as the transformation of a quasi-white, obscurantist writer into a black, accessible one. "Originally writing in the obscure Greenwich Village idiom, his recent identification with the black masses has caused him to write with more clarity and force," Dudley Randall wrote.[5] Baraka's work and career have received far more attention than those of any other African American experimental writer, largely due to the conversion narrative that's now put at the heart of it, a narrative that leaves the grid of expectations intact. The social text it foregrounds is a simple one, much easier to decipher than a text by Melvin Tolson or Russell Atkins or, earlier on, Baraka himself.

American society's appetite for simplicities is not to be underestimated.

It poses a challenge to all experimental writers, an especially stiff one to those hailing from a group expected, more than most, to feed and affirm that appetite. A few years ago I received a paper in a class on the Harlem Renaissance in which a student praised James Weldon Johnson's poetry because, as he put it, "Johnson, unlike T. S. Eliot, doesn't display his intelligence." An occupational hazard I suppose you could call it, but what struck me was its resonance with more skillfully worded assertions to the same effect by critics and academics, black as well as white, bent on promoting African American literature as the alternative to modernism, recondite writing, art for art's sake, and other targets. To be let in only on those terms is enough to put one at peace with being left out. As an old calypso puts it, "I don't give a damn, I done dead already."

But we should give a damn, and do, and I don't want to paint too bleak a picture. The relevance of experimentalism to African American writing and of African American writing to experimentalism needs to be insisted on and accorded its place in the discourse attending African American literature and in the discourse attending experimental writing. I wouldn't want to conclude without mentioning a development or two that brighten the prospects of doing so, that are already doing so—things like Harryette Mullen's critique of the hegemony or potential hegemony of the "speakerly text" paradigm; C. S. Giscombe's "Maroon Writing" section in the *American Book Review* a few years ago; Aldon Nielsen's *Black Chant: Languages of African-American Postmodernism*, and the two-volume anthology of black experimental poetry that he and Lauri Ramey are editing; Paul Naylor's *Poetic Investigations: Singing the Holes in History*; Bernard Bell's forthcoming anthology of essays on Clarence Major's work, *Clarence Major: The Portrait of an African American Postmodernist*; or sections devoted to the work of Harryette Mullen and Will Alexander in recent issues of *Callaloo*. Another such development, of course, is this conference, which I'm glad is taking place.

Editing *Hambone*

The first issue of *Hambone* was published in the spring of 1974. It was then dormant for several years before being revived, the second issue appearing in the fall of 1982. Since then it has appeared at a rate just a bit slower than an issue per year. My comments here will focus on the period commencing with the revival of the magazine in 1982, as it became a significantly different journal upon resuming publication at that point. For one, I became the sole editor and publisher, whereas the spring 1974 issue was a group effort initiated by the Committee on Black Performing Arts at Stanford University, where I was a graduate student. The journal in fact had a different name and a different editor at its inception; I was asked to take over when that editor, midway through the year, left Stanford for a teaching job in another part of the country. I thus, for that first issue, inherited material that had been gathered and selected by others. To this material I added contributions that I solicited from writers and artists whose work I admired. I also gave the magazine the name *Hambone.* Shortly after the appearance of the first issue, I, too, left Stanford for a teaching job elsewhere. No one at Stanford took up the job of continuing to put out the journal, so for several years I carried around the idea of someday reviving it in a somewhat different form—which, as I've mentioned, I did in 1982.

The aim of the Committee on Black Performing Arts was to publish a journal presenting work by African American writers and artists. This the first issue did, and subsequent issues have continued to do so. The name *Hambone* carries African American references and resonances, conjuring and alluding to the vernacular rhyme and the vernacular figure of that name, the dialogical "'Hambone, Hambone, where you been?' / 'Around the world and I'm goin' again.'" I also, in choosing the name, had in mind a composition of the same name by saxophonist Archie Shepp, itself based on this rhyme, a signal, suggestive meeting of the vernacular and the avant-garde. The name of the journal thus accents an African American provenance while also marking a propensity to range or to roam ("Around the world and I'm goin' again"), a propensity I brought more emphatically to the fore when *Hambone* began to appear again in the 1980s. Whereas the 1974 issue was comprised entirely of works by African American writers and artists, I decided that, beginning with issue number 2, *Hambone* would include work by contributors from a variety of racial and ethnic backgrounds, albeit continuing to present work by African American writers and artists. It would, I decided, attempt to offer an informed, coherent eclecticism, publishing work by writers and artists from various communities inside and outside the United States, bringing together contributors who, actual and ostensible differences notwithstanding, share certain formal, linguistic, and social concerns. It would lean toward and feature the experimental and the esoteric, divergent artistico-cultural practices, advancing a noncentrist, counter-mainstream aesthetic. "Cross- cultural work with an emphasis on the centrifugal" is how I characterized the journal's focus for the Coordinating Council of Literary Magazines' directory.

The editorial agenda that has informed *Hambone* since resumption of publication in 1982 has thus been: (1) to create an eclectic but not haphazard mix in which writers from a variety of communities both inside and outside the U.S. are brought together; (2) to highlight shared as well as contrasting concerns and artistic orientations, favoring work bent on testing and extending the conceptual and technical possibilities afforded by writing; (3) to compose each issue with an eye toward continuity, counterpoint, overlap, and overall coherence; (4) to publish unknown and less-known writers deserving greater exposure alongside well-known writers; and (5) to include relevant forays into the nonliterary arts (music, the visual arts, etc.). I want to emphasize the fact that *Hambone* has been the work of a single editor, that solicitations and editorial decisions have been made not by an editorial board or an editorial staff but by one individual. It has not aspired to be or to appear to be other than the small press publication, the one-man operation, the little magazine that it is. One of the influences on my sense of the little magazine's function was the proliferation of such journals in the United States during the postwar period, a variety of publication I became acquainted with in the late 1960s. The little magazine explosion, as some have called it, accentuated plurality and particularity, bestowing upon the literary landscape a growing number of small-scale but often far-reaching journals that made no claim to institutional authority. Indeed, implicitly on the whole and explicitly in many cases, they countered the notion of such authority, which tends toward centralization, consensus-making, and canon formation, with a valorization of individual energy, idiosyncratic vision, and centrifugal or polycentric judgment and address.

Of the magazines I read during the 1960s and '70s, those that most influenced my practice as an editor were magazines that were shaped by the engagements, enthusiasms, and aesthetic inclinations of an individual editor—*Caterpillar, Coyote's Journal, Credences, Io, Isthmus, Montemora, New Wilderness Letter,* and *New World Journal,* to name a few. In most cases these editors were themselves writers, and their editorial work could be seen to be an extension of their writing, clearly of a piece with vantage points and valorizations advanced by their writing. They were, among other things, mapping the context they saw their writing situated in, creating the context in which their writing could be situated; editing and writing worked hand in hand. This reflects the fact that, for a variety of reasons, it had become increasingly necessary for writers, especially those outside the mainstream, to take more initiative and to assume a larger role in the dissemination of their work and the definition or cultivation of the place it seeks to occupy. Editing had joined writing as a vehicle of self-definition. This was the model from which my sense of the little magazine's function took its cue. *Hambone,* then, has been greatly informed by my predilections as a writer, reader, and critic, by lines of affiliation within a community of concerns and dispositions that I share with certain other writers, artists, and critics. The publication of *Hambone* has thus been something of a personal undertaking—or, better, a particularist undertaking—yet with a certain drive, which every magazine should have, toward ensemblist identity and definition.

In a book of critical essays published in 1993, *Discrepant Engagement: Dissonance, Cross-Culturality, and Experimental Writing,* I called conventional boundaries and groupings into question, calling for mixes that challenge the normalizing authority of such boundaries and groupings. The book itself advanced a mix of this sort in the range of writers dealt with by the essays it contained—black writers from the United States and the Caribbean and the so-called Black Mountain poets primarily. Toward the end of the introduction I wrote,

> [B]ecause of preconceptions regarding who belongs where and with whom, which have been shaped and reinforced by existing rubrics and academic

> practice, there are readers who will find the mix of writers dealt with in this book incongruous and problematic. In this respect, the book's title refers to its own practice, its willingness to engage what will be seen by some as an unlikely or an unsanctioned fit, a non-fit. Though I have attempted in this introduction to offer some of my senses of how these essays and the writers with whose work they deal fit together, I have also offered its fortuitous, figurative title, "And All the Birds Sing Bass," as a discrepant note meant to call attention to the problematics of rubric-making, a caveat meant to make the act of categorization creak. Such creaking is always present, even in the case of more customary groupings—groupings that appear unproblematic, proper, only because we agree not to hear it.[1]

In *Discrepant Engagement* I was concerned with widening the scope of discussions of experimental writing, with gaining greater recognition of the cross-cultural, multiracial range of experimental writing and of innovative artistic practices more generally. I was concerned with diversifying the group of writers—mostly white, and, more often than not, male—whose work tends to be seen as innovative and experimental. I wanted to combat the reduction of the work of writers from minority or socially marginalized groups to simplistic social documentation, to insist that experimental writing, the aesthetic margin, is not the domain solely of those from socially nonmarginalized groups. In the editing and publishing of *Hambone* I've been similarly motivated, hoping to offer something of a corrective to the situation that critic, editor, and translator Eliot Weinberger complained of when he wrote in the early 1980s, "On the aesthetic Left, the magazines are publishing many more women than they used to, but are not attracting young writers from the minorities, despite the presence of major avant-garde minority figures."[2]

On *Hambone*, then, I've brought to bear the aims, inclinations, and priorities that are important to me as a writer and critic. My editorial sensibility owes a great deal to the aesthetic tendencies that have most interested me as a reader and a critic and stimulated me as a writer. These include poetry in the imagist/objectivist tradition, African American modernism and postmodernism from the Harlem Renaissance to the present, surrealism's New World offshoots, the alternative U.S. writing represented by Donald Allen's anthology *The New American Poetry 1945–1960*, Caribbean writing, ethnopoetics, and jazz. Several of these strains were reflected in the list of contributors to issue number 2, with which publication resumed in 1982, all of the work for which I solicited. My aim in composing the issue entirely of solicited work was to delineate the magazine's intended range and reach, to sketch out some of what I intended to be its defining dispositions and concerns. An editor should know not only what sort of work he wishes to publish but specific artists whose work the journal will include. Among the contributors to issue number 2 were Kamau Brathwaite, Beverly Dahlen, Robert Duncan, Wilson Harris, Susan Howe, Clarence Major, Paul Metcalf, Ishmael Reed, Sun Ra, John Taggart, and Jay Wright. Several of the contributors to that issue have published again in subsequent issues. It has, for example, been a particular aim of mine to make the work of the Caribbean authors Brathwaite and Harris better known in the United States; their work has appeared repeatedly in *Hambone's* pages. Likewise, certain areas of focus have been returned to on more than one occasion. The lecture by Sun Ra, for example, itself preceded by an interview with Anthony Braxton in issue number 1, has been followed, in subsequent issues, by interviews with postbop musicians Billy Bang, Steve Lacy, and Cecil Taylor, the jazz-influenced sculpture of Bradford Graves, and jazz-influenced writing by a number of authors. Still, that issue was a call, a summons, an invitation to those who located themselves in the terrain it mapped to submit work. I've continued to solicit work for *Hambone*, to rely primarily on solicited work, but I've been especially gratified to receive a good deal of unsolicited work that fit, to be introduced to the work of writers I wasn't previously aware of but who, in some cases, have become regular contributors, to be taken, especially by the work of such writers as Anne-Marie Albiach, Max Aub, Julio Cortázar, Mahmoud Darweesh, and Alejandra Pizarnik submitted by translators, in directions I hadn't planned or foreseen. As in the music the journal's name refers to, this is what one wants: that the call not go without response.

PART V

Interview by Christopher Funkhouser

The following interview took place in Santa Cruz, California, on September 3, 1991.

CHRISTOPHER FUNKHOUSER: In your work you take improvisation, jazz, and other styles of music and use them as a wellspring. Could you describe how you came to this and manage to keep it such a prominent part of what you do?

NATHANIEL MACKEY: Probably the earliest aesthetic experiences for me were experiences with music, going back to when I was a kid. Certainly that's what that comes from and it has continued to be a very important part of my experience. Not that I started off listening to a lot of the music I listen to now. But music has always been a very important part of my life—even when I was seven, eight, nine years old. Why I didn't take up an instrument and become a musician remains a mystery to me but I didn't, and that has to do with circumstantial things which are just circumstantial things. Late in high school I got into reading poetry and fiction on a more serious level, as something other than what you did because it was assigned. I was actually beginning to do it because I was interested in it, because it was speaking to me in a meaningful way. Some of the literature I got into had analogies with music, though I wasn't always aware of it. Some of the writers who had an early impact on me were also engaged with music. William Carlos Williams was a writer whose work I got interested in when I was in high school. I didn't know about his interest in music, which wasn't that strong or that extensive, but later I found out about it, though it wasn't necessarily that I was hearing music coming through in Williams's work. Among those writers I was reading early on was Amiri Baraka, whose engagement with music is enormous, tremendous. It was one of the things that galvanized the relationships among writing, reading, and music which began to develop for me.

FUNKHOUSER: Was there anything equally as important as music as an influence?

MACKEY: The music was pretty close to and bound up with the religious for me. Some of the earliest music I was exposed to was the music in the Baptist Church, so the relationship between music and the spiritual was very strongly imprinted very early through the church experience. Seeing people respond to music in ways that were quite different from music being listened to in a concert situation, I mean, people actually going into states of trance and possession in church, had a tremendous and continuing impact on me. It's no doubt one of the reasons I so often refer to and incorporate aspects of, say, Haitian *vodoun*, Cuban *santería*, and other trance rituals that involve music—dance as a form of worship. That was part of the music experience, the wider context into which the music experience extends. I don't know what else. Obviously one of the things is that I was interested in a variety of things, even as a kid, so there are a variety of things that were pertinent to my early development. I was a precocious reader, read a lot of different kinds of things and had an interest in mathematics and science early on. I don't know to what extent that comes in but it does. There was a time when I was reading philosophy, although it's been a while. I think all of those things play a part. It's easier to see the role that music plays because it's so pronounced and it has become a central preoccupation or the trope for a variety of preoccupations that such a work as *From a Broken Bottle Traces of Perfume Still Emanate* builds upon. The poems participate in that in their own way, in both the musicality of the writing and the overt referentiality to music in the writing. For me music is so much more than music that when you ask "What else besides music?" it's hard for me to answer because music includes so much: it's social, it's religious, it's metaphysical, it's aesthetic, it's expressive, it's creative, it's destructive. It just covers so much. It's the biggest, most inclusive thing that I could put forth if I were to choose one single thing.

FUNKHOUSER: In the work—the prose and the poetry—there is an extreme lyricism that's transmitted from somewhere. What lineage do you see your work aligned with?

MACKEY: Well, I've already named Williams and Baraka. The larger tendencies in American poetry that they are a part of I relate to and relate myself to. Oppen, for example, whose line "bright light of shipwreck" I use as a subtitle to one of the poems in *Eroding Witness*. Some of the so-called New American Poetry, the poets in Donald Allen's anthology, which I read and was very much impacted upon by in the mid-sixties. The Black Mountain projectivist poets were very important: Charles Olson, Robert Creeley, Robert Duncan. Denise Levertov early on was an important poet for me. I began reading poetry seriously in high school. I graduated from high school in 1965. It was when I went to college that I began to read more, began to read more contemporary, more recent stuff, more postwar poetry. Those were the people I was reading at that time. And, you know, one goes on reading and building on what one has read, and I've gone on to other people since then. A couple of Caribbean writers have been very important to me, Wilson Harris and Edward Kamau Brathwaite. Other Caribbean writers as well, like Aimé Césaire, and other writers, a range of writers. If I start naming them I'll name all day. There was a period when, for example, the new novelists of France, Alain Robbe-Grillet, Nathalie Sarraute, and others—I read their work quite attentively. I was a big fan of a Polish writer named Witold Gombrowicz. I remember reading and rereading his novels. You know how it is: you read and you read and you read and some stuff you reread.

FUNKHOUSER: Did you write at Princeton?

MACKEY: Yes. I had written a little bit, had gotten the impulse to write in high school, but hadn't written a whole lot. It was when I was in college that I started writing more and started thinking about that as something I wanted to do if I could. It was in college that I really began to invest in and investigate the sense of myself as a writer.

FUNKHOUSER: There were teachers there that helped you?

MACKEY: Not particularly. It wasn't so much that setting or any particular teachers there. There were teachers there that I talked to and liked and whose classes were an influence, but not in a direct sense of there being writers there who were teachers of mine. It was more the exposure to literature that I got in literature classes, the exposure to readings that took place on campus, and Princeton being only an hour-and-a-half drive from New York. I would go in and hear readings there, although there wasn't really a heavy reading scene at that time. Mainly what I did when I went into New York was hear music. That was one of the big stimuli that that allowed. I wasn't a creative writing major or anything like that—I think I took one creative writing course the whole time I was in college and that was enough. But I wrote and published in some of the campus literary magazines.

FUNKHOUSER: You manage to place, by virtue of being a publisher and via radio broadcasting, some of your creative output within the context of Western culture, not limiting it to African or Asian or some of the other reference points. Are you striving at all to facilitate any type of social change or awareness, or is it just art?

MACKEY: Well, if it can facilitate social change and awareness in a positive and progressive direction, then, certainly, more power to it. I don't want to overestimate or inflate what work of that sort—doing a radio program, or editing a magazine, or writing poetry and prose—can do. But certainly to the extent that categories and the way things are defined—the boundaries among things, people, areas of experience, areas of endeavor—to the extent that those categories and definitions are rooted in social and political realities, anything one does that challenges them, that transgresses those boundaries and offers new definitions, is to some extent contributing to social change. The kind of cross-cultural mix that a radio program like *Tanganyika Strut* offers diverges from a prepackaged sense of what appropriate content for a radio program is, where one is usually offered a homogeneous program. There's a challenge in heterogeneity, whether it's radio programming, editing a magazine, one's own work, putting together a syllabus for a class, or whatever. These are questions that resonate with all of the political and social urgencies that have to do with how do you get different people to live together in society in some kind of positive and productive way.

FUNKHOUSER: So where do you find your audience? Are you directing what you are transmitting as poet, as radio programmer, as teacher, to any specific audience or are you just throwing it out there?

MACKEY: I'm not just throwing it out there. I'm putting it out there, but I can't say that I am putting it out there with a particular audience in mind because the way in which audiences are defined is often dependent upon those categories that I mentioned earlier that are fixed and static and I think misrepresent reality in most instances. Therefore I can't let those senses of possible audiences be what dictates what I do. So I don't think about the given categories of audience. I think about doing what makes sense to me, what is meaningful to me, with the conviction that there are other people that it will make sense to, be meaningful to, and with the hope that what I'm doing will find its way to them and they'll find their way to it. That's the sense of audience I work with. To me it's more the work finding or defining, proposing an audience, than the work being shaped out of some idea of an audience, consideration of an audience, "this is what such and such a group of people wants to hear. . . ."

FUNKHOUSER: There are writers, especially at this time, who are thinking that way because there's money in it. That's not why I was asking you, though. Mostly I ask because a lot of the references in your writing are almost completely obscure to someone who is not really on top of it as far as world music goes, as far as "outside" musics go. Someone naively picking up your books might think they were Pound's *Cantos*, with so many obscure reference points. For instance, most people would have no idea who Albert Ayler was, and so on. Automatically you might, in a way, sever some understanding.

MACKEY: Well, obviously you can say certain things about the audience for a work by looking at the character of the work. In many ways the work itself answers the question "What is the audience for this work?" If you look at a work that is making mention of Albert Ayler, then obviously that work is aimed at people who know who Albert Ayler is or are interested in finding out, would want to find out. You have to talk and write from what you know, about what you know, with what you know. You have to take the risk of speaking to people about things they may be unfamiliar with, just as there are things other people know that you are not familiar with. I have read people whose work spoke of things and made reference to things that I didn't know about, and reading that work has been an impetus for me to find out about those things. Since that has been my experience as a reader, why wouldn't it be the experience of others? One doesn't have to be constantly looking over one's own shoulder asking, "Can I say this? Is the reader still with me?" I think you have to go with the faith that there are readers who are with you. You may not know who or where they are but you have to take that risk.

FUNKHOUSER: In a way it seems that that's what a lot of the outside jazz improvisers were doing, hoping by putting it out there that somebody would hear it at some point and be able to have some transcendence, or at least some type of unification with them.

MACKEY: Yes. When I first started listening to improvised music in my early teens—up to that point I had mainly been listening to R & B and rock 'n' roll, popular music you hear on the radio—it didn't make a whole lot of sense to me. I don't know what it was about it that made me go back and give it a chance, but it was something I had to learn how to listen to. And I did learn how to listen to it, by going back and listening on repeated occasions. That was how I got into the music of Miles Davis, John Coltrane, and others in the early sixties. I came to the outside players later and had a similar experience with them. In high school I kept reading and hearing about Ornette Coleman in places like *DownBeat.* There was a lot of fuss being made about what he was up to, so I wanted to check it out. I remember buying an Ornette Coleman album and it just sounded very strange and weird. I couldn't figure it out but I kept listening to it and after a while it not only made sense to me, there was a beauty to it. It was unlike the beauty that I heard in Miles Davis or John Coltrane, but it was beauty. The ability to get into something that initially is forbidding or intimidating or just doesn't speak to you at all is one that is tested and proven. I tend to stay with things which may, on first or second or third hearing or reading, present me with difficulties that make it seem like it isn't going to go anywhere. You're right. What any experimental art is trying to get you to do is move beyond your preconceptions and your expectations regarding what should be happening, what's going to happen, what kinds of effects it should have, and enter a liminal state in which those things can be redefined in the way that the particular artist or piece of art is proposing.

FUNKHOUSER: A more specific question: At a "Poets For Peace" reading in February you read a poem called "Slipped Quadrant." You mentioned that the poem operates out of Islamic and Arabic materials or concepts. Which ones? Is your interest in these materials primarily poetic or is it something else?

MACKEY: Well, "Slipped Quadrant" makes reference to Sufis in Andalusia, and one of the particular Islamic thinkers I had in mind is Ibn 'Arabi, who wrote a book called *Sufis of Andalusia.* There's a point where the poem says "to be alive / was to be warned." A sense of omen, more than concepts per se, is how Islam comes into it. Ibn 'Arabi, in a famous episode early in his life, was asked by the philosopher Ibn Rushd, Averroes, what solution had he found in mystical trance, in divine inspiration, and did it agree with what one finds through speculative thought. He answered, "Yes and no. Between the yea and the nay the spirits take their flight beyond matter, and the necks detach themselves from their bodies." More generally, I'm interested in the Islamic/Moorish presence in Spain, and have been for a long time. How I got into reading about Islam I'm not sure. One of the early places where just the presence of

Islam in the world was made apparent was that many of the black musicians I was listening to were interested in it and in many instances were converts to Islam. Yusef Lateef, for example. Then just learning more about history and the role of Islamic and Arab civilization in history. Later I became interested particularly in Islamic mysticism and heterodoxy. My introduction to Ibn 'Arabi came by way of Charles Olson, who got very interested in him via Henri Corbin's books, a book on Ibn 'Arabi and a book on Avicenna. Those are some of the places I was finding people making use of thought from the Islamic world. I read around some, and have listened to a great deal of music from the Muslim world. An early musical interest of mine that continues is flamenco, which I began listening to back in the early sixties, partly because of Miles Davis's *Sketches of Spain.* At the time I was taking Spanish in school and some attention to flamenco was a part of studying Spanish culture. The contributions of Moorish and Gypsy cultures to flamenco were very clear and obvious, its connections to North Africa, and so on. So it's part of my larger interest in the movement of cultural influences and exchanges over wide geographic areas, the cross-cultural mix that the planet is. As I said, some of the earliest articulations and manifestations of that I encountered in the music that was coming out of outside players, the black musicians of the sixties. There's an Indian musician who plays the shenai called Bismillah Khan. The first time I ever heard of Bismillah Khan was on a record by one of the Chicago reed players out of the AACM, Kalaparusha Maurice McIntyre. He has a piece on one of those Delmark albums called "Bismillah." I have forgotten which instrument he plays on it. I don't think it's a shenai, but it's obviously imitating a shenai. About that same time I saw someone else mention Bismillah Khan and I decided to get hold of one of his records. A lot of the music and other things from other countries I have gotten into I have been led to by these musicians—Don Cherry doing an album called *Eternal Rhythm,* on which he uses Balinese gamelan instruments, and things like that. There's this "world ear" that many of the musicians were blessed with that led me to a lot of these things. Islamic music and the Islamic literature are entwined with one another in that way, and that mix comes up in *Bedouin Hornbook,* for example, where at one point a book such as *Conference of the Birds,* which is a Sufi text, is referred to. It's also the name of an album by David Holland, *Conference of the Birds,* with Anthony Braxton, Sam Rivers, and Barry Altschul on it. Those kinds of musical-textual, musical-literary-religious, music-literary-spiritual confluences are very much what *Bedouin Hornbook* and the poems are often touching the notes of and applauding. The Gulf War and all of the warmongering rhetoric that led up to it had a great deal to do with and came out of anti-Arab racism, a sense of Arab inferiority. That was one of the reasons it was so easy to mobilize and launch that war. What I said in prefacing the poem, which didn't specifically have to do with the war—in fact it was written considerably before the war—was simply that one of the things that made it so easy to go into that war was, first of all, the sense that the people that this country would be fighting against were nonentities culturally, historically, that they had never done anything that amounted to anything. In a very simple way, I invited people to think about the fact that we use Arabic numerals. One could go on and catalog the ways in which Western civilization likes to propose itself as the superior antithesis of Arab civilization when in fact it is indebted to Arab civilization. Arabs pulled Europe out of its Dark Ages, reintroduced it to what it likes to think of as its roots, the Greek philosophers, Aristotle, Plato, and so forth. In saying that to preface the poem I wanted to underscore the way in which our intellectual activities can be a part of something that is oppositional to the formation of social attitudes and biases in a country such as this—how as intellectuals, poets, writers, we're engaged in something that is looking at the complex interconnectedness of people, of cultures, in a way that is finally in opposition to the oversimplifications of experience and of identity that dominate the politics of this and too many other countries. That's what I was trying, in a nutshell, to say.

FUNKHOUSER: Those complexities seem to somehow possibly relate to the intricacies of mathematics, also the scientific realm. The title "Slipped Quadrant" might also imply this.

MACKEY: In "Slipped Quadrant" not in any extensive way, though when I was younger I was very involved with math and science. In fact, when I was in junior high school and high school I considered that the field that I would go into. But it's been a long time since I last sat down with a book of differential equations. It's also been a long time since I've gone through or even looked at a book on physics. But as reference points every now and then they have come in. "Slipped Quadrant" was playing with two things, two senses of the word *quadrant,* one of which is that when you have a pair of Cartesian axes you have each of those four parts as a quadrant. There was that sense, so you're right. There was a mathematical meaning to that term I had in mind. But also it's a poem that has to do with generations and wandering and so it was also a quadrant in the sense of a navigational device. The idea of "Slipped Quadrant" was the idea of a dislocation, something out of joint, talking not about Cartesian symmetry, equilibrium, settledness, but something that's shaken, something that is in trouble, something that's unsettled. Another reference in that title is Cecil Taylor's music. He has an album called *Winged Serpents (Sliding Quadrants)* and I was thinking about that: slipped quadrant/sliding quadrants, this whole idea of slippage and erosion, disequilibrium, unrest—which his music is so majestic and outrageous an expression of.

FUNKHOUSER: Getting back to *From a Broken Bottle Traces of Perfume Still Emanate,* I was wondering what you think the effect is of publishing in serial format, and how much of it is outlined in thought beforehand. Was there a concept from the start or is it just happening as it happens? As far as process goes, are the letters journalistic writing? Dreams? How edited is it? How is it progressing? Will it be a trilogy specifically or might it continue? Is the protagonist going to get killed at the end of the third book by the CIA?

MACKEY: Well, I don't proceed with some mapped-out plan or some blueprint. I can't tell you how it's going to end. I didn't really know what I was getting into when I started that series. In fact, I would have thought you were crazy if you had told me years ago that I would be doing a third volume, at some point, of these little prose things that I had started to do. I started in the late seventies with the first few of those "Dear Angel of Dust" letters, and I didn't really know what was happening. "Dear Angel of Dust" is a phrase that really just came into my head. It came into my head before there was really even a letter or occasion, just "Dear Angel of Dust." At that point I didn't know whether it was something that would be a line or an image in a poem or what, but it spoke to me and intrigued me, resonated for me, and just held on and held on. The letters got started from an actual correspondence. A friend of mine to whom I'd sent a couple of poems or something wrote back with some questions. By way of talking about or addressing those questions I wrote it out in the form of a letter which began "Dear Angel of Dust" and made a copy and sent it to this friend. So it began in actual correspondence but it was like proposing another correspondence that I was allowing this friend to eavesdrop on, so to speak, though the thoughts were provoked by his questions. At that point I was getting interested in prose as something which could include, in a more explicit way, certain types and areas of information that I was interested in but that I couldn't work into poetry, at least not in such an explicit way as I could in prose. One can be discursive and one can use various modes of address, so I started writing a few of these letters. I didn't know how to think of them, whether they were prose poems or what. In any case, a couple of the first few that came occurred in the context of poems and are included in *Eroding Witness.* So it started off being meditational/ manifesto-type assertions which were making certain propositions about poetics that were related to the poems that they occurred in the context of. Then this idea of having N. form or be a member of a band came about and they really sort of took off in a direction of their own—more narrative, and longer. When I started doing those first few I still didn't know just how much of that there would be. It just turned out to be something that grew on me. And it continues to go on.

FUNKHOUSER: It's a terrific form.

MACKEY: Yes, it's right there, very immediate. It goes right back to the roots of the English novel and the fact that we often end up reading the letters of this, that or the other writer. It seemed like that form, which is episodic, which doesn't seek to totalize but to be just the expression of a particular occasion, fit my commitment to process. The serial form that you ask about—I use it in poetry too—is something that has been around for quite a while and has been increasingly used by poets and the advantages of it have been talked about quite a bit. It gets you away from, among other things, the idea of the well-made little poem that is self-contained and static. You begin to have work that carries over and that you pick up the resonances of and carry forth. It invites you to think about work that you've already done as incomplete and open to further articulation or modification, variation, which is a lot of what improvisation is, working out the suggestions that reside within a previous statement, a musical line or whatever. You start pulling things out of it that you didn't know were there. For example, the poem sequence "Septet for the End of Time," a sequence of eight poems at the end of *Eroding Witness,* for a long time was just that one poem "Capricorn Rising" which is the first of the eight. But I found that those three words that begin each of the poems, "I wake up," just kept coming back.

FUNKHOUSER: And you do wake up . . .

MACKEY: Right. So the next thing I knew I had written another poem that began "I wake up" and it took up with some of the imagery of "Capricorn Rising." I began to consciously go back in and work with that kind of literal rearticulation and further articulation of things that were resonant in "Capricorn Rising," letting it unfold into a particular sequence. That's one of the senses of open-form poetry to me: when something is apparently closed, you can break it open and pull further implications and explications out of it. That's the process that I work with, in both verse and prose. Often writing is a form of rereading for me, just going back and seeing things in something I've written that I didn't see before. So much writing comes out of reading anyway, reading other people, so why shouldn't it come out of reading yourself?

FUNKHOUSER: It is exciting, not just for the writer but for someone who is interested in the writer who can wait with interest for what is to come, and it's definitely a way to enliven literature. Then again, I've been thinking of your work as more than just literature, as something more like anthropology, especially with all the musicology and different spirits that come into it. Beyond this, there may be political implications as well, which brings me to ask you about your experience with being a black publisher, editor, poet, and teacher. Obviously it is intricately interwoven through the material, but is there any particular direction you're taking it?

MACKEY: Do you mean literary politics?

FUNKHOUSER: Sure; also cultural and social politics.

MACKEY: Well, some of this stuff we've already touched on. I think that politics is, among other things, laying claim to one's own authority. And that is obviously something people from socially marginalized groups are not encouraged to do. So simply being an author, and laying claim to one's authority, in that sense, is already fraught with political resonances, especially in the case of African Americans, who less than 150 years ago were forbidden to read and write. There were laws against African American literacy for decades and decades in this country. The monopolistic claim to literacy by the dominant white culture is one of the things that the African American literary tradition has been at odds with and up against from the beginning. And we continue that. It hasn't gone away. There are other forms of authority besides one's writing. Being an editor, being a publisher. All those things are a part of doing it, of putting oneself in the position of making decisions, saying, "This is how I'm going to write" or "These are the pieces I'm going to publish." These are things that can't help being social and political in those senses, which seem to me perfectly obvious.

FUNKHOUSER: But it's not always stated forthrightly in discussions or in print. By and large, a lot of people aren't thinking of it that way, with such fortitude, of the poet or writer as an authority. Poetry seems to be a very subversive form of communication, almost, and can be very political. Maybe it's not politicized enough . . .

MACKEY: We have to make some distinction between literary politics—which is the politics of power and distribution of power among writers and groups of writers—and politics in the society at large, which is why I ask. What we've got is politics within politics. Certainly anybody who publishes or seeks to publish, who becomes a writer, is immediately involved in some arena of literary politics. "You write more like certain people than you do certain other people." "Your writing speaks more to certain groups than it does to other groups." "You have affinities with certain writers and certain audiences and certain other audiences can't stand you." Things like that. So that's inevitable. Inevitably you're doing something that is probably rubbing against somebody else.

FUNKHOUSER: Another reason I asked the question is because Western culture is overtly racist. Your experience with that is without doubt very different than mine. At the same time, you really thrive within it.

MACKEY: Well, like I said, people who are not supposed to speak with any authority claiming their right to speak with authority goes against the kinds of racism that you're talking about. The kind of challenging and questioning of categories that I spoke about earlier is very important to that too. Mixes of things that defy and redefine boundary lines are very important in the literary politics, cultural politics, and marginalized social politics of the time we're living in. What kinds of groupings, what kinds of work you publish in your magazine, what kinds of intellectual and other sorts of influences and predecessors you bring together in your work, all of those things speak to an order or possible order of things. I think that to the extent that they diverge from and challenge the accepted orderings and accepted boundary lines, the accepted, monolithic senses of what is possible, there's a seed in that. How long it will take to germinate, how big it will grow—I think that when we're talking about things of this sort we're talking about a long-range thing, we're not talking about immediate gains. All of this is trying to do something. The writing and these other activities come out of living, come out of the desires and demands we make upon living. Those desires and demands call for change because we're not doing the kind of living often enough that we want to be doing. The reasons for that include factors that can be changed, factors that we have some control of as human beings. Poetry, music, sculpture, or painting that speaks from that discontent and unrest is mobilizing an awareness that things are not what we want them to be and there has to be a movement toward them becoming what we want. That's the politics of art. That's always been the politics of art. Certainly in the foreseeable future it will continue to be the politics of art.

FUNKHOUSER: I remember from somewhere in your work the phrase "Antediluvian sense of design." I guess in a way that's what I just heard from you, at least in terms of the politics of art. Who are the visual artists of the time that you are interested in?

MACKEY: I'm not really up on visual arts. I can't really say much about visual arts. I consider myself not a terribly visual person. I'm just really not. I don't seek out the visual arts in the way I seek out music.

FUNKHOUSER: In sections I've read from the prose book that's about to come out there are descriptions of the Mystic Horn Society's "Quantum-Qualitative Increments." I am wondering if you've ever actually experienced this yourself in writing or performing.

MACKEY: Yes. I've certainly experienced it in writing. Since I'm not a musician I can't say that I've actually experienced it in musical performance, and I can't say that I've experienced it in reading my work, although there are some readings where your voice is dealing in nuances that it hadn't dealt in before. Some readings are better than others. Some readings you are able to hear, see, think implications in the words, or between the words, or among the words, that you are somehow able to translate in a way that you didn't foresee or think about in advance in your vocal rendering of a piece. That's happened, and I think it has something to do with the character of the occasion and the audience that one is reading to. There are certain times when I've read when I've sensed a quality of attention in the audience that had an impact on the way I read, in a way that I'm often writing about in the "Angel of Dust" letters, that sense that N. is often talking about of picking up on what's going on in the audience and that becoming a part of the performance, having an impact on the performance in some way. I've had that kind of experience in readings. One doesn't have that sitting by oneself and writing, but I've had the experience of breakthroughs when writing, words and formulations of a certain sort, new and unprepared for, that I didn't know were there, experiences where I had to ask, "Why now?"

FUNKHOUSER: Have you ever performed with music as texture or performed with musicians?

MACKEY: Not very much. I read at the University of San Francisco about a year and a half ago in a reading that included Allen Ginsberg, Diane DiPrima, and others. Don Cherry, who was there to accompany Ginsberg, came up while I was reading with flutes and some percussion instruments, gourd rattles and stuff, and began to play. This was not planned, was very spontaneous, about halfway through my portion of the reading. I knew he was going to show up because Ginsberg had mentioned it, and apparently he showed up while I was reading. I didn't see him come up on stage but I was reading and heard this flute and knew immediately who it was. So I had to alter my reading a bit. I had to listen to him, and he listened to me. Apparently it turned out pretty well. I haven't heard the tape but people said so. I haven't done a whole lot of that. The other thing that's kind of close to that, but really different, is that last spring, in a program called "Exercises for Ear," Dave Barrett, who's a musician in the Bay Area—part of the Splatter Trio—put together at Small Press Distribution and at New Langton Arts a program for which he got a number of writers and composers to come up with compositions that he and several other musicians performed. He invited me to take part in that. What I did was use a portion of the text from *From a Broken Bottle Traces of Perfume Still Emanate* which describes a composition. In fact, it's from that section that's in *Conjunctions 16.* There's a piece that's called "Udhrite Amendment." I simply sent that with some accompanying texts, because that portion refers to other things, some sections of *Bedouin Hornbook.* I sent those texts and simply said, "Can you get a performance of 'Udhrite Amendment' based on what's written here?" And they did. There was a performance of that at New Langton Arts in early June. But I haven't done a whole lot of that sort of thing. I've thought about doing it, reading to musical accompaniment, but just never found a musician who's around on a regular basis. Because the rhythms of the poems I write are so cut to my voice and my sense of placement and space and so on, it would really take some work to get to where I could, with some musicians, have the kind of interplay that would do both the music of their music and the music of my music justice. I realized that at the reading when Don Cherry showed up, that I had to alter some of my rhythms, in some ways make them less idiosyncratic to fit the music that he was making.

FUNKHOUSER: With regards to education: by and large, in the academy, when poetry is taught it is left on the page. Written and printed texts are read. There usually isn't as much exploration of audiotexts and sound as a part of poetry, when in actuality that's where the roots of poetry are. In your own teaching do you bring this in as an element?

MACKEY: When I teach I include as a part of the experience of a poem, to the extent that it is possible, hearing the poetry. That means in some cases getting recordings, when they're available, of the poet in question and playing them in class. If they're not available, and it's a poet I've heard read, I'll give students some sense of how that poet reads, how that poet sounds. If it's a poet whose work I haven't heard, I'll ask if there are any students who have heard the poet read. Just stressing how the poem sounds is not only important but indispensable to the experience of the poem. I'll have people read the work out loud, offer their senses of how it sounds, and talk about certain aspects of how the poem sounds, the rhythm, where the stresses are falling—not in some scansion sense but what that has to do with what the poem is saying, how it's being said. I try to get the poem off the page. I think the experience of how the poem is on the page is important too. For me it's not an either/or situation. Both of those things are important. I write with the sound of the poem in mind. But I don't write poems that I expect to be fully digested simply by being heard. I write with the fact that people can go to the text in mind. I try to write a type of poetry that takes advantage of the possibility of reading and rereading, even though I don't think that simply reading the poem on the page is enough. In some cases of poets who write poetry that is put forth as poetry that needs to be heard, has to be heard, is primarily oral, sometimes it makes for a poetry that is not very satisfying or interesting when it's on the page. I want both things to be happening. I want it to be interesting when you hear it, and I want it to hold your attention in both kinds of readings. I want it to hold your attention when you hear it and when you're reading it on the page.

FUNKHOUSER: I wanted to ask you about *Hambone.* How did it come about? Is it a lifelong project? I'm fascinated by the *Hambone* network, by and large very unknown poets—on a wide scale—but the magazine in itself coming together so incredibly, and the last issue, number 9, tied together by the interaction and interview with Brathwaite, your relationship with him. It astounds me how few people know about *Hambone.*

MACKEY: It doesn't astound me! Going back a little bit, to something we were talking about earlier, which is the idea of networks of association and communities of interest, inclination, and affinity—the cultivation and pursuit of that, the registration of that, is one of the central reasons for editing a magazine as far as I'm concerned. That was a central ambition I had when I started to edit and publish *Hambone* in the early eighties. I was actually reviving a magazine whose first issue had appeared in 1974 when I was still a graduate student at Stanford. It was in a different format and in a different situation, which we don't need to go into, but in many ways when I started *Hambone* again in the early eighties it was a different magazine, although I called the first issue I did in the eighties *Hambone 2*. For one thing, I was the sole editor, whereas in '74 I was working with other people. In any case, in the eighties my idea was to simply put my sense of a community of writers and artists on a kind of map, in one place. So in *Hambone 2*, in which all of the material was solicited, that meant having a talk by Sun Ra and poems by Robert Duncan, poems by Beverly Dahlen, Jay Wright, fiction by Clarence Major, Wilson Harris, poems by Edward Kamau Brathwaite and so on. That issue was sort of saying, "Okay, here's my map, a significant part of it, and we're going to call it *Hambone*." It seems to me that's what little magazines do, and do best. They put a particular editor's sense of "what's up" out there, and you find out who out there is interested in that. There are poets and writers that I have come to publish in *Hambone* since that issue, and have published several times, who have become repeat *Hambone* contributors, people I have gotten to know that I didn't know before I started publishing *Hambone* that I have gotten to know—at least their work—through them reading *Hambone* and seeing *Hambone* and feeling that this was a map that they had a place on. That's the function of a magazine, I think—to create those kinds of contacts and those kinds of connections. Whether it will go on my whole life? I'm pretty sure that it won't. I don't know how much longer it will go on. Again, it was to make a particular mix available that one would not normally find—for instance, Sun Ra and Robert Duncan in the same publication.

FUNKHOUSER: So are you teaching out of necessity, or are your feelings about it stronger than that?

MACKEY: I teach out of necessity but at the same time it's a necessity that I try to make useful in ways that further my concerns and things that I'd like to get done. The teaching I do is folded in and connected to the other things that I do. When we were talking about *Hambone*, you mentioned the interview with Brathwaite, and your sense that it didn't seem fortuitous, I guess, that I was talking to Brathwaite and I seemed to be talking about concerns that were his concerns and vice versa. Well, Brathwaite is someone whose work I got interested in in the early seventies, and have read, and taught, and written critical work about. So I've been influenced by his work, I've been turned on to things by his work. That's one instance of how my work as a teacher is connected with my work as a writer. I'm at the university and one of the things that I do at the university besides teach is write literary criticism about some of the writers that I have published in *Hambone.* For example, in *Hambone 2* there were writers like Brathwaite whose work I had been reading, in some instances teaching, and in some instances had written about, like Duncan and Harris. Paul Metcalf is someone whose work I have taught, although I haven't written on his work. Susan Howe was in that issue. I've taught her work. Jay Wright's work I've taught, though I haven't written extensively on it. Clarence Major I've taught and written on. So that's just talking about the connection between teaching and editing. Those are also writers who have informed my own work, and my own sense of what's possible in writing in various ways. Those things all go around in a circle with one another. I try to get teaching and being in the university to work with, complement, and reinforce the work that I do as a writer and as an editor/publisher. The occasion of that interview with Brathwaite was the fact that Brathwaite was here as a Regents Professor for a couple of weeks at UCSC. He was here because I nominated him for it, in the same way that a few years ago Wilson Harris was here as a Regents Professor because I nominated him. Both those visits resulted in me getting to know those writers better, resulted in some publication of interviews or whatever in *Hambone,* and student interaction. The quarter that Brathwaite was here I was teaching a course on Caribbean literature and we were reading, among other things, his work. He came and spoke to the class one day while he was here. I think we were reading George Lamming's work, who's also from Barbados, and Brathwaite talked a bit about Lamming's novel *In the Castle of My Skin,* about the Caribbean situation—Barbados particularly—and students asked questions and he answered them. So, again, regarding the question of audience, as an editor I'm interested in cultivating, creating certain kinds of audiences, reaching people with the work of people I think they should be reading. As a teacher I'm trying to do the same thing, and those things lend themselves to one another. It is no accident that I publish and teach some of the same people.

Interview by Edward Foster

The following interview took place in Santa Cruz, California, in August 1991.

EDWARD FOSTER: In a recent review of *Eroding Witness,* Leonard Schwartz defines what he calls the "transcendental lyric," saying that in your poems you explore "subjective access to modes of being prior to personal experience." Could you comment on where you feel he is situating your work and how that is distinct from conventional representations of subjectivity in lyric poetry?

NATHANIEL MACKEY: Well, it would be modes of being prior to *one's own* experience, which I think is probably what that statement is aiming at—to free it of the immersion in the subjective and the personal. Records of experience that are part of the communal and collective inheritance that we have access to even though we have not personally experienced those things are prior to one's own experience in the sense of preceding what one personally experiences, while also being available to one's personal experience of the world. I found the emphasis he was placing on alternate traditions that have not so compromised subjectivity with a history of oppression important. I think that he rightly situated the predicament of subjectivity in the lyric that we inherit within a Western tradition which has legacies of domination and conquest and moral complication that make those claims to subjectivity and sublimity hard to countenance. His emphasis on my recourse to, say, African traditional wisdoms and neo-African and Caribbean sources of access to a kind of subjectivity—or just the whole realm of subjectivity that is called into question as one of the repercussions of that oppressive legacy of the West—I think that way of situating the current predicament within the Western sensibility was a necessary move. It is a move that is not often made. It is a move that is necessary to make in order, for one, to situate that problematic, to historicize it, to see it as something that is not some universal condition that is shared by all people in all parts of the globe, to see that the bad taste or aftertaste that haunts Western subjectivity has to do with a particular Western history and a particular imposition upon the world that has been made in the name of that subjectivity.

FOSTER: Could you give an example of how subjectivity dominates in poetry—how it speaks for more than itself in other than political ways?

MACKEY: Well, I think that it's not possible to dissociate in any radical way the subjectivity that comes across in many of the poetic works and cultural works from the political imposition, the political subjectivity that we're talking about. For example, you find in something like John Donne's poetry the registration of the fact of European incursion into the New World in the tropes and imagery he begins to use, where he refers to a woman's body as his "new-found-land." Or, later, you get a related imagery of incursion, similar tropes of expedition, when Baudelaire writes of a "languid Asia" and "blazing Africa" in his mistress's hair, resorting to figures of ships, ports, and so forth. That sense of the poetic subject being related to and in some way implicated in the movements of European subjectivity into the larger world is one of the things I've got in mind when I talk about the connection between the poetic and the political in a specifically Western context of imperial expansion, colonialism, and so on.

FOSTER: Do you feel there is something implicit in Western subjectivity that leads to domination?

MACKEY: Yes, it's the Cartesian separation of the ego from the rest of the world in order to achieve knowledge of and power over the rest of the world—knowledge of and power over nature and knowledge of and power over non-European people, who are seen as being closer to nature than Europeans are. The subjugation of nature and the subjugation of those people identified with nature, viewed as being more natural, native, etcetera, have gone hand in hand. That's one of the things that is troubling the tradition of the Western "I."

FOSTER: So then you are saying there is a distinctive Western identity which is inherently corruptive?

MACKEY: There's a distinctive Western identity that has been constructed and maintained by the West, which has posed as one of its defining attributes an ability to dominate and govern the world. Whether that's inherent or not I wouldn't venture to say, but it is certainly an historical development that has been sustained by a sense of people in the West that it is their role to dominate, their role to govern, that it is their role to impose a Western will and a Western order on the rest of the world.

FOSTER: Is Western subjectivity or at least the lyric tradition in the West so compromised by a will to dominate that at this point it should simply be passed over?

MACKEY: Leonard Schwartz mentions Robert Duncan in that review, and Robert Duncan is someone whose work is very important to me. One aspect of that importance is the fact that Robert was so insistent upon the heterodox tradition in the West, that marginalized tradition within the West which was in significant ways victimized by the very will to order that we've been talking about being imposed on other parts of the world. You know, the suppression of witchcraft, the suppression of the occult, the suppression of the irrational, so on and so forth. The way in which the heterodox lyric tradition in the West has tried to avail itself of those things that go counter to and are contrary to that very rationalist Cartesian order is one of the things that makes the question of the lyric and of subjectivity not as cut-and-dried as some of the dismissals of the lyric and of subjectivity have tended to suggest. I see it all as something that is not over and done with by any means.

FOSTER: But I assume the tradition of the lyric isn't some kind of absolute standard or reference or model for your work—the way it seems to be for some academic poets and the neoformalists. It's not something you use to judge your own work.

MACKEY: No, I don't think there are any absolute references that I evaluate my work in relationship to—otherwise, there wouldn't be any reason to do my work. One of the things that impels my work is the sense that there's still work to be done and that areas of necessary inquiry and, hopefully, accomplishment have not been closed off by some tradition which is now absolute and monolithic, some obstinate, solid thing that simply sits on and squashes us. I don't see it as an absolute reference, but at the same time, because this thing is prone to so many oversimplifications, I feel I have to be careful in also underscoring something else that Leonard Schwartz said in his review, which is that we are working with the English language and that brings with it a certain history, a certain poetic tradition which I inherit and I work with. I can talk about the ways in which English has been altered by the consequences of its imperial history—the other Englishes that are now being spoken in other parts of the world and in England as well—but at the same time the English language as such is what I'm working in. Therefore, what has been done in English by previous poets is of necessary relevance to my work.

FOSTER: In that sense, you do identify with the traditions of Western lyricism.

MACKEY: Yes, those would be some of the earliest instances of poetry that I read, and they certainly formed my earliest senses of what poetry was.

FOSTER: Who among recent generations did you read and like?

MACKEY: Not to go way back to reading stuff like Longfellow and Tennyson back in junior high school and high school, the work that has been more immediately of relevance to me has not been so much English poetry as American poetry, the work of poets I became interested in in high school and college. I became interested in the work of William Carlos Williams and the work of Amiri Baraka—LeRoi Jones at that point—and many of the poets who were featured in Donald Allen's anthology *The New American Poetry.* That particular tendency in American poetry is one that was very important to me as I began to develop some sense of myself as possibly a poet, possibly a writer. So I was reading in the middle to late sixties, in addition to Williams and Baraka, Olson's work, Creeley, Levertov, Duncan, and others. I read the Beat poets, Ginsberg, Ferlinghetti, and so forth, and other poets as well, getting into some of the poets outside of the United States that I saw mentioned by various poets whose work was important to me—poets like Lorca and Césaire and Neruda. Vallejo came later.

FOSTER: In what you are describing, there is no separate black literary tradition.

MACKEY: Well, the black literary tradition has been intertwined with the white literary tradition in ways which don't tend to be acknowledged because of the ghetto that black literature has been consigned to in academic and institutional practices having to do not only with the university but with publishing and with ways of marketing and promoting literature. The black writer who was most important to me early on, Amiri Baraka, was important to me at a time when he was very much involved with a literary scene that was predominantly white, that was in many instances otherwise white were it not for him—publishing, for example, *Yugen,* a magazine in which one could read not only Olson but a black writer like A. B. Spellman. The separateness of the black literary tradition has to do with the segregation of black people, the subtle and not-so-subtle apartheid which is the history of this country and continues to be part of the social fabric and the assumptions that govern a great deal of social life, most of social life in this country. I don't feel an obligation to assert a sense of a separate black literary tradition. The tendencies and the inclinations that do that are so pervasive and so dominant that in many ways it goes without saying that it is separate, but the thing that needs to be emphasized is that that separation is a consequence of social practices that we're supposed to be against.

FOSTER: So I gather you don't accept that argument you often hear in academia that you can understand a particular tradition only if you're part of it—the idea, for example, that there should be only women teaching in a women's studies program, only African Americans teaching in an African American studies program, and so forth.

MACKEY: Well, I know that argument. I mean, I'm a university professor, and, being in that arena, I know what that argument is about. That's a political argument. The epistemological claims of that argument have not been worked out in any sustained way, so I won't even engage it as an epistemological question. It's a political question first and foremost, and I think that's the way it has to be understood. It is a battle for turf, a battle for space that I very much understand and am very much a part of. And it is that more than it is some claim that only those who are part of a tradition can understand a tradition. Those who are part of a tradition are in a different position with regard to that tradition, and that difference we have to respect and value. It has not been sufficiently valued within those institutions and institutional practices that the argument you are talking about is now challenging. But I don't think that to reduce that argument to an epistemological question of who understands what is to do it justice. In fact, it does it a disservice by creating a straw target that it's then very easy to knock down. I'm trying to look at it in a more complicated, maybe more dialectical way.

FOSTER: Then to go back to Leonard Schwartz's discussion of the lyric as an act of transcendence, do you think that transcendence is free, or at least potentially free, of ethnic, gender, racial, and other forms of collective identity?

MACKEY: Yes, as I read that review I think that what Leonard Schwartz is talking about is a reach, an attempted reach beyond such confinements of identity. It's a funny situation, because the lyric has a bad name for being subjective and solipsistic on the one hand, and it has another bad name for being inflated and reaching for positive transcendence in some fatuous way. Obviously the lyric, when it is speaking to us in that compelling and convincing way that it does, is doing something that is neither one of those extremes but is somewhere in between. It's in some kind of liminal state that is acknowledging the claims of the particular, and the limitations that go with that, along with the aspirations to, and inklings of, some liberation from those limitations that might be available to us. It of necessity does that with a certain hesitation and tentativeness that has to do with being in that complicated liminal area in which there are no easy assurances. But, at the same time, the other problem is to so take it as a given that the confines of one's particular identity, based on whatever determinants one would name in a particular instance—historical, regional, ethnic, gender, etcetera—that one is so bound by those that one mustn't even bother, in effect that one is guilty of some kind of naïveté or presumption to even bother to aspire to something beyond that, something that troubles those boundaries, battles with those boundaries, bumps up against them and in some way wants to get beyond them. I think the assumption that it's a futile aspiration, and therefore something not to be undertaken, is as guilty of oversimplification as that inflated transcendentalism that we seem to be in reaction against at this time.

FOSTER: Susan Howe, in *My Emily Dickinson*, said that poetry transfigures beyond gender. You're saying in effect that it transfigures beyond any social demarcation or identification.

MACKEY: I think we have to keep both in view. We live in a social world and certainly nothing that Susan is saying wants to dismiss or diminish the ways in which the social determinations of our being impact and impinge upon us, but at the same time I think she rightly doesn't see that as justification for caving in, capitulating to a rigidly historicist view that is often complicit with the very limitations and oppressive formations it seems otherwise interested in moving us away from.

FOSTER: In the talk which you gave last spring at the Detroit Institute of Arts, you said that artistic "othering" involves "innovation, invention, and change," whereas social "othering" is a matter of "power, exclusion, and privilege." It sounds as if you are opposing poetry and politics and saying that they are fundamentally different forces.

MACKEY: Yes, I think that they are much more different than they are similar, and maybe in that I'm a minority voice in more ways than one, since it does seem a tendency nowadays to conflate them, the poetic and the political. There is a long tradition of poetics as an alternative to politics, a sense of poetry as an alternate government, so on and so forth. In talking about othering and contrasting artistic othering to social othering, I tried to accent the fact that often the recourse to artistic othering by people who are subjected to social othering is a poetic which is political in that it enacts a resistant variation that is otherwise blocked in its more political-qua-political manifestations. That dialectic between what I call, in a broad sense, poetics and politics goes beyond an easy, cut-and-dried distinction between poetry and politics. It is quite obviously and manifestly true that poetry and poetics has done and does do political work, but the political work that it does is often a consequence of more immediately political work not being doable. One historical example that comes to mind immediately is the Harlem Renaissance, which was quite announcedly and self-consciously, on the part of many of the thinkers and writers and artists involved, an attempt to win in the realm of artistic activity—poetics, call it—gains that could not be won in the political arena due to the backlash and repression to which such political-qua-political activity as the Marcus Garvey movement and the black socialist journal *The Messenger* were subjected. The shutting down of those various political activities created a situation where you had people like Alain Locke and James Weldon Johnson saying that literature now had to do the job, to the extent that it could, that those more genuinely political activities had not been able to do because of the repression. And that generally tends to be the case, I think, more for marginalized, socially othered people than it does for people who come from the dominant center. Social othering consists primarily of a political, social, and economic disenfranchisement of those people, which diminishes their ability to act politically in the institutional ways that give political results that count in material, quantifiable ways. A distinction between the political and the poetic is a distinction between the rhetorical kinds of politics that art activity often is and political activities with consequences beyond the rhetorical, the decisions that impact upon and largely determine the way we live. I think that needs to be remembered, that distinction needs to be kept in mind. That reminder would be a part of political seriousness in the simplest sense, as I see it. To make outlandish claims for the political efficacy of poetry is to be guilty of a very naive politics that is not political, so I do think it is important to acknowledge and to talk about the differences between poetry and politics.

FOSTER: There seems to be a suggestion in what you're saying that in some ways the person identified as the other may be the one better situated to be a poet. In your essay, "Sound and Sentiment," you say, "Music and poetry, if not exactly a loser's art, is fed by intimacy with loss and may in fact feed it." Oddly it seems that if poetry had political effect, and I rather doubt it ever does, it would dismantle the circumstances that makes poetry possible.

MACKEY: That's a possibility. Perhaps, to go back to the question of the lyric, one of the reasons the lyric is in a troubled position is the elegiac tradition with regard to the lyric, the investment in loss that tradition brings with it, where you seem to be at odds with a political will to overcome loss. In saying that poetry, if not a loser's art, is intimate with loss, I'm talking in part about the elegiac tradition, which does build on and lament loss in a way which becomes in some ways self-perpetuating, in some ways a consolation to losses that a more manifestly political will toward social change might tell you are unnecessary and not inevitable. The argument would be that there are losses that can be turned around and that one's job is to be about the business of achieving that turnaround rather than lamenting loss. So, yes, again I don't want to be reductive about it, and I wouldn't want to just make a bald statement that if you are too well off, you can't be a poet—if you don't have the blues, you can't sing the blues—but, you know, those are formidable problematics. How do you lament loss without investing in loss? I think the lyric tradition is troubled by that problematic, but it's also a problematic that the lyric tradition has acknowledged.

FOSTER: The ultimate loss, or threat of loss, that the lyric confronts is loss of the self, and that is something that *Bedouin Hornbook*, as well as your poetry, deals with. That's also very much Jack Spicer's territory, of course, and I'm wondering if you identify him in the background in your work.

MACKEY: The practice of outside? Well, it has to do with that mixed inheritance that the self is—which is, to put it in more common terms, a blessing and a curse. One index or measure of having a self is, in that sense, a need to get beyond it or to expand it or widen it or to make it something other than a prison of sensibility and possibility. That's very different from the denial of self and the reduction to a state of nonentity that I call social othering, but to come up against the limitations of the self is to understand the self, I think, in a deeper and finally more accurate and compelling way than some blissful, unproblematic enjoyment of residing in the self. For me it's a symptom of one's residence in the self that there is this impulse to get beyond it or at least posit the possibility of some reach beyond it, to want to be in touch with that or in its service, if only in a dialectical way. Jack Spicer's concern with dictation, the poet becoming a kind of medium, is certainly of importance and relevance to that pursuit and is one of the things that has informed my understanding of it, although I don't see my work as being very much like Spicer's except maybe in the prose, following the real jolt and eye-opening enthusiasm that I felt for *After Lorca* and that I acknowledge in the very first of the "Angel of Dust" letters that appears in *Eroding Witness*—it's CC'ed to García Lorca and Spicer—acknowledging the correspondence, the letter form, the sense of being in conversation with the dead, the sense of things that is entailed in Spicer's idea of dictation, that one is writing beyond one's self or at least aspiring to write beyond one's self. That goes back to a way in which that English tradition we started off talking about would be relevant. I mean, Blake's statement, "I'm the secretary," seems very much a precursor of Spicer's sense of dictation and would be another instance of where poetry in the Western tradition has often been at odds with the totalizing imperial project that another poetry in that Western tradition can be seen as being complicit with and some kind of reflection of. One has to make these distinctions and one has to, while acknowledging and acceding to the necessity of speaking in these rather large and global terms that tend to create monoliths like "Western subjectivity," then deal with that in a more nuanced way that comes in and complicates it and which shows the other sides of it. So, yes, Spicer would be one. I think that Duncan's sense, too, that even—you know, Robert was very much into a sense of the occult and of the heterodox, but he would also speak of it in a way that is less sensational. You know, in language we inherit the voices of the dead. Language is passed on to us by people who are now in their graves and brings with it access to history, tradition, times and places that are not at all immediate to our own immediate and particular occasion whether we look at it individually and personally or whether we look at it in a more collective way and talk about a specific community. A lot of theory and criticism that has been coming from Europe is simply trying to catch up with the unspectacular practice of outside and to keep in mind the different levels on which a practice of outside is understandable. It doesn't have to be seen in sensational terms of Martians and so forth. It's an everyday and unspectacular fact of life that we are often in touch with much more than we presume ourselves to be in touch with.

FOSTER: Spicer found that his work was more an expression of his self than he had assumed.

MACKEY: I'm certainly not going to make any claims to have left my self behind. There are aspects of sensibility and of personality that I would like to think of as having been left behind, but leaving them behind is probably more a variation on a theme than it is a completely discontinuous break with what has gone before. It's othering, but it is participial, and it's ongoing. It's pretty obvious in my work that I'm back at some of the same material and some of the same obsessions and problematics and issues and so forth, over and over again. It's not as though my sensibility is a tabula rasa every morning. So it's a difficult thing to talk about this, to talk about it as an achieved erosion of the self. I don't have that sense of it and would not be comfortable with that claim.

FOSTER: In your critical essays, you are often concerned with the importance to people like Robert Duncan of writing, or art in general, as process. In your essay on Baraka, for example, you discuss his work in connection with Olson and Jackson Pollock and Ornette Coleman and so forth and make connections among them in terms of their respective aesthetics of process. And your own work seems to involve an aesthetic of process, and yet at the same time there is considerable containment and rigor as if you were working with an aesthetic of revision. And your essays have generally followed a conventional academic format. Even *Bedouin Hornbook* has a certain traditional formality and restraint. It's less pronounced in the poetry, at least for me, but even there it can be felt.

MACKEY: I don't think that process is necessarily an abandonment of form or formality. It is an acknowledgment of the provisional character of forms and of certain attitudes of formality, tones of formality—tonal, formal properties. But the formal character of the essays I've written and of the prose in *Bedouin Hornbook,* as against the poetry—I see them on a continuum. They're different instruments that I use to do different things. I avail myself in poetry, verse, of a compression and an elliptical way of going about things that I don't, for the most part, resort to in prose. And in prose my intellectual bearings and academic bearings are more evident than in verse. The tension between the formal and the informal has been very important in my work. It's something that I have worried over, and it is something that has produced some of the characteristic gestures or mannerisms in my prose. You mention the academic essays. One of the things that's been a source of some annoyance to people within the academic community has been a tendency I have in essays to introduce, or to try to introduce, an informality in an otherwise very formal tone through the use of colloquialisms, contractions, and so forth. What's going on there is my own awareness of and discomfort with some of the formalities of that sort of writing. I don't think I necessarily pulled off any great marriage of the formal and the informal, but what you find in that is an unrest, discontent with any easy dwelling in the one or the other. It makes for shifts in register that are not always felicitous and that are not always smooth and that are sometimes awkward in ways that call attention to themselves and, whether consciously or unconsciously, call attention to what I'm feeling as a problematic with regard to the boundaries between the formal and the informal. In *Bedouin Hornbook,* because it's not so strictly the formal occasion that writing academic literary criticism is, it probably is smoother or at least it's lubricated with humor in a lot of instances where the different modes of address or registers are juxtaposed in a way that is self-conscious and that extracts a certain humor, a certain comic element. And in that sense it's another way of doing it. It's a way you can do it when you're writing something that is fictional and that is pointing to and worrying the line between any number of things—between genres, between fact and fiction, between music criticism and music composition, etcetera.

FOSTER: What I was trying to get at was more the fact that, for example, in *Bedouin Hornbook,* a great emphasis is placed on change and process, but the prose itself becomes almost Jamesian—highly convoluted, syntactically complex. It seems closer to a language of definition than a language of process.

MACKEY: It's a language of reflection. Well, there's Bud Powell, and then there's Cecil Taylor, and Cecil Taylor comes after. Cecil Taylor comes also after an academic experience in conservatories devoted to Western art music that Bud Powell didn't have, etcetera. When you talk about this particular mix of formal writing—formal in a kind of Jamesian way—that is extolling and explicating music whose key ethic is improvisational, constant redefinition of the formal, I think of Cecil Taylor, who, in his way of accommodating that conservatory, academic background of his with the improvisational tradition that his music is performed in the context of, would be one of the models that I have had in mind. I'm post-bebop. I come after Bud Powell and Bird and Monk and so forth, and my sense of things very much has the imprint of coming up in the sixties, of beginning to think about writing in the sixties, at a time when we had the black avant-garde, the new black music, the new jazz as it's called by some people, in which a significant break was made with the tradition of the black musician as an embodiment of instantaneity, instinct, pure feeling, in some unmediated way uncomplicated by reflection and intellect. We had a kind of emergence, a coming out into the light, of the black improvisational music tradition as an intellectual tradition—whether or not we're talking sociohistorically about the fact that many of the brighter members of the black community became musicians because it was one of the few avenues open to them where they had a relative degree of autonomy and self-definitional freedom, given the kinds of hurdles and impediments black people were up against when it came to occupations. You really did have a channeling of an intellectual impulse and energy into music which ironically got understood by the dominant culture, and even to a great extent by black culture itself, as prioritizing immediacy, feeling, emotion, etcetera—which music does in fact tend to do, but with the emergence of musicians like Cecil Taylor, Archie Shepp, Marion Brown, Bill Dixon, and later Anthony Braxton and others, you had a much more outfront acknowledgment of the intellectual component that had been driving the music. The kind of intellectuality that the formal character of the writing in *Bedouin Hornbook* conjures is in part an outgrowth of that, a very deliberate impulse on my part to foreground that intellectuality in a writing which does not try to shed its reflectiveness in the service of a presumed immediacy, instantaneity, or emotionality that black music has in too many instances and for too long been burdened with being the embodiment of or seen as the embodiment of. One of the things that Marion Brown said about the new music of the sixties is that he sensed that many of the people who were bothered by the music and were reacting against it were bothered by the level of abstraction of the music and the way in which that level of abstraction being engaged in by black musicians diverged from and called into question certain notions regarding black people's relationship to abstraction, the idea that black people, if not in fact incapable of abstraction, tend to shy away from it in the direction of the immediate, the physical, the athletic, the performative. That's one of the things that informs the writing of *Bedouin Hornbook* and that whole series. In fact, one of the things that a friend and former student of mine wrote to me and said when *Bedouin Hornbook* appeared was exactly to that effect, that he thought one of the useful things done by the book was to highlight that component and that aspect of the music, as against that tendency to celebrate in a really naive way the improvisational nature of the music as somehow being immediate and instinctual and instantaneous in a way that anybody who has ever familiarized themselves with the technical procedures of music knows does not apply. All the practicing that you do, all the internalization of a repertoire that your time in the woodshed is meant to leave you with—when somebody is standing up there improvising, the last thing they're doing is creating stuff that's just happening as they create it. They have recourse to a process of selection and combination that draws on a repertoire that they have developed through repetition, that they have developed through going over the same stuff over and over and over again and working things out. There's quite a reflective and, I would insist, intellectual process that goes on in the music that tends to be obscured by the myths about the music, what it has been made to symbolize, what black people have been made to symbolize, and also by the setting in which the music is presented and heard for the most part, nightclubs, etcetera. So that's very deliberate, that insistence upon the formality that you noted, a formality that is not embarrassed by what you might hear as Jamesian echoes in the same way that Cecil Taylor doesn't seem to be embarrassed by echoes of Bartók or Messiaen. But then you have neoconservative critics like Stanley Crouch come along and accuse him of just retreading Messiaen and the like. That sort of mind is more comfortable with cut-and-dried definitions and discriminations, but Cecil's bigger than that, and that's one of the things we should be instructed by in his music.

FOSTER: What do you think of Kerouac's appropriating bop as a model for his own prose?

MACKEY: I have to say that Kerouac has never been a writer who has spoken to me. I have tried to read Kerouac again and again over the years, but his work has never become a primary text for me, partly because of some of the things I just said. The sensibility of Kerouac is that of a refugee or would-be refugee from the white center who is seeking some alternative to himself, a self he sees as too hung-up in convention and tradition—the ratiocinative, the reflective, the intellectual—while in black music he sees a model of spontaneity and of gut feeling that is exactly what I'm saying has been the problem: an oversimplified "understanding" of what the music is about and where it's coming from. The romanticism and frequent romantic racism in Kerouac are simply an extension of that on a thematic level—you know, the notorious passage in *On the Road*, walking through the black section of Denver, which Baldwin and others have pointed to. That impulse and that project were simply not mine and simply did not speak to me. This is where my particular location in a culture, being of a people, shows its impact on what I see to be my job or my project. I don't identify with the white center that sees itself as burdened with a ratiocinative intellectual tradition that it wants to dislocate through identification with an emotive other. Quite the opposite. I am a black intellectual. Among other things, I'm an intellectual among a group of people who have in recent history been denied an intellectual dimension, who have been characterized as being incapable of intellectual performance and pursuit and who have been made to symbolize the opposite of that, have been caught in a binary opposition between intellect, reflectivity, identified with whiteness, the dominant center, and impulse, instinct, instantaneity. And that dominant center's appreciation of black people, even when it has been quite genuine and quite benign in its motivations, has tended to be guilty of a binary opposition which extolled black people for the emotive, anti-intellectual or nonreflective presence, immediacy, or alternative that they were taken to be. I understand why Kerouac's work did not speak to me. I don't think that Kerouac was aiming his work at young black intellectuals who were in high school reading Sartre and Camus and listening to Ornette Coleman. The popularity of Kerouac is made up of a different constituency, a constituency of which I am not a part. In an academic way I understand and recognize the principles and the cultural and aesthetic tendencies that were coming together to make for Kerouac, but again, as a model for prose, his is certainly not mine. And as far as the meaning of black music goes, the writings of Baraka are infinitely more on the mark for me. At that point, LeRoi Jones, a young, black intellectual trying to bring two modernisms together—literary, predominantly white modernism together with black musical modernism—and bring a lot of other stuff together, too, definitely spoke to me. His work had a lot more resonance and applicability to my situation than Kerouac.

FOSTER: I think Baraka mentions, and you quote approvingly, an observation that in fact has often been made—the observation that in the 1940s bop and abstract expressionism and literature came together in a shared aesthetic of spontaneous, improvisational work. But you seem to be suggesting now that that's not altogether valid.

MACKEY: No, I'm not suggesting it's not valid. I'm just suggesting that the proportions in which one takes that mix vary. They vary as a function of what one's particular situation, needs, inclinations, temperament—and who knows what other factors—happen to be. I think that my work, though very much influenced by Baraka, is obviously very different. With Kerouac, I can say I identify him with a white center. I can't say that about Baraka obviously. Baraka is different from me in other ways. He's another generation, for one thing. There are class differences—in his black, middle-class upbringing and certain kinds of turmoil and self-critique that grow out of that for him. I'm not from the black middle class—I'm from a working-class family—and some of that doesn't apply to me. Some of those anxieties about identity that come of a class position that I didn't occupy growing up don't apply to me. Some of the tone of Baraka that derives from that is not a tone that you'll find me making use of. But also there is a different historical moment. I have to respect the fact that he had to fight fights that I didn't have to fight. There are all kinds of ways we have to relativize all this stuff because there are no absolute models for the way in which our particularity and our differences determine the direction in which we go. The confluence that Baraka is talking about in *Blues People* when he talks about abstract expressionism, bop, and certain tendencies in writing—that was a different moment from the one I came in on. It seemed to me that to try to pretend that that moment was still there when it demonstrably wasn't didn't make any sense. All of these things are partial articulations, and as partial articulations they are subject to revision and alteration. There are no final truths or last judgments, and it would simply be stupid to act as though any particular confluence or formation was the last word, especially if you're somebody who is impelled to move with and be moved by writing, by language, to write. I see what they were doing, but I also see that the equation of improvisation with spontaneity in too simplistic a sense is something that we are now in a position to see as such, to be critical of.

FOSTER: At what point did you become aware of the complexity of black culture and the new direction in which it was moving? Was that something that came with the sixties, with what was happening then in colleges and universities?

MACKEY: Well, first I'll say I don't know, then I'll go on to answer in some tentative ways. In the most general and applicable way, the thing I've been saying throughout this conversation is something that warns against the construction of monoliths, and one thing about the cultures of marginalized peoples is that those cultures tend to be subjected to oversimplification and tend to be made into monolithic and often homogeneous entities that in actual fact they are not. So I would say that my impulse to acknowledge the complexity of black culture, its variousness and its several-sidedness, is not something that necessarily came with college. I don't think you could locate it in that exact or limited a way. It came from growing up black and seeing the character of experience within a black community in its multiplicity and seeing on the other hand the assumptions made about black people, black culture, and black communities in the dominant culture as reflected in writings, the media, and so forth, being very aware of the fact that there's a great gulf between the two, that the latter is much more simplistic than the former, and acknowledging the reasons for that simplification, that one aspect of that simplification is what we all acknowledge to be the racist character of the society and its history. I don't think that it comes at any particular point; it just comes in part from what Du Bois called "double-consciousness" back in 1903—seeing that there's one's reality and then there are the versions of that reality, representations of that reality, that one has to contend with in the dominant culture. That apprehension has certainly been contributed to by my going on to be in places like Stanford or Princeton that it wasn't the design of this country to have open to black people. But that heightens the contradictions and complicates them further in many ways. I was a kid who was into books, among other things, which didn't preclude my being into sports and all that stuff, but I was into books, and I was viewed as anomalous because of that—you know, a young black male who was into books wasn't what was expected. You find a lot of that expression in Baraka's early work. And it's not just in Baraka's work. It's something that comes up in African American literature a great deal because literacy has been a dividing line between black and white going back to the laws against teaching slaves how to read and the enforced illiteracy of the black population in the time of slavery and to a disproportionate degree continuing after slavery. So Baraka says, in the preface to *Home,* "I was taught that literature was what white people do." The sense that books are alien terrain is a notion that is very consciously and deliberately instituted socially and perpetuated. There are a host of assumptions of that sort that one is up against.

FOSTER: Before we end, I'd like to go back to something we were talking about before, the apparent conflict between, on the one hand, an aesthetic of process that results from artistic othering and, on the other, the sense that there is at this point a kind of intellectual definition in black culture.

MACKEY: Well, I don't think it's reached a point of intellectual definition and certainly not a point of terminus, a terminal point. Interesting things are happening, which include impulses toward definition. Necessarily partial or provisional definitions are being offered as to the black cultural tradition, but it seems to me to be more a sign of ferment and of trying to get work done that needs to be done than a sign of having come to be living in a museum. These very questions about how we understand what is already on the table and the necessary expansion of the discourse that attends to what is already on the table are enough to assure various paths, often divergent to the point of being diametrically at odds with one another, being taken in the near future. There is also the work of getting onto the table stuff that is not on the table yet. So, on the one hand, if I hear you correctly, there is developing something of a canon, and I guess one sign of that would be the imminent appearance of a Norton anthology of African American literature and the institutionalization of certain aspects of African American culture in universities and in other places. These institutionalizations are always partial, especially at the beginning, especially in the early stages when you are dealing with material that has not made it into those institutions yet, and that's very contentious ground, those institutional arenas. So there is a great deal of work to be done there, and there's a great deal of discussion. There's a great deal of thinking and conversation that's going to go on. I don't think that has come to a point of exhaustion, myself. In many ways I think it's just beginning. It's just getting interesting. Younger African American writers that I've been coming into contact with in the past few years seem to be energized by the increase in the level of serious and sophisticated intellectual attention that's being given to African American culture and literature and artistic practices in previously not-so-accessible institutions and places.

FOSTER: But don't you think this recognition in some ways alters the adversarial position African American culture has traditionally held in the larger culture and so diffuses one of its principal sources of energy?

MACKEY: That's obviously one of the dangers, and that's one of the threats that it poses. That's one of the interesting jobs that needs to be done, to keep that adversarial edge even in the face of this very necessary inclusion of black practices and paradigms in the larger cultural conversation. One doesn't want to be frozen out. Again, it's that thing: you don't want to invest in your wounds. You don't want to see your wounds as the sole source of your identity, and you also want to make distinctions among those wounds—which of those wounds come from where and why are they there and which ones can be dealt with, something be done about, and which ones can't. I don't see any imminent incorporation of black people and black culture that will blunt that adversarial edge. The danger is that a kind of token accommodation tends to be blown up as though it were an entry en masse into the mainstream, which it is not. But there are enough people who know it's not and have the experience of the fact that it's not that those adversarial tonalities and reflections will definitely remain a part of the larger picture. They will inform, on a number of levels, what's going on.

Interview by Peter O'Leary

The following interview took place in Chicago on May 18, 1996. Also present and contributing to the interview was Devin Johnston.

PETER O'LEARY: You've written critically about Robert Duncan, Charles Olson, Black Mountain poets, Caribbean writers; you've written about Amiri Baraka. There's a way in which someone coming upon this might think that these were just discrete areas of your interest, but I have a sense that they are part of a synthetic periscoping in which you're taking in an imagined or envisioned whole. I'm wondering, then, if this is the case. I wonder how you relate to this eclecticism. It's not discrete, is it?

NATHANIEL MACKEY: All of those writers that I've written about are writers who have had an enormous impact on me. They just spoke to me in some way that was very compelling and that went very deep and that made me want to stay with them more, read farther into them, go farther into them. I find that that doesn't happen with everything; it doesn't happen with many things. Now, what that impact is and what they have in common to have achieved it, I don't know if I can say. And they've also come in at different times. The Black Mountain poets I began to read in the mid-sixties: that was part of reading Baraka when he was LeRoi Jones and seeing him associated with that group, and becoming interested in that group partly because of this association, and also because I had an interest in William Carlos Williams's work and the Black Mountain writers were taking from Williams, taking up the Williams initiative in various ways. They've held sway in different ways and to different degrees at different times. There was a period, for example, when Robert Creeley was probably the dominant influence in my writing . . .

O'LEARY: Was that when you were writing the poems of short line lengths?

MACKEY: Yes.

O'LEARY: The ones that appear in *Eroding Witness*?

MACKEY: More before that. When I was in college I was writing Robert Creeley poems. And they really were Robert Creeley poems [*laughing*].

O'LEARY: Good Robert Creeley poems?

MACKEY: I don't know. Some people thought they were very good. But, you know, they were Robert Creeley poems. So, different people have come in at different times. I began reading Wilson Harris and Kamau Brathwaite about the same time. That would have been around 1973 or 1974. Yes, that's when I picked up *The Arrivants* by Brathwaite.

Earlier than that, Amiri Baraka was somebody whose work was very important to me and his work continues to be so. He was probably the first writer whose work was really important to me that I met. It must have been 1967, because that was the year *Tales* came out. I met him in Greenwich Village. It just happened that we were in this bookstore at the same time—in fact, I had just bought *Tales*. I looked a few rows over and there was Amiri Baraka. I saw him and went over and started talking to him. I was interested in him giving a reading at Princeton, where I was an undergraduate at the time, and I asked about that. It worked out eventually that he came to give a reading at Princeton. This was something put on by the Black Students Union at Princeton, and he was quite distant and disdainful of us. He gave a speech—this was when he was really in a fiercely black-nationalist phase—and as part of his reading/presentation he brought some people with him from Spirit House, which he was running up in Newark, and they put on a skit. He gave this speech that was directed at us and said that we were being trained like Pavlov's dogs. He really laid into us, publicly, before everybody there. At the same time, he didn't want to meet with us to have dinner or a reception or anything like that. He just came in and gave the reading and took off. I won't say it was disillusioning, because I knew from his work and from stories about him that he could be a very difficult person, that he was irascible and believed in what he believed in very fiercely, and was quite willing to tell anybody what he thought with all the fierceness of those beliefs. So, in that sense, it wasn't disillusioning, but at the same time it wasn't an endearing experience. That might have contributed to this wariness about meeting . . .

O'LEARY: Meeting your masters. I know that Robert Duncan was an early influence, and that you wrote your dissertation on his work. Did you ever meet him?

MACKEY: I think the time I first met him was at Stanford. He came down to Stanford on this occasion not to read but to accompany someone who came to give a talk on Black Mountain College. I can't remember the guy's name, but, anyway, Robert came down with him and there was a reception afterwards and that was the first time I ever talked to him. I think that would have been around 1971. But I didn't get to know him in a way in which I was seeing him on any kind of regular basis and outside of those formal occasions—seeing him as a private citizen, so to speak—until the late 1970s. He came to give a reading at USC, where I was teaching, and I introduced his reading and I spent a lot of time with him, just walking around with him during the day and going out to dinner with him that night. He seemed to be struck by the fact that I had done all this work on his work but I had never sought him out. He said, "You must be—you're quite discreet." I was, you know, scared of him. Anyway, we talked a lot and we got on well. And he said, "When you're in San Francisco, we should get together." And, in fact, we did. Then when I moved up to begin teaching in Santa Cruz in 1979 I saw him a lot more. I would visit him in San Francisco when I was there and often we would go out to lunch or dinner, to bookstores—that sort of thing.

O'LEARY: Similar to your eclectic reading of contemporary writers is the way you've taken to or made use of different kinds of mythologies, the West African myths and their variations in the Caribbean. Do they play a similar role in your work? Are they part of the same process? I guess I have a sense that arching over your work is an almost mythological panorama, that in a certain way—Black Mountain poetics, Duncan, the story of Gassire's lute—all of these different things play a part in this arch.

MACKEY: There are overarching concerns, and you see them coming up in my work as you will see recurrences coming up in any writer's work. There are these recurrent—I don't even know if *concerns* is quite the word. There are recurrent figures; there are recurrent strains of exploration and implication; there are recurrent sites of investigation—whether the site is a particular myth or a particular trope or a particular theme—sites not only of investigation but sites of performance: you're doing something with the possibilities that reside within that trope or that myth or that problematic. So, in that sense, there's an overarching—there's an umbrella of some sort. But I haven't been anxious to designate that umbrella other than through the terms of the practice that has been emerging under it. In bringing, for example, those essays together in *Discrepant Engagement,* I wanted to be careful not to present it as something wholly synthesized and thought out, with no cracks and no gaps and no leaks and no ellipses. It's not that. They are moments that constellate a possible umbrella but it's not an umbrella whose empty spaces I've been interested in filling in, for myself or for others.

O'LEARY: It strikes me that the way that you've used a lot of these mythologies—whether you're quoting from folktales or you're quoting from anthropological sources—that the thing that always interests you are the slippages or the puns. I'm thinking specifically of the way Aunt Nancy appears in *From a Broken Bottle Traces of Perfume Still Emanate.* Aunt Nancy originally was a male figure, at least as Ananse, the storyteller, who was brought over in folklore from Africa to the Americas, and then in your work Aunt Nancy's a she, literally.

MACKEY: And also in African American folklore, black folklore in the United States, Aunt Nancy . . .

O'LEARY: Is Aunt Nancy a female?

MACKEY: Yes, a female. She develops out of Ananse.

O'LEARY: That would be a kind of slippage I find your writing accentuates, in the critical work but especially in the poetry.

MACKEY: It's a transformation. And it's a case in point of the fact that these traditions—the mythology, the lore—are not being gone to as some kind of fixed, given entity that one then has to have a subservient relationship to. They are active and unfinished; they are subject to change; they are themselves in the process of transformation and transition. They speak to an open and open-ended possibility that the poetics that I've been involved in very much speaks to as well. To see cracks and incompleteness as not only inevitable but opportune has been one of the things that these writers and musicians and others I've been interested in writing about and talking about and reading—that possibility has been one that they've been there to apprise us of.

O'LEARY: One of the things I've been struck by is that much of the material you make use of comes to you through Western, academic inroads, such as anthropology. And yet you turn it into a wholly other thing. You show how these inroads' slippages and incompletions can lead to artistic transformations and unexpected adaptations. I guess I see a parallel between your work and the way mostly black jazz musicians use Western, European instruments, like trumpets and saxophones, to create a whole new project that is not necessarily Western or European. Do you see yourself using specifically academic resources or traditionally white, American projects like Black Mountain poetics in a similar way or toward similar ends?

MACKEY: Well, the things that are being done in the example that you give of African American musicians improvising upon a theme provided by Tin Pan Alley, bebop taking a Tin Pan Alley tune and making something else out of it, or the tradition of taking an instrument like the saxophone and really finding new use for it—that's part of a larger improvisational process where people find out what they can use. You take what comes to hand and you adapt it to your uses. That's in the face of ideas of orthodoxy that would dissuade you from doing that, that would say that you have to take it in this form and take it as meaning this and then find some way to comport yourself in such a way that you defer to that given meaning and that given form. People don't do that. They didn't do it in Europe and they didn't do it anywhere else. And they certainly didn't do it when they got over here. You start having different cultural dispositions coming into contact with one another and alternative ways of not only viewing the world, that is, through the lens of another cultural disposition, but also alternative ways of viewing your *own* cultural disposition through the encounter with that difference. This then came as a reminder of the fact that these verities, that these cultural dispositions, installed and invested in as though they were unmovable and fixed and eternal, are not that. We're always making and remaking the traditions and the precepts that inform our moment and that we inherit from the past.

That's why music has been such a prominent concern of mine. The African American improvisational legacy in music has been instructive way beyond the confines of the venues in which it takes place and the particular musical culture in which it takes place, way beyond music itself. It's become a metaphor for all kinds of processes of cultural and social revaluation, cultural and social critique, cultural and social change.

O'LEARY: I see, at least as far as your use of mythologies or raw myth goes, two areas which have their branchings-off: West African mythology, especially the myths of the Dogon, and Middle Eastern religions and mythology, especially as they relate to North Africa.

MACKEY: Those two things—the West African mythology, say, in recent poetry that I have written is intertwined with allusions to or evocations of Bedouin culture, really a very specific moment in Bedouin culture which is the school of Udhra, the Udhrite school of poets, Djamil being the founding poet there.

O'LEARY: When was that school around?

MACKEY: Boy, it's going way back. It goes back to the seventh century. Djamil comes in at the end of *Bedouin Hornbook* as the founder of the school of Udhra—the poets who, the saying has it, "when loving die"; it's in the last section of *Bedouin Hornbook*. Anyway, there was the idea of the ecstatic love-death which is both secular and sacred, and the confusion between the secular and sacred that the traditions of Islamic mysticism play upon is part of what shaped my understanding of that phrase when I encountered it. That's in correspondence with Western traditions of a similar sort. The troubadours certainly made use of that trope. One of the places they got it from was the Arab tradition in Spain. So in some ways my receptivity to the Udhrite school denotes a certain familiarity with it that I had via the Western poetic tradition to which it had contributed . . .

O'LEARY: To which you were corresponding . . .

MACKEY: Yes. You know, one of the things I've read into and studied is Pound's interest in the troubadours and things of that sort. The fact that there were Arab and Islamic correspondences with the troubadours, going into Dante as well, is something that I was reading about in the 1970s. That was long before I read this short little thing I happened upon about the poet Djamil.

O'LEARY: Where did you read about it? Do you remember?

MACKEY: It was in *The Encyclopedia of Islam* and it was when I was writing *Bedouin Hornbook*. There's this one character, Djamilaa, and one of the things I was doing in writing it was—there're a lot of name changes and playings on names and unpacking of names in that work. In going to see what was packed into that name that I didn't know about already, I went to *The Encyclopedia of Islam* and read an entry on "Djamila," where I found out certain things about the root of the name in Arabic and what it means and also found out about this historical figure, the singer Djamila. And right above it was an entry on "Djamil," so I read that too, which is where I found out about the school of Udhra. So reference to both Djamila and Djamil come into that last section of *Bedouin Hornbook*. I call them Djamilaa's "adopted namesake parents." One of the things I was doing with that, again highlighting this process I was talking about earlier, where to adopt a parent is to create a lineage, to create a genealogy—what I was highlighting was the fact that, yes, we have given genealogies, but we also have adopted genealogies. We create our genealogies as much as they are given to us and fixed for us. We find the traditions that feed us; we make them up in part, we invent the traditions and the senses of the past, the genealogies, that allow us to follow certain dispositions that we have, to be certain things we want to be, to do certain things we want to do. But it's a complicated process. It's not like we decide what we want to do and then we go find a genealogy to justify it. We're looking for what we want to do and what we want to be and we're looking for a disposition as we go through things. Some things speak to you and some things open doors for you while other things don't.

O'LEARY: Even that looking is full of slippages . . .

MACKEY: Yes. And you see a lot of things that don't open doors for you. You see a lot of things you don't follow up; in fact, you see more things that don't take for you, that don't make for those possibilities for you. That seems to me to be a mysterious process, why certain myths are resonant for you while others aren't. It's not like this is a better myth [*laughing*] or anything like that, but some of them speak to you and seem to be bursting with possibilities that you are impelled to explore, while others don't.

O'LEARY: Let me ask you a question, then, about the flamenco concept of *duende* that Lorca was so concerned with, and then also about the "Song of the Andoumboulou." Duende is a longing, and the "Song of the Andoumboulou" is a song sung to a people who no longer exist. Both of these seem related to the concept of the dream of the phantom limb that you use in *Bedouin Hornbook.* All these things have to do with loss. They come across as figures of desire for something you want but can't obtain.

MACKEY: Or it's finding out what you have but don't have. You have it in the form of a disposition but that disposition is not the same as the possession of it. So you have it as a reaching toward something. In many ways, you have it as a reaching through things, so that there's a way in which that reaching is not satisfied even when it does seize upon something. It goes on reaching. The phantom limb bespeaks that reach, which continues beyond the grasping of something. It speaks of loss, it speaks of lack, but it also speaks of an insufficiency that's indigenous to the very act of reaching. Reaching wants to go on, in some sense that's troubling to the things it does settle upon and take hold of. It's not that it empties those things. It simply finds that those things are in place in a certain way that the reaching wants to continue to be free of. Duende, as Lorca talks about it and as singers and musicians in flamenco talk about it, is that kind of reaching. It's that quality of discontent, it's that refusal to be satisfied with mere material achievement—whether we're talking about technical elocution or technical virtuosity—so I think there's something very spiritual about it. It is a spiritual discontent with the very nature of material achievement, no matter how exquisite. These figures of ghostliness and absence and incompletion are meant to suggest a spiritual supplement to the world that both invests it with a certain urgency and divests it of any ultimacy.

O'LEARY: And are the Andoumboulou ghostly in the same kind of way? Or do they have a different kind of presence?

MACKEY: The Andoumboulou are related to that but they're a little bit different. The Andoumboulou are, in Dogon mythology and cosmology, an earlier form of human beings who were flawed and failed to sustain themselves or failed to be the thing that human beings would eventually be. So they're a version, an earlier attempt, an earlier draft of human being that didn't work out. But they are invoked at the time of Dogon funeral ceremonies; the "Song of the Andoumboulou" is a Dogon funeral song. It is as if they are harking back to the failure of the Andoumboulou as a prefiguration of mortality in the more fully realized form of human being that the Dogon are, that we are. I haven't read anything that has explained that, so I've had to guess. Why do they sing the "Song of the Andoumboulou" at funeral time? Why do they hark back to these failed earlier human beings? My understanding of it is that the Andoumboulou become relevant in a ritual that is marking death and mortality, the failure of human life to sustain itself indefinitely, because they are figures of frailty and failure. Mortality is a reminder of frailty and failure. But that song is also a song of the spirit of the person who has died and is moving on to another realm. It's a song of lament and of rebirth.

There's a trumpet-like instrument that is blown to indicate the movement of the person who has died on to another realm. When I heard that—and this is another example of the kinds of things that make an impression on you—that series of poems comes out of my hearing a performance of the "Song of the Andoumboulou" on a record of music by the Dogon. This was something I heard in the early 1970s and I was just struck by it, struck by the music of it, the sound of it. It was aurally impressive in a way that I found ineradicable from my thinking. This was before I knew anything about this stuff—because the liner notes to the album don't say anything, really, about who the Andoumboulou are, and I didn't find out anything about what or who the Andoumboulou were until I read *The Pale Fox* by Marcel Griaule and Germaine Dieterlen, from which I took an epigraph for the first section of *School of Udhra.* So the "Song of the Andoumboulou" is related to what I'm saying. It's addressed to the spirit; it's a spiritual. It's speaking to the spiritual vocation of music, the spiritual vocation of art, the spiritual vocation of poetry. In that way, it's related to what the figure of the phantom limb and the other things you've alluded to are getting at. And it's related in my mind to duende and to flamenco by that raspy tonality that is resorted to in the voice of the singer of the "Song of the Andoumboulou," which is the thing that really struck me. I seem to be very susceptible to these raspy vocal qualities, so much so that I've had to become self-conscious about it and to think about it, because it's become so abundantly clear that I'm susceptible to it [*laughing*]. So you find me thematizing it in different things I've written.

JOHNSTON: Does that have an impact formally on your poetry?

MACKEY: I don't know. I don't know that it has. Or I don't know how it has, if it has. Probably if I thought about it I could talk about ways in which there are analogies to raspiness in what I'm doing. Among other things, raspiness suggests a certain roughness, suggests a certain friction, things rubbing together in a way that makes noise. I talk about making noise in the introduction to *Discrepant Engagement* and about the fact that the word *discrepant* comes from a word meaning "to creak."

O'LEARY: "The creaking of the word."

MACKEY: Yes, "the creaking of the word," which recurs in *Bedouin Hornbook* and *Djbot Baghostus's Run.* The process of bringing things together that are, in the most widely accepted senses of the terms, "disparate" and "disengaged," bringing them into contiguity with one another, is analogous to the roughness you get and the rub you get when you bring things that are not homogenous together. In that sense, there is a kind of raspiness in the discrepant mix of materials that I have been working with, which is also in the discrepant mix and changes of reference and register that one finds in my writing. In some sense, that's to accentuate a certain roughness as against a certain smoothness. What you do is find a certain smoothness in the way you put those materials together. There is a kind of flow and continuity even though you're moving among different domains of discourse and you're going from one realm of the world to another. It's not that as a reader of poetry I'm doing anything at the vocal level that has that kind of raspy and discordant quality.

O'LEARY: But you are indicating it in a kind of adventuresome lineation that you have increasingly put to use, which seems to me to echo a lot of the jazz you're interested in, especially free jazz and experimental jazz, but also something of Duncan in "Passages," also something similar to Amiri Baraka. Is your sense of this adventuresome line—as I've called it—is it drawing from all these things? Or is it drawing from your longing toward the raspiness?

MACKEY: That line is suggesting a certain jaggedness which is a visual analogue of raspiness, a visual embodiment of raspiness. There's also a visual rhythm there. Robert Farris Thompson in his book *Flash of the Spirit,* which is on African art and philosophy—there's a section in there where he pays some attention to African fabric and certain graphic traditions, visual traditions in Africa, and says that these are really the visual counterparts to the kinds of rhythmic displacements that you hear in African music. You have textile practices in which staggered patterning and unexpected placement achieve an unsettled, irregular rhythmicity that you can see.

O'LEARY: It's somewhat synesthetic then.

MACKEY: Yes. There's a kind of visual syncopation going on. Thompson is drawing the connection between the more obvious manifestation of that kind of rhythm in acoustic space that we readily notice in music, speech, etcetera, and its manifestation in visual space. Likewise, in that line, in the lineation of my poetry, there is a visual rhythm, a visual stagger, a visual syncopation.

O'LEARY: Let me ask a question about your serial poems, "mu" and "Song of the Andoumboulou." I'm wondering if you think of them—they're comprised of these jagged clippings of speech—do you see them cohering with the books they are a part of, or do you see them each as a discrete series?

MACKEY: They are bounded by the book. I write with the book as a unit in mind. "Song of the Andoumboulou: 1–7" is a part of *Eroding Witness*; "8–15" is part of *School of Udhra.* Within the book they work with what else is in the book. Yet they are both within the book and within the sequence that continues in other books. So they're in more than one place at the same time: they are discrete *and* continuous.

I'm attracted to the sense of closure that the book offers but I'm also—I'm attracted to it but I'm not content with it. I want to have something that opens it up, that reminds us of the openness and the "openedness" that it is susceptible to, that it can't in fact escape.

O'LEARY: But there's a way in which the poems that you write, especially as they appear in *School of Udhra,* really do go beyond their bounds: they end and then there are subsequent sections that appear beneath a marginal line, almost a footnote line. I'm curious, first of all, about how you developed this move as a technique, and then, second, on a practical level or on the readerly level, are they read as progressive extensions of the poem or are they read as "alternate takes" of the poem?

MACKEY: When you read them, you go through them sequentially, so they read as further sections of the poem. But they have an unsettled relation to the poem that precedes them and the poem that follows them. And sometimes, in giving a reading, I don't read those sections that fall under the bar, under the line.

O'LEARY: Really? In some of them, there's more poem under the bar than there is poem above the bar.

MACKEY: [*Laughing.*] Yes.

O'LEARY: "Song of the Andoumboulou: 15" has *four* of them.

MACKEY: Yes. I was trying to suggest that even within the book there is another book, there's this "under-the-line" book. And by citing them specifically that way in the table of contents, it's like saying they are works unto themselves in some ways. I was trying to suggest the possibility of a multiple reading in which one could go through and read those poems that are under the line, go through *School of Udhra* and read the poems under the line sequentially without reading the other ones. And, similarly, one could go through and read the—let's call them "above-the-line"—the regular poems without reading those that are under the line. And also one could read them together. It was another way in which I was working to unsettle and multiply the possible relations of the parts. That occurred to me as a possibility in the course of writing *School of Udhra,* because there were things that were alternate takes in a sense, or continuations of things that had already been written. I wanted to keep that mark of process in the work. Also, it varied the rhythm in a sense, because I was getting into writing these long poems that run out over a number of pages. It was these shorter—and for the most part they are shorter—these shorter pieces were punctuative and percussive in ways I wanted to include. I didn't want all the poems to go on for three, four, five pages. I wanted to vary the measure as to what a stretch of utterance could be.

O'LEARY: I wonder if they are—I said "alternate takes" before. Are they almost a kind of revision? Do you revise?

MACKEY: I do revise but that's not the form of my revision. They *revisit* in many instances, but they revisit in a way that's differently marked. There's a great deal of revisitation in my writing anyway; these do it in a way that's marked visually and underscored visually in the way that they are put on the page, where they're placed at the bottom of the page, beneath a line. I was getting into using the page, using the visual display that the book offers, that print offers, to further announce and articulate senses of recurrence and rhythm and periodicity that are operative in the varieties of revisitation going on in the work.

JOHNSTON: With these serial sequences, do you foresee any conclusion? Or do you plan on continuing them indefinitely?

MACKEY: I think I'll know when they're over, after the fact. The "mu" series may well be over. I haven't written anything in that series for a while. But it was a conscious decision on my part to stay within "Song of the Andoumboulou." Again, it's one of those—I arbitrated that decision myself [*laughing*]. "This is the space I'm going to work in." I haven't worked in the "mu" series at all since I finished *School of Udhra.* And I haven't thought about it much. Probably when I finish this book of poems I'm working on now, I'll give some thought to whether the "mu" series is still alive. I think the serial poem suggests the possibility of going on and on, but in reality you have to find out whether in fact that is the case. Is this thing still going on? Can I continue this? Do I want to? Things like that. It's not that you just put it on automatic pilot and they go on out into infinity.

O'LEARY: The first appearance, as far as I know, of the letters to "Angel of Dust" is in "Song of the Andoumboulou." And then they achieved a much fuller, more serial form in *Bedouin Hornbook* and *Djbot Baghostus's Run.* Was *From a Broken Bottle Traces of Perfume Still Emanate* originally conceived poetically, since it appears in a sequence of poems? Or was it developed as a way for you to say things in a form that you couldn't say in poetry or you weren't saying in poetry? The letters give you a platform to lecture, to write essays, to be very discursive . . .

MACKEY: I didn't have a plan when I first started writing them. The first couple occur in "Song of the Andoumboulou" in *Eroding Witness.* I just saw them—yes, as you say—as a way to speak without the constraints of verse. There are constraints in verse that disallow certain kinds of statement and certain declarations.

O'LEARY: You can't really just talk about how much you like Jackie McLean in a poem. Well, you can . . .

MACKEY: You can, but I don't write that type of poetry. So it was a way of getting some other kinds of stuff in. At that point, it was very modest, occurring in the context of those poems. And the first one occurred out of an actual correspondence with a friend.

O'LEARY: So there was a "real" Angel of Dust.

MACKEY: I'm trying to remember if I actually—it was sent to a friend but it wasn't addressing the friend as Angel of Dust. I wrote the Angel of Dust and I sent a copy to the friend. I was allowing the friend to overhear this conversation with the Angel of Dust, which was prompted by questions raised by this friend, who had written me about a poem. Anyway, it started there. One of the impulses was—because it came out of questions about my poetry raised in correspondence with this friend—one of the impulses was to unpack the poetry in some ways but not do it in verse. To unpack; not to explain. To speak at greater discursive length about the content, the perspectives, the different dispositions that inform the poetry. Those first two were statements of poetics, kind of flirting with being prose poems, but delivered in an epistolary form which was invoking a certain audience, a rather spectral audience. At that time I was writing out of a sense of isolation that was rather severe. It seemed that letters addressed to an angel were appropriate to that situation. I didn't have any plan that, okay, I'm going to write two of these and then I'm going to start writing these books called *From a Broken Bottle Traces of Perfume Still Emanate.* I wrote those first two and then I wrote some longer ones that turned out to be the first half-dozen that after a period of time appeared in *Bedouin Hornbook.* After the first three of those, I still didn't know what this was. Was this some kind of prose poetry that was going to be a section of a book of poetry? In an early version of a collection of poems, which was not at that point called *Eroding Witness* but included much of what came to be collected in that volume—those longer letters were included in that collection. You see, I was constantly collecting poems and making books out of them to see if they worked that way for me. And seeing if they worked for publishers [*laughing*], which they didn't. At that point, I didn't know what was happening with these letters, but I kept writing more and more of them, and I started reading them at readings. It became clear after a while that they were a work apart from the books of poetry. And I liked that. I liked having this other venue in which to work. It allowed me to do other things, to range around in ways that I felt a great need for.

O'LEARY: Early on, in fact, in the first appearance of these letters, "Song of the Andoumboulou: 6," N. refers to himself as the author of "Song of the Andoumboulou: 3." Early on, N. is writing your poetry; later on, he takes on a more fully formed character. Has he become that as the work has progressed? Is he more fully formed for you?

MACKEY: Early on, he's not so much writing my poetry—well, I guess N. *is* writing the poetry, because he does, as you note, answer for it. Yes, N. is writing the poetry. I was going to say N. is *intruding* on the poetry, but [*laughing*] he could be doing both.

JOHNSTON: *You* may be intruding on the poetry.

MACKEY: Yes [*laughing*]. But, N. as a more fully-formed character? I don't know.

O'LEARY: You never had cowrie shells in your forehead.

MACKEY: [*Laughing*] I did have bits of glass in my forehead.

O'LEARY: Oh, you did?

MACKEY: From my head hitting the windshield of a car in a car accident, which is evoked in one of the letters in *Bedouin Hornbook.* N. and I have some things in common. We overlap.

O'LEARY: Shared experiences.

MACKEY: Shared experiences. Some shared proclivities.

O'LEARY: Do you see *From a Broken Bottle Traces of Perfume Still Emanate* as serially as the poems we've been talking about? Or do you see an end?

MACKEY: Oh, I see an end to all of them. I mean, I'm not going to be around forever. The question for all of them is when will I stop writing them. And that is still an open and unanswered question for *From a Broken Bottle Traces of Perfume Still Emanate.* I've seen that series referred to as a trilogy and I don't know where anyone got that idea. I've said I'm working on the third volume, but I didn't say that it would necessarily be the last. It *may* be the last one. Again, I have to find out.

O'LEARY: When the fourth one comes they'll start comparing it to *The Ring,* Wagner's tetralogy. At this point, though, it is serial.

MACKEY: It is serial and I don't know if I'm going to continue, if I'm going to go on with it in this particular way. There's a way in which writers go on writing and the books they write turn out to be installments of this big single work, finally. I don't know whether—I have a strong feeling

I'm going to go on writing about music, that I'm going to go on writing about it using some of the linguistic modalities, if not all of the linguistic modalities, that enter into *From a Broken Bottle Traces of Perfume Still Emanate*. But whether I will do it consciously and explicitly within that framework, using letters and that kind of thing, I don't know. There are other possibilities. There are possibilities of dropping the epistolary framework, for one thing. It's possible that these things that are called "after-the-fact lecture/libretti" are pushing a possibility that now resides in those letters, that are enclosures or attachments to those letters. They could take on a certain life of their own and could exist without letters or incorporate letters or references to letters in some kind of way. These other kinds of formal possibility are swimming around in my head. What's going to prove to be interesting and compelling enough to make me do it remains to be seen.

Interview by Charles H. Rowell

The following interview took place via telephone between Charlottesville, Virginia, and Santa Cruz, California, on February 21, 1997.

CHARLES H. ROWELL: As you know, contemporary poetry, as opposed to fiction, has a very small audience. That small group of general readers is familiar with a particular kind of poetry, most of which has that autobiographical or confessional bent—that is, the first-person voice which almost echoes the reader's or someone whose experiences the reader recognizes. In other words, the familiar first-person voices of contemporary poetry usually recount experiences or issues that seem everyday and immediate. Your poems, on the other hand, operate from a site that is not immediately familiar. In that sense it is different from the contemporary poetry we regularly read. Your poetry operates in an epic field, in a cosmic field, a field beyond what is immediate in our daily lives. We do not associate ourselves with the first-person voice in your poems. Your poems take leaps. Your poems inhabit spaces that we don't immediately know. They are spaces of the spirit. They are spaces in meditation. They are spaces in musical frames. They are spaces beyond this physical landscape. They are spaces beyond time. What is the uninitiated reader to do? After all, you're providing for us a new way of reading the world. And that new way we don't know until we get locked into the text. But can the general reader go that far without help?

NATHANIEL MACKEY: You're right that the confessional or autobiographical mode is a disposition that many writers of poetry write out of and many readers read with the expectation of finding. But it's also one that has been, at least in my reading of twentieth-century poetry, critically interrogated by the theorizing and the practice of a good number of poets. I write informed by the fact that there is a strain, especially in twentieth-century poetry, which does not presume that the poem is the vehicle for representing and revealing the travails of a discrete first-person subject, with consistencies of tone and voice and perspective and with constraints upon what that voice can chart, both in literal spatial and temporal terms and in terms of what that single voice can believably be taken to know or to be able to utter. There are a number of different senses of poetry in circulation. While there may be a dominant model, a model that most readers would be expected to bring to the poem, the models that I've been most engaged with as a reader, as a writer, as a teacher, and as a scholar haven't been that mainstream or dominant model. I have to pause a little bit to even think about what my practice is and what it must look like in relationship to that model. But you're right. I haven't been concerned with prioritizing a plausibly autobiographical "I" in the poem. That has a lot to do with my initial senses of what was possible in poetry, with the reading I was doing that drew me into wanting to pursue writing poetry of my own. Among the modernist poets that I was introduced to as a student there was, in T. S. Eliot, for example, the insistence upon the impersonality of the poet and the collagelike effects that he uses, especially and most famously in "The Waste Land," to dislodge the univocal speaking voice that dominates most poems and anchors most poems in the sense of a secure, stable, and discernible first-person speaker. So I see a long tradition, a pretty widely recognized tradition, behind the sorts of things that I'm doing and the sort of approach that I'm taking. It's not that I was terribly influenced by T. S. Eliot. I'm just saying that it goes back, if not beyond Eliot, to at least as canonical a figure as Eliot, so that there's a sense in which what I'm doing is not that far beyond the pale. It has come down through other poets that I've been interested in as well, whose names I could go into and probably will in the course of our conversation get into. But, for starters, let me say that I wonder, really, at this point in the twentieth century, in 1997, how radical and shocking it is to open a book that's not presenting poems that offer a discrete picture of a discrete narrating voice that tells bounded stories of a believable sort about the doings and the travails and the triumphs of the person whose voice one presumes it to be.

It depends on the disposition of the poet. If it's a sense of who the writer is that the reader wants, it says something about the sensibility of a particular poet that he or she would choose this option, the one that I've chosen. It speaks to my concerns. One of the things that poetry has become for me is an instrument to articulate not simply my personal experiences and my emotional reactions to those experiences but also my engagement with intellectual matters, with philosophic, aesthetic matters, with world traditions of various sorts and local traditions of various sorts. It's become something that allows me to express, to the extent that I can push the medium to do it, my sensibility at large, so to speak. And there are ways in which that sensibility reaches beyond or at least wants to reach beyond the confinements of the everyday, of the empirically verifiable, the sorts of things that we assume to define the realm in which relevant events occur. That realm has been extended by a number of things that we maybe take for granted in the twentieth century. The world in which we live is widened and deepened by what we read—books, but also, you know, periodical literature—and obviously by the electronic media that put us in touch with, if not distant parts of the world, images of distant parts of the world. The flow of information and such really has, in a way, shrunk the world. I think that the sensibility of a poem that allows that kind of information in is saying something very valid. It's testifying to—and is itself evidence of—the fact that the world is a more snug place these days and that individual consciousness is often being impressed or imprinted upon, impinged upon in some instances, by what's going on in various places at various times and at various levels at various times. That would be, off the top of my head, what I would begin to say to the reader you're speaking about. That's how I would begin to explain some of those differences that you speak about, some of the unexpected challenges the poetry might pose to that reader.

ROWELL: I want to try to explore another issue: tradition and your readings. We know that you have read much, that you have read in a most critical way, and that you have read deeper than the usual reader, deeper than the traditional scholar; we know that you have read and absorbed and synthesized many, many texts and many, many traditions. But the point is that your readers—if they read as I usually do—feel something new when they face your poems as aesthetic and ideational constructs. In the use of disparate materials you have gone far beyond the poetry of T. S. Eliot and Ezra Pound and Louis Zukofsky, for example. Your poetry reminds me more of that of Jay Wright. Is Jay Wright an influence on your work? Is the voice in these lines from your poem entitled "Capricorn Rising" that of a prophet, the same kind of voice I hear in some of Jay Wright's poems?

I wake up mumbling, "I'm
        not at the music's
    mercy,"   think damned
        if I'm not, but
        keep the thought
                    to myself.

Sweet mystic beast on the
        outskirts of earth,
    unruly airs, an awkward
                        birth
        bruises the bell of its
                        horn . . .

Just listen to what I read. That takes us far beyond the world we read in most contemporary poetry. It's your synthesis that I'd like you to talk about.

MACKEY: Yes. Well, if I could just spring off from that particular poem: that's a poem dedicated to Pharoah Sanders, a tenor saxophone player who quite famously came onto the scene playing in John Coltrane's group in the mid-1960s. If we got into talking about what a passage such as that is synthesizing, I'd say it's certainly synthesizing a sense of danger and alarm that Pharoah Sanders's music conveys, as does Coltrane's music and that of a great number of other musicians that I've been listening to and influenced by. It plays with that fact. It plays with the fact that the attainment of a certain level of chops or imaginative virtuosity among these musicians is often marked by referring to the musician in question as a "monster": "He's a monster of a pianist." That term was one of the things that I had in mind in speaking of a "sweet mystic beast"—this monstrous eruption onto the world that music of that order seems to announce and to impose. That would be one of the senses in which the music is something one would have a mixed feeling about being at the mercy of. There is something very numinous about that experience of being in the control of a music that is so powerful. But it's also part of the ecstatic tradition of music and it's also a part of those privileged moments that musicians aspire to and live for and that we as listeners get a bit of a taste of. So something of that is in that passage, but I think you're right to detect in it a sense of poetic vocation, a sense of the writerly vocation, maybe with music as an analogue, that does perhaps take the poetry to a different conception of what writing is for and what writing does than do the predominant and most prevalent conceptions. It's a sense of the writing as—*ceremonial* is perhaps the word, *sacramental* is perhaps the word.

You mentioned Jay Wright. I know that one of the things that Jay has been very insistent about over the years is that the space for poetry in our society and in our culture has lost touch with those ritual and sacramental roles and spaces that it has traditionally occupied throughout the course of world history and throughout the various sites of world culture that you find poetry in, which is essentially everywhere. He has been quite adamant about insisting that poetry needs to reclaim that role and that space, with almost a priestly or a prophetic task being taken on by the poet. I'm informed by a lot of that, and there are impulses in me that tend very strongly in that direction. Those impulses are complicated by other influences, among them the fact that we do live in a secular age and in a secular culture, an age of skepticism and doubt. I'm also in touch with that. Some of the manner in which the poetry moves—because movement conveys and is a vehicle for meaning and implication as much as overt statement—some of the way in which it moves, I think, is a carrier of that anxious or not altogether settled relationship to the desire or the need for a poetry that would carry a hieratic voice or at least a desire for reaching after a hieratic voice. Maybe that's, if not new, at least different from what is encountered in a lot of poetries—and there are so many poetries—these days. That might be a place to begin to open up onto what it is that is, if not being synthesized, at least being reached toward or sought after in an admittedly unpropitious climate.

ROWELL: "Capricorn Rising" is a favorite of mine, but I like "Passing Thru" more. I think if one were to place these two poems together with one of the "Angel of Dust" poems one would get a sense of the variety in your poetry, and one would also get, as I said earlier, a sense of the poem as a new form in your hands.

MACKEY: Well, I think it goes back to being open and improvisatory as to what can come into the poem, trying to make the poem a place where not just the usual content of poetry appears but where all kinds of other things can appear: new information, new discoveries of a scholarly sort, an intellectual sort, intellectual excitements, intellectual disappointments, things like that. As you've noticed, I'm something of a bookish poet and I try to leaven that bookishness with musicality. I mean, music is very important in my work in a lot of different ways, including rhythm and explorations of a variety of rhetorical tonalities, and maybe that's what's opening it into novel or innovative areas. The poem "Passing Thru" simply came out of my reading Ivan Van Sertima's work. Actually, it began before I'd really read his work in any depth. I happened to hear him give a talk and in the course of that talk he mentioned and showed photographs of an inscription in an ancient Libyan alphabet that he had found in the Virgin Islands. He showed some photographs that later appeared in his *Journal of African Civilizations.* I was very taken by the look of this script and also by the facts surrounding it: that this was an alphabet that was used in North and West Africa and that here we find it inscribed above a rock pool on one of the Virgin Islands. Obviously, this was part of his thesis, which he has written about at length in his book *They Came before Columbus,* that there were African expeditions to the Americas prior to Columbus's voyage to the Americas. I was struck by that because it's an unrepresented or underrepresented or hidden aspect of history, a history that doesn't make it to mainstream venues for the most part, mainstream historical texts, mainstream historical curricula. I was drawn to it as a kind of hidden or secret history. Of course, poetry has throughout the ages been a vehicle for imparting and keeping alive secret knowledge, secret information, secret wisdom. Not only did there seem to be something very ancient about that text, that old North and West African script that Van Sertima was talking about, but it also seemed to spark in me this old and ancient sense of the role of the poet. I had a great desire, when I saw that script while listening to his lecture, to write a poem, write something that would somehow come out of and honor—recognize, acknowledge—the fact of that inscription that he was showing the photographs of. That's a poem that I eventually did write some time afterwards, after reading *They Came before Columbus.*

It's kind of faint now, it's been a long time, but I think it was in 1978 or 1979 that I heard this lecture. It was at the University of Southern California, where I was teaching at the time. I think I actually wrote the poem in the summer of 1979 after reading *They Came before Columbus.* Anyway, there's a chapter in the book about a prince of Mali, Abubakari, who, like Columbus but before Columbus, had this sense that the world was round or, as the imagery that's used in the book says, like a bottlegourd. It seems that he set out to the west and was never heard from again. What triggered the poem was the fact that Mali was one of the places where this Libyan alphabet that Van Sertima had found in the Virgin Islands was used, this alphabet called Tifinagh. He doesn't make anything of it in *They Came before Columbus.* I don't think he makes the connection and maybe there is no connection, but I made a connection between this Malian prince/navigator, Abubakari, setting out and not having been heard from again and the fact that this alphabet that was used in Mali, among other places, was found in the Americas—evidence, perhaps, that Abubakari did make it here. The poem was sparked by the possible connection between those two things and it plays with that. And it *is* play. I mean, I wasn't trying to write a historical treatise proving this hypothesis, but it was an intriguing and appealing hypothesis and I ran with it a little bit, allowing speculation of that order to become the catalyst for a poem and feeling that the excitement that that speculation sparked was justification enough for a poem.

ROWELL: Risking unnecessary repetition, I want to return to the issues I raised at the opening of this interview. Will you for a moment imagine me as a general reader and help me to enter *Eroding Witness,* then guide me through the text by commenting on its architecture? First, perhaps, talk to me about the untitled opening poem. Is it an African diasporic piece searching for a name and a voice? Look at the last line, "an undertow / of whir im- / mersed in / words." Now look at the end of the volume, section four, entitled "Septet for the End of Time," with its series of eight poems, each beginning with "I wake up . . . ." Will you talk about the form of this book and about the meaning of its title?

MACKEY: I try to make books work as books and try to get beyond the book of poetry as just a miscellaneous collection of poems that happen to have been written over a certain period of time and happen to have arrived at a certain number of pages that qualify it to be a book. I wanted to order the book in a way that made some kind of sense. One of the things that makes that not only appealing but imperative is the fact that one of the things that my reading of poets associated with open form—the William Carlos Williams of *Paterson,* Amiri Baraka, Charles Olson and his theories of open field composition, Robert Duncan and his idea of the "world-poem" and what he calls the "grand symphony"—one of the things that's happening in these ideas of open form is a discontent with and a critique of the individual poem as a bounded, discrete, self-sufficient achievement, the well-made poem that stands by itself as if everything that needs to be in it is in it. The tradition that

I hooked up with was questioning that and instigating another kind of practice which sees the individual poem as always incomplete, always partial, always part of a larger work that is ongoing and that continues to feed upon previous work. I remember early on reading Robert Creeley quoting Louis Zukofsky, who said that we write one poem all our lives. The sense that each poem is just an installment in the development and inscription of this longer poem which is one's body of work I found to be a very freeing idea, in that it allows you to work in the poem with a certain intensity that does not have to be resolved in that particular poem. It allows you to get into areas that are alive and resonant in ways that you can't shut down and wouldn't want to shut down in a resolute way within the boundaries of a single poem. So my poems echo and anticipate one another. They lean on one another. They read back on one another. There's a kind of intertextuality going on among the various poems that I write within a book and even from book to book. There's also a conversation going on between the different books. I would say to that reader you've postulated that one way to get onto the turf that *Eroding Witness* is on is to keep that in mind: that the poems do share space with one another, that their borders are not hard borders and that there are flows among the various poems.

The book is divided into four parts and two of the parts, parts 2 and 4, are in fact serial poems. Part 2 is the first seven installments of "Song of the Andoumboulou," which is a poem that I've continued to write. There were eight more installments of it in *School of Udhra*, and the book that I've just completed is made up entirely of installments of "Song of the Andoumboulou," numbers 16 through 35. It's made up of twenty of them and it's divided into two sections of ten each. But, anyway, getting back to *Eroding Witness,* section 2 is "Song of the Andoumboulou" and section 4 is "Septet for the End of Time," which is, again, a set of poems, a set of eight poems that are tied together. One of the things that ties them together is that each begins with the three words "I wake up." Those three words are important to the whole book, because the book, from the first poem on, signals a task which the poetry has set for itself or which I have set for it or which poetry has set for me, which is the task of trying to enter a realm which it images as a submerged realm. That could be the realm of sleep or the realm of dream, as it comes to be in section four, or it can be the realm of the underwater, the subaquatic, an oceanic realm, as it's imaged in that first poem—"Waters / wet the / mouth"—which is both an invocation of the muse and a prefatory poem, significantly untitled, as you point out, that is meant to signal to the reader something of what's to come. I mean, it's a poem about speaking: "At the tongue's / tip the sting / of saltish / metal, rocks / the wound." It's a poem about the material of the book, words: "An undertow / of whir im- / mersed in / words." Those last four lines give an image of something that the poetry is in other ways enacting, which is a determination to serve that dimension of linguistic activity and possibility which is imagined here as whir. *Whir* is what you might call a more unruly semantics than that which we normally use language for, than that of the instrumental and functional uses that we employ language for. The first poem, then, is announcing that the poems are going to pull us into another disposition with regard to language, a disposition that it images almost as a drowning: "An undertow / of whir." It's announcing an ability to dwell in or a willingness to dwell in an area of resonance and implication that are not entirely domesticated by the instrumental, utilitarian senses of language which, because language is such a practical part of our everyday lives, we come to regard as perhaps the only valid deployment of language.

That poem is trying to say something about the poetics which inform the book. It's something of an *ars poetica* and it reinforces the suggestion in the book's title that writing or language as witnessing is here being brought into a kind of complication that can appear erosive, that can appear to be pulling the ground or the foundation out from under what we normally expect in the speech acts and the writing acts that we encounter. The book, overall, is informed by that trope, this title, *Eroding Witness.* If somebody were to say to you that poetry is an act of witnessing, that would conjure some pretty definite images, pretty reassuring and familiar images of what the function of poetry is. But for someone to say that the function of poetry is to simultaneously witness and erode its witness, to witness and erode its witnessing, as this title suggests, announces a different vocation for poetry, a trajectory for the poem that differs from that more common understanding. That first poem, as I said, really begins to flesh out what is already there and implied by the title. The first and third sections of the book are really more like miscellaneous sets of poems, although there are connections among them as well. I tried to organize them in such a way that some connections flow through them. As you move through the book, you find, for example, the epigraph from the liner notes to a record album of Dogon music, which talks about the song of the Andoumboulou, saying that the song of the Andoumboulou is addressed to the spirits. That's another statement in the book or another way of asserting in the book that there is a different sense of the rhetorical situation of the poem being practiced and advanced in the book, a sense which, as you noted earlier, doesn't take the constraints of the dominant model as its constraints. We're speaking to an audience of secular modern readers who won't buy into certain kinds of talk or evocations of certain kinds of realities—spiritual, ecstatic, etcetera—but to take the Dogon song of the Andoumboulou as the namesake for a serial poem is to say that there is a wider sense of audience that's being sought by that work, that's being sought not only by that work but by the body of work that it's included in.

The last section, "Septet for the End of Time," has a number of epigraphs as well, and they go some further distance in showing the importance to my work of ancient texts and ancient cosmological traditions. There's a citation from Marcel Griaule's *Conversations with Ogotemmêli,* which is about Dogon cosmology; there's a citation from the Koran; and there's a citation from one of the Egyptian pyramid texts. These epigraphs all play on numbers, seven and eight, and that kind of play, a play of resonance and implication as against an arrival at resolution and conclusion, is also saying something about the way I work, which is that I like to inhabit that play rather than try to close it down—not only inhabit that play but try to heighten and expand it. "Septet for the End of Time" is a set of poems that grew out of the first poem you brought up, "Capricorn Rising," which I did not embark upon as a poem that would be a part of a set. I just found, after I had written it, that there was a lot of imagery and implication in it that the subsequent poems revisited and began to further explore. This again says that the poem is a partial articulation that has within it the seeds of new articulations, that the poem continues to live beyond its own boundaries. "Capricorn Rising" continues to live in the subsequent poems that are a part of that set, both in the fact that those subsequent poems echo the first three words, "I wake up," and in, for example, a concern with music, ideas of danger within music and music within dangerous situations. The fourth poem in the set, "Winged Abyss," is dedicated to the French composer Olivier Messiaen and has largely to do with music, particularly music composed in dangerous and dire circumstances. Messiaen composed *Quartet for the End of Time* while he was a prisoner of war during World War II. One of the things of concern in those poems is war. They were written in the early 1980s. There's an apocalyptic tone to them. The Reagan administration had just come into office and was talking about a winnable nuclear war, things of that sort. The words "end of time" seemed apropos.

ROWELL: You mentioned your next book, *Whatsaid Serif*, your third volume of poetry. You told me some time ago that it has traces from *Eroding Witness* and from *School of Udhra.* Will you talk about its relationship, for example, to *School of Udhra*? Will you also discuss the genealogy of *Whatsaid Serif*?

MACKEY: Well, it continues, as I've already pointed out, the serial poem "Song of the Andoumboulou," which runs through the first two books. There are sections of the first two books that are devoted to installments of "Song of the Andoumboulou." The twenty installments in *Whatsaid Serif* pick up on a number of threads that run through *School of Udhra.* For example, in *School of Udhra* there's a poem called "Tonu Soy," a poem that I dedicated to Jay Wright. It came out of rereading Jay's work one summer, vaguely with the idea of writing an essay on his work, an essay that never got written. That rereading immersed me in the way in which Jay's work weaves together a variety of places—Latin America, the U.S., Spain, Portugal, Africa—a number of cultural traditions, mythological traditions, historical episodes and what have you from those places. A lot of those places are places I share his attraction to. The Dogon of Mali are very important in his work, and in fact the title, "Tonu Soy," is Dogon for "word seven." One of the things that happened in writing that poem is that I was weaving together references to the Arabic world and the Iberian world, to the diasporic extensions of those worlds. So references to and incorporations of flamenco are in there, as are references to some aspects of Cuban culture, reference to a Brazilian musician, Martinho da Vila, things like that. That kind of mix, especially the inclusion of the Arab world, came more and more into the later poems in *School of Udhra,* came up again, for example, in "Aspic Surmise" and "Slipped Quadrant." One of the things that *Whatsaid Serif* does is continue that.

The first poem in *Whatsaid Serif* is prefaced by an epigraph, a statement made by a flamenco singer, Manuel Torre, to García Lorca in the 1920s. He was talking to Lorca about the quality called *duende* that flamenco singers strive for. He said, "What you must search for, and find, is the black torso of the Pharaoh." I'm sure you can hear all the resonances in that. So I got going with "Song of the Andoumboulou: 16," which carries evocations of flamenco and evocations of Arab music. I wrote an essay at about the same time, which began as a talk at the Naropa Institute, called "Cante Moro," which means "Moorish Song." I got the title from an old Manitas de Plata album on which one of the singers says, "Eso es cante moro"—"That's Moorish singing." I thought it was pretty astounding to hear these Gypsies singing in southern Spain and calling it Moorish singing. In fact, Stephen Jonas, who was a poet in the Boston area associated with Jack Spicer and Charles Olson, among others, wrote a poem in the 1960s that takes off from that recording. Anyway, this talk that I gave at Naropa was about the connections between Lorca's theories of duende and the work of a number of recent American poets: Robert Duncan, Amiri Baraka, Bob Kaufman, and Jack Spicer. It also took off into talking about how the idea of duende not only applies to flamenco music but, as I hear it, to certain qualities of African American music, blues and other forms of African American music. I was very much immersed in these sorts of things at the time, so one of the things that flows through *Whatsaid Serif* is a kind of musicological emphasis which, like I said, picks up on some of the musical and cultural motifs that are in *School of Udhra.* But it brings in some other things as well. There is the city of Zar that comes out of African American folklore. You find reference to it in Larry Neal's poem, "The City of Zar," and you find reference to it in Zora Neale Hurston's field work. The third section of *School of Udhra* is called "Zar." In *Whatsaid Serif* there are references to Zar and there are anagrammatic rearrangements of the word's letters: "Zra," "Arz," "Raz." That continues an interest in and a use of anagrammatic play that arises in *School of Udhra* with the poem "Alphabet of Ahtt," dedicated to Cecil Taylor. So it's very much a book that takes up the idea that the work you do always leaves unfinished business and proceeds to try to, if not finish some of that business, at least extend the doing of it. There are a lot of connections, a lot of ways in which it continues things that were initiated in *School of Udhra* and, before that, in *Eroding Witness.*

ROWELL: What I find interesting, too, about your volumes of poetry is that you have successfully embedded in them performance qualities as well as musical traditions. But the performance attributes of your poetry are not one-dimensional, as they are in that of so many contemporary "performance poets." You have succeeded in putting performance on the page. Your poems are for the eye and the voice, the page as well as "the stage." Is that a self-conscious effort on your part?

MACKEY: Yes. I've never bought into the dichotomy that's often postulated between poems for the page and poems for the ear. The page and the ear coexist. Not only do they coexist, they can contribute to one another. A fact of life for most poets is that we write for both those occasions. I mean, we write poems that are published and appear on a page and we also give poetry readings, where the poem is addressed to the ear rather than to the eye reading the page. Knowing that fact, I think it's important to honor both those sites of reception for the poem. So I try to write poems that are on the page in a fruitful and fertile way, poems that repay rereading, poems that can be gone back to and read again and again, poems that have enough action in them and enough life in them that those rereadings can find something fresh or can find something that hadn't been seen before or simply emphasize something that's been seen before but not seen with that emphasis before. At the same time, I want to write poems that, when heard, appeal to the ear's desire for rhythm, for music, for the quickness of movement and the shifting of reference and register that is meaningful to a listening audience—that is not only meaningful in the thematic sense but meaningful in the sense that that's one of the things that exercises the ear, exercises the listening faculties in a way that as listeners we enjoy and find instructive, find pleasurable, find challenging, any number of things. I try to get the poems to do both. In the way I put the poem on the page—with variable spacing and variable margins and such—I try to give some sense of a visual dance, a kind of choreographic—though it's frozen choreography—a sort of choreographic relationship among the words, which I think it's easier to pick up on when you hear a poem read. The uniform spatial arrangements that most poems are put on the page with—uniform except for the ragged right margin where you have the line breaks—impart or imply a uniformity or a homogeneity to the space the words occupy that is not really there in the way that we speak words and not there in a poem when we hear a poem read or hear a poem spoken, so one of the things going on with the way I put the poem on the page is an attempt to give the sense of a visual dance, a visual rhythm or rhythmicity on the page, and a sense of the poem as it appears on the page as a sculpted inscription. I'm just trying to use the medium in as many ways as I can, be that medium the spoken word, the poem in the air traveling from speaker to listener, or the printed word, the page being looked at by the reader.

ROWELL: Will you talk about the relationship of your texts to musical traditions?

MACKEY: Well, one of the relationships is that I've been an avid listener to music for most of my life. Though I'm not a musician and though the extent of my musical training is, to put it charitably, rudimentary, music has always been a very important and nourishing part of my life. That's reflected in my writing. It's reflected in the fact that some of the poems are dedicated to musicians, that some of the tropes are musical tropes, that some of the reference material comes from the world of music. Of course, in the prose it's even more obvious because I write these letters that are penned by a musician/composer who signs his letters "N." This engagement with music has partly to do with trying to free the sense of what language does and what writing does by invoking the example of music, where, especially in instrumental music, what we're listening to are by no means denotative sounds yet we have the sense that something very meaningful is being conveyed nonetheless. That fact serves as a provocation for language uses that cultivate apprehensions of meaning which are not carried at the denotative level, uses of language which get into areas of resonance and gesture that can be as meaningful and as expressive as the denotative functions of language. We hear a word and it denotes something, but in addition to that there are communicative and expressive properties that have to do with the tone of voice with which the word is uttered, the connection of that word to other words, rhythmically, phonologically, and syntactically, and so forth. Different grammatical arrangements, for example, elicit different responses. Music has been and continues to be a teacher and a case in point for me of such nondenotative possibilities. For example, I listen to a lot of vocal music from other countries, in languages that I don't understand. I don't get the lyrics at the denotative level, but I respond nonetheless, learning to listen to language without the amenities of its denotative content. Doing that has probably had a significant influence on some of the ways in which I go about writing, an influence that I'm not able to talk about in an extended or explanatory way but that I know to be there nonetheless.

ROWELL: I have already asked you whether Jay Wright influenced you as a writer. Are there other writers who have been important to you? I also wonder whether Wilson Harris has influenced you. The ritual and spirituality in Wright and Harris, for example, must have had an impact on you.

MACKEY: Both of them have been very important as kindred spirits, elder kin. Both of them I've corresponded with over a number of years now. I first wrote Wilson Harris in the late 1970s—I think it was 1978—and we've been corresponding regularly ever since. Jay I think I first wrote not too long after that, in the early 1980s—1980 or 1981—and we've been corresponding since then. I wrote both of them out of admiration for their work and a sense of affinity with what they were doing. They were very important guiding spirits for me in their engagement with the African diaspora and beyond, the human diaspora which another poet important to me, Robert Duncan, spoke of as being articulated, inscribed, and advanced within what he calls the "world-poem," a heterogeneous poem in which elements from various spaces on the map come into the weave. You're quite right. Those two poets in particular, those two writers in particular—I say "poets" because I consider Wilson a poet even though he writes novels. To call his novels *novels* is to use a term of convenience. They have the compression and the imagistic muscle of poetry and they have the compacted thought of philosophic, theoretical discourse, with a whole lot more going on than what we normally think of when we think of the novel. The confounding of genre that we were talking about earlier is very active in his work. He's an acknowledged influence in my prose, but he's also been an inspiration in my poetry. One of the poems in "Septet for the End of Time" is dedicated to him. As for other influences, there are a number of figures who come to mind, more than we have time to go into. I'm rereading Ralph Ellison's *Invisible Man* this week for a course I'm teaching, so I'll mention him. Again, rereading the novel, I see things that have influenced me, though I've never talked about Ellison very much as an influence. The open manhole that N. dreams about in *Bedouin Hornbook*'s opening letter may well have been a subliminal homage, but Ellison's isn't one of the names I'm first to name when I start talking about influences. Perhaps it's because he's influenced so many people, his influence is so pervasive, I take it it goes without saying. But the idea he floats early on in the novel that writing is an impulse to make music of invisibility has teased me for years with its inversion of music's literal invisibility—usefully teased me, I think. I try to align writing with that invisible ability to make a mark.

Interview by Brent Cunningham

The following interview took place in Santa Cruz, California, on August 16, 1998.

BRENT CUNNINGHAM: Your new book from City Lights is called *Whatsaid Serif* and subtitled "Song of the Andoumboulou: 16–35." In the eighteenth song you write, "Rethought what Andoumboulou / meant." Possibly you could speak, in this context, about your own sense of what is rethought in the new work.

NATHANIEL MACKEY: One of the things that's happening is that I'm getting more into what I found out later about the Andoumboulou, which first comes up in *School of Udhra.* As I've explained before, when I first began the series I didn't know certain things about the Andoumboulou. In fact, there's not a whole lot that I've been able to find out about the Andoumboulou. I took the title from a Dogon funeral song that I heard on a record in the early 1970s. It was only in reading *The Pale Fox* years later, in the late eighties, that I learned that the Andoumboulou are a failed earlier form of human being in Dogon cosmology, a premature form or premature attempt at human being. What's being thought or rethought are the implications of these figures of failure and prematurity. I've thought about that in a number of contexts. One of the contexts that comes up a lot in *Whatsaid Serif* is gnosticism. In one of the early installments in *Whatsaid Serif* I quote, as an epigraph, from Jacques Lacarrière's book *The Gnostics,* which I had recently read. One of the things that comes up in that book is the gnostic idea of human beings as a premature creation. That idea resonated with the figure of the Andoumboulou, so in *Whatsaid Serif* there's a good deal of thinking about the Andoumboulou in gnostic terms. There are other ways it is being rethought as well, more than we have time to go into. Just to give one example, I was also rethinking the literal sound of the song of the Andoumboulou, a certain stridency and raspiness of voice that struck me and appealed to me from the beginning. One of the things that comes into *Whatsaid Serif* is hearing a kinship or an affinity, a sense of similarity, between that sound and, say, the sound of flamenco, *cante jondo,* deep song, of which there's a great deal of invocation and to which there's a great deal of allusion in the book. So I'm bringing the Andoumboulou and the "Song of the Andoumboulou" into harmonic interplay with a number of other references and traditions.

CUNNINGHAM: When you say the subject is this shift, this learning about the Andoumboulou, do you mean the subject is what you are learning or the process itself, the fact that one begins with less knowledge and learns more later?

MACKEY: It's really, for me, discovering the range of things that this figure can apply to. I haven't found out a great deal about the Andoumboulou as the Dogon conceive of them. In the three or four books on Dogon cosmology that I've read, there isn't a whole lot on the Andoumboulou, so it's not finding out in that sense. It's partly finding out and it's partly making. It's not a passive act of finding out; it's also constructing, creating what "andoumboulouousness," which is a neologism that comes up in *Whatsaid Serif,* means. It's really extending the implications and resonances that reside in the figure as it presides over certain areas of my life and work. It becomes more inclusive and more elastic and, again, vibrates with other traditions and with my own experience. I've taken to joking lately that the Andoumboulou are a form of failed, flawed human being and that that's something I can identify with.

CUNNINGHAM: I wonder if you would apply this idea of expanding the resonances that reside in a figure to a line that stood out for me from "Song of the Andoumboulou: 23": "And were there one its name was / Ever After, a story not behind but in / front of where this was . . . ." The "one" refers, I take it, to a universal point of reference yoking all stories together. The line strikes me as both difficult and suggestive, asking one to conceive of the plane of the reader, or perhaps even a plane somehow in front of that plane, as precisely the hidden reference of the text, subjectivity as text's objective ground. Is this relevant to the idea of a figure taking on more and more resonances in the writer's life, picking up new resonances in front of the text? How is one to think of this "in front of" as opposed to the more familiar debate between meaning taking place "in back of" the text versus meaning taking place on the text's "surface"?

MACKEY: It does relate to what we've been talking about. There's the obvious sense of the phrase "Ever After." It evokes fairytale endings and by implication—which is an implication I intended—it suggests that the story behind the story is closure, and that closure is a fiction, a fairy tale, that the impulse toward closure, which is often made to be coincident with meaning, sets up false expectations, expectations that lead us astray. I also hear other meanings in the phrase "Ever After." If you hear the word *after* in the sense of *pursuit*—as in, "this is what I'm after"—the phrase then suggests that the story is a story of pursuit, that "Ever After," fairytale closure, is in front of us, that we're in pursuit of it, ever after it. "Ever After" names both a goal and our relationship to it. One works toward, writes toward, pursues meaning as much as one tries to find the names to express a meaning that one already has, that one has already found. That's one of the ways in which the process I've been talking about is related to "Ever After." One of the things I've been doing is finding out what "Andoumboulou" means; I've been after the meaning. There's that phrase of Whitehead's that the Black Mountain poets liked so much, "a lure for feeling." Well, for me the Andoumboulou is a figure that's not just a lure for feeling but a lure for meaning as well. That sense of pursuit, a sense of transit and movement and search that is so much a part of *Whatsaid Serif*, is talking about the microlevel of the poem itself, about the language itself, at the same time that it's talking about the macrolevel, the sense of quest and migration in geographic space and historical time.

CUNNINGHAM: I wonder if that phrase, the "lure for feeling" or "lure for meaning," relates to a phrase you used in some of your earlier critical work, "a self-supporting myth." I think of it as similar to Michael Davidson's phrase "enabling fictions," where the perspectives one takes—outside any question of their "objective" truth—tend to justify themselves by the fact that they generate a kind of work, or a kind of being in the work, whatever your particular poetics are. They "lure" you into doing the work.

MACKEY: Yes, I've thought of them in terms of motivating fictions. Often, I think, poetic theory and poetics get into the realm of motivating fictions. They are ideas, figures, tropes, stances or attitudes that don't just make your writing possible but motivate you to write, move you to write, compel you to write. It's not that you make them up yourself; you find yourself spoken to by certain myths, certain tropes, certain figures, certain ideas, certain thought systems. They seem to have the role of lure not only for feeling and meaning but for further expression. In fact, experiences in one's life are often like that. When people talk about "watershed experiences" they are talking about something like that, experiences that one finds oneself going back to again and again, dreaming about again and again, even though one would think, "That's thirty years back there; that's already been resolved." But there is a way in which they don't resolve or haven't been resolved. They continue to secrete meaning and motivation. They impel you to revisit them, to look at them again, to perform further acts of inspection and expression. That's one of the things, again, that the "Ever After" suggests.

CUNNINGHAM: In some of your earlier critical work—say, for example, your comments on Williams in the essay "The World-Poem in Microcosm" or your comments on Olson in "That Words Can Be on the Page"—you appear skeptical of what you call their "Adamic sense of language," roughly their belief in an almost prelinguistic authenticity located in the notion of the word as object rather than the word as social construction. At the same time, the attempt in your own work to articulate a different kind of "world-poem" can be open to a similar criticism, that such an ambition, no matter how fluid and well-intentioned you or Wilson Harris or Robert Duncan might be, inevitably becomes "the private property" of the poet or groups writing it, inevitably partakes of an Adamic pretension. Are you concerned about that kind of reification? Is there a way to avoid that?

MACKEY: I'm always concerned with reification, if you mean that term in the way that I understand it, as a kind of rigid consolidation of what appears to be asserted in someone's work, especially if he or she has taken pains in that work to complicate it, to be as mobile as one can and to be as many-sided as one can. Yes, I think we need to be concerned with the tendency of critical discourse to do that kind of thing. But, if I hear correctly the implications in your question and in the term *private property*, then what you're saying is that this apparent engagement with the world, reaching out to the world, lending oneself to and incorporating the world, what we think of when we hear the expression "the world-poem," can simply become an act of solipsistic appropriation, where the world is pulled into a privatized realm of discourse that is the property of the poet. If that's your concern, if that's what's in your question, I would have to say yes, we have to be concerned. That's one of the risks we run. We have to exercise a certain kind of vigilance and awareness that comes with the consciousness of that risk.

I should point out that I've never applied the term *world-poem* to my work. Paul Naylor has used it in relation to my work and I understand how my work can be read in relationship to Duncan's idea of a world-poem. Obviously there are certain attractions that I found in his postulation of it, certain affinities that can be found in my work coming out of that influence, but I wouldn't say that I've been trying to write a world-poem. The term suggests all-inclusiveness and I balk at that. It's a misnomer. The thing about the world-poem that needs to be stressed is that it is not an all-inclusive poem. In some of the earlier instances of it that Duncan talks about—notably Pound's *Cantos*—there was a desire to be all-inclusive, to be conclusive and comprehensive, to reach some kind of closure. But, of course, the *Cantos* didn't end with Canto 100. He couldn't include all of human knowledge and all of human history in the poem. The amazing thing is that anyone would have ever thought that could be done. That doesn't seem to me to be what Duncan is doing—in "Passages," the very title suggests otherwise—and it's certainly not what my work, which draws on traditions from various parts of the world, is trying to do. It's a selection. It's a selection where one often feels that one has been selected as much as that one has done the selecting. I mean, why "Song of the Andoumboulou"? There are other pieces of music I've heard, other pieces of ritual music, funeral music, from other parts of Africa and from the U.S. and elsewhere. Why does that one grab me at a certain point and hold on to the point where I continue to elaborate a work under that title?

It's a selection. Being up front about the fact that it's a selection, that one is not making claims to comprehensiveness and closure, should inhibit, if not altogether prohibit, the reification process. It's an open-ended endeavor that doesn't end with one's own work. Duncan had the sense that his work was part of a larger work that included every poet that there ever was, and all future poets. One acknowledges one's particularity and partiality, one's placement as an individual, but also allows for that particularity and that placement to be susceptible to something outside or beyond it. The world-poem is more an aspiration than an accomplishment. I would be very uncomfortable with any claim that comprehensive globality had been achieved by Duncan's "Passages" or by my work.

Here *world* is just a relative term. It's the way we see the term *world* being used when we go into a record store and there's a section called

"World Music." What that means is just that it's stuff you don't normally hear, it's some part of the rest of the world. I'm a disc jockey at a radio station here in town, KUSP, and the program I do falls into one of the "world music" slots. But I tend to go to the same places on the map over and over again. I've never played any music from Transylvania on the program, but I play music from Brazil again and again. It's particular places in the world that we select to go to or that we're drawn to. It's the same thing, I think, in this world-poem business we're talking about.

CUNNINGHAM: This idea of the particular and the specific has been important in your work, but it's been important in a specific way—i.e., there's not a "poetics of place" as there is in the case of many of your influences, say Williams. I'm also thinking of Robert Creeley, who talks so often about his family and where he comes from, but in your work it's not overt. There aren't many specific references to Florida, Princeton, or Santa Cruz, for example. Was there a point when you decided this was the place you would go, away from a discussion of, say, your day-to-day experiences?

MACKEY: I couldn't say there was a specific point at which I decided that. One thing that has led me away from that was the fact that those people did it so adamantly, to the point where it no longer needed to be done with such obsessional energy. That would be one reason: it had been done. There was no need for me to do it quite that way again. But that's not to say that I didn't, especially early on, feel some anxiety about the fact that I didn't seem to be much given to doing that sort of thing, to locating myself in that way, in terms of geographic space, personal biography, family history, and so forth. One can find gestures in my work that come out of the anxiety I felt about whether I was doing that or not. Tellingly, those gestures get complicated by a swerve. In "Ohnedaruth's Day Begun," speaking as John Coltrane, I talk about playing at the Village Gate one night in late '65 and "some kid comes up and says he'd / like to hear 'Equinox.'" Well, in fact, I was at the Village Gate in late '65 and I heard John Coltrane play. Between sets he was sitting at the bar, not too far from where I was sitting, and I walked over, said hello, and asked if he would play "Equinox." So at that point, in 1977 when the poem was written, I was playing with bringing myself into the poem, but in a skewed way. It's in a poem in which I'm speaking as John Coltrane, speaking through a persona, and referring to myself and a piece of my own personal history in an oblique and refracted way.

Or, in that same poem, "my divorced mother / daddied me to death." Now, that's Coltrane speaking but that's not true to Coltrane's personal history. That's some of my personal history bleeding into the figure of Coltrane. We share the "I." My sensibility has been projected onto Coltrane.

Location, where I got into location, would be complicated by dislocation, by senses of drift. There's a lot of location in my work. It's hard to see it for what it is because it's layered or refracted or brought into some kind of play with multiplicity. The epistolary prose series *From a Broken Bottle Traces of Perfume Still Emanate* was begun when I lived in L.A. The band that the series is about continues to reside in L.A. although I no longer live there. A lot of biographical material comes in there, but neither there nor in my poetry am I writing autobiography. I'm using biographical material as elements of a composition, in the same way that I use things I've read, things I've listened to, stories I've heard about other people. The point is not to reduce the composition to one site of origin. You don't reduce the composition to my living in Los Angeles. You don't reduce the composition to my having heard *A Love Supreme*. The composition brings them into an order of its own. That is their site, that's where they exist. We still have a critical discourse that is more concerned with narratives of origin and looking for sites of origin than the supposed sophistication we've arrived at would suggest.

CUNNINGHAM: It seems to me, from some of the other interviews, that as you developed as a writer you were never reliant on a poetic community per se—not, that is, in the sense of having weekly contact or conducting extensive epistolary communication, and this seems different from what one finds among some of your influences, thinking here of the Olson-Creeley letters, the Beat scene, the Duncan-Spicer circle, and so on. Your ideas seem to have been built far more from reading and listening to music, a privately assembled aesthetic that equally avoids becoming self-oriented. I wonder, first, if this is a true impression and, if it is, how you think being—I don't know if I like the word *isolated*, but I'll say isolated—has shaped your work and your thinking. Did you ever seek out such a community?

MACKEY: I think there's a good deal of truth in that, although I would inflect it differently. I don't feel like I've been in isolation, but you yourself picked up on the problem with the word *isolated*. Again you note a difference from some of my influences. I think one *should* be different from one's influences. Still, it's not just that. The situation one finds oneself in is different. The situation of the people you name in the forties and the fifties was very different from my situation in the seventies and eighties. One big difference is that I pursued an academic career, which meant that I was not in a situation that caused me to seek out a community of writers in the way I otherwise might have. I was already in a kind of community, a community that increasingly included writers in a way that it didn't for, say, Duncan and his generation. Of course, the antiacademicism of some of the writers I've been influenced by made for some perturbations on my part about what in the world I was doing in academia. That was something that had to be worked through, and I worked through it. Though I haven't sought to be a part of a scene or a part of a movement, I have had contact with other writers, others who wrote, and that's been the case from the time I was an undergraduate beginning to take seriously the hope of being a writer. You're right, I didn't meet weekly, there was no group I was part of. But I did talk to others who had a writing aspiration, I did take one creative writing course when I was at Princeton, I did contribute to and publish in student literary magazines there and at Stanford. I wasn't at Stanford as a creative writing student; I was in the Ph.D. program in English, but there was a creative writing program there and I got to know some of the people in it. I met aspiring writers there who I talked to as an aspiring writer. You know, we talked to each other as aspiring writers, in addition to whatever else we were aspiring to. That's been the case in all the places I've been. I went to Wisconsin and that was the case there. But none of these associations ever aspired to be a movement or a school. I haven't sought out that kind of community. Movements get a lot of attention but they distort our vision of how writing is done. There are a lot of reasons why movements get attention, most of them obvious. Writing outside of movements is probably the rule rather than the exception, and in that sense I feel like I haven't been in a weird place. I've been in the place where most writers have been, which is where you find yourself influenced from a number of different directions. I see myself as having done what most writers do, just finding out what works for me, what speaks to me, what resonates for me. Of course, writers who are involved in movements also do that. That's why movements often fracture; the writers involved are different, have different sets of concerns. I've certainly, though, sought out contact, communication. I've corresponded with other writers, though this has come later, for the most part. I've been corresponding with Wilson Harris for twenty years now. I've corresponded with Jay Wright for almost the same amount of time. I feel like I've been in touch to the degree I needed to be. Editing *Hambone*, for example, which I began to do again in the early 1980s, has been a way of being in contact and conversation, creating something of a sense of contact and community. I've been in touch, but it hasn't been in the day-to-day sense of walking down the street and running into eight writer friends.

CUNNINGHAM: The reference points for much of your work are located in Africa or the Caribbean. Have you been to those regions?

MACKEY: Yes, to a degree; 1975 was the first time I ever went abroad; that trip included a week in Morocco. But I haven't been to Africa since then. I applied for and got a Fulbright to teach at the University of Cape Coast in Ghana in the late eighties. I wasn't able to go because the university was shut down by the government in response to student strikes. I still would like to go to Africa, south of the Sahara. I'm not much of a tourist; I found that out by doing the tourist thing. I prefer to have something take me somewhere, some reason to go, as with the Fulbright. But there were problems with that, especially the conditions at the universities in Ghana. The more I found out about those conditions and the living situation there, the more wary I became of taking that on. Then it became a moot question when the universities were closed down.

I have also been to the Caribbean, but not much. In the last few years, I've been to Trinidad and Tobago a couple of times, and before that to the Bahamas. I went to the Bahamas a few years back, in the mid-eighties. One of the reasons I was interested in going to the Bahamas is that I have family lineage that goes back to the Bahamas. My father, who was born in the Panama Canal Zone, was actually Bahamian. His mother and father were from the Bahamas. They went to the Canal Zone, as did many West Indians, to work on the canal. I remember talk of the Bahamas and of Bahamians from my childhood, growing up in Miami, and after, when we moved to California. That was one of the connections I felt, one of the ways I felt a connection with the Caribbean. I went to Nassau for a poetry conference in 1985.

That's the extent of my traveling in those regions. I'm doing more traveling now, usually in connection with my work, which is the way I like it. I get fidgety and bored just being somewhere as a tourist.

CUNNINGHAM: It must be striking to arrive at a place you've imagined so much, written about so much.

MACKEY: Well, there's the place in your imagination and then you bring that place into conversation with the literal place. I've had some occasion to do that. But, again, that's my sense of displacement and palimpsestic overlay. There's a way in which that old line of Stein's, "there's no there there," is always true. "There" is a construction of where you are, the "here" that you inhabit, and once you go to that place you think corresponds to that "there," it's a "here"—it's not quite the place you've carried over in your head. There's very fertile slippage between those two senses of location. It's a slippage, a discrepancy, that I've both lamented and felt good about.

As I said, 1975 was the first time I went abroad. One of the things I had to deal with was a romance of travel that I had absorbed, which the traveling didn't live up to. I was quite disappointed. In some ways, I've never gotten over that disappointment. It has figured into, I think, a lot of the concern with location, locus, and dislocation that comes into my writing, the sense of itineracy that is increasingly accented, say, in *Whatsaid Serif*, where tropes of vehicular movement—bus, boat, train—recur and senses of arrival and/or frustrated arrival are articulated over and over again. A lot of *Whatsaid Serif* comes from my experience of travel and gets transposed in various ways. That's the term I've seized upon in recent months to talk about that concern: *transposition*. It's a word that speaks to those kinds of complications, one's fulfillments and disappointments as a traveler. It's finding out that you had an appointment other than the one you thought you had. Your disappointment is that the appointment you thought you had wasn't kept, but you find there were other reasons for you to be there. You had an appointment you didn't know you had. That disappointing travel experience in 1975 is one of the places that the figures out of North Africa come from, all that concern with the Bedouin and the desert. Some of that is me revisiting that experience, keeping appointments I only come to see later. Then, of course, it gets overlaid with subsequent kinds of travel.

Interview by Paul Naylor

The following interview took place via e-mail between March 1999 and February 2000.

PAUL NAYLOR: I thought I'd start off with a sweeping and ill-defined question, so feel free to answer it in an equally sweeping and ill-defined way. One of the aspects of your work that sets it apart from a great deal of contemporary thinking and writing is your commitment to "mystical" traditions and experiences. For the record, let me say that I have a fairly restricted definition of mysticism as an affirmation of the possibility of knowledge gained from sources other than "reason" as it is traditionally conceived in Western thought. Your poetry, fiction, and critical prose all explore such possibility. I understand your dissertation at Stanford is titled "Call Me Tantra: Open Field Poetics as Muse," and your latest collection of poetry, *Whatsaid Serif*, is full of references to gnosticism. In between those works are your appeals to Dogon cosmology and all those cowrie shell attacks N. undergoes in *From a Broken Bottle Traces of Perfume Still Emanate.* So my sweeping question is, what attracts you to the various forms of mysticism that run throughout your work? Do they resonate with your own experience, or do they perhaps represent a desire for certain kinds of experience?

NATHANIEL MACKEY: That's actually not so restricted a definition. On the contrary, it's very inclusive and elastic, very capacious, and the very sweeping aspect of it begins to answer the question you pose. It seems to me that by juxtaposing the mystical to reason, as you do, you're giving it the status and the scope of an alternative reason, much the way in which Pascal, in that famous formulation of his, writes of the heart having reasons that reason knows nothing about. So we're talking about a recognition, even within the Western tradition, of the limits of reason, a recognition of other ways of knowing, multiple ways of knowing. Poetry—art in general, really—has long been concerned, characteristically been concerned, with giving such reasons their due. My attraction to mystical traditions simply continues that line of endeavor. Yes, to answer your question more directly, the attraction is based on both resonance and desire. I feel the need to keep head and heart together, to have them, if not exactly connect, at least correspond. In putting it so I'm echoing Jack Spicer, of course, but that echo also recalls Baudelaire's poem "Correspondences," which I first read in my late teens in *The Forest of Symbols,* one of Victor Turner's books on Ndembu ritual. Turner uses the poem as an epigraph to the book, whose title is a phrase found in the poem. The book is about how the Ndembu intuit and enact correspondences between themselves and their environment and how they sustain or, when it's ruptured, restore such a sense. So the poetry/anthropology nexus was there early on. It has continued in such things as the recourse to Dogon cosmology that you mention. What you call my commitment to mystical traditions—my respect for the intuitive, the uncanny, the oneiric, the sympathetic, the coincidental, the ecstatic, the intangible, the paradoxical, the oceanic, the quirky, the psychosomatic, the quixotic, the religioerotic, and so on—has to do with temperament, experience, and a good deal of textual reinforcement. The latter ranges from having read, say, Jacques Maritain's *Creative Intuition in Art and Poetry* in my late teens to more recently reading Michael Sells's *Mystical Languages of Unsaying* or Catherine Clément's *Syncope,* from (and this is why Pascal came to mind) being taken with Henri Corbin's coinage "cardiognosis" in his books on Islamic mysticism to seeing Harriet Jacobs, in *Incidents in the Life of a Slave Girl,* refer to the heart as a "mystic clock."

NAYLOR: I like the phrase "alternative reason" in your reply. Forms of thought that aspire to an "anti-reason" rather than alternative reason make me nervous, to say the least. And your positive example of the Ndembu and the correspondences among themselves and their world that they intuit gets right at my concern. The members of the jazz band you create in *From a Broken Bottle Traces of Perfume Still Emanate* correspond among themselves like the Ndembu. In all three volumes of that work, a great deal of important "information" is shared among the band members through their music rather than through words. In the opening scene in *Djbot Baghostus's Run,* for example, Aunt Nancy and Djamilaa, the two female members of the group, make their argument for recruiting a female drummer by performing a musical composition—an argument none of the men in the band fail to grasp immediately. Since these kinds of experiences happen outside the realm of discursive reason, they're mystical, but they're anything but irrational. N.'s "translations" of these musical arguments are represented as highly articulate, tightly reasoned exchanges, so the call and response between the musicians does seem to be an alternative form of reason. One consequence of the way you represent these mystical exchanges of music as sequential dialogues is that they have a quality of duration, of unfolding in time, that works against more traditional representations of mystical experiences as being sudden flashes of insight that collapse space and time. Like the Ndembu, the intuitive correspondence among the band members takes place in and through time.

I'd be interested to hear about the compositional practices and problems involved in creating these scenes in your fiction. What are some of the difficulties you confront when trying to write about what is outside writing or to make reasonable that which draws reason into question by exposing its limits? What correspondences or dissonances do you experience in representing the kinds of temporality that distinguish music and writing?

MACKEY: Yes, there's a tendency to identify the mystical with sudden epiphanies that transcend or obliterate normal time and space constraints. That's a central and salient strain in the mystical tradition, but there's also a strain that recognizes and works with temporality, even in pursuit of such "atemporal" epiphanies, a strain that posits a tendency toward fulfillment or fruition working through time, posits and seeks access to it. Alchemy, for example, in both the East and the West, built on ancient metallurgical beliefs that all metal, given time, grows into gold and that this growth can be assisted and accelerated by human effort, that time can be speeded up, heated up. One's transmutation of metal through mastering fire takes time where it was already headed, only faster. It's interesting that Charles Olson echoes these ideas in "Against Wisdom as Such," saying with regard to poetry that we invoke other times when we master the flow of time, that we take time and heat it, bend it to serve ourselves and to serve form, that a song is heat, and so on. There are, of course, large-scale teleological and eschatological beliefs that these ideas are folded into, beliefs a certain sophistication tends to back away from (as, by the way, Olson does even as he echoes them). But certainly we persist in believing in the promise of consummation or disclosure proffered by time on a smaller scale, persist in believing time will tell. The old spiritual "We Will Understand It Better By and By" carries and comes out of that older, larger-scale understanding but it continues to resonate—so much so I echo it at points in *School of Udhra* and *Whatsaid Serif.* There's an unforgettable version done by the Pindar Family and Joseph Spence on an album called *The Real Bahamas,* notable not least of all for the ambiguous laughter they break into when it's over.

I've drifted a bit, but what I was on my way to saying relates to the questions you raise in that, while it's poetry Olson's talking about, the connection between time and telling, timing and telling, obviously applies to a piece of fiction or a piece of music as well. Each not only unfolds in time but uses features of its unfolding in time (rhythm, sequence, pattern, pace, etcetera) in significant, constitutive ways. The kinds of temporality involved in music and writing can, as you note, be very different, but they also have much in common. *From a Broken Bottle* builds in large part on the sense of correspondences between music and verbal discourse that has long had a good deal of currency among African American musicians and audiences (Lester Young saying a solo should tell a story, Eric Dolphy saying he tries to get his horn to speak, Anthony Davis calling his publishing company "Mindspeech Music," and so forth). I tend to view the differences not as difficulties or problems of an especially pressing sort but simply as features or facts which come with the territory. Simultaneity, for example, is something fiction has struggled with for quite some time, resorting to "meanwhile-back-at-the-ranch" tactics of one sort or another. Two or more instruments can play separate lines at the same time but a piece of writing is univocal; it can't reproduce polyvocal simultaneity. It describes or narrates the line the instruments play not simultaneously but one at a time, however much it may work to weave them together. Still, one understands, in the world of correspondences, that one isn't dealing with reproductions or even congruent mappings. The time it takes to describe a note will in most cases be longer than it takes that note to sound, but we're always dealing with different temporalities, even when it's not music that's being written about. A paragraph read by a reader in half a minute may have taken three days to write.

NAYLOR: I do think you're right about writing being ultimately univocal, and it's the visual dimension of writing that makes it so. I remember hearing four people and a pianist performing Louis and Celia Zukofsky's

"A-24," which does have multiple lines of language happening simultaneously, so heard rather than read language can be polyvocal—although the demands of meaning imbedded in language make it difficult, to say the least, to follow more than one line at a time. I bring this up because I'm interested in the ambivalence toward the visual that runs throughout *Atet A.D.*, the third volume of *From a Broken Bottle.* I'm thinking in particular about N.'s attitude toward music videos, which seems to spill over into his attitude toward those cartoon balloons with captions that first come out of Penguin's oboe in the band's concert in Seattle and then out of Djamilaa's trumpet in San Francisco. Later in the book, N. sets up, in his last "After-the-Fact Lecture/Libretto," a kind of genesis and/or hierarchy of the senses that moves from smell to sound to sight: "Founding nose would elide founding noise as what preceded so-called founding script." Is this ordering of the senses consonant with the strains of mysticism you wrote about in your last reply, or is it more particular to your own sensibilities? Do you think smell and sound open us more readily to alternative forms of reason?

MACKEY: There may well be something particular to my own sensibilities in this, though it's not only that. My experience has been that auditory and olfactory sensations have greater transportive power than do visual ones. The ability of sound or smell to usher one away from the immediate moment and circumstance into some other tends to be stronger than that of sight, more palpable and penetrative, more corporeally felt, internally felt. They get to you and into you, inside you, to a degree I don't find arrived at by sight. I recall Amiri Baraka getting at something like this in a very early poem, "The Clearing": "The eye is useless. Sound, Sound, / & what you smell / or feel." As for the place of this in the strains of mysticism I've mentioned, I don't think it's that strongly put. In alchemy there's a lot of emphasis on the visual (changes of color and such), albeit olfactory apprehension figures prominently as well—the acrid odor of sulfur, etcetera. In Eastern traditions you have Om, you have mantras, you have chanting, you have Inayat Khan writing *The Mysticism of Sound,* but you also have the mandala. It's not so much an either/or situation; the different senses coexist and are given their due. Even so, there's a tendency to identify visual apprehension with the snares of ordinary reality, the snares of unenlightened or illusory perception, so figures involving darkness or blindness, the eclipse of the eye, abound in the esoteric traditions. Wilson Harris draws on this in *Palace of the Peacock* when he speaks of a "dead seeing material eye" and a "living closed spiritual eye." I was struck, to again mention one of the books I mentioned before, by Catherine Clément's discussion, in *Syncope,* of a reversal or distillation of odors, the saint's, the yogi's or the mystic's transformation of the fetid odors of bodily exertion, breakdown or putrefaction into spiced aromas, floral aromas. She in fact says that the saint, the yogi, and the mystic are "living perfume bottles." I couldn't help thinking of this in relation to funk, the African American transformation of offensive odor into a canon of approval, aesthetic approbation, an analogously mystical distillation of the otherwise or ostensibly offensive into perfume. There's also a social, cultural critique bound up in this. So, yes, getting back to *From a Broken Bottle,* N. does express a certain wariness with regard to the visual. He identifies it with the ruling episteme and with certain temptations that episteme puts in one's way: commercialism, oversimplification, and so on. He's more genuinely tempted, however, by this very line of thought, by a risk of overreaction he runs in valorizing the non-visual as he does. He himself is aware of this, so it gets a bit complicated. It's really more the hegemony of the visual than the visual itself that has him worked up; he's not asking to have his eyes plucked out. It's an equilibration of the senses he's after, hence the inklings throughout, some explicit, some implicit, of synaesthetic alliance, transaction or translation, the sort of translation achieved by funk's equation of sound and scent (though he'd want to avoid the commercialization funk fell into). He offers, in the lecture/libretto you mention, the rendering "no(i)se," which allows nose and noise, sound and scent, to converge. But the visual is also there, both in the recourse to the scribal medium so crucial to suggesting such convergence and in the punning, parenthetical "i" (eye) the rendering is built around. He's not unaware of this. Though he's a musician, deeply invested in sound, he also feels a very strong need for the amenities and effects afforded by writing.

NAYLOR: I'm glad you mentioned Wilson Harris in the context of a discussion about mysticism and writing, since I've been planning to ask about his work in relation to yours, to *From a Broken Bottle* in particular. With the notable exception of Robert Duncan, you've devoted more of your critical writing to Harris than any other writer I can think of. You've guest-edited an issue of *Callaloo* on Harris, and there are four essays on his work in *Discrepant Engagement,* so you've had your say about his work from the perspective of a reader-critic, but what about from the perspective of a fellow writer of fiction? I know this question must make your head spin (not to the extent of a cowrie shell attack, I hope), so perhaps you could begin by discussing where and when you first encountered Harris's work, and then discuss some of the consequences of that encounter on *From a Broken Bottle.*

MACKEY: Trying to specify the impact of Wilson's work does make my head spin, so, yes, let me focus mainly on factual matters. I first read his work in 1975, during my first year teaching at the University of Wisconsin in Madison. A graduate student who as an undergraduate at the University of Texas had taken a class with him during a visiting stint spoke very excitedly about him; when he heard of my interest in the Caribbean he recommended Wilson's work. So I read *Palace of the Peacock,* his first novel, and pretty much from the first page I became a devotee. I'd never read anything quite like it. It was lyrical, it was weird, it was metaphysical, it was audacious, it was loaded, it was concrete—a tight but rangy poetic prose working on so many levels, doing so much. I set about reading everything of his I could find—not only all the novels but also his essays and the early book of poetry, *Eternity to Season.* One of the things that interested me was that he was a poet turned novelist, that the poem became a novel, the novel a poem. *From a Broken Bottle* didn't really get going until about three years later, but Wilson's work definitely made me think about the possibilities of prose. I had written a couple of short stories as an undergraduate but by this point I was writing only—outside of criticism—verse.

It was in early 1979 that I began corresponding with Wilson. I was teaching at the University of Southern California and Ivan Van Sertima came to lecture on pre-Columbian African voyages to the Americas. I went up to talk with him afterwards and, knowing he was from Guyana and also a poet (I'd read a couple of his poems in the anthology *Breaklight*), I asked if he knew Wilson. It turned out he not only knew him but had written on his work. Hearing of my interest, he suggested I write Wilson and gave me his address at Yale, where he had a visiting position. So I wrote him. I enclosed copies of two essays on his work I'd written. One of them, on *The Eye of the Scarecrow,* had recently been published, and the other, "Limbo, Dislocation, Phantom Limb," was in manuscript. I also enclosed a copy of my chapbook *Four for Trane,* which had come out the previous year, and he commented kindly, in the letter he wrote back, on its (I still remember the phrase) "layers of sensibility." We've corresponded regularly since. It was almost three years later that we actually met—at a conference on Caribbean literature at the

University of Dijon in late 1981. He was the featured guest and speaker. I presented a paper on *Ascent to Omai.* Then I nominated him for a Regents Professorship here at UC Santa Cruz, which brought him here for a two-week visit during the spring in 1983. I saw him again during a summer visit to London in 1984, but it wasn't until this past summer that we had a chance to get together again. While in England for a few days I visited him one afternoon in Chelmsford, where he now lives.

As for the relation of my work to his, it's hard for me to separate my perspective as a reader-critic from my perspective as a fellow writer. As with my reading of and work on other writers, these modes are bound up with one another and rub off on one another, different aspects or facets of a single effort. So alongside the essays you find a poem in *Eroding Witness,* "The Sleeping Rocks," dedicated to Wilson, and just this fall I wrote another such poem, "Eye on the Scarecrow," for a special issue of *Journal of Caribbean Literatures* devoted to his work. This has to do with the fact that his work, like that of other influences, has resonated for me in multiple ways. It both spoke to interests and concerns I already had and sparked or inspired new ones. The phantom limb phenomenon, for example, is one which has fascinated me since I first heard of it as a kid, so Wilson's recourse to it as a figure for cultural and psychic redress in one of his early essays not only struck a responsive chord but stuck, stayed with me. I comment on his use of it in "Limbo, Dislocation, Phantom Limb" and make further use of it in another essay, "Sound and Sentiment, Sound and Symbol," as well as in poems and in *From a Broken Bottle,* where N. cites Harris in the very first letter. Indeed, one of the things I was most struck by and tried to learn from was figural knowledge's consistently high status in Wilson's critical as well as creative work and the tendency of distinctions between the two to dissolve. *The Eye of the Scarecrow,* his sixth novel but, significantly, the first on which I wrote, brings the metafictional and metacritical strains discernible in his earlier novels more emphatically to the fore. It features a heterogeneity or an indeterminacy with regard to genre I was very much drawn to, just as I'd been several years earlier reading Borges's fictions. When I began writing the letters which comprise *From a Broken Bottle,* I wasn't at all clear what they were or would become. For a long time I was uncomfortable with them being called fiction and with the individual volumes being called novels, but I eventually got used to it. Anyway, to finally wrap this up, I should also mention that I found the evocations of music in Wilson's work among the closest to the actual experience of music I'd read and that this musicality appeared to extend into and crucially consist of a propositional fervor peculiar to language.

NAYLOR: I'm intrigued by your statement that you "eventually got used to" the works comprising *From a Broken Bottle* being called novels. That suggests that you still don't consider them novels but have adjusted to others characterizing them that way. What is it about terms like *fiction* and *novel* that makes you uneasy about applying them to *From a Broken Bottle*?

MACKEY: No, that's a statement about the past, not the present. My uneasiness was ultimately a matter less of something about those terms than of something about me and how I saw what I was doing. I'd written, as I mentioned already, a little bit of fiction, a very little bit, but by the time I began writing the letters I'd long since given up on the idea of myself as a fiction writer. I'd learned or accepted or decided that I wasn't much inclined in that direction, seeing as I hadn't written more than three or four short stories, didn't have plots and characters and such filling my head and certainly didn't have plans for anything the length of a novel. I thought of the first few letters in the context of the poems I was writing. The first two, as you know, went into the "Song of the Andoumboulou" series. At that point I thought of them as some kind of cross between prose poem, *ars poetica*, and apologia, a clipped aesthetic tract or treatise of an offhand sort. The third letter signaled a change, though I wasn't all that aware of it at the time, and it eventually became the first letter of *From a Broken Bottle.* It was longer, and it announced the formation of the band, a move which essentially introduced characters and plot. I continued, however, to think of the letters not as fiction but as a kind of extended prose poem, an extension incorporating aspects of several genres (essay, diary, liner notes, etcetera) alongside the now more overt narrative elements. Rilke's *Notebooks of Malte Laurids Brigge* had had an impact on me years before and it sometimes came to mind as a possible model for what I was doing: a patchwork of ruminative intensities not necessarily seeking narrative linearity and resolution. But the work grew on me and even as it grew and as I increasingly availed myself of narrative possibilities and techniques I shied away from the terms *fiction* and *novel*—largely due to my sense of myself as not being a fiction writer. My attraction to generic indeterminacy or multiformity in the work of Harris or Borges or in something like Jean Toomer's *Cane* or Paul Metcalf's *Genoa* also, as I've mentioned, had a hand in it. I was wary of the expectations those terms trigger. I tended to focus more on the things I wanted to do which were not typically done in fiction than on the aspects of the work which conformed to common fictional practice. But as people more and more applied those terms I got to the point where I said why not, although not everyone, I should point out, agreed that the terms applied. There were publishers I sent *Bedouin Hornbook* to who evidently had definitions of those terms it failed to comply with, who felt its lack of classificatory clarity was a liability. In a more positive vein, Jed Rasula has called its categorization as fiction a misnomer, valorizing what he terms its "transgeneric fabric," and Charles Bernstein has cited it as an example of "reworkings of the essay form." Still, I'm not uncomfortable with *From a Broken Bottle* being called fiction or the individual volumes being called novels and it hasn't been simply, as my statement may have suggested, a matter of getting used to it. Those terms do apply, if for no other reason than that they include so much, even the antithetic. You look at something like *Tristram Shandy* and you see that the novel has spawned and incorporated the antinovel pretty much from the beginning.

NAYLOR: One of the things that draws together your work as a fiction writer and as a poet is a commitment to the serial form. It's nearly impossible to characterize your work without using the term *ongoing.* You've finished three volumes of *From a Broken Bottle,* and *Whatsaid Serif,* your third book of poetry including poems from the "Song of the Andoumboulou" series, has recently been published. You've been asked about the serial form in previous interviews, so I don't necessarily want you to rehearse what you've already said. But I imagine the process of writing six books in two serial forms over the past fifteen or so years has enriched your experience of that form. How has your theory and/or practice of the serial form changed over time?

MACKEY: I'm not sure there's been a great deal of change. That probably has to do with my having been pretty well prepped, so to speak, by the theories and practices of a range of writers whose recourse to seriality informs my own. In a sense, they taught me what to expect, if only in a very general way. Early on, for example, I absorbed a couple of principles or propositions from Robert Creeley, two precepts which he himself took from the work of others. It was in Creeley's early essays that I first encountered Louis Zukofsky's assertion that a poet writes one poem all of his or her life. This idea of an ongoing work of which there's a series of installments may pertain to work which isn't announcedly serial, but the serial work makes a point of it, even where there's more than one series. There's a content and a contention to the very form. The second precept occurs as an epigraph to Creeley's novel *The Island,* which he takes from Parmenides: "It is all one to me where I begin; for I shall come back again there." The ongoing work not only goes on but circles back, repeats. It entails exact and oblique echo, recurrence, recursiveness. If there's been a significant change in my involvement with serial form over the years it's been an increased awareness of repetition, of the inevitability of repetition, odd as that may seem. Indeed, recursiveness has probably been what most informed me that I was involved in serial work. This no doubt accounts for my increased commitment to seriality in recent years, my increased or more explicit acknowledgment that I'm involved in certain patterns, concerns, and resonances I don't pretend I've left behind. Hence *Whatsaid Serif* is devoted entirely to the "Song of the Andoumboulou" series, whereas *Eroding Witness* and *School of Udhra,* while including installments from that and the "mu" series, are more miscellaneous, outwardly at least. Similarly, *From a Broken Bottle,* which I thought might have ended with the third volume, *Atet A.D.*, flared up again about a year after I finished that volume. But then again, I had thought it might have ended with *Djbot Baghostus's Run* before that and with *Bedouin Hornbook* before that.

As for theorizing serial form, lately I've been more attentive to a dark accent or inflection running through its recourse to repetition, the sense of limits one again and again bumps up against, limits one would get beyond if one could. This qualifies, if not brings to a crisis, the form's promise of openness, possibility, advance. The form lends itself to a feeling for search but to one of insufficiency as well, to prospects of advance as well as to the not always happy fact of déjà vu. I've lately been looking at this especially in relation to James Snead's essay "Repetition as a Figure of Black Culture," which, to put it roughly, poses a cultural disposition which prioritizes repetition against one which prioritizes progress. Still, I don't know if this is all that new to my thinking. I was asked by Donna Hollenberg to write an essay on my relation to H.D.'s work for a book she's editing and in doing so a year ago I found myself insisting upon apprehensions of destitution in *Trilogy, Helen in Egypt,* and *Hermetic Definition,* apprehensions I picked up reading those poems in the early 1970s. I noted a singularity she took to exist beyond or beneath seriality, a singularity the sequencing of poems can't capture but is included by. I noted the way recursiveness appears to mark or to symptomatize the sense of deprivation or dispossession fostered by failed capture, the sense of disquiet and susceptibility to endless revisitation and variation, a meandering transit through mixed emotional states. I talked about her use of the labyrinth—and the senses of beguilement and even entrapment that go with it—as a figure for recursive movement. Such movement's desert ethic or nomadic measure I went on to call a desperate measure. The note of desperation or dispossession is what I mean by dark. But the affirmative take on this is that the dark accent or inflection issues out of a largeness of appetite, a utopic appetite. I recently read Graham Lock's forthcoming book on Sun Ra, Duke Ellington, and Anthony Braxton, in which he addresses a utopic assertion found in their work, a utopic assertion shaded by a blue, dystopic recognition of the world as it is. The book's title is a neologism he borrows from one of Ellington's compositions, a neologism I very much like, *Blutopia.* Seriality's mix of utopic appetite and recursive constraint I'd call blutopic. If you look at a work like Langston Hughes's *Montage of a Dream Deferred,* which I think of as a serial poem, this is obvious. I haven't spelled all this out as yet myself, but I find Rachel Blau DuPlessis's recent essay on segmentivity and seriality in Robin Blaser's and George Oppen's work very useful and suggestive, especially in two places. One is where she cites Oppen's notion of the line break or, more generally, the cut of segmentivity speaking to the vertical dimension. The other is where she uses Gary Saul Morson's notion of sideshadowing to say that seriality, in the absence of a teleological guarantee, offers what she calls voices to the side, a way of speaking to the side, a way of speaking not assimilable to a single, totalizing story. I seem to have been intuitively involved with claims or ideas of this sort. N., after all, addresses his letters to an angel and *Whatsaid Serif*'s homophonic counterpart to *seraph* denotes a short line stemming horizontally from the upper or the lower end of the stroke of a letter, a lateral additive. In Kalapalo storying practice, of course, the what-sayer invites or instigates asides, invites or instigates detours. Small wonder, I guess, that the poems repeatedly tell of being taken aside.

NAYLOR: How does the genre you're working in affect your approach to serial forms of composition? Does either fiction or verse tap in more to the "dark accent or inflection" that shows itself in repetition? Is the mix you mention between "utopic appetite and recursive constraint" in serial form more pronounced in fiction or verse? Is the phenomenon of "being taken aside" something that happens mostly in poems?

MACKEY: Genre, in my case at least, doesn't make much difference with regard to those issues. Normally, I suppose, verse would tend to emphasize and utilize repetition more than fiction does. Rhyme, after all, is a form of repetition, as are assonance and alliteration and, even more obviously, the refrain and other such devices. In verse, even at the level of its name, turning and returning seem to be centrally at issue. Fiction, on the other hand, we normally associate with linearity, a certain forward motion which seeks and achieves closure and resolution. My fiction, however, is strongly influenced by my coming to it from verse. It's significant that I chose to use the epistolary mode, a mode for which, at the formal level, given the conventions of salutation, etcetera, a certain amount of repetition is built-in; the letters all begin exactly the same, "Dear Angel of Dust," and all end pretty much the same, "Yours" and so forth. In addition, letters tend, for the most part, to be short, so there's a lot of interruption, so to speak, in the epistolary mode, a greater prominence given to the cut, to the segmental, to the episodic, and, accordingly, more amenability to drift and detour than in more usual forms of narration. Last but not least, of course, is the fact that I've consciously cultivated repetition and reverberation in fiction no less than in poems. It doesn't surprise me that two different people have written me about two different books in two different genres—one about *Djbot Baghostus's Run* several years ago and the other about *Whatsaid Serif* more recently—and applied the same term, "echo chamber," to them. The answer to your question might normally be that poetry lends itself to the things you name more than fiction does, but I've tried to make that not the case or at least less the case.

NAYLOR: Your fictive or narrative writing does strike me as having been "poetic" from the start; what intrigues me is the extent to which your poetry becomes more narrative in *Whatsaid Serif.* The sense of a journey is much more explicit in that book—lots of trains, boats, and buses moving through those poems. I don't mean to suggest that the installments of "Song of the Andoumboulou" in *Eroding Witness* and *School of Udhra* are pure lyrics, but the narrative dimension seems much more in play in *Whatsaid Serif.* Any particular reasons why?

MACKEY: Contagion perhaps. That or transmigration. While I was writing *Whatsaid Serif,* I sometimes had the feeling that *From a Broken Bottle,* which I was going for unusually long periods of time without working on, was making its way into the poems. It was as though the narrative impulse, blocked or boxed in on one front, sought an outlet on the other. That may be too hydraulic or too compensatory a way of looking at it, but the narrative pressure in the poems came aligned with a musical/musicological bent, an alignment recalling N.'s letters. It wasn't long before the band-of-travelers motif I had recourse to in the poems could also bring a traveling band to mind, as in lines like "Tenuous Kin we called / our would-be band, Atthic Ensemble." Still, the narrative dimension isn't all that new. It's there already in such early poems as "Dream Thief" and "The Shower of Secret Things" in *Eroding Witness,* so what you note is more a matter of degree and, I think, of a greater accent on the fact or the filter of narration, a metanarrative or narratological dimension found in *Whatsaid Serif,* the "he'd say" or the "she says" of the two early poems I just mentioned extended, spun within a more intricate weave. The greater intricacy or accent is hopefully a ripening or a maturation the work has undergone, an impulse to put more at stake, an amplification. "Whatsaidness" ups the ante on witness, not wanting to abide by simple oppositions between narrativity and reflexivity, expressivism and constructivism. The what-sayer is the recipient of a narrative and a co-producer of the narrative, a weave or a tangle of roles the Kalapalo, I think, usefully acknowledge.

NAYLOR: Speaking of contagion, I'm intrigued by the gnostic cosmology that infiltrates *Whatsaid Serif* and the way it adds another narrative line to your serial poem. What sparked your interest in gnosticism, and what work do you see it doing in your new poems?

MACKEY: Over the years at various times I've read up on gnosticism, but I don't recall exactly when I first got into it or why. My guess is that it was fairly early, during my late teens and early twenties when comparative religion interested me a lot. I do recall being struck during the early 1970s by the references to gnosticism in Robert Duncan's work, especially *The H.D. Book,* and in the work of Henri Corbin, whom I've already mentioned, especially *Avicenna and the Visionary Recital* and *Creative Imagination in the Sufism of Ibn 'Arabi.* Duncan and Corbin both tie gnosticism's insistence on estrangement to a core precept or proposition of esoterism, the idea that meaning or essence is veiled rather than openly available, a proposition which Duncan deploys as analogous to poetic espousal at the very least and which Corbin poses as intrinsic to a poetics of theophany. The idea that essence is alienated rather than immediate and the linkage of gnostic estrangement, esoterism, and poetics are among the things that struck and stayed with me and that led me to read Hans Jonas's *The Gnostic Religion* and Elaine Pagels's *The Gnostic Gospels* in the early 1980s. This all caught up with me, I guess, in *Whatsaid Serif,* sparked (reignited, really) by my reading Jacques Lacarrière's *The Gnostics* at about the same time as I was writing some of the poems which open the book. "Rethought what Andoumboulou / meant," for example, are lines which occur in "Song of the Andoumboulou: 18" and refer to my linking the Andoumboulou, a failed, early form of human being in Dogon cosmology, to the gnostic assertion that, as Lacarrière puts it, we are all premature births. My adoption of the Andoumboulou as a figure for our present as well as past condition, the suggestion that the Andoumboulou are a rough draft of human being and that we're (still) that rough draft, is a gnostic one. That, in the most general sense, is the work gnosticism is doing in the poems.

But it's also working in some rather specific and connected ways. I use a passage from Lacarrière's book as an epigraph to "Song of the Andoumboulou: 17," a passage having to do with Simon Magus's aim that *we* supersede all other pronouns, a passage meant to resonate with the epigraph to "Aspic Surmise" in *School of Udhra*: "inchoate pronouns which are in need of movement," from James Fernandez's *Performances and Persuasions.* These newer poems continue the concern with "an abducted / 'we,' an aborted / history," found in an earlier poem in *School of Udhra,* "Sweet Mystic Beast," adding an explicitly gnostic frame or inflection. This addition is part of the amplification or attempt at amplification I spoke of before, an amplification in which varied frames or inflections overlap and coexist. One needs to view gnosticism as one of several frames, though the very insistence on multiple framing, if one likens frames, as I do, to folds in a veil, can be said to be gnostic—multiple frames veiling and unveiling, albeit neither all at once. One of the things that appeals to me about gnosticism is its antiliteralism. Most famously, of course, it rejected the literal interpretation of the resurrection, which the Church Fathers used to consolidate power. Its opposition to that particular brand and use of historicism implies a lateral, nonliteralizing step, an acute sense of unarrested play between letter and spirit, the very play that poetry seeks to ride rather than resolve. This too, I realize, is a bit on the general side, but it pertains to the multiple framings and reframings of particular gnostic figures found in *Whatsaid Serif*: Sophia, the world as inn, the awakening from sleep, and so on. The senses of sojourn and journey that you remarked on, for example, bespeak the sorts of uprooting and transplantation that give rise to such phenomena as gnosticism, which was, as Jonas points out, a syncretic religion. As such, it encourages the syncretizing impulse the writing subjects it to, an impulse already encouraged by New World *vodoun* and other such responses to dislocation.

NAYLOR: That "syncretizing impulse" gnosticism lends to the poems of *Whatsaid Serif* seems to be offset by a more acutely historical treatment of the Diaspora enforced by the slave trade. The opening poems of that book invoke precise locations—"The same cry taken / up in Cairo, Córdoba, / north / Red Sea near Nagfa, / Muharraq"—that, as I read them, serve to counterbalance a tendency to allegory an unchecked allegiance to gnosticism might cause. In general, the result is a dynamic tension between drawing together and pulling apart that runs throughout the book, but I also think that tension brings up specific issues of racial conflict to a greater degree than in the earlier installments of "Song of the Andoumboulou." Did you begin the poems of *Whatsaid Serif* with a conscious desire to raise those issues more concretely?

MACKEY: In a way. I'm conscious of the fact that syncretism is a product of the schisms it aims to resolve, that it's a symptom as much as it is a solution since the unequal social relations that bring it into being tend to persist. One of the precursor poems to *Whatsaid Serif,* "Tonu Soy" in *School of Udhra,* says it: "syncretist wish to be beyond schism, / recollected bliss to erase the / movement of troops, wall of money." The syncretic equation of African loas with Catholic saints in New World *vodoun* doesn't erase, outside of the minds of its adherents (and, to an extent, not even there), the dominant position of Catholicism relative to *vodoun,* Europe relative to Africa, white relative to black. The equation itself is a recognition of that dominance, a combative response to it. It differently inflects the social divisions to which it responds. It may move in a millenarian, utopic direction which envisions eventual harmony between contingents currently at war, but that move is itself a combative one, itself a maneuver within that war. Sometimes the equation is not an equation at all, as in the Cuban *santeria* practice that William Bascom writes about and that "Song of the Andoumboulou: 4" cites, where the chromolithographs and plaster images of the Catholic saints which are displayed in the *santeria* shrines are regarded as empty, powerless, mere decor. The real power is believed to reside in stones hidden behind a curtain and the most powerful of these stones are said to have been brought from Africa, concealed in the stomachs of slaves. The poem braids a contention of black and white, darkness and light, saying that "The light arrives wrapped in / shadows" and ending by saying, "The rocks / inside our stomachs / want blood." I wanted those rocks to be many things: historical, allegorical, the rumblings of hunger, David's rocks against Goliath, the philosopher's lapis. That was back in *Eroding Witness*, so what you note in *Whatsaid Serif* is a continuing attempt to fulfill an aim that's long been there.

The other matter you mention, the specificity of location and the like, is the outcome of seeking a measure which could accommodate it and of gaining confidence that the marshaling of such particulars, which one can neither stop to explain nor presume to be common knowledge, at least conveys a specifying intent. That intent exists within tendencies to contrast and to homologize over distances—cultural, geographic, temporal and social distances, as well as distances within the work itself. Those places in the passage you cite, locations in Spain, Egypt, Ethiopia, and Bahrain, are points on a musicological mapping which hears a certain cry that flamenco's *cante jondo* has in common with Arab music. Those places are obviously not part of the African diaspora brought about by the middle passage, but that cry is a characteristic they share with New World black music for historical reasons that John Storm Roberts and others have gone into. You hear it in field hollers and work songs, for example; hence the images of sisyphean labor the poem begins with and the subsequent mention of the martinete, a flamenco song backed by a hammer pounding an anvil. That cry is the cry of estrangement, later called "flamenco's gnostic / moan." In calling it gnostic, I'm attempting to serve history and metaphor both. I'm also taking my cue from certain strains in African American music. Trombonist Grachan Moncur III has a piece called "Gnostic" on one of his albums from the 1960s, *Some Other Stuff*, and I've long thought of Sun Ra as something of a latter-day gnostic, a view that John Szwed appears to share in his biography of Ra.

NAYLOR: That "syncretizing impulse" also points toward an aesthetics of collaboration to some extent—the desire to incorporate in the work elements of another's work—which leads me to a question about a more directly collaborative project you've been involved in. My question concerns *Strick: Song of the Andoumboulou 16–25*, the compact disc recording you made with Royal Hartigan and Hafez Modirzadeh. The poems on that recording make up the first half of *Whatsaid Serif*, and I was wondering if working with musicians on those poems had much of an effect on the composition of the poems in the second half of *Whatsaid Serif,* songs 26–35. Did you "hear" the new poems differently after working with Hartigan and Modirzadeh? I don't mean to be so crude as to suggest that you somehow had a soundtrack installed in your head as a result of that collaborative recording, but I imagine there were some effects. Am I wrong on that score?

MACKEY: Outside of "Hafez / blew a chicken-bone clarinet / he'd / brought back from Iran," which comes up in "Song of the Andoumboulou: 33," I can't think of any way in which the collaboration had an effect on the poems in the second half of the book. It added another dimension to the traveling-band motif I touched on earlier, fleshing out, in a way, the figure of the band or the fantasy of being in a band which has long been a part of my work. I was in a trio, with the book or the poem or the voice as my instrument. Such was the manner, at any rate, that Royal and Hafez suggested I think of it in. So the "we" within the poems picked up another prompter, another localization joining those it was already shifting among. The lines I quoted came out of a rehearsal for the Monterey Jazz Festival we had in September 1995. Hafez had recently returned from a year in Iran and among the instruments he brought back (he was showing them to Royal and me) was one he called a chicken-bone clarinet. It was a small "horn" made from the legbone of a chicken, only a few inches long. I liked the sound of it, both the sound it made when blown and the sound of the name *chicken-bone clarinet*; *chicken-bone* and *clarinet* evoke such different images. Anyway, it made its way into the poem. But that entrance or effect is a matter of content, not one of hearing the poem differently in the process of writing, not one of writing differently. That kind of collaboration does, of course, have an impact on the sound or the reading of the poem, the sounding out of the poem, but that's a different matter. I read the poems a bit differently when accompanied by Royal and Hafez, different from the way I read them when unaccompanied. My basic approach to reading is the same in the two situations; whether I'm reading accompanied or unaccompanied I try to read the poem the way I heard it when I wrote it. But there's the element of interaction in the collaborative situation that makes a difference. There are times when what the musicians are doing causes me to read louder, read slower, read faster, lengthen or shorten a phrase, place accents differently or in some other way read the poem differently than I would were I simply reading by myself. Still, that doesn't carry over into how I hear a poem when I'm writing.

NAYLOR: I thought I'd shift directions here and ask a few biographical-bibliographical questions. In your interview with Chris Funkhouser, you talked about your early experiences with music in the Baptist Church and a little bit about your initial experiences with poetry. You mention William Carlos Williams and Amiri Baraka as formative influences on your sense of poetry. When and how did you come across their work? What in particular made their work so important for you at that time?

MACKEY: I came across their work while I was in high school. I don't recall exactly when, but I graduated in 1965, so it would have been sometime during the year or two preceding that. Williams's was the work I came across first and that was pretty fortuitous. I simply pulled a book of his off a shelf at the public library out of curiosity, drawn by his name, which I thought was an odd one. I don't recall whether I'd come upon it before, though perhaps I had in something I'd read or through mention of him in school, but I remember that the first name and the surname being more or less the same struck me as peculiar and that the Spanish middle name made it all the more so. That was enough to get me to take a look. The book was *Pictures from Brueghel,* and I found I liked it. For someone like me, new to modern poetry, it offered enough surface clarity and gnomic assertion to keep anxieties over meaning and allusion at bay. My encounter with the more hermetic side of Williams waited a couple of years until I picked up *Paterson* in college, but even in *Pictures from Brueghel* I got inklings of it and that was part of the appeal, part of what held my interest, intrigued me. Another part was the placement of the poem on the page, in particular the stepped or staggered, tripartite lineation—what Denise Levertov calls the triadic line—that he uses throughout the last two-thirds of the book. The spatial arrangement had an appeal that showed me early on that such arrangements are among the ways in which a poem speaks or signifies or insinuates—in a glyphic sense, not as a scoring device.

Baraka's work I encountered not all that long after beginning to read Williams. If I recall correctly, I'd actually read something about him before I first read his work. It was a short profile or some such mention of him in a magazine. I think it was *Esquire.* Anyway, the first things I read were the poems of his in Langston Hughes's anthology *New Negro Poets: USA* and his liner notes to a John Coltrane album, *Coltrane Live at Birdland.* The latter made a particularly strong impression. I've said before that liner notes were among my first literary influences and that's especially so for those Baraka wrote, as they were tied to a literary practice. The music was music which, for me, since my early teens, had become an increasingly strong and suggestive force. Baraka's simultaneous involvement with it and with tendencies in contemporary writing of which I was just becoming aware made him extremely important. The challenge of catching, in writing, some of the spirit of the music was one he was beautifully taking on. The poems in Hughes's anthology, from the period represented by his first book, *Preface to a Twenty Volume Suicide Note,* didn't grab hold of me as strongly as the *Birdland* liner notes did, but not long after that I picked up his second book, *The Dead Lecturer,* and it became my bible, remaining so for quite some time. The way the poems moved, as early commentators noted, appeared to obey an aesthetic analogous to that of the music—mercurial, oblique, elliptical—and what particularly caught my attention in that was the ratio of statement to imaged evocation, the way it kept changing.

In both cases, the work, over the years, stayed with me and I with it. Both are writers whose work I read more and more of and came eventually to deal with critically and academically. I wrote my undergraduate thesis at Princeton on Baraka's work and Williams figured prominently in my doctoral dissertation at Stanford. I've taught their work and written on them in critical essays and in Baraka's case there's been some personal contact as well. I met him in 1967—bumped into him in a bookstore in Greenwich Village. It was quite a coincidence, as I'd just picked up a copy of his book *Tales,* which had recently come out, when I spotted him an aisle or two over, thumbing through a book. (I still remember: it was David Cronon's biography of Marcus Garvey, *Black Moses.*) A reading at Princeton resulted from that, but it wasn't until about ten years later that I had further contact with him—again on the occasion of a reading, this time at USC while I was teaching there. It was about ten more years after that, in the spring in 1988 when he was at UC Santa Cruz for a week as a Regents Professor, that I really got to spend some time with him. Since then we've had a bit of correspondence in connection with my publishing work of his in *Hambone,* and I've gotten together with him a couple of times during trips back east. I last saw him just a few weeks ago in fact, when he was here for a reading in May—as ferocious as ever.

NAYLOR: I'd like to ask a few questions about your critical writing, about "Gassire's Lute: Robert Duncan's Vietnam War Poems" in particular. When did you write that work? Is it a development of your dissertation? I was also wondering about your decision to publish it serially in four issues of *Talisman*. In that respect, it resonates with Robert Duncan's *H.D. Book*, which you draw on quite a bit in "Gassire's Lute." Was that resonance intentional?

MACKEY: Yes, it grew out of a section of my dissertation. I wrote it in 1980 at the encouragement of the University of California Press. I had sent them my dissertation to consider for publication, and they'd made some encouraging noises about it. They ultimately decided it was too unconventional for them but suggested I rework some of the Duncan material for their Quantum Books series, a series in which they put out books of about a hundred pages in length, short books. I said okay, I'd make the focus Duncan's Vietnam War poetry, and again they made encouraging noises, but when I sent them the book they said it was too unconventional as well. I tried two or three other presses, but with no success, so I put it away. I showed it to Ed Foster, the editor of *Talisman*, years later, though I've forgotten exactly how it came about that I did. Anyway, this was in the late 1980s, 1989 I think, and he said he liked it and wanted to publish it in *Talisman*. The decision to publish it serially was a practical one. One of the problems I had with trying to place it after UC Press sent it back was that it was too long to be a journal article or essay and too short, in the eyes of the publishers I approached, to be a book. (A couple of them, unaware of its history, suggested that it would be perfect for UC Press's Quantum series.) The solution, as far as journal publication was concerned, was to publish it serially. I wasn't thinking of resonances with *The H.D. Book* in that regard, but it's nonetheless the case that I was under its influence and had been even more so in my dissertation. The dissertation's title was "Call Me Tantra: Open Field Poetics as Muse" and the subtitle was meant to suggest a methodology as much as a topic or a thesis. I was trying to make it a performative work, one which advanced an open field critical practice. *The H.D. Book* was prominent among a group of works of criticism or commentary I was inspired by, a group ranging from such obviously pertinent works as Olson's *Call Me Ishmael* and Williams's *In the American Grain* to less obviously related work such as that of Gaston Bachelard. In one section, for example, I made use of the collagelike manner of presentation found in parts of *The H.D. Book*, where diaristic entries that are separated by asterisks relate more by way of suggestion, juxtaposition, recursiveness, and associative leaps than through linear argument or exposition. While not as obviously influenced by *The H.D. Book* as the dissertation in this way was, "Gassire's Lute" necessarily drew on it to explicate Duncan's poetics but was touched by it in other ways as well.

NAYLOR: So you were engaged in writing "Gassire's Lute" at the same time you were writing the initial installments of your long poem, "Song of the Andoumboulou." Given that much of "Gassire's Lute" is about "the dangers of poetry" as they manifest themselves in the long poems of Pound, Williams, Olson, H.D., and Duncan, did writing that book impact the way you proceeded in your own long poem? In particular, how does "Song of the Andoumboulou" participate in the "willingness to question or to corrupt its own inspiration" that you find so admirable in Duncan's "Passages"?

MACKEY: I'm not sure that the actual writing of the book had an impact in that respect or how much, if it did, of an impact it had. Much of the reading and the thinking that went into the book took place over a number of years prior to its writing, as did the writing of the initial installments of "Song of the Andoumboulou," which began in the early 1970s and the first publication of any of which was in 1974. The first seven, which eventually appeared in *Eroding Witness,* had already been written by the time I sat down to write "Gassire's Lute," but my address of the book's concerns had been going on for some time, as I've already said, so it's no surprise to see those concerns, the willingness you ask about among them, enter "Song of the Andoumboulou" as well. "Song of the Andoumboulou: 5," after all, is subtitled "gassire's lute" and says early on: "'Sad bringer of love, / born singer of sorrow,' / she warns / me, 'beware the false beauty / of loss. . . .'" The realization that poetry's ability to console suffering or to compensate or sublimate trouble could in fact instigate trouble, look for trouble, was on my mind and had been for some time. That one could so rhapsodically lick one's wounds as to acquire and promote a taste for woundedness was something I was finding out on various fronts. The tale of Gassire's lute seemed to be getting, among other things, at that. The co-dependency of rhapsody and wound it outlined or accented I associated with the old rhyme about singing the blues and paying dues, caught up as I was in the fact that the tale comes out of Mali, a region in whose traditional music, that of Bazoumana Sissoko in particular, I was hearing something very close to Delta blues. There were other aspects to it as well. For one, the lost, idealized city of Wagadu, "now in the mind indestructible," as Pound, in *The Pisan Cantos,* put it, stood for me for idealization itself, idealizing memory or expectation and the trouble in mind and outside the mind it can create. That the caveat is voiced by a "she" partakes of and tries to tamper with a poetic tradition of idealization, the woman-as-muse tradition, and this continues in "Song of the Andoumboulou: 6," where the willingness to question or corrupt or, at the very least, interrupt a romance of inspiration gives rise to a switch from poetry to prose in the form of the first of the "Dear Angel of Dust" letters, a recourse to prose that occurs again in "Song of the Andoumboulou: 7" with the inclusion of the second of the letters. These are probably the most obvious examples, but that willingness gives rise as well to such things as the role of wary auditor often adopted by the "I" in *Whatsaid Serif.* But it's not only in "Song of the Andoumboulou" that you find that willingness. It's there in poems outside that series, as well as in the prose work that's led to by those two letters, *From a Broken Bottle.* In fact, it's the writing of some of the early letters in *Bedouin Hornbook* that coincides with the writing of "Gassire's Lute," a fact that's evident in the references N. makes to Wagadu, Gassire, the notion of a riff requiring dues of itself, and so on.

NAYLOR: Throughout "Gassire's Lute," you're concerned with fleshing out the many profound and often productive contradictions in Duncan's poetry and poetics. In particular, you write of "two contrary impulses [that] intersect" in Duncan's work, "one of them a desire to issue poetry a clean bill of health—to say, as H.D. does, that 'we have not sown this'—and the other an assertion that even poetry bears something like 'a burden of original sin.'" H.D.'s and Duncan's evaluations of poetry arise in the context of conflict—World War II for H.D. and the Vietnam War for Duncan. My guess is that your evaluation of poetry is as ambivalent as Duncan's, but I thought I'd alter the terrain of the issue somewhat and ask about your evaluation of the present state of poetry in the context of another kind of conflict—racism in America. What role does poetry play in causing or healing the rift between races in America? How much has that role changed during the time you've been engaged with poetry?

MACKEY: Whatever ambivalence enters my evaluation of poetry has nothing to do with presuming ties of an intrinsic sort relating it to racism.

Poetry is neither the cause of nor the cure for the rift between races, but it can, depending not only on the writer but also the reader, be symptomatic of that rift and/or involved in an effort to overcome it. I say "and/or" because it's possible for it to be both at the same time, possible for it to be symptomatic of the very problem it wants to redress. The recognition of this possibility with regard to war fuels a certain hesitation or moment of hesitation in Duncan's and H.D.'s work, a moment in which the ability to derive a poetic return from war, to in that sense invest in war, is confused with motive and causation. H.D. wonders in *Helen in Egypt* whether Troy was lost for a new rhythm on the lute, lost for the sake of the lute, but it's worth remembering that Homer, whom she echoes in asking that question, didn't start the Trojan War. The question is loaded with the return it's after, which in H.D.'s case comes out of a Romantic/Modernist impulse to make poetry matter by putting it at the very heart and source of things. Duncan continues that line of endeavor and thought but I think it's possible for poetry to matter without recourse to a centralizing impulse, without rushing it to a presumed center or equating it with a putative source. I think it's possible not only for it to matter in other ways or for other reasons but for it to significantly not matter—not in Eliot's late sense but in the way suggested by Wilson Harris's idea of an apt irrelevance. In any case, poetry's role with regard to the rift between races is a relatively small one, a rhetorical one. It runs the gamut between furthering the rift and attempting to combat it, sometimes, as I've said, doing both at the same time. Exactly where along that spectrum it functions and how exactly it functions depend, among other things, on whose poetry it is, on whether it's George Moses Horton's or Jupiter Hammon's, Frances Harper's or Thomas Nelson Page's, Walt Whitman's or Russell Irwin's, Paul Laurence Dunbar's or Sterling Brown's, Gwendolyn Brooks's or Mina Loy's, and so on. Other factors bear as well. I don't know if it's a role so much as a fact of life, but poems reveal more than poets and critics intend. They carry marks of their context and register their occasion, register and interact with their context and occasion, in ways that go beyond the poet's or the critic's control. The discourse that proposes a role for poetry is typically concerned with intent and determinate effects. That being the case, as it was with so much of the discussion during the Harlem Renaissance and later in the Black Arts Movement, discussion of how poetry could help combat racism, such a discourse misses a vital point. One of the useful changes I see having taken place during the time I've been engaged with poetry is that that point, more and more, albeit not yet as often as I'd like, is not missed. The variability thus afforded or recognized might eventually have a part—an admittedly small one—in uprooting reductive patterns of thought and expectation, racial shorthand among them. That's my hope at least.

NOTES
DISCOGRAPHY

Notes

Introduction: Door Peep (Shall Not Enter)

1. Wilson Harris, *Explorations: A Selection of Talks and Articles 1966–1981* (Mundelstrup, Denmark: Dangaroo Press, 1981), 99.

2. Pablo Neruda, *The Heights of Macchu Picchu*, trans. Nathaniel Tarn (New York: Farrar, Straus and Giroux, 1966), 47. Hereafter cited parenthetically as *HMP*.

3. Georg Lukács, *The Theory of the Novel*, trans. Anna Bostock (Cambridge, Mass.: MIT Press, 1971), 91.

4. William Bronk, *The World, The Worldless* (New York: New Directions/San Francisco Review, 1964), 13.

5. H.D., *Trilogy* (New York: New Directions, 1973), 53. Hereafter cited parenthetically as *T*.

6. Nathaniel Mackey, *School of Udhra* (San Francisco: City Lights, 1993), 44.

7. Sun Ra, "Your Only Hope Now Is a Lie," *Hambone*, no. 2 (1982): 111.

8. "An Interview with Edward Kamau Brathwaite," *Hambone*, no. 9 (1991): 44.

9. Jerome Rothenberg, "The Commentaries," in *Technicians of the Sacred: A Range of Poetries from Africa, America, Asia, Europe and Oceania*, ed. Jerome Rothenberg (Berkeley and Los Angeles: University of California Press, 1985), 541.

10. Stephen Jonas, "Cante Jondo for Soul Brother Jack Spicer, His Beloved California and Andalusia of Lorca," in *Selected Poems* (Hoboken: Talisman House, 1994), 160–64.

11. Billy Cobham, quoted in Paul Tingen, *Miles Beyond: The Electric Explorations of Miles Davis, 1967–1971* (New York: Billboard Books, 2001), 70–71.

12. William Carlos Williams, "To Daphne and Virginia," *Pictures from Brueghel and Other Poems* (New York: New Directions, 1962), 78. Hereafter cited parenthetically in the text as *PB*.

13. Marcel Griaule, *Conversations with Ogotemmêli: An Introduction to Dogon Religious Ideas* (London: Oxford University Press, 1965), 78–83.

14. Nathaniel Mackey, *Bedouin Hornbook* (Lexington, Ky.: Callaloo Fiction, 1986), 201.

15. Nathaniel Mackey, *Djbot Baghostus's Run* (Los Angeles: Sun and Moon Press, 1993), 40.

16. Nathaniel Mackey, *Atet A. D.* (San Francisco: City Lights, 2001), 78–79.

17. Zora Neale Hurston, *Their Eyes Were Watching God* (New York: Harper and Row, 1990), 183.

18. Robert Duncan, *The Opening of the Field* (New York: Grove Press, 1960), 41.

Phrenological Whitman

1. Quotations from Whitman's work are taken from *Complete Poems and Collected Prose* (New York: Library of America, 1982). There being so many editions of Whitman's work, I take the liberty, throughout this essay, of citing his poems and essays by title rather than page number.

2. Madeleine B. Stern, *Heads and Headlines: The Phrenological Fowlers* (Norman: University of Oklahoma Press, 1971), 100. Hereafter cited parenthetically as *HH.*

3. Edward Hungerford, "Walt Whitman and His Chart of Bumps," *American Literature*, no. 2 (1930–31): 362. Hereafter cited parenthetically as WWCB.

4. Thomas Hardy Leahey and Grace Evans Leahey, *Psychology's Occult Doubles: Psychology and the Problem of Pseudoscience* (Chicago: Nelson-Hall, 1983), 50. Hereafter cited parenthetically as *POD.*

5. John D. Davies, *Phrenology: Fad and Science; A Nineteenth-Century American Crusade* (New Haven, Conn.: Yale University Press, 1955), 8. Hereafter cited parenthetically as *PFS.*

6. Jorge Luis Borges, *Other Inquisitions, 1937–1952*, trans. Ruth L. C. Simms (Austin: University of Texas Press, 1965), 68.

7. Allen F. Roberts, "Insight, or, *Not* Seeing Is Believing," *Secrecy: African Art that Conceals and Reveals*, ed. Mary H. Nooter (New York: Museum for African Art, 1993), 71.

8. Frederick Merk, *Manifest Destiny and Mission in American History: A Reinterpretation* (New York: Alfred A. Knopf, 1963) 13. Hereafter cited parenthetically as *MD.*

9. Justin Kaplan, *Walt Whitman: A Life* (New York: Simon and Schuster, 1980), 100. Hereafter cited parenthetically as *WW.*

10. See Walt Whitman, "Anti-Slavery Notes," in *Walt Whitman's Workshop: A Collection of Unpublished Manuscripts*, ed. Clifton Joseph Furness (New York: Russell and Russell, 1964), 71: "I was a decided and out-spoken anti-slavery believer myself, then and always; but shied from the extremists, the red-hot fellows of those times."

11. Robert Farris Thompson, *Face of the Gods: Art and Altars of Africa and the African Americas* (New York: Museum for African Art, 1993), 131–33.

Wringing the Word

1. Edward Brathwaite, *The Arrivants: A New World Trilogy* (London: Oxford University Press, 1973), 34. Hereafter cited parenthetically as *A.*

2. Edward Kamau Brathwaite, *Mother Poem* (London: Oxford University Press, 1977), 108. Hereafter cited parenthetically as *MP.*

3. Edward Kamau Brathwaite, *Sun Poem* (London: Oxford University Press, 1982), 3–4. Hereafter cited parenthetically as *SP*.

4. Edward Kamau Brathwaite, *X/Self* (London: Oxford University Press, 1987), 32. Hereafter cited parenthetically as *XS*.

5. For a discussion of such use of Caliban by West Indian and African writers, see Rob Nixon, "Caribbean and African Appropriations of *The Tempest*," in *Politics and Poetic Value*, ed. Robert von Hallberg (Chicago: University of Chicago Press, 1987), 185–206.

6. Stewart Brown, "Interview with Edward Kamau Brathwaite," *Kyk-over-al*, no. 40 (1989): 85.

7. Marlene Nourbese Philip, *She Tries Her Tongue, Her Silence Softly Breaks* (Charlottetown, Prince Edward Island: Ragweed Press, 1989), 16.

8. Marlene Nourbese Philip, *Looking for Livingstone: An Odyssey of Silence* (Stratford, Ontario: Mercury Press, 1991), 52–53.

9. Ihab Hassan, *The Literature of Silence: Henry Miller and Samuel Beckett* (New York: Alfred A. Knopf, 1967), 9.

10. Kamau Brathwaite, *Middle Passages* (Newcastle upon Tyne, England: Bloodaxe Books, 1992), back cover.

11. Wilson Harris, *The Eye of the Scarecrow* (London: Faber and Faber, 1965), 95.

Palimpsestic Stagger

1. Nathaniel Mackey, *Bedouin Hornbook* (Lexington, Ky.: Callaloo Fiction, 1986), 17.

2. H.D., *Helen in Egypt* (New York: New Directions, 1974), 174. Hereafter cited parenthetically as *HE*.

3. H.D., *Trilogy* (New York: New Directions, 1973), 23. Hereafter cited parenthetically as *T*.

4. Robert Duncan, *Roots and Branches* (New York: New Directions, 1969), 176.

5. Nathaniel Mackey, *Eroding Witness* (Urbana: University of Illinois Press, 1985), 38.

6. Antonio Benítez-Rojo, *The Repeating Island: The Caribbean and the Postmodern Perspective*, trans. James Maraniss (Durham N.C.: Duke University Press, 1992), 16–17.

7. René Char, *The Dog of Hearts*, trans. Paul Mann (Santa Cruz, Calif.: Green Horse Press, 1973), no pagination.

8. Charles Olson, *The Maximus Poems* (Berkeley and Los Angeles: University of California Press, 1983), 175.

9. Robert Duncan, *Bending the Bow* (New York: New Directions, 1968), 6.

10. Robert Duncan, *Tribunals: Passages 31–35* (Los Angeles: Black Sparrow Press, 1970), 7–8.

11. H.D., *Hermetic Definition* (New York: New Directions, 1972), 109. Hereafter cited parenthetically as *HD*.

12. Nathaniel Mackey, *School of Udhra* (San Francisco: City Lights, 1993), 23.

Gassire's Lute: Robert Duncan's Vietnam War Poems

1. Robert Duncan, *Bending the Bow* (New York: New Directions, 1968), 114. Hereafter cited parenthetically as *BB.*

2. Douglas C. Fox and Leo Frobenius, *African Genesis* (New York: Stackpole Sons, 1937), 97. Hereafter cited parenthetically as *AG.*

3. Leo Frobenius, *Leo Frobenius, 1873–1973: An Anthology,* ed. Eike Haberland, trans. Patricia Crampton (Wiesbaden: E. Steiner, 1973), 140. Hereafter cited parenthetically as *LF.*

4. Robert Duncan, "From the Day Book—Excerpts from an Extended Study of H.D.'s Poetry," *Origin,* 2d ser., no. 10 (1965): 35. Hereafter cited parenthetically as DB.

5. Ezra Pound, *The Cantos of Ezra Pound* (New York: New Directions, 1970) 442. Hereafter cited parenthetically as *C.*

6. Robert Duncan, *The First Decade: Selected Poems, 1950–1956* (London: Fulcrum Press, 1969), 88.

7. William Carlos Williams, *Selected Essays* (Norfolk, Conn.: New Directions, 1954), 180. Hereafter cited parenthetically as *SE.*

8. Robert Duncan, "Rites of Participation," in *A Caterpillar Anthology,* ed. Clayton Eshelman (Garden City, N.Y.: Doubleday, 1971) 48. Hereafter cited parenthetically as RP.

9. Charles Olson, *The Distances* (New York: Grove Press, 1960), 38.

10. Charles Olson, *Muthologos: The Collected Letters and Interviews,* vol. 2, ed. George F. Butterick (Bolinas, Calif.: Four Seasons Foundation, 1979), 79.

11. Roland Barthes, *Mythologies,* trans. Annette Lavers (New York: Hill and Wang, 1975) 158–59.

12. Robert Duncan, "Man's Fulfillment in Order and Strife," *Caterpillar,* nos. 8–9 (1969): 248. Hereafter cited parenthetically as MF.

13. *Robert Duncan: Scales of the Marvelous,* ed. Robert J. Bertholf and Ian W. Reid (New York: New Directions, 1979), 181. Hereafter cited parenthetically as *SM.*

14. Robert Duncan, "Preface to a Reading of Passages 1–22," *Maps,* no. 6 (1974): 54–55.

15. David Bromige, "Beyond Prediction," *Credences,* no. 2 (1975): 105.

16. Charles Olson, *The Maximus Poems,* ed. George F. Butterick (Berkeley and Los Angeles: University of California Press, 1983), 510. Hereafter cited parenthetically as *MP.*

17. Ishmael Reed, *Conjure* (Amherst: University of Massachusetts Press, 1972), 43.

18. Charles Olson, *Reading at Berkeley* (San Francisco: Coyote, 1966), 15. Hereafter cited parenthetically as *RB.*

19. Edith Porada, quoted in Charles Olson, *Human Universe and Other Essays,* ed. Donald M. Allen (New York: Grove Press, 1967), 19. Hereafter cited parenthetically as *HU.*

20. H.D., *Trilogy* (New York: New Directions, 1973), 15. Hereafter cited parenthetically as *T.*

21. Imamu Amiri Baraka (LeRoi Jones), "Poetry and Karma," in *Raise Race Rays Raze: Essays since 1965* (New York: Random House, 1972), 17–26.

22. Robert Duncan, *The Opening of the Field* (New York: Grove Press, 1960), 93. Hereafter cited parenthetically as *OF.*

23. Robert Duncan, *The H.D. Book*, part 1, chapter 1: "Beginnings," *Coyote's Journal*, nos. 5–6 (1966): 8–31. Hereafter cited parenthetically as HDI.1.

24. Robert Duncan, *Roots and Branches* (New York: Scribner's, 1964), 16. Hereafter cited parenthetically as *RB.*

25. Robert Duncan, *The H.D. Book*, part 2, chapter 4, *Caterpillar*, no. 7 (1969): 48–49. Hereafter cited parenthetically as HDII.4.

26. Robert Duncan, *Ground Work: Before the War* (New York: New Directions, 1984), 33. Hereafter cited parenthetically as *GW.*

27. Robert Duncan, *The H.D. Book*, part 2, chapter 5, *Sagetrieb* 4, nos. 2–3 (1985): 40–41. Hereafter cited parenthetically as HDII.5.

28. Robert Duncan, *Derivations: Selected Poems 1950–1956* (London: Fulcrum Press, 1969), 11–12. Hereafter cited parenthetically as *D.*

29. LeRoi Jones, *Black Magic: Collected Poetry, 1961–1967* (Indianapolis: Bobbs-Merrill, 1969), 41.

30. Robert Duncan, "Changing Perspectives in Reading Whitman," in *The Artistic Legacy of Walt Whitman: A Tribute to Gay Wilson Allen*, ed. Edwin Haviland Miller (New York: New York University Press, 1970), 97. Hereafter cited parenthetically as CP.

31. James F. Mersmann, *Out of the Vietnam Vortex: A Study of Poets and Poetry against the War* (Lawrence: University Press of Kansas, 1974), 179–82.

32. Erich Heller, *The Disinherited Mind: Essays in Modern German Literature and Thought* (Cleveland: World, 1959), 138. Hereafter cited parenthetically as *DM.*

33. Robert Duncan, "Pages from a Notebook," in *The New American Poetry*, ed. Donald M. Allen (New York: Grove Press, 1960), 402. Hereafter cited parenthetically as PN.

34. Edward Dahlberg, *Alms for Oblivion* (Minneapolis: University of Minnesota Press, 1964), 118–19, and *Can These Bones Live* (Norfolk, Conn.: New Directions, 1960), 45–46.

35. Robert Duncan, *The Years as Catches: First Poems (1939–1946)* (Berkeley: Oyez, 1966), vii–viii. Hereafter cited parenthetically as *YC.*

36. Robert Duncan, *The H.D. Book*, part 2, chapter 3, *Io*, no. 6 (1969): 135. Hereafter cited parenthetically as HDII.3.

37. Robert Duncan, *The H.D. Book*, part 2, chapter 9, *Chicago Review* 30, no. 3 (1979): 42.

38. Robert Duncan, *The H.D. Book*, part 1, chapters 3–4, *TriQuarterly*, no. 12 (1968): 72.

39. Robert Duncan, *The H.D. Book*, part 1, chapter 5: "Occult Matters," *Stony Brook*, nos. 3–4 (1969): 5–6.

40. Robert Duncan, *The H.D. Book*, part 2, chapter 1, *Sumac* 1, no. 1 (1968): 111. Hereafter cited parenthetically as HDII.1.

41. William Carlos Williams, *Paterson* (New York: New Directions, 1963), 233.

42. Unpublished manuscript, Robert Duncan Archives, Poetry/Rare Books Collections, State University of New York–Buffalo.

43. Robert Duncan, *Caesar's Gate* (Berkeley: Sand Dollar, 1972), xl.

44. *The Iliad of Homer*, trans. Richmond Lattimore (Chicago: University of Chicago Press, 1951), 162.

45. H.D., *Helen in Egypt* (New York: Grove Press, 1961), 238. Hereafter cited parenthetically as *HE*.

46. Jean Giraudoux, *Tiger at the Gates*, trans. Christopher Fry (New York: Oxford University Press, 1955), 74.

47. My discussion of Cao-Daism is based on the following sources: Joseph Buttinger, *Vietnam: A Dragon Embattled* (New York: Praeger, 1977); Piero Gheddo, *The Cross and the Bo-Tree: Catholics and Buddhists in Vietnam*, trans. Charles Underhill Quinn (New York: Sheed and Ward, 1970); Gerald Cannon Hickey, *Village in Vietnam* (New Haven, Conn.: Yale University Press, 1964).

48. George Oppen, *Collected Poems* (New York: New Directions, 1975), 191.

49. *The Presocratics*, ed. Philip Wheelwright (New York: Odyssey Press, 1966), 79.

50. Ibid.: "People do not understand how that which is at variance with itself agrees with itself. There is a harmony in the bending back, as in the cases of the bow and the lyre."

51. The exchange is quoted by Gary Snyder as an epigraph to his poem "What Steps," in *Turtle Island* (New York: New Directions, 1974), 62.

52. Denise Levertov, *Relearning the Alphabet* (New York: New Directions, 1970), 26. Hereafter cited parenthetically as *RA*.

Cante Moro

1. See the discography at the end of this volume for recordings referred to in the text.

2. Federico García Lorca, *Poet in New York*, trans. Greg Simon and Steven F. White (New York: Noonday Press, 1988), 214. Hereafter cited parenthetically as *PNY*.

3. Federico García Lorca, "Theory and Function of the *Duende*," in *The Poetics of the New American Poetry*, ed. Donald M. Allen and Warren Tallman (New York: Grove Press, 1973), 91.

4. Federico García Lorca, *Deep Song and Other Prose*, trans. Christopher Maurer (New York: New Directions, 1980), 43. Hereafter cited parenthetically as *DS*.

5. Leon Forrest, *Two Wings to Veil My Face* (Chicago: Another Chicago Press, 1988), 192.

6. Jack Spicer, *The Collected Books of Jack Spicer* (Los Angeles: Black Sparrow Press, 1975), 12. Hereafter cited parenthetically as *CB*.

7. Robert Duncan, *Caesar's Gate: Poems 1949–50* (Berkeley: Sand Dollar, 1972), xxi–xxii. Hereafter cited parenthetically as *CG*.

8. LeRoi Jones, "Lines to García Lorca," *New Negro Poets: USA*, ed. Langston Hughes (Bloomington: Indiana University Press, 1964), 55.

9. LeRoi Jones, *Black Music* (New York: Morrow, 1967), 160.

10. LeRoi Jones, *Black Magic: Collected Poetry, 1961–1967* (Indianapolis: Bobbs-Merrill, 1969), 38.

11. Steve Abbott, "Hidden Master of the Beats," *Poetry Flash*, no. 155 (1986): 1.

12. Bob Kaufman, *The Ancient Rain: Poems 1956–1978* (New York: New Directions, 1981), 4. Hereafter cited parenthetically as *AR*.

13. Nathaniel Mackey, *Eroding Witness* (Urbana: University of Illinois Press, 1985), 73.

14. Nathaniel Mackey, *Bedouin Hornbook* (Lexington, Ky.: Callaloo Fiction, 1986), 43.

15. Alejo Carpentier, *The Lost Steps*, trans. Harriet de Onís (New York: Noonday Press, 1989), 184. Hereafter cited parenthetically as *LS*.

16. LeRoi Jones, *Tales* (New York: Grove Press, 1967), 91.

17. Jalaluddin Rumi, *Teachings of Rumi: The Masnavi*, trans. E. H. Whinfield (London: Octagon Press, 1979), 1.

18. Robert Kelly, *Songs I–XXX* (Cambridge, Mass.: Pym-Randall Press, 1968), 53.

Blue in Green: Black Interiority

1. All quotations up to this point are taken from *The Miles Davis Radio Project*, an eight-hour documentary produced by Steve Rowland for American Public Radio, first broadcast in October 1990.

2. Miles Davis with Quincy Troupe, *Miles: The Autobiography* (New York: Simon and Schuster, 1989), 83. Hereafter cited parenthetically as *M*.

3. James Hillman, "Alchemical Blue and the Unio Mentalis," *Sulfur*, no. 1 (1981): 39.

4. William Gass, *On Being Blue: A Philosophical Inquiry* (Boston: Godine, 1976), 57.

5. Kamau Brathwaite, "Improvisations and Dreams," June 1992, cited in Graeme Rigby, "Publishing Brathwaite: Adventures in the Video Style," *World Literature Today* 68, no. 4 (1994): 708–9.

6. Ornette Coleman, "Something to Think About," *Free Spirits: Annals of the Insurgent Imagination*, ed. Paul Buhle, Jayne Cortez, Philip Lamantia, Nancy Joyce Peters, Franklin Rosemont, and Penelope Rosemont (San Francisco: City Lights, 1982), 117.

7. Cassandra Wilson's rendition of "Blue in Green" appears on her 1986 recording *Point of View* (JMT 860004).

8. LeRoi Jones, *Black Music* (New York: Morrow, 1967), 67.

9. Nathaniel Mackey, *Bedouin Hornbook* (Lexington, Ky.: Callaloo Fiction, 1986), 86. Hereafter cited parenthetically as *BH*.

10. Nathaniel Mackey, *Djbot Baghostus's Run* (Los Angeles: Sun and Moon Press, 1993), 18–19.

Paracritical Hinge

1. Nathaniel Mackey, *Discrepant Engagement: Dissonance, Cross-Culturality, and Experimental Writing* (New York: Cambridge University Press, 1993), 19. Hereafter cited parenthetically as *DE*.

2. Oliver Lake, *Ntu: Point from which Creation Begins* (Arista/Freedom AL 1024).

3. Vera M. Kutzinski, *Against the American Grain: Myth and History in William Carlos Williams, Jay Wright, and Nicolás Guillén* (Baltimore: Johns Hopkins University Press, 1987), 180–82.

4. Art Lange and Nathaniel Mackey, "Editors' Note," in *Moment's Notice: Jazz in Poetry and Prose*, ed. Art Lange and Nathaniel Mackey (Minneapolis: Coffee House Press, 1993), ii. Hereafter cited parenthetically as *MN*.

5. Nathaniel Mackey, *Atet A.D.* (San Francisco: City Lights, 2001), 48–61, 118–22.

Sight-Specific, Sound-Specific . . .

1. Stewart Brown, "Interview with Edward Kamau Brathwaite," *Kyk-over-al*, no. 40 (1989): 89–90.

2. Robert Duncan, *Roots and Branches* (New York: Scribner's, 1964), 169.

3. Lorenzo Thomas, *Chances Are Few* (Berkeley: Blue Wind Press, 1979), 44–45.

4. Nathaniel Mackey, *Whatsaid Serif* (San Francisco: City Lights, 1998), 21.

Expanding the Repertoire

1. Charles Olson, *The Maximus Poems* (Berkeley and Los Angeles: University of California Press, 1983), 18.

2. LeRoi Jones, *The Dead Lecturer* (New York: Grove Press, 1964), back cover.

3. LeRoi Jones, *Home: Social Essays* (New York: Morrow, 1966), 10. Hereafter cited parenthetically as *H*.

4. LeRoi Jones, *Black Magic: Collected Poetry, 1961–1967* (Indianapolis: Bobbs-Merrill, 1969), 207.

5. Dudley Randall, "Three Giants Gone," *Negro Digest* 17, no. 1 (1967): 87.

Editing *Hambone*

1. Nathaniel Mackey, *Discrepant Engagement: Dissonance, Cross-Culturality, and Experimental Writing* (New York: Cambridge University Press, 1993), 21.

2. Eliot Weinberger, "Montemora," *Poetry East*, nos. 9–10 (1982–83): 61.

Discography

Camarón, *Calle Real.* Phillips 814–466–1.

———. *La Leyenda del Tiempo* Phillips 63–28–255.

Miles Davis, *Bitches Brew.* Columbia GP 26.

———. *Kind of Blue.* Columbia CS 8163.

———. *Sketches of Spain.* Columbia CS 1480.

Miles Davis and John Coltrane. *Live in Stockholm 1960.* Dragon DRLP 90/91.

Folk Music of Iran. Lyrichord LLST7261.

Fred Ho and the Afro-Asian Music Ensemble. *Tomorrow Is Now!* Soul Note SN 1117.

Ketama. *Ketama.* Hannibal HNBL-1336.

———. *Songhai.* Hannibal HNBL-1323.

———. *Y Es Ke Me Han Kambiao Los Tiempos.* Mango 539.879–1.

Rahsaan Roland Kirk, *I Talk with the Spirits.* Limelight LS82008.

Oliver Lake. *Ntu: Point from which Creation Begins.* Arista/Freedom AL 1024.

Juan Peña Lebrijano and the Andalusian Orchestra of Tangier. *Encuentros.* Ariola I-207240.

Lole and Manuel. *Casta.* CBS S-26027.

———. *Lole y Manuel.* CBS S-82276.

———. *Nuevo Día.* Movieplay 15.2320/3.

Nathaniel Mackey with Royal Hartigan and Hafez Modirzadeh, *Strick: Song of the Andoumboulou 16–25.* Spoken Engline Company.

Manitas de Plata. *Manitas de Plata—Flamenco Guitar, Volume 2.* Connoisseur Society CS-965.

Manzanita. *Poco Ruido y Mucho Duende.* CBS S-83188.

José Heredia Maya and the Andalusian Orchestra of Tetuan. *Macama Jonda.* Ariola I-295400.

Mississippi Fred McDowell. *I Do Not Play No Rock 'n' Roll.* Capitol ST-409.

Pata Negra. *Blues de la Frontera.* Hannibal HNBL-1309.

Pastora Pavón. *La Niña de los Peines.* Le Chant du Monde. LDX 74859.

Pepe de la Matrona. *Pepe de la Matrona, Volume 2.* Hispavox 150–055.

Sonny Rollins. *East Broadway Rundown.* Impulse! A-9121.

Singing Preachers. Blues Classics BC-19.

Cassandra Wilson. *Point of View.* JMT 860004.

Index

CONTEMPORARY NORTH AMERICAN POETRY SERIES

Bodies on the Line: Performance and the Sixties Poetry Reading
By Raphael Allison

Industrial Poetics: Demo Tracks for a Mobile Culture
By Joe Amato

What Are Poets For? An Anthropology of Contemporary Poetry and Poetics
By Gerald L. Bruns

Reading Duncan Reading: Robert Duncan and the Poetics of Derivation
Edited by Stephen Collis and Graham Lyons

Postliterary America: From Bagel Shop Jazz to Micropoetries
By Maria Damon

Among Friends: Engendering the Social Site of Poetry
Edited by Anne Dewey and Libbie Rifkin

Purple Passages: Pound, Eliot, Zukofsky, Olson, Creeley, and the Ends of Patriarchal Poetry
By Rachel Blau DuPlessis

On Mount Vision: Forms of the Sacred in Contemporary American Poetry
By Norman Finkelstein

Writing Not Writing: Poetry, Crisis, and Responsibility
By Tom Fisher

Form, Power, and Person in Robert Creeley's Life and Work
Edited by Stephen Fredman and Steven McCaffery

Redstart: An Ecological Poetics
By Forrest Gander and John Kinsella

Jorie Graham: Essays on the Poetry
Edited by Thomas Gardner
University of Wisconsin Press

Gary Snyder and the Pacific Rim: Creating Countercultural Community
By Timothy Gray

Urban Pastoral: Natural Currents in the New York School
By Timothy Gray

Ecopoetics: Essays in the Field
Edited by Angela Hume and Gillian Osborne

Racial Things, Racial Forms: Objecthood in Avant-Garde Asian American Poetry
By Joseph Jonghyun Jeon

We Saw the Light: Conversations between the New American Cinema and Poetry
By Daniel Kane

Ghostly Figures: Memory and Belatedness in Postwar American Poetry
By Ann Keniston

History, Memory, and the Literary Left: Modern American Poetry, 1935–1968
By John Lowney

Paracritical Hinge: Essays, Talks, Notes, Interviews
By Nathaniel Mackey

Behind the Lines: War Resistance Poetry on the American Homefront
By Philip Metres

Poetry Matters: Neoliberalism, Affect, and the Posthuman in Twenty-First Century North American Feminist Poetics
By Heather Milne

Hold-Outs: The Los Angeles Poetry Renaissance, 1948–1992
By Bill Mohr

In Visible Movement: Nuyorican Poetry from the Sixties to Slam
By Urayoán Noel

Reading Project: A Collaborative Analysis of William Poundstone's Project for Tachistocope {Bottomless Pit}
By Jessica Pressman, Mark C. Marino, and Jeremy Douglass

Frank O'Hara: The Poetics of Coterie
By Lytle Shaw

Renegade Poetics: Black Aesthetics and Formal Innovation in African American Poetry
By Evie Shockley

Questions of Poetics: Language Writing and Consequences
By Barrett Watten

Radical Vernacular: Lorine Niedecker and the Poetics of Place
Edited by Elizabeth Willis